ECONOMIC EPISODES
IN
AMERICAN HISTORY

Mark C. Schug

William C. Wood

WOHL
PUBLISHING

A Note from the Publisher

I am very proud to be the publisher of *Economic Episodes in American History* by Mark C. Schug and William C. Wood. It has been a great honor to have worked on it with them and with the team of publishing professionals and educators that have been a part of the entire effort. We hope that you will find the results of their work to be valuable to you and to your students, and that you will decide to integrate our textbook within your curriculum by having your school adopt it for classroom use.

Given the tight budgets that many schools now face, some publishers have scaled back their activities on projects that fall outside of traditional, core textbook programs. We have taken an opposite approach, believing that the need is greater than ever for unique and innovative teaching materials that engage students in new and creative ways about issues that really matter. We hope that you find that this book is such a text, and that the teaching and learning that happens in your classes every day are enriched by its use.

—Rich Wohl

Development Editor: Barbara A. Conover
Copy Editor and Production Manager: Richard Western
Book Design and Photo Editor: Jeremy C. Munns
Indexer: Jennifer Petersen
Printer: Malloy, Inc.

Cover image:
Vendors along Mulberry Street, center of the
Italian neighborhood in New York City, 1890s.

North Wind Picture Archives

Credits and acknowledgements borrowed from other sources and
reproduced, with permission, in this textbook appear on appropriate
page within the text and/or in credits sections at the end of this book.

Wohl Publishing, Inc.
45 S. Park Place #223
Morristown, NJ 07960
www.wohlpublishing.com

10 9 8 7 6 5 4 3 2 1

ISBN 978-1-935938-11-8 (Hard Cover)
ISBN 978-1-935938-12-5 (Soft Cover)

ABOUT THE AUTHORS

Mark C. Schug, Ph.D.

Mark C. Schug is Professor Emeritus at the University of Wisconsin Milwaukee. He taught for 36 years at the middle school, high school, and university levels. A widely recognized scholar, he has written and edited more than 200 articles, books, and national curriculum materials. He has received awards for leadership and research in economic education from the Council on Economic Education. He has been the guest co-editor of six issues of *Social Education*, the flagship journal of the National Council for the Social Studies. He serves on the boards of the Association of Private Enterprise Education, Business and Economics Academy of Milwaukee (BEAM), Economics Wisconsin, and the Wisconsin Governor's Council on Financial Literacy.

William C. Wood, Ph.D.

William Wood is Professor of Economics and Director of the Center for Economic Education at James Madison University. Wood was the recipient of teaching awards at the University of Virginia and at James Madison University, where he was the 2001–2002 Distinguished Teacher in the College of Business. Wood was named in 2002 as an inaugural winner of the Southern Economic Association's Kenneth G. Elzinga Distinguished Teaching Award. Wood is also a past recipient of the Alpha Kappa Psi-Clifford D. Spangler award for research in risk and insurance and Best Paper award for the *Journal of Private Enterprise*. He is the author of three books, more than 30 scholarly articles, and national economic education materials for school and adult audiences.

ADVISORY BOARD

Preface

Near the end of the classic 1946 American movie *It's a Wonderful Life*, George Bailey (played by Jimmy Stewart) is a crestfallen man. He has sunk to a low point in his life; he has decided that he is a complete failure. But then something important happens. Thanks to a surprise visit and some guidance from a helpful angel, George suddenly realizes that life in his hometown would have been much worse if he had not been a part of it. This insight enables George to see the world differently. He races down the street shouting, "Hello Bedford Falls!" He calls out to the buildings he recognizes—the Bijou movie theater, the Emporium, and the Bailey Bros. Building and Loan. Returning home, he bursts through his front door and is *delighted* to find the bank examiner, who uncovered his financial problems, and the local sheriff, who has a warrant for his arrest. He joyfully embraces his children and kisses Mary (Donna Reed), his wife, repeatedly. His new insight has changed his life.

Looking Beyond the Everyday, Taken-for-Granted World

We know that reading *Economic Episodes in American History (EEAH)* will not change your life in the magical way George Bailey's life was changed. But we do think that a careful reading of *EEAH* can position you to see certain things differently. That opportunity depends, as George's opportunity did, on gaining new ideas from outside the everyday, taken-for-granted world. The outside source in *EEAH* is nothing like an angel, of course. Instead, it is something we call the economic way of thinking. The economic way of thinking differs in important ways from other approaches to understanding our world. It emphasizes paying close attention to the choices people make, and to the costs related to those choices, and to the incentives that influence people as they make choices. We use the economic way of thinking in the following chapters to help you *think through* several important issues from U.S. history, rather than asking you merely to accept taken-for-granted interpretations.

Using Economics to Think about U.S. History

The main purpose of *EEAH* is not to teach economics. Its main purpose is to help you understand U.S. history. Toward that end, *EEAH* introduces a few basic economic principles and shows, over several chapters, how these principles can be used in efforts to think about topics and issues from U.S. history—ranging from war and slavery, for example, to immigration and information technology. Students often find that efforts of this sort cast events from the past in a new light—illustrating, at the same time, a powerful new way to examine human behavior. Not a George Bailey moment, but maybe one resembling it.

EEAH is not meant to serve as a substitute for a history textbook. History textbooks are important. They provide readers with carefully crafted chronological accounts of political, military, and cultural history. They usually offer some observations about economic issues as well, but economic analysis is not their main purpose. As a result, they do not provide accounts of the past that describe and explain people, events, and ideas by reference to choices, costs, and incentives. Enter *Economic Episodes in American History*. Its goal is to engage students in formulating economic analyses of key events from America's past—analyses yielding insights they are not likely to discover in traditional textbooks.

The Organization of *Economic Episodes in American History*

Chapter 1 introduces the economic way of thinking as an approach to understanding history. Students should read this chapter first and use its introductory remarks as a basis for their work with other chapters. The other chapters are designed to be self-contained; they may be used selectively (though of course we hope you'll use them all) and in any order.

Topically, chapters 2–32 follow a chronological order, from the colonial era to current issues about trade policy and federal government programs. Analytically, the chapters unfold according to this set of categories:

- In an opening section called "Framing the Issue," each chapter tells a story about a person in history. The personal stories introduce the time periods focused on in the respective chapters.

- The next section in each chapter, the "Historical Context" section, briefly describes the period in history being discussed, as a foundation for the explanation of that history developed later in the chapter, by reference to the principles of economics that apply to it.

- The heart of each chapter is a section titled "The Economics of . . . ." Each of these sections focuses on principles of economics as they pertain to the chapters' main contents— homesteading, the desegregation of major league baseball, women in the workforce, and so on.

- Next comes "Historical Questions and Economic Answers"—sections featuring a lively question-and-answer format to show how economic reasoning yields answers to key questions.

- The Questions and Answers sections are followed by "Primary Source" sections. Each Primary Source section focuses on an original document, photograph, or art work related to the chapter's contents, so that students can examine historical evidence first-hand.

- Each chapter concludes with a "Then and Now" section, focused on a modern-day example related to the chapter's main contents.

We Are Interested in Hearing from You

We hope you enjoy reading the book as much as we enjoyed preparing it for you. We would love to hear from students and teachers who are using *EEAH*. Please contact us with questions or comments through the publisher's website at **www.wohlpublishing.com** or e-mail us at **economicepisodes@wohlpublishing.com**

Mark C. Schug
William C. Wood

TABLE OF CONTENTS

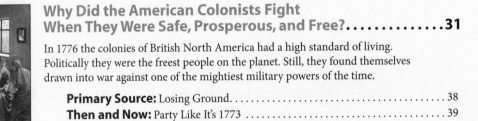

CHAPTER 16

CHAPTER 17

CHAPTER 18

CHAPTER 19

CHAPTER 20

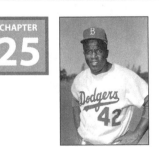

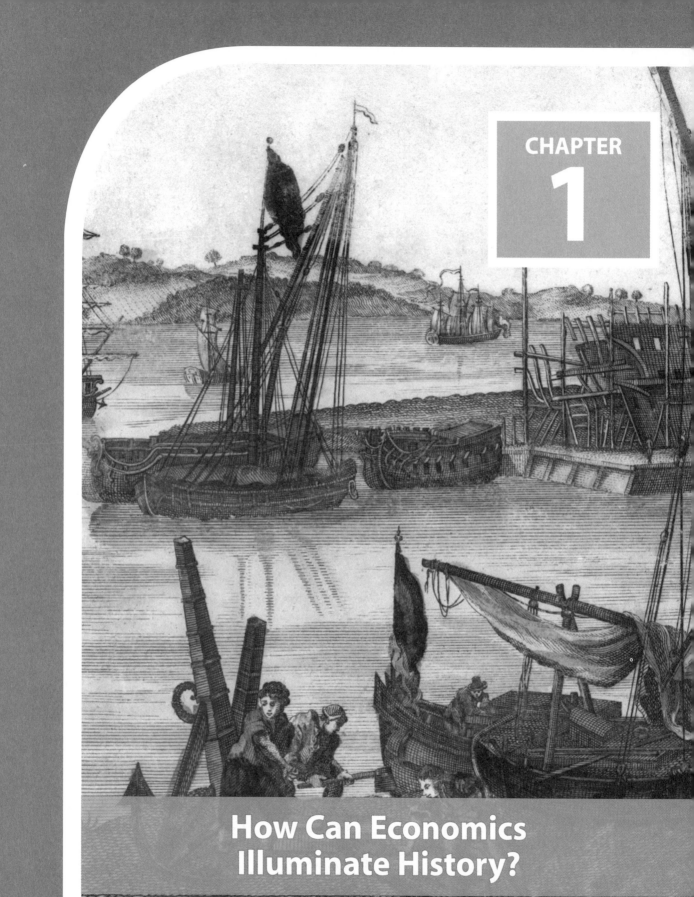

CHAPTER

1

How Can Economics Illuminate History?

Workers tend to ships on the waterfront in Salem, Massachusetts, 1770s.

Economic Thinking: New Views of Old Events

Istory matters because we see our future through the past. The better we understand our past, the better we can shape our future. Douglass North, who was awarded a Nobel Prize for explaining how societies develop, stated the point simply: "History matters."

Have you noticed how things have changed since you were younger? You may have begun recently to use an iPhone or to view 3D video. Your parents must have experienced many changes on that order during their lives. The same is true for your grandparents or great grandparents. The choices they made as things changed around them affected your parents' lives. And your parents' choices have certainly affected you. Your life wouldn't be the same today if your parents had made different choices. Knowing something about their choices can help you understand where you were born, where you grew up, how you and your family and friends live. Understanding anything—yourself, for instance—depends in part on knowing how it came to be the way it is now.

Of course history involves more than family decisions. It also provides accounts of our nation and the world. These accounts are valuable because, when they are well done, they provide accurate chronologies of events from the past: this happened, then this happened, then that happened.

This focus on chronology helps reveal how events unfolded. But the focus on chronology can mislead us if we are not careful. For example, most of us already know that:

- Americans declared their independence on July 4, 1776, and General Washington went on to defeat the British in the Revolutionary War.

- President Lincoln preserved the Union, and worked to end slavery in the United States.

KEY ECONOMIC CONCEPTS

Competition	Profit
Economics	Rules of the game
Economic way of thinking	Scarcity
Free Trade	Self-interested behavior
Globalization	Specialization
Incentive	Unintended
Market economy	consequences
Opportunity cost	Voluntary trade

- President Roosevelt and the Prime Minster of Great Britain, Winston Churchill, led the United States and its allies to victory in World War II.

- Martin Luther King, Jr., and Rosa Parks were central figures in the Civil Rights Movement.

- Barack Obama was the first African American elected to the presidency of the United States.

The events in this list are common knowledge to many Americans. That is well and good, so far as it goes. But merely knowing *what happened, how events turned out*, is the easy part. It is not the same as understanding *why events occurred as they did*. This question—call it the *Why?* question—invites us to think about explanations, not merely outcomes.

Unfortunately, many students of history never quite get to the *Why?* question. Why not? One big stumbling block is that the question itself may seem strange. Didn't events turn out as they did because they just *had to* turn out that way? And if that's so, isn't it a bit silly to go on asking about explanations? The correct answers here are *no* and *no*. Water has to freeze at certain temperatures, but nothing in the human world ever *has to* turn out the way it does.

Events from our past might have turned out one way or another, depending on the choices people made and the actions they took. It was not at all certain, in 1776, that the American colonists would defeat the British in the Revolutionary War. It was not at all certain, late in the 1960s, that the Civil Rights Movement would overcome deeply entrenched patterns of racial segregation in the United States. History is replete with examples of unexpected outcomes. And the outcomes themselves don't answer the *Why?* question.

Historian David McCullough states the point this way:

> [Y]ou must remember that nothing was *on track*. Things could have gone any way at any point. As soon as you say "was," [your remark] seems to fix an event in the past. But nobody ever lived in the past, only the present. The difference is that it was their present. They were just as alive and full of ambition, fear, hope and all the emotions of life. And, just like us, they didn't know how it would all turn out.
>
> The challenge is to get the reader [of history] beyond . . . thinking that things had to be the way they turned out and to see the range of possibilities of how *it could have been otherwise.*[1]

Suppose we accept McCullough's point that, in history, it always could have been otherwise. What's next? How do we move from that point to begin looking for explanations instead of mere chronology? The answer, we suggest, is that in order to find explanations it is necessary to go beyond chronology. It is necessary adopt a certain perspective or way of looking at the events we find in chronologies. And here there are several possibilities. We might look at events in the way psychologists look at them, or political scientists, or evolutionary biologists, or geographers. Each of these disciplines provides a distinctive perspective on people and their activity, and each perspective can yield important insights.

Our perspective—the perspective that informs this book—derives from economics. **Economics** is the study of human behavior that emphasizes the choices people make. It provides a distinctive set of ideas and a particular way of thinking that can be especially helpful in the study of history.

How do you get started thinking about history from an economic perspective? Let's begin by considering some key assumptions of that perspective, as stated by American economist Paul Heyne:

> All social phenomena emerge from the choices that individuals make in response to expected costs and benefits to themselves.[2]

Now, let's briefly examine these assumptions as they might be applied in the study of history.

- Historical events are produced by the choices individuals make. We are all members of groups—families, friends, and organizations—but the economic way of thinking focuses on individuals making choices. Individual choices, in turn, shape institutions and influence the activity of groups and nations.

- Individuals make their choices by taking account of possible costs and benefits. **Benefits** are positive consequences; **costs** are consequences that people try to avoid.

- People make decisions that they think will make them happier or more satisfied. The sources of happiness or satisfaction might be material gains (a new car, perhaps, or a better salary, or a new kitchen counter) or nonmaterial rewards (perhaps the satisfaction gained by volunteering to work at a homeless shelter).

- Finally, the use of the word "expected," in Heyne's term "expected costs and benefits," is important. Since we never know how things will turn out, and we can never have perfect information when we make a choice, we make our choices as best we can and hope they are the right ones. Often we make good decisions; sometimes we make mistakes. Our mistakes do not mean that choosing is a bad thing to do.

The Economic Way of Thinking

Heyne's statement of assumptions can help you think about how to approach a historic event from an economic perspective: Pay close attention to choices, costs, and benefits. But there is more to the story. With a bit of elaboration, Heyne's assumptions can be restated as six principles of economic thinking. The application of these principles can cast historic events in a new light and suggest explanations of why and how they occurred. Here are the six principles.

1. People make choices because they face scarcity.

Would you like to have a new cell phone? Take a vacation in Florida for spring break? Maybe you would like more time to study, be with friends, or work at a part-time job. Economists assume that the things individuals want are, for all practical purposes, unlimited. Most of us want to have more goods and services than we now have, or will ever have. All this would not be a problem except that, individually and as a nation, our resources are limited. We have only so many *labor resources*—people in the workforce with specific skills to produce the goods and services we want. We have only a limited supply of *natural resources*—timber, fertile soil, sunshine, coal, oil, and so on. We have only so many *capital resources*—the factories and equipment used to make the things we want. Economists call this condition **scarcity**. It is a condition everybody faces—rich or poor. It is found in all societies. We can increase the number of wants we satisfy, but scarcity isn't going away.

Because resources are scarce, we have to make choices. Economists claim that people manage their lives by making choices, even though they sometimes prefer to believe that they do not. Think how often you hear people say, in one situation or another, that they had "no choice" but to act as they did. In this respect, young people and older people are much alike. They sometimes deny that they are making choices when that is exactly what they are doing. They sometimes explain certain actions of theirs as matters of necessity rather than choice—forced on them, perhaps, by a challenging situation.

The economic way of thinking is about understanding choices.

Imagine that Derrick, a high school student, arrives four minutes late to his third-period history class. He explains to the teacher, "Sorry to be late, but I had no choice. I had to stop by my locker to pick up my history textbook. It's too heavy to lug around to all my morning classes, and you said we should bring our book to class every day." Set the economic way of thinking aside and you might see things the way Derrick did. His lateness was really the teacher's fault. Economic thinkers, however, would see the situation differently. They would see the outcome as a consequence of Derrick's choices. He chose not to carry his book from class to class. He chose to race to and from his locker. He decided that the convenience of not carrying the history book was worth the possible cost of being late to class. He could have made other choices.

2. People's choices involve costs.

Choices come with costs. The costs are obvious enough in the case of decisions to buy goods or services. If you choose to go to Florida for spring break, you need to find a way to pay for your travels. But not all costs are dollar costs. For example, you might decide to go for a run after school. This decision might seem to involve all benefits and no costs, especially if you enjoy exercise. But it takes time to go running, and you could use that time in other ways. The cost of running after school might be homework not done, or a favorite television show missed.

Although there are many kinds of cost, economists stress the importance of opportunity cost. In any decision, the **opportunity cost** is the person's second-best choice. It is not *every* alternative not selected. You might have done all sorts of things instead of running after school. Of all the possibilities, the opportunity cost is the second-best alternative, the alternative or set of alternatives you would have chosen next. For example, let's imagine that you narrowed your choice down to two alternatives—run or do homework after school. If you choose running, the opportunity cost is homework not done. If you choose homework, the opportunity cost is running. This idea of opportunity cost explains why economists like to say "There is no such thing as a free lunch." Even if somebody bought your lunch, you spent your time eating it. Every choice involves a cost.

3. People respond to incentives in predictable ways.

Incentives are benefits offered to encourage people to act in certain ways. Money is a powerful incentive because it can be exchanged for other things. But not all incentives are monetary. Another sort of incentive has to do with the satisfaction that comes from doing the right thing. Many people perform acts of virtue that involve nonmonetary rewards. They donate blood, pick up trash in a park, and show up to vote on Election Day. Other people, including police officers and firefighters, risk their lives daily for reasons that go beyond the salaries they earn.

In a market economy, profit is an important incentive to producers of everything from iPads to Honda Civics. **Profit** is the money left over after a business has paid all its costs—wages, rent, utilities, taxes, and so on. The prospect of earning profits provides an incentive for producers to provide the goods and services consumers want. When a consumer buys a widget produced by Acme Widget, the transaction is voluntary. Acme didn't have to produce widgets; the consumer didn't have to buy an Acme widget. Because they can't force consumers to buy their products, businesses try to produce goods and services people actually want to purchase.

In their efforts, businesses compete with other businesses. **Competition** in this context is rivalry between two or more firms, each seeking to earn the business of consumers by offering quality products at reasonable prices. In a market economy, competition acts as a control mechanism to reduce prices and improve the products and services that businesses offer.

4. People create economic systems that influence individual decisions.

In economics, the emphasis on individual choice prompts some people to charge that economists are unrealistic, since individuals don't make choices in a vacuum. Individuals live within families, usually, and they are members of the larger society. These associations influence their choices. All this is well known, even to economists. They emphasize that economic behavior occurs in a climate of rules and institutions, formal and informal. The **rules of the game** (drive on the right side of the road, for example) act as incentives and influence the choices people make in particular cases. ("I believe I'll drive on the right side of the road, since I'd rather not have a head-on collision.") Governments establish many rules of the game (other rules are established by custom and private contracts). Tax laws, for example, create incentives that influence behavior. If a city government places a heavy tax on the width of buildings, tall, narrow buildings soon begin popping up. If a state government places a large tax on savings accounts, people soon look for other places to put their extra money.

Within our system of laws, government is authorized to enforce its rules, subject to public oversight. Government can impose fines and even send people to jail for refusing to pay taxes or violating regulations. Private businesses have no such authority. McDonalds cannot force anyone to buy its hamburgers; Starbucks can't force anyone to buy its coffee. Only government can use the prospect of force or coercion as an incentive to encourage people to comply with its rules.

5. People gain when they trade voluntarily.

"Voluntarily" here refers to lack of fraud or coercion. "Your money or your life!" does not describe an instance of voluntary trade. "Gain" refers to money gains, of course, but also to other benefits. Examples of voluntary trade are everywhere. Purchasing a movie ticket, filling your car's tank with gas, buying a stock—all involve **voluntary trade** in which people exchange something they value less for something they value more. That's why the store clerk often thanks the customer and the customer often thanks the clerk at the end of a transaction.

Voluntary trade encourages cooperation, even among people who don't know each other, as is often the case in international trade. Trade involves specialization. **Specialization** occurs when people concentrate on producing goods and services they can produce with relative ease and at a relatively low cost. Some people in Wisconsin specialize in producing cheese; some people in Florida specialize in producing oranges. Wisconsinites *could* grow oranges, by using greenhouses, and Floridians *could* devote more resources to producing milk and processing it into cheese. The problem in both cases is that it would be more expensive for Wisconsinites to grow oranges, and more expensive for Floridians to produce cheese. It is better for them to specialize and then trade for other things they want. Specialization and trade benefit all parties involved in the exchanges.

Purchasing gas is an example of voluntary trade.

6. People's choices sometimes create unintended consequences.

Thinking economically involves analyzing secondary effects. The *primary effects* of an action are the immediate, visible effects. Put 50 cents in the parking meter and you get a place to park, right away. The *secondary effects* of an action are indirectly related to the initial effects; they may appear only after some time has passed. Low parking fees for parking meters may have the secondary effect of encouraging consumers to shop at nearby stores.

Here is another example of primary and secondary effects at work. In 1990, Congress approved a 10 percent tax on yachts sold in the United States at a price higher than $100,000. The intended primary effect was to increase government revenues by imposing a tax on wealthy people who buy yachts.

What were the secondary effects? A 10 percent tax on a yacht selling for $300,000 amounted to a $30,000 price increase. How did potential yacht buyers respond? As you might guess, many decided not to buy new, American-built yachts. Instead, they bought used yachts, or yachts made in other countries, or they didn't buy yachts at all, choosing instead to do other things with their money. These decisions caused a decline in yacht sales that almost destroyed the U.S. yacht industry. Nearly 8,000 workers lost their jobs. These were often highly skilled workers—carpenters, fiberglass and metal workers, and electricians. Moreover, tax revenues from the new tax fell far short of expectations. While people who built yachts were not rich, they depended on customers who were rich. Those rich people had alternatives when it came to buying yachts. Politicians had apparently never thought any of this through. They were horrified when they learned about the secondary effects of what they had done. The yacht tax was repealed in 1993.

As the yacht tax illustrates, an economic system is in some ways like an ecological system. An action here may create **unintended consequences** there. Congress intended only to raise more revenue to help pay for the costs of government. It did not intend to destroy the jobs of 8,000 workers. But that is precisely what it did. Wise policymakers are mindful of unintended consequences.

Adam Smith and the Economic Way of Thinking

The economic way of thinking provides an approach to describing and explaining human behavior. The approach has developed over time, with ideas and methods of analysis contributed by many thinkers. Of these thinkers, one of the most important is Adam Smith (1723–1790). He is best known for writing a book now known by its shortened title, *The Wealth of Nations* (1776). Ideas presented in this book have influenced economists ever since Smith's time, including such notables as David Ricardo, John Maynard Keynes, and Milton Friedman.

Smith was born in the small village of Kirkcaldy, Scotland. He attended Glasgow University and Oxford, and later returned to Glasgow University to teach moral philosophy. He traveled throughout Europe from 1764 to 1766. He met and exchanged ideas with other great intellectuals of his time including David Hume, Voltaire, Jean-Jacques Rousseau, and French economist François Quesnay. Most people who knew him regarded Smith, personally, as a delightful dinner guest and loyal companion; one acquaintance, Samuel Johnson, said Smith was "as dull a dog as he had ever met with." Johnson himself was a brilliant but very quirky man.

Smith returned from his travels to Kirkcaldy in 1766 and devoted much of the next 10 years to writing *The Wealth of Nations*. It has proved to be a work of historic importance. It describes and explains how a market economy works—the sort of economy found today, for example, in the United States, Canada, the United Kingdom, Germany, Japan, and South Korea. A **market economy** is one in which individual choices and voluntary exchanges determine what is produced. In markets, sellers voluntarily provide what buyers are willing to pay for. Consumers are free to save or spend their money as they wish; individuals are free to start businesses or to sell their labor as they

Adam Smith, author of The Wealth of Nations.

think best. A market economy thrives when individuals have the freedom to make their own economic choices.

Smith is especially well known for his explanation of why societies as well as individuals benefit from self-interested behavior in market activity. His explanations emphasize the importance of self-interested behavior. He wrote:

> …man has almost constant occasion for help from his brethren, and it is in vain for him to expect it from their benevolence only…. It is not from the benevolence of the butcher, the brewer, or the baker, that we expect our dinner, but from their regard to their own interest. We address ourselves, not to their humanity but to their self-love, and never talk to them of our necessities but of their advantages.[3]

The butcher, the brewer, and the baker do not offer their goods and services to others out of love and kindness—and we should be grateful that they do not. If we depended on love and kindness to encourage people to produce goods and services for others, it is likely that store shelves would be empty. Instead, Smith contends, people produce goods and services for others because it is in their self-interest to do so.

But self-interested behavior is not the same as selfishness or greed. **Self-interested behavior** helps people to do things that matter to them. In 1979, Mother Teresa received the Nobel Prize for Peace. Mother Teresa, a Catholic nun, was offered a sum of $190,000 along with the prize. Did Mother Teresa, known for her tireless work on behalf of Calcutta's poorest people, accept the money? Of course she did. Was her willingness to accept the money an act of selfishness and greed? Of course not. Mother Teresa accepted the money and used it to construct a hospital for leprosy patients.

Smith would regard Mother Teresa's decision as one made in regard to her own self-interest. Mother Teresa lived to help poor people. She found satisfaction in her work with the poor. Given an opportunity to provide even more help, thanks to a $190,000 award, she took advantage of it. Her decision to accept the money was both self-interested and generous. Knowing that people respond to opportunities to earn money tells us little about their character. Saints and sinners alike have reason to be interested in money.

Smith also explained the benefits of **free trade**—that is, trade that is not heavily restricted by tariffs (taxes on imports), quotas, and other barriers to exchange. Most economists today remain strong supporters of free trade, but it is a controversial idea in some circles. Domestic businesses and unions often lobby Congress and federal regulatory agencies for protection from foreign competition. The argument for protection is usually that unfair competition from foreign firms threatens American firms and the jobs of American workers. Smith and other proponents of free trade suggest instead that individuals and firms should specialize, producing goods they can produce at a low cost, and then engage in voluntary trade with others, including suppliers in other countries. Both sides will be better off as a result:

> It is the maxim of every prudent master of a family, never to attempt to make at home what it will cost him more to make than to buy. The [tailor] does not attempt to make his own shoes, but buys them of the shoemaker. The shoemaker does not attempt to make his own [clothes], but employs a [tailor]….What is prudence in the conduct of every private family, can scarce be folly in that of a great kingdom.[4]

Smith argued that free trade benefits consumers by giving them access to lower prices and a wider selection of goods and services. Simultaneously, free trade opens new global markets for domestic businesses. Today, this increase in international trade is called **globalization**. Finally, free trade puts pressure on domestic producers to work hard; if they don't provide well for their customers, their customers might find another place to buy.

Smith's ideas about trade amounted to more than topics for pleasant discussion and debate. They touched directly on issues of war and peace in his time. He published *The Wealth of Nations* in 1776; shortly thereafter, the British were at war, fighting to keep their American colonies. Smith boldly argued that the cost of keeping the American colonies would not be worth the benefits. The benefits could be achieved without the costs of war, he claimed, by allowing the colonies to be free and then trading with them; that would be a better economic option.

Smith's ideas about free trade have had lasting, widespread impact. To cite one example: they influenced a decision by the English Parliament to repeal the Corn Laws in Great Britain. The Corn

The Peterloo Massacre was a consequence of protests against the Corn Laws in Britain.

Laws, enacted in 1815, imposed tariffs (taxes) on corn (and wheat and grain) imported into Great Britain and Ireland. The tariffs prevented nearly all foreign grain from entering Britain. Prices for bread went up. Consumers suffered, especially in Ireland, where a potato blight had caused famine. Domestic producers nonetheless supported the Corn Laws. An Anti-Corn-Law League sprouted up to advocate for repeal. The League was part of a growing movement among England's middle class in support of free trade. Repeal of the Corn Laws came in 1846. With free importation of corn, wheat, and grain, prices for bread came down. Corn prices held steady for another generation, and with better times there was a greatly increased consumption of bread.[5]

What's Next?

Each of the following chapters focuses on a particular episode in American history. The chapters call on you to examine these episodes in light of economic concepts, including some we have introduced here. The choices colonists faced as they decided whether to fight a risky war of revolution, the opportunity cost of the Civil War, the incentives for immigrants to leave their home nations, the contribution competition made to the desegregation of major league baseball—these and other economic aspects of American history will be revealed and clarified, we believe, as you analyze them by applications of the economic way of thinking.

Our goal in these chapters is to show you how the economic way of thinking provides a deeper and more complete understanding of why people made the choices they did and why history happened as it did. Economic thinking can improve your ability to use historical information to understand human actions. In most cases, the behavior in question can be explained by reference to a few simple but powerful economic ideas. As you continue reading the chapters, be sure to keep these ideas in mind:

- The choices people make as a result of scarcity.
- The costs and benefits involved.
- The incentives in play.
- The rules of the game, and any changes in those rules.
- The gains from voluntary trade.
- The unexpected consequences.

Along the way—in light of information about spending, earning, prices, taxes, and other economic factors—you will learn more about how people have earned a living in the U.S. economy, how businesses have operated, and how interaction between market institutions and government institutions has often resulted in unexpected outcomes. Your insights into economic episodes in American history will enrich your understanding of the past. Understanding the past will enrich your understanding of economic episodes as they unfold in the present.

QUESTIONS for DISCUSSION

1. Briefly stated, what is the economic way of thinking?
2. How did Adam Smith contribute to the economic way of thinking?
3. What is a market economy?
4. Why did Adam Smith support free trade?
5. Allison is a junior at Washington High School. She shows up on time every day for her U.S. history class and she completes all the assignments and quizzes even though history is not her favorite subject. Citing at least three principles of the economic way of thinking, and using your imagination (going beyond the information provided above), write a short paragraph that describes and explains Allison's behavior.

The Wealth of Nations
http://www.econlib.org/library/Smith/smWN.html

This site includes the complete text of Adam Smith's masterwork, The Wealth of Nations.

Adam Smith's *The Wealth of Nations*
http://www.c-spanvideo.org/program/292116-1

This site includes a video (running time 1 hour, 5 minutes) in which Samuel Fleischacker and Russell Roberts talk about The Wealth of Nations.

EH.Net Economic History Services
http://www.eh.net

Resources for historians of economic thought provided by EH.Net and the History of Economics Society. Resources include databases and an online economic history encyclopedia.

Why Did the British Colonies Succeed Economically—Without Finding Gold and Silver?

John Rolfe, a colonial entrepreneur, with his bride, Pocahontas.

John Rolfe's Shipwreck

When the English gentleman John Rolfe found himself shipwrecked on the Atlantic's Somers Isles (later to be called Bermuda) in 1610, his plans for gaining wealth and fame went badly off track. Rolfe had sailed on the *Sea Venture* bound for Jamestown, Virginia, the colony English settlers established in 1607. Rolfe's ship had been headed for the colony with fresh supplies and new settlers.

After the shipwreck it took Rolfe's party a year to build new ships and continue the journey to Jamestown. In the meanwhile, things had gone badly for the colonists, who suffered from conflict among themselves and starvation. When Rolfe and his party finally arrived, they found only a ragtag remnant of the original Jamestown settlers. The survivors had been ready to abandon the colony, but receiving new supplies caused them to change their minds.[1]

Rolfe was a new kind of fortune-seeker in his time. Rather than hunting for gold and silver, the resources colonial governments expected to be most rewarding, he had a less exciting plan: he wanted to grow tobacco for export back to England. In this chapter we will see how John Rolfe's approach to colonial development succeeded far beyond anything the treasure hunters had dreamed of. But how did John Rolfe and his fellow British settlers make it happen? How did the British colonies succeed economically without finding gold and silver?

The Historical Context
Comparing the British and Spanish Colonies in America

Do people need kings and queens to tell them what to do? Just as surely as we answer "no" today, the accepted answer was "yes" in John Rolfe's time. Central authority then seemed necessary for two main reasons:

KEY ECONOMIC CONCEPTS

Economic growth	Mercantilism
Entrepreneur	Specialization
Exports	Trade
Imports	

1. Politically, it was thought, people could not be trusted to govern themselves. They were not well schooled and did not have the same wisdom as the ruling classes. Self-government would lead to chaos, whereas rule by a king or queen would be orderly.

2. Economically, people might make bad decisions or take advantage of others if they were allowed too much freedom. Their choices about buying, selling, and employment needed to be reined in by custom, tradition, or royal authority. In practice, this meant that people would experience little or no upward mobility. Most people born into the lower class would live their lives without hope of economic advancement.

In many ways, American history is the story of disproving these two points. The United States has thrived under a measure of self-government and economic freedom unheard of in old Europe.

Although at this time both Britain and Spain were ruled by kings and queens, there were important differences in how their monarchs ruled. Britain by this time had developed a political system in which royal power was limited. The British Parliament had taken control of many governmental responsibilities once held by kings and queens. (In England, Parliament is a legislative body, similar to the United States Congress.) In Britain, moreover, the law protected certain individual rights against the exercise

Attack on a Spanish treasure ship in 1620.

of royal power. Spain had no parliament, nor did it have effective laws to protect individual rights. As a result of these differences, the two countries took different paths in their colonial ventures. Britain's colonies enjoyed considerable autonomy—freedom to make decisions about local political and economic activity. Spain exercised more direct control over political and economic activity in its colonies.

Britain's success in America was unexpected. Spain was the original colonial power in the New World. Its explorations and conquests, starting with Christopher Columbus, enriched the Spanish treasury with gold and silver. The British, arriving more than 100 years after the Spanish, found little gold and silver. Instead, they occupied a strip of Atlantic coast land that offered only rocks, forests, and mosquitoes. The outcome of the colonial power game seemed clear: Spain had succeeded and Britain had failed.

But by 1776, the North American British colonies had actually become prosperous.[2] In the American experience, kings and queens and gold and silver proved unnecessary to a prosperous civil society.

The Economics of Mercantilism, Economic Growth, Specialization, and Trade

The colonial powers' determination to acquire precious metals reflected their belief in **mercantilism**: the idea that colonies have an obligation to assist the mother country in gaining wealth. As the Spanish applied the doctrine of mercantilism, they measured economic success by the mother country's holdings of gold and silver. Thus it was considered a boon for the economy whenever Spain's ships returned from the New World loaded with treasure for the king and queen.

Other Spanish mercantilist policies included the following:

- A nation should increase its domestic production of goods and services, to be traded for gold and silver from other nations.

- A nation should prohibit the export of gold and silver. (**Exports** are goods and services sold to other countries.)

- A nation should discourage imports of consumer goods where possible. When imports were necessary, they should be paid for with other consumer goods, not gold and silver. (**Imports** are goods and services brought in from other countries).

Spain's strict form of mercantilism, with its focus on accumulating gold and silver, went hand-in-hand with Spain's tradition of rule by a powerful central government supported by a strong navy. Spanish mercantilism fit well within a system of royal rule and a tightly controlled economy. The British pursued a looser form of mercantilism, partly because they found almost no gold or silver in their colonies and partly because they followed a less centralized approach to political and economic control. The English economy was not controlled by the King or by Parliament.

Instead of finding precious metals, the Jamestown colonists found themselves struggling to survive harsh winters. Even after two years, they did not have a secure food supply. By 1610, only 60 of the 204 original settlers remained. "The Starving Time" had been so severe that the colonists ate cats, dogs, horses, and rats; some even turned to cannibalism and grave robbing to avoid starvation.

In 1610 success seemed unlikely, but by 1776 it was assured. What caused this turnaround? Economic growth—fostered by entrepreneurship, specialization, and trade—was the key.

Economic growth is an increase in a society's production of goods and services over time. Colonial America experienced substantial economic growth from 1607 to 1776. Slow at first, it rapidly gained momentum. Colonial America possessed, in abundance, some resources that were in short supply in Europe: land, water, and fishing grounds. It did not have a large labor force; but, early on, labor was not its most pressing need. What the early settlers needed most was knowledge of which enterprises would succeed. It was in fact a new world for them, and they did not know which activities could generate profits in this new environment. They quickly learned that exploration for gold was not the answer.

Jamestown in 1614.

In an environment of such uncertainty, mercantilism based on a quest for gold and silver, with strict central controls, would not work. The English king and queen held power an ocean away, and they showed no inclination or ability to dictate exactly which enterprises should be attempted in their colonies. The time was right for experimentation by **entrepreneurs**, individuals who would assume the risks of starting new enterprises.

Many entrepreneurial experiments failed. Successful ventures included timber harvesting, shipbuilding, and the production of crops. England provided a ready market for exports from the colonies, and the export trade fostered economic growth. Most important for John Rolfe was success that came from specializing in growing tobacco. Rolfe had managed through his shipwrecked journey to hold onto Spanish tobacco seeds he had bought for the trip. The seeds grew well at Jamestown, and the tobacco crop he produced was eagerly sought by British consumers.

Growing tobacco for trade worked so well for Rolfe that he became a wealthy planter. He and many other entrepreneurs thrived in the British North American colonies, but entrepreneurs generally did not thrive in Spain's Latin American colonies. What made the difference? Although there is no single answer, several reasons help to explain the outcome:

- The Spanish colonies had both gold and silver, and the Spaniards created mines to extract these resources. According to mercantilist thinking, that was enough. These precious metals were the reason for exploration and colonization. There was little reason to consider other enterprises.

- The Spanish colonies, in part because the gold and silver they held was valuable, were tightly controlled by the crown. The British colonies were not tightly controlled by the British government. Entrepreneurs in Britain's colonies could easily try out new ventures.

- Private ownership of resources was prevalent in the British colonies; thus, entrepreneurs could keep most of the profit they generated.

Their earnings motivated them to expand production and trade.

- Risk-takers like John Rolfe were naturally attracted to the British colonies by the abundance of land, the personal freedom the colonies allowed, and the opportunities for trade to be found in the colonies.

As colonial America succeeded in export markets and more settlers arrived, economic growth increased. A larger colonial population meant larger markets for the goods and services being produced. Selling to those larger markets increased incomes and production in turn. With internal and export markets thriving, both Britain and its colonies benefited.

Specialization occurs when individuals choose not to be self-sufficient in producing everything they need. Instead, they concentrate on (they specialize in) producing those goods and services they can best produce, and they trade for other things. Some British colonists, early on, had been subsistence farmers, supporting themselves and their families but producing no surplus goods for trade. Before long, however, economic growth created other opportunities. A skilled carpenter, for example, could enjoy a much better food supply by working in shipbuilding and then using his earnings to buy food. A tobacco farmer could specialize in growing tobacco and use his earnings to buy more and better food than he could raise himself. Specialization and trade served as complementary economic activities, fostering economic growth in a climate of economic freedom.

In the Spanish colonies specialization and trade proceeded under constraints: the crown's demand for gold and silver, managed by strong central control. In the race between the Spanish and British colonial empires, the Spanish began their quest earlier and found gold and silver quickly. The British began later but caught up and passed the Spanish in colonial prosperity. This outcome would have been hard to foresee in 1607, when the first British settlers arrived, but it became reality as British entrepreneurs pursued growth through trade and specialization.

Was mercantilism a well-worked-out economic theory?

No. Unlike more recent economic ideas, mercantilism never became a fully developed system of economic thought. Rather, it was a loose collection of ideas about how nations become wealthy.

Was mercantilism the same everywhere it was applied?

No. As applied by the Spanish, mercantilism had very simple goals: bringing back gold and silver from the New World to enrich the homeland treasury. The Spaniards were able to focus on gold and silver because of their early lead in colonizing the new world, with protection provided by the Spanish navy.

Though the British might have wanted to emulate the Spanish, the lack of gold and silver in their colonies forced a different approach. Britain's legal and economic systems also made a difference. They traditionally had provided freedom for entrepreneurs. As a result, Britain's colonies could contribute to Britain's accumulation of wealth, but in a different way. Instead of expecting gold and silver to be provided directly from the colonies, Britain's mercantilists came to expect that the colonies would provide raw materials for British manufacturing, as well as markets for finished British goods. The increase in overall economic activity, together with exports to the rest of Europe, would eventually bring in the gold and silver so valued by mercantilists.

Did gold and silver foster economic growth in Spain's colonies?

No. Money is used to purchase goods and services, but the exchange of money does not by itself create economic growth. Rather, it is the *investment* of money—in starting up new businesses, buying equipment, farmland, ships, houses, and so on—that creates economic growth, as that investment yields new goods and services, produced for trade. When Spaniards mined gold and silver in America and shipped it back home, they were in essence shipping money. Rather than investing that money for specialized production and trade in the colonies, they shipped it back to Spain where it was used in support of military activities and to provide luxury goods for the royal family and the nobility. These uses of gold and silver did not foster economic growth in the colonies.

What makes a nation wealthy?

Mercantilism's answer to this question was simple: gold and silver. Adam Smith, whom we met in Chapter 1, thought mercantilism's answer was wrong. Instead, Smith wrote, it was growth in production and consumption that would make a nation wealthy. Such growth would enable all the people, not only the royalty, to gain some luxuries in addition to the necessities of life. To Smith, a large royal treasury did not mean that an economy had succeeded. He wrote: "No society can surely be flourishing and happy, of which the far greater part of the members are poor and miserable."[3] In *The Wealth of Nations*, Smith explained how economies could succeed. His work was inspired partly by his knowledge of the success of the British American colonies.

Is central control necessary for prosperity?

Smith considered and rejected the idea that an economy must be centrally controlled to ensure that people will have adequate incomes. Instead, he thought that government should provide the proper institutions (a legal system, for example) and then step aside to let private initiative succeed. Smith's formula for economic growth was "peace, easy taxes, and a tolerable administration of justice."[4] Mercantilism and royal rule had all too often led to the opposite: high taxes, arbitrary administration of justice, and war.

Writing against the popular sentiment of his time, Smith maintained that self-interest is actually good for an economy. In Smith's view, people would be better off if they were allowed to choose

Farmers harvest tobacco in Jamestown.

their own occupations and enterprises. A self-interested person, he wrote, is "led by an invisible hand to promote an end which was no part of his intention."[5] Smith's metaphor of an "invisible hand" became a powerful symbol of the benefits of markets.

What lesson about economic growth did the experience of the British colonies suggest?

The colonists' experience, in a remote frontier not closely controlled by royal rule, provides a clear example of how an economy can grow without central planning. The British colonies' economic success was a by-product of Britain's informal policy of "salutary neglect"—that is, lax enforcement of laws for control of the colonies. The economic historians Gary M. Walton and Hugh Rockoff found that by 1776 colonial Americans "lived very well, both by today's standards in many areas of the world and in comparison with the most advanced areas of the world."[6] The year 1776 was important both in intellectual history and American history: Smith's *Wealth of Nations* was published then, in the year that Britain's American colonies declared their independence.

QUESTIONS for DISCUSSION

1. What was the main economic goal of mercantilism?
2. Could the king and queen of England have done a good job directing the growth and development of the colonial American economy? Why or why not?
3. Why would a settler who wanted to have a lot of corn concentrate instead on growing tobacco?
4. To Adam Smith, what was the significance of a large royal treasury? Did it mean that an economy had succeeded? Explain your answer.

Pastime and Merry Exercises

Captain John Smith led the English settlement in North America at Jamestown, Virginia. The colony struggled before it became firmly established.[7] Smith wrote the account below, describing a time when laziness threatened the survival of the colony. Ensuring survival was a full-time job, but some colonists worked on it only part-time, spending the rest of the day in "pastime and merry exercises." Smith responded with a proclamation in which he concluded that "he that will not work shall not eat." Here is an excerpt from his proclamation:

But now casting up the store and finding sufficient till the next harvest, the fear of starving was abandoned .... Six hours each day was spent in work, the rest in pastime and merry exercises, but the untowardness of the greatest number [caused the president to] advise as followeth. Countrymen, the long experience of our late miseries, I hope is sufficient to persuade every one to a present correction of himself, and think not that either my pains, nor the adventurers' purses, will ever maintain you in idleness and sloth. I speak not this to you all, for diverse of you I know deserve both honor and reward, better than is yet here to be had: but the greater part must be more industrious, or starve, how ever you have been heretofore tolerated by the authorities of the Council ....You see now that power rests wholly in myself: you must obey this now for a Law, that he that will not work shall not eat (except by sickness he be disabled)[,] for the labors of thirty or forty honest and industrious men shall not be consumed to maintain an hundred and fifty idle loiterers.[8]

QUESTIONS for DISCUSSION

1. When the colonists took inventory of their food ("casting up the store"), what did some of them conclude? How did this conclusion affect their behavior?
2. How long did the Jamestown settlers work each day? Does this strike you as appropriate behavior?
3. The "adventurers' purses" referred to in Smith's proclamation were the funds provided by investors in the Jamestown venture. What was Smith warning the lazy members of the party against in that sentence?
4. Smith stated that the majority of the settlers must now be "more industrious." What does he say the alternative is if they do not work harder?
5. Did Smith's proclamation include an exception for disability? Does our society today require that disabled people work or starve? Explain.

Is China the New Mercantilist State?

Mercantilism fell out of favor in the 1700s, as the advantages of less restrictive economic systems became apparent. Is there a nation that favors mercantilism today? Some economists believe that China is pursuing a modern form of mercantilism. Although the Chinese government does not focus on accumulating gold and silver, it has, under its current leadership, been accumulating large amounts of wealth from foreign trading relationships.

The growth of Chinese exports—goods and services sold to other countries—has been dramatic in recent years. Author Philippe Legrain calculates that China now exports as much every six hours as it did in the entire year of 1978.[9] In return for China's many exports, the rest of the world pays with its currencies and other forms of wealth.

Consider these parallels between the mercantilists of old and China today:

- Mercantilism called for increasing domestic production of goods and services, to be traded to other nations for gold and silver. China follows a similar path today, but accumulates currency and other forms of wealth rather than gold and silver.

- Mercantilism prohibited the export of gold and silver. China maintains strict controls on the flow of currency and other forms of wealth.

- Mercantilism discouraged imports of consumer goods, as China does today.

- Mercantilism required a strong central government, which China has today.

China's leaders believe that export-led growth has been responsible for China's recent economic success. However, China's leaders now also favor reducing the income inequality that came with that economic success. Some Chinese people saw sharply increased incomes as the Chinese economy grew, but others, especially in rural areas, saw little improvement. In a 2007 address, President Hu Jintao pledged to reverse this growing disparity of incomes. Hu called for "a reasonable and orderly pattern of income distribution," adding that a large middle class of Chinese citizens was an important goal.[10]

QUESTIONS for DISCUSSION

1. In what ways does China's policy of promoting exports resemble old-fashioned mercantilism?
2. In what ways is China's policy of promoting exports different from old-fashioned mercantilism?
3. If a nation's economy grows, increasing average income levels, does that mean that all of its residents are better off? Why or why not?
4. Is it a sensible strategy to try to make an economy grow first, and then to worry about any income inequality that might result? Why or why not?
5. Is creating a large middle class a worthwhile goal for the Chinese economy? For the U.S. economy?

Jamestown Rediscovery

http://www.preservationvirginia.org/rediscovery/page.php?page_id=1

This is the official website of the Jamestown Rediscovery Archaeological Project at Jamestown Island, Virginia, the first permanent English colony in North America. It includes recent information about continuing digs at the historic site.

The Voyages of Captain John Smith

http://www.smithtrail.net/captain-john-smith

This site provides biographical information about the leader of the Jamestown expedition, along with links to the text of Smith's writings and maps.

Virtual Jamestown

http://www.virtualjamestown.org

The Virtual Jamestown Archive is a digital research, teaching, and learning project that explores the legacies of the Jamestown settlement and "the Virginia experiment."

Is China the New Mercantilist State?

http:www.chinatoday.com

This site provides links to Chinese government information, Chinese news outlets, and news accounts about Chinese events.

Why Did John Harrower Sell Himself into Bondage?

Colonial workers dig ditches.

The Story of John Harrower

I n the late 18th century, John Harrower was a poor Scottish merchant—probably a peddler. He was married and had children, and he was desperate to find work. After leaving Scotland to look for work in England, he eventually arrived in London. Still he had no luck. In fact, he was destitute. Finally he made a bold choice. Here is an excerpt from his diary:

> *Sunday 18th [January 1774]*
> This day I got to London and was like a blind man without a guide, not knowing where to go being freindless and having no more money but fifteen shillings & eight pence farthing a small sum to enter London with; But I trust in the mercys of God who is a rich provider and am hopefull before it is done some way will cast up for me.

> *Wednesday 26th*
> This day I being reduced to the last shilling I hade was obligded to engage to go to Virginia for four years as a schoolmaster for Bedd, Board, washing and five pound during the whole time. I have also wrote my wife this day a particular Accot. of every thing that has happned to me since I left her untill this date; At 3 pm this day I went on board the Snow Planter Capt. Bowers Comr. for Virginia now lying at Ratliff Cross, and imediatly as I came on board I reed, my Hammock and Bedding.[1]

Harrower arrived in Virginia after a long and difficult voyage. His indenture was sold to William Daingerfield, who wanted Harrower to tutor his three sons. An indenture was a **contract**—a legally binding agreement between the individuals involved that could be enforced by the courts.

Harrower had sold himself into indentured servitude. In other words, he had signed a written document in which he agreed to provide his labor for four years; a man named William

KEY ECONOMIC CONCEPTS

Contract	**Market economy**
Incentive	**Opportunity cost**
Indentured servitude	**Voluntary exchange**

Daingerfield bought the contract, thus buying the right to Harrower's labor. Hundreds of thousands of others made choices similar to Harrower's. Most of the indentured servants were English; others were Scottish, German, and Irish. In contrast, few people in Spain and France made the choice to indenture themselves. Why did so many people like Harrower choose to indenture themselves in Britain's American colonies? Why did the British rather than the Spanish and French colonies attract large numbers of colonists through the indenture system?

The Historical Context
The British Colonists Arrive and Few Others Come

Britain got off to a late start in the race to establish colonies in the New World. By the time Britain had established its colonies along the northeast coast of North America, all the "good" land in the New World had been seized by Spain and France. At the time, the good land was thought to be land that held gold and silver, the minerals that nations prized most highly. Spain had dispatched its *conquistadores*—the men who were to conquer native people and their land—to plunder the gold and silver of the Americas. Although the Spanish established plantations and other enterprises, overall they failed to bring substantial numbers of settlers to their colonies. Between 1509 and 1740, about two million British settlers came to the New World, compared with 150,000 Spanish.

The French, arriving after the Spanish, pushed their colonial claims aggressively. France established settlements in Quebec and eventually claimed lands stretching from the Great Lakes to Louisiana. Although the French were highly successful at establishing trading posts, they also failed, like the Spanish, to attract large numbers of settlers. In 1756, 60,000 French people lived in Canada and the Caribbean.

The Economics of Labor in the Colonies

Scarcity of labor was a long-standing problem in Britain's North American colonies. Demand for labor was high. Owners of businesses and farmers needed workers of all types. They sought many kinds of artisans including blacksmiths, brewers, butchers, glassblowers, silversmiths. Owners of large farms and plantations needed farm hands and unskilled laborers.

The potential supply of labor from across the Atlantic was also high. Farmland was abundant in the colonies, but it was scarce in Britain and mainland Europe, where young sons knew they had little chance to inherit farms of any workable size. Then, late in the 17th century, there was a series of crop failures in England, as well as religious and political persecutions in Britain and parts of Europe. These conditions provided strong **incentives**—positive benefits— encouraging individuals to leave Britain in search of better conditions.

But wait. Despite the incentives that encouraged people to set sail for America, there was a practical problem. People were seeking economic opportunities in Britain, where the opportunities were scarce; other people were offering economic opportunities in the colonies, where opportunities were abundant. But passage to North America was expensive; it would cost more than a year's income for a typical person. How could people seek a better life in the colonies when the price of passage was so high? A new sort of labor market emerged to bridge the gap.

The London Company

wants settlers to go to
Virginia
Free land!
Free Ship fare!

sign up now to work
for a Virginia Planter

Work for seven years to pay back the planter for your fare to Virginia. After seven years, you will receive land, clothing, some livestock, and tools.

Come! Be an indentured servant. Then start a life of your own!

Indentured Servitude

John Harrower and hundreds of thousands like him decided to participate in a new sort of labor market for indentured servitude. **Indentured servitude** enabled people of modest means to travel to North America by selling their labor for a specified period of time to an owner who would have control over their employment and other aspects of their lives. In other words, people like John Harrower voluntarily sold themselves into a form of bondage. Although this concept might seem startling today, it was not unusual at the time. Parents in 17th and 18th century Britain and mainland Europe often indentured their children to craftsmen and shopkeepers for six or seven years so that they might learn a trade. In return, the employers fed and clothed the children and taught them a trade or a business.

To allow people to leave Britain and Europe and travel to North America, the concept of indenture was modified. Here is how the system worked:

- Ship owners or their agents advertised their offer of indentures (contracts) for passage across the Atlantic.

- A person interested in migrating to the colonies signed a contract with the ship owner. He or she then became an indentured servant.

- Indentures typically required an indentured servant to provide a specific number of years of service to an owner, in return for food, clothing, housing, and perhaps training in a craft. Some indentured servants received money or land at the end of the contractual period.

- Most often, the length of a contract was for four to seven years.

- The ship owner transported the indentured servants to a port in North America.

- The indentured servants, if they survived the rigors of the voyage, remained on the ship until the ship owner could find someone to buy the contract. Ship owners often advertised on shore that they had indentures available for sale.

- Once the indenture was sold, the indentured servant was legally obligated to serve out the time of the contract.

- The owners were legally obliged to meet their obligations under the contract, such as providing food and education.

- Once all terms of the contract were fulfilled, the former servant was free.

Soon, a highly organized labor market built around the indenture system developed in the colonies. Agents, advertising for potential clients, attracted people of all sorts, including farmers, artisans, domestic servants, and unskilled workers. Here, identified by name, are a few of the thousands of people who came to Virginia under terms of indenture from 1654 to 1686.

- John Davis was a tanner (tanners make leather out of animal skins) from Berrow, Worcestershire. The date of his indenture was October 16, 1654. He was to serve for four years.

- Robert Fox was a collier (colliers made charcoal) from Bristol. The date of his indenture was December 11, 1654. He was to serve for four years.

- Susan Selfe was from Chippenham, Wiltshire. The date of her indenture was December 1654. She was to serve for four years.

- Robert Smith was a house carpenter from Kingsale, Ireland. The date of his indenture was October 8, 1655. He was to serve for four years.

- Peter Whitingham was from Middlewich, Cheshire. The date of his indenture was September 4, 1655. He was to serve for three years.

- John Worgan was a laborer from Covert, Monmouth. The date of his indenture was October 2, 1656. He was to serve for eight years.[2]

HISTORICAL QUESTIONS & ECONOMIC ANSWERS

Why did Britain succeed in settling North America with assistance from an indenture system while Spain and France did not?

Britain and Spain had different economic systems. The British economy was much closer to being a market economy than was the economy of Spain. Private ownership is the key to a market economy. As described in Chapter 1, **market economies** involve private ownership of natural resources, capital resources, and labor resources. Individual choices and voluntary exchange determine which goods and services will be produced, not the government. Individuals are free to start businesses or to sell their labor as they think best.

Private property rights were not as well developed or secure in Spain as they were in Britain. In Spain, during the years of colonial ventures, decisions made by the royal family still dominated the economy. Private land ownership had not been firmly established. Britain was far more accustomed to the operation of free markets and individual decision making. Parliament had limited the powers of the royal family. The right to private ownership was well established and enforced.

The British colonial system encouraged settlement over other colonial activity—over, for example, establishing military outposts. The establishment of permanent settlements in Britain's colonies resulted in the development of privately owned farms. This set the stage for increased demand for labor, a resource that was always scarce in the British colonies. In response to this demand, a new type of labor market developed in Britain and the British colonies: the market for indentured servitude. Although it was controversial at the time, the British Parliament allowed this market to operate. The result was that British economic and political institutions became dominant in North America.

Spain chose to use most of its new gold and silver resources to purchase luxury items and fight wars in Europe.[3] Although Spain brought substantial military forces to the Americas, it did not attract many settlers. Since it had little regard for private ownership of enterprises, it relied on using American Indians for labor.

The overall experience of the French in North America is not much different from the experience of the Spanish. Like the Spanish, the French were slow to develop institutions of a market economy. A specialized labor market for bringing French settlers to North America never materialized. The French at the time were also distracted by religious wars and other conflicts at home. The French authorities never chose settlement as a high priority.

What incentives encouraged people to sign indentures?

Land, it turns out, was a big motivator. The chance to own land—to become a farmer— was a major incentive to many potential setters living in England, Scotland, Ireland, Germany, and elsewhere in Europe. In addition, other employment opportunities for skilled and unskilled workers were abundant in North America. The indenture contract itself offered positive rewards. It provided that a person would be free after the period of the indenture. In Maryland, for example, an indentured servant was entitled at the end of his or her term of service to 50 acres of land, a suit of clothes, various tools, and three barrels of corn. "The former servant then could set up as a . . . farmer, vote, and even be elected to the [Maryland] assembly."[4]

What were the costs of the indentures?

Signing an indenture involved a high opportunity cost. **Opportunity cost** is the next-best alternative a person gives up in making a choice. What was the next-best choice for a person who signed an indenture? It probably would have been to stay home and keep trying to find opportunity there. People who signed indentures had to be willing to leave behind family and friends and any alternative economic opportunities they might be able to find in their homelands. By all accounts, the voyage across the Atlantic was difficult. Poor food, disease, foul air, and overcrowded living conditions were common on board ships. A voyage might take 12 weeks. Poor weather conditions often prolonged the trip. People often became very sick during the voyage. Some died on the way.

There was also another risk. What sort of a person would purchase the contract? Would the person be a kind owner or a ruthless tyrant?

People who signed indentures were willing to take risks. Individuals like John Harrower were willing to make enormous sacrifices in the hope of improving their economic condition. Remember, most people stayed behind in their home lands, unwilling to take such a gamble.

Were most indentured servants criminals?

No, although this is a popular misconception. In 1718, the British Parliament passed the Transportation Act, under which Britain began sending its imprisoned convicts to be sold as indentured servants in the American colonies. It was customary for a convict to serve 7 years for a minor offense and 14 years for a major offense. The "export" of convicts caused much consternation among the American colonists. However, the number of exported convicts was not very large. About 35,000 convicts were exported as indentured servants, compared to the total of more than 350,000 indentured servants.

Was indentured servitude brutal?

Indentured servitude certainly appears to be brutal or harsh, by today's standards. But life for poor people back in their homelands was often harsh, too. And of course working conditions for indentured servants varied with the owners. John Harrower described his life as a tutor as a good experience—certainly better than his economic experiences in Scotland and England. Other indentured workers were not so lucky. Cruel owners were reported to whip their servants for trivial wrongdoing and work them until they were exhausted. And if indentured servants ran away, time was added to their length of service. An indentured servant could even be resold to another owner without his or her permission.

Were indentured servants slaves?

No. Most indentured servants were British subjects with the rights of British subjects. They signed a contract to provide their labor to an owner for a specified period of time. But the contract was enforceable both ways. If an indentured servant ran away, the owner could use the local police and courts to find the person, get him or her back to work, and add time to the contract. If an owner failed to meet the terms of the contract, the indentured servant could and sometimes did take the owner to court. If the judge ruled in favor of the indentured servant, he or she could be set free. In comparison, enslaved Africans had no such rights. They had no legal means to redress their grievances.

The voluntary exchange system built into indentured servitude provided strong incentives to owners and indentured servants to stick to their agreements. **Voluntary exchange** means that both sides in an exchange believe that what they are getting is worth more than what they are giving up. With the indenture system, owners

Colonial lumber and wood production.

were able to obtain workers and workers were able to obtain improved economic opportunities in a new land. Most indentured servants worked out their indenture periods without having to petition the courts and without feeling so desperate as to risk running away. Once indentured servants completed their obligations, they were free to live their lives as they wished.

Why did indentured servitude disappear?

Indentured servitude was controversial even at the time. People often criticized the methods of the recruitment agents. Agents had reputations for exaggerating or simply lying about conditions in North America. Sometimes people signed contracts after the agent had gotten them drunk, and they would have no idea what they were signing. At the worst, there were reports of actual kidnappings.

The British Parliament did act to regulate the market. For example, agents and potential indentured servants were required to sign contracts before a judge. This step helped to drive scoundrels out of the business and to protect the reputations of honest agents. Indentured servants were also registered in order to keep track of those involved in the trade and what eventually happened to them.

Indentured servitude was never abolished by Parliament, nor was it regulated out of existence. Why did it disappear? There were three primary reasons.

- First, the cost of passage across the Atlantic declined over time. With wages gradually rising in Europe, it made economic sense for individuals to save up money and purchase a ticket for passage rather than selling their labor.

- Second, as individuals in America became economically successful, more were able to save money and purchase tickets for family members to come to North America.

- Third, in some colonies, slavery provided labor at a lower cost than the costs involved in maintaining indentured servants. This was especially true for southern colonies engaged in the production of rice and tobacco.

QUESTIONS for DISCUSSION

1. Why were there more settlers in the British colonies than in the colonies of Spain and France?
2. What were the main elements of an indenture?
3. How was indentured servitude an example of voluntary exchange, which benefited both parties?
4. What was the opportunity cost of signing an indenture?
5. Why did indentured servitude gradually disappear?
6. What points might one of the indentured servants identified by name in this chapter (John Davis, Robert Fox, Susan Selfe, Robert Smith, Peter Whitingham, or John Worgan) make in a letter written to loved ones back home?
7. A claim could be made that the development of indentured servitude set the stage for the development of a prosperous new nation. How could that be true?

Richard Lowther Signs an Indenture

Indentures were signed by hundreds of thousands of individuals. Because of widespread interest in the market for indentures, the contracts gradually became standardized. The following is an indenture signed by Richard Lowther in 1627.

The Last day of July/ Anno Dom 1627 … between Richard Lowther of Broome in the Parish of South well [i.e., Southill] in the County of Bedford brewer of the one party and Edward Hurd Citizen and Iron monger of London of the other party witnesses that the said Richard Lowther … has hired himself and is become and by this presents does Covenant and agree and bind himself to be remain and Continue the Covenant servant of him the said Edward Hurd his heirs and assigns to be by him or them sent and transported unto the Country and land of Virginia, … & to be by him or them employed upon his plantation there, for and during the space of Four years … during which said term the said Richard Lowther shall and will truly employ and endeavour himself to the utmost of his power knowledge and skill to do and perform true and faithful service unto the said Edward Hurd his heirs and assigns in for and concerning all such Labor and business as he or they shall think good to use and employ him the said Richard Lowther in ….IN CONSIDERATION whereof the said Edward Hurd for himself his executors administrators or assigns … do covenant promise and grant to and with the said Richard Lowther his heirs executors administrators and assigns … not only transport and furnish out the said Richard Lowther to and for Virginia aforesaid and there find provide and allow unto him sufficient meat drink apparel and other necessaries for his livelihood and maintenance during the said term But also at the expiration of the said term shall and will grant assign and allot unto him the said Richard Lowther the quantity of Fifty acres of Land in Virginia aforesaid to hold to him his heirs and assigns for ever …
In witness whereof the said parties to theis present writings indented Interchangeably have set their hands and seals given the day and year first above written.

Richard Lowther

Sealed and delivered in the presence of us John Davies and Andrew Ball
Servants to Tho: Thompson Ser.

Source: http://etext.lib.virginia.edu/etcbin/jamestown-browsemod?id=J1046

PRIMARY SOURCE QUESTIONS for DISCUSSION

1. What benefits did Richard Lowther gain according to the terms of the contract?
2. What benefit did Edward Hurd gain according to the terms of the contract?
3. What characteristic of a market economy is illustrated by the agreement made between Richard Lowther and Edward Hurd?

THEN & NOW

Are You Army Strong?

Are there examples of modern-day indentured servitude? Not really. But getting started in some careers—for example, enlisting in the armed forces—does resemble signing a contract for indentured servitude. If you decide to sign up for active duty in the U.S. Army, you sign up for a definite period of time; and, like the contracts for indenture, the agreement you sign for Army service provides no easy "opt out" clause.

Individuals who join the armed forces do so in response to a variety of incentives. Undoubtedly, many young people who enlist do so for nonmonetary reasons—out of a sense of duty and patriotism. Other incentives, more material in nature, probably include basic pay, according to years of service, and programs to help pay for education after service is completed. Here are some examples of the latter from www.goarmy.com:

- **Montgomery GI Bill (MGIB) & Army College Fund (ACF)**
  As a soldier, you can take advantage of the Montgomery GI Bill and the Army College Fund to pay for your college education. Depending on how long you enlist with the Army and the job you choose, you can get up to $83,448 to

help pay for college. All you have to do is give $100 a month during your first year of service. If you select the Army College Fund, the total amount is combined with the MGIB.

- **Post 9/11 GI Bill**
  Soldiers who served at least 90 days on active duty on or after 11 September 2001 are eligible to take advantage of the Post 9/11 GI Bill, which provides up to 36 months of benefits for education at an institution of higher learning. Benefits of the program include tuition, fees, a monthly living allowance, books, and supplies. Benefits may be transferred to a spouse or dependent children.

The Army also offers extensive fringe benefits, including:

- health care coverage,
- life insurance, and
- vacations.

In regard to opportunity cost, however, a person who joins the U.S. Army must sign a contract that commits him or her to three to six years of military service. Most recruits sign up for four years. Once a recruit has shipped to basic training, penalties may be applied for breaking the agreement.

THEN & NOW QUESTIONS for DISCUSSION

1. In what ways does service in the U.S. Army resemble indentured servitude?
2. In what way does service in the U.S. Army not resemble indentured servitude?
3. Why do you think the armed forces continue to require individuals to sign up for a specific period of time?

The Diary of John Harrower

http://www.archive.org/stream/diary00harr/diary00harr_djvu.tx

An archive from the Library of Congress that includes the full text of The Diary of John Harrower.

Indentured Servants in Maryland

http://teachingamericanhistorymd.net/000001/000000/000183/html/t183.html

Contains a listing of Maryland state archives concerning indentured servants and the laws relating to them.

Background Information on Indentured Servants

http://picketteducationalresources.com/images/indser.pdf

Includes information on the daily lives of indentured servants, pictures, and additional questions for discussion.

Are You Army Strong?

http://www.todaysmilitary.com

This site provides detailed information about the costs and benefits of serving in the U.S. armed forces.

Why Did the Colonists Fight When They Were Safe, Prosperous, and Free?

A wealthy colonial household in Virginia.

Was the Revolutionary War Inevitable?

John Greenhow was born in England in 1724.[1] He seems to have gotten off to a rough start in business; apparently he filed for bankruptcy in England in 1752. Then somehow he made his way to Williamsburg, Virginia, where he established himself as a successful merchant running a popular store. He owned a schooner—an eight-ton sailing vessel—called *The Robert*. *The Robert* carried peas, pork, lard, and butter northward to markets in Philadelphia; it returned to Williamsburg carrying pottery, flour, bread, bar iron, chocolate, coffee, iron skillets, soap, and furniture. Greenhow also operated a store in Richmond, Virginia. Advertisements listing the variety of imported goods Greenhow sold appeared regularly in the *Virginia Gazette* and attracted many customers.

Greenhow is not an isolated example. By 1776, many colonists had become economically successful as farmers, planters, and merchants. Widespread success among the colonists suggests that life in colonial America had clear advantages. We might wonder, then, at the colonists' decision to rebel. They had much to lose.

KEY ECONOMIC CONCEPTS

Opportunity cost	Rules of the game
Market economy	Subsidy
Incentive	Mercantilism

In fact, it is by no means obvious why the colonists decided to fight the Revolutionary War. At least until 1775, radical separatists in the colonies had failed to gain majority support among their countrymen for the revolutionary cause. This isn't much of a surprise. As the colonists looked toward the last quarter of the 18th century, they could have cited at least three powerful reasons not to fight: they were safe, prosperous, and free. (This generalization does not, of course, apply to African Americans held as slaves in the colonies.) Under these favorable circumstances, why would the colonists—English subjects themselves—fight a revolution against Britain, one of the world's most powerful nations?

A prosperous Yorktown, Virginia, in the mid-18th century.

The Historical Context
Why Fight?

The colonists were safe. The colonists lived and worked in relative safety, given the protection provided by Britain's Royal Navy and ground troops. This was no small matter. Throughout the earlier colonial era, imperial rivals and American Indians often posed serious threats to the colonists' lives and property.

The British spent heavily to protect the colonies from French forces and their American Indian allies during the French and Indian War (1755–1763). And the Royal Navy protected American shipping along the North American coast, in the Caribbean, and in the Mediterranean, where Barbary pirates conducted raids, stole cargoes, and sold captive sailors into slavery. All this protection was provided at a relatively low cost to the colonists; in taxes per person, they paid little—only 20 to 25 percent of taxes paid by the average British resident.

The colonists were prosperous. By today's standards, colonial life was rough indeed. But by the standards of their own time, the colonists enjoyed a high quality of life and material well-being. Production had increased at high rates throughout the colonial period. The colonists lived longer and better than most of their contemporaries in other places. Their incomes on average were apparently as high as or higher than average incomes for people living in Britain. Research by T.G. Burnard suggests that the wealth per person of the American colonists in 1774 was higher than that of people living in England and Wales. Burnard estimated that wealth per person in England and Wales equaled £42.30 (pounds sterling), compared to £46.50 in the colonies.[2] Referring to other data from 1774, economic historians Gary M. Walton and Hugh Rockhoff write, "Even today, relatively few countries generate average income levels that approach the earnings of free Americans on the eve of the Revolution."[3]

The colonists were free. In the words of American historian Samuel Eliot Morison,

> British subjects in America, excepting of course the Negroes, were then [about 1763] the freest people in the world . . . . They argued and then they fought, not to obtain freedom but to confirm the freedom they already had or claimed. They were . . . more advanced in the practice of self-government than the mother country. There was slight pressure from ancient custom, and few relics of feudalism. . . . [By] 1735, almost complete freedom of speech, press, and assembly was enjoyed. Trades and professions were open to the talented . . . . The hand of government rested lightly on Americans.[4]

In part, this climate of freedom reflected simple practicalities. The colonies were a long way from the British Isles. Transportation and communications were slow. It took a long time for anybody in London to learn of anything that looked like wrongdoing in a colonial legislature or seaport, and a long time, again, to respond with efforts to intervene. British authorities, accordingly, had been inclined to leave the colonists more or less alone, or to back away when the colonists resisted an unpopular policy. Moreover, the British system of colonial administration favored local control. Colonial legislatures, acting with a measure of democratic legitimacy, made most policy decisions in the colonies. In these bodies, members of the upper legislative houses were appointed by the Crown (as were colonial governors), but members of the lower legislative houses were elected.

The Economics of the Decision to Fight

Economists emphasize that events flow from the choices people make. The American colonists certainly were making choices as they moved toward war. They were not acting out of necessity or blindly, or without regard for consequences. They decided that fighting the Revolution somehow offered the best combination of the costs they might bear and the benefits they could attain.

What Were the Costs?

The economic costs of fighting were substantial. They involved an **opportunity cost**—the second-best choice that is given up in every choice people make. War would bring death and injury to many colonial fighters. The productive skills of the fallen would obviously be lost or diminished. War also would threaten the colonists' lucrative trade in tobacco, grains, wood, rice, and indigo. The second-best choice, we might suppose, would have been to avoid war and thus avoid these human and material losses. In choosing to fight, however, the colonists gave up that alternative, electing instead to pay the opportunity cost.

For further exploration of this decision and the costs it entailed, it is helpful to consider a basic feature of market economies. A **market economy** is one in which individual producers and consumers make their own economic choices. They are free to engage in voluntary exchanges and to compete with one another in various ways. They carry out their economic activity in the context of a legal system that enforces their contracts and protects their property, including privately owned businesses, personal possessions, and savings.

British governance of the American colonies imposed many policies that were contrary to the operation of a market system. Some of these policies hurt the colonists. For example, to protect its status as the colonies' primary trading partner, Britain imposed restrictive trade policies. British authorities sought to restrict the products the colonists could import from other nations; they also sought to prevent the colonists from trading with their European rivals.

Other British policies helped the colonists. England's restrictive trade policies required that ships built in New England would be sold directly to buyers in Britain. Colonial shipbuilders thus enjoyed favored status compared to ship builders in other nations. Rebellion against British rule would put them at risk of losing their guaranteed market.

Britain also provided the colonists with direct subsidies to produce certain products. A **subsidy** is a form of financial assistance—a special economic favor—provided by government to a business, to individuals, or to some group. Some subsidies are provided to encourage the production of certain goods. Britain, for example, provided subsidies to colonial producers of indigo dye and also paid for several forest products including tar, pitch, turpentine, and lumber. These subsidies would be lost if the colonies went to war.

These details elaborate the point that colonists on the eve of war faced steep opportunity costs—in lost lives, the loss of guaranteed British customers, lost income, and lost military protection provided under the umbrella of the British Empire—if they chose to fight. Yet they decided at some point that the benefits of fighting would outweigh the costs.

What Were the Incentives?

An **incentive** is a benefit that influences the choices people make. Incentives can take many different forms. In the United States today, for example, tax rules create various incentives, influencing the choices people make about working and investing.

Before 1763, the American colonists had often objected to tax and trade policies imposed by British authorities, but they had been able in many cases to successfully resist such policies. After 1763, however, Britain changed the **rules of the game**, imposing many new regulations and taxes and enforcing them more strictly. These changes created additional incentives for the colonists to consider war.

Some of the changes had to do with opportunities for colonists to establish new settlements by moving westward. For the colonists, one early benefit had emerged as a result of the defeat of the French in the French and Indian War. They had previously regarded the French and France's American Indian allies as dangerous rivals for land in the colonial West. The defeat of the French eased fears of rivalry. Americans who sought to settle in outlying areas would no longer face French interference or competition. Many colonists were eager to move west.

But an even more serious threat to the prospect of westward settlement soon emerged. British authorities introduced new measures of their own to control the frontier and contain the colonial population largely within the eastern seaboard area. These measures included the Royal

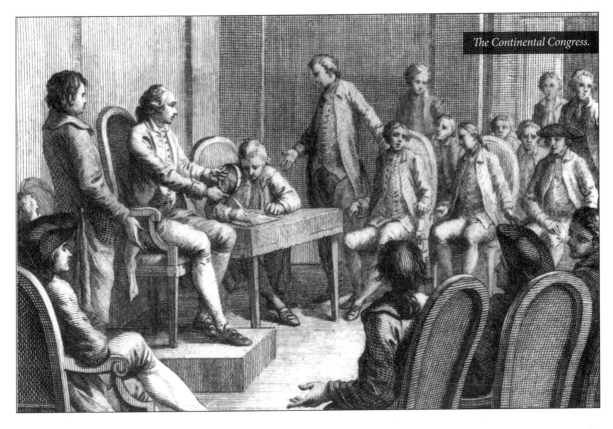

The Continental Congress.

Proclamation of 1763 and the Quebec Act of 1774, which restricted colonial settlement throughout a large area ranging from what is now Georgia to the north shore of Lake Superior. The prospect of land ownership was a huge attraction—an incentive—to many colonial Americans. That the British would prevent colonists from acquiring cheap, unsettled western land struck many of them as an act of theft. The threat to future land ownership, moreover, affected people from all walks of life, not only merchants on the eastern seaboard. The prospect of regaining land for settlement thus created another incentive to fight.

Other incentives also were changed by changes in the rules of the game. Traditionally, spending and tax decisions had been made by the lower houses in colonial legislatures. In most colonial legislatures, members of the lower house were elected, as they were in Britain's House of Commons. But as the Crown and Parliament increasingly exercised direct control over taxation and other policies after 1773, the colonists more and more resented being treated as "colonials"—

as second-class citizens. In 1774 the Continental Congress published a list of grievances, emphasizing ways in which colonial self-governance had been eroded. The idea that the British could impose taxes and other legislation on the colonists without their consent created a strong incentive to fight.

Britain's new policies and enforcement procedures threatened to raise prices and reduce income among some colonists; they also marked a change in the climate of freedom to which the colonists had become accustomed. The sense of grievance therefore was widespread: "debtors objected to the Currency Act; shippers and merchants to the Sugar Act; pioneers to the Quebec Act; politicians, printers, and gamblers to the Stamp Act; retailers and smugglers to the Tea Act."[5] The losses that the new acts implied—in material well-being and autonomy—created an incentive for the colonists to fight. Successful revolution would enable them, in a new republic, to secure the rights and benefits to which they felt entitled.

HISTORICAL QUESTIONS & ECONOMIC ANSWERS

In taking actions that caused such a strong reaction among the colonists, was Britain acting unreasonably?

Not if you look at events from the British point of view. British policy for the American colonies was based on **mercantilism**, the idea that colonies have an obligation to assist the mother country in gaining wealth. For American colonists in the 1760s, this meant providing Britain with many raw materials it desired, such as iron and naval stores including tar, pitch, and tall timbers for ship masts. The colonies were also expected to generate income by selling colonial products through Britain to other nations. In addition, mercantilism meant that American colonists were to buy goods produced in Britain.

Between 1645 and 1761, Britain enacted several laws known as the Navigation Acts to enforce mercantilist policy by protecting British and colonial trade from competition. All imports from Europe to the colonies were to be shipped through British ports. And certain products from the colonies—"enumerated goods"—could be exported only to Britain. The enumerated goods included tobacco, sugar, cotton, indigo, rice, molasses, and naval stores.

Most economic historians argue that the colonists felt little incentive to break away from Britain until 1763. Until then, the list of enumerated goods had grown slowly over time, and the colonists would have bought most of their manufactured goods from Britain even without the Navigation Acts. But after 1763 the Crown and Parliament became increasingly demanding in the new rules and enforcement procedures they imposed. Britain had, after all, paid for protecting the colonists during the French and Indian War, at a high cost to British taxpayers. In return, Britain sought ways to extract more revenue from the colonies.

Did all the colonists favor the fight against the British?

No. Historian Robert Calhoon estimates that the patriots were supported by perhaps 40 to 45 percent of the white populace—at most, by no more than a bare majority.[6] There were patriots and loyalists in all the colonies, but some colonies were more vigorous than others in support of revolution. Colonists in Virginia and Massachusetts appeared to be highly supportive. (It is noteworthy that many colonists in Virginia and Massachusetts held claims to western land that were denied by the Quebec Act of 1774.) New York City, however, was home to many loyalists. And some colonists, including the Quakers, wanted to stay out of the fight altogether.

Did Britain's tightening of the Navigation Acts hurt the colonies economically?

Without a doubt. New restrictions imposed by the Navigation Acts meant that the colonists would pay higher prices for imports from outside the Empire. The colonists also anticipated paying higher prices for goods that could be purchased (legally) only from Britain. And colonial exporters anticipated paying higher prices to ship their products. Merchants and ship owners in port cities such as Boston, where the Revolution began, were especially hard hit.

Still, the tightening of the Navigation Acts seems insufficient to explain the decision to fight, given the costs the colonists were bound to incur in fighting a war they might well lose. Were there other reasons?

Yes. The Townshend Acts (1767) placed new taxes on English manufactured goods entering America, including tea, glass, paper, and pigments for paint. The colonists reacted angrily with boycotts and, eventually, the Boston Tea Party. Britain backed away from the Townshend taxes in 1770, except for the tax on tea. The tax on tea was particularly offensive to the colonists. It represented, in their eyes, Britain's power to tax the colonies even though the colonies were not represented in Parliament. Moreover, the tea tax allowed the East India Company to ship tea directly to the colonies, cutting American merchants out of the trade. Whose trade would be eliminated next?

What was the importance of the Quebec Act?

In hindsight, it seems unlikely that these changes in tax and trade policies, unpopular though they were, would suffice to make the case for rebellion. After all, agriculture, not trade, was the most important sector of the colonial economy. Colonial farmers achieved success in producing corn, wheat, tobacco, rice, indigo, and products (especially timber) used in ship building. Why would a far-flung rural populace support a war stirred up by grievances among colonial merchants? Here, another change in the rules becomes relevant—the policy change regarding western land. The Quebec Act of 1774 greatly enlarged the size of Quebec, thus reducing western land areas available for settlement by Americans; it also nullified the western land claims of many colonists from Massachusetts, Connecticut, and Virginia.

For many colonists, including many young adults of fighting age, land ownership represented an opportunity for economic success in the future. To them, the Quebec Act was especially offensive. As Britain took steps to prevent colonists from settling in the West, the colonists feared that these lands would be sold instead to outsiders, not Americans. They also feared that Britain's new controls on the fur trade would interfere with exploration and settlement.

Why did Britain approve the Quebec Act of 1774?

For three main reasons. First, restricting access to western lands would help Britain maintain its political control of the colonies. Second, restricting access would help reduce conflicts with American Indians, thus protecting the fur trade that had been established by the French. Finally, restricting access would allow British authorities to reward British subjects by giving away or selling land to those whom they favored.

Summing up: what prompted the colonists to fight for independence?

Taken together, changes in British policies created new incentives, shaping the decisions of colonists who eventually came to support the Revolutionary War. From 1763 to 1775, the colonists had to make decisions about which path would lead them to a better future. As we have seen, they had become accustomed to a relatively high standard of living. But changes in British policies put the future in doubt. Under British rule, the colonists faced what seemed to be diminishing prospects for continued growth in prosperity. Before 1763, they had been for the most part self-governing and free to pursue their own economic interests. After 1763, these benefits were diminished in ways that threatened their freedom in matters of trade, taxation, land ownership, and self-government. The prospect of securing those benefits by going to war eventually outweighed everything else.

QUESTIONS for DISCUSSION

1. What did the colonists risk losing when they decided to fight the British?
2. What incentives encouraged the colonists to fight?
3. What did the British expect from the colonies? Do you think these expectations were reasonable? Explain your answer.
4. What do you think the most important reasons were for the colonists' willingness to risk fighting a war against one of the world's most powerful nations? Explain your answer.

Losing Ground

The following map shows various changes to colonial boundaries. Note the new Quebec boundary that was established in 1774. Note also the western land claims of Virginia, Massachusetts, and Connecticut. These land claims were eliminated by the Quebec Act of 1774.

PRIMARY SOURCE

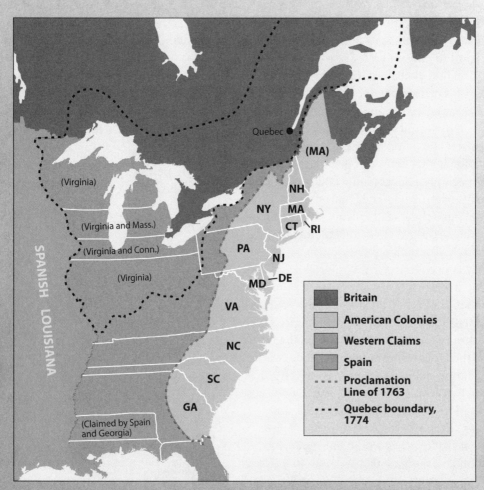

PRIMARY SOURCE **QUESTIONS for DISCUSSION**

1. Describe the expanse of land claimed initially by the colonies but later given to Quebec. Which of today's states would have been included?
2. Why do you think the Quebec Act was described by some of the colonists as one of the "Intolerable Acts"? Explain your answer.

Party Like It's 1773

This chapter stresses the point that Britain's changes in the rules of the game changed, in turn, the incentives facing the colonists. The changes included alterations of the tax structure and changes in land policies. The colonists had achieved a relatively high standard of living. They feared that changes in British policies threatened their prospects for continued economic success.

Taxes are once again on the minds of Americans. A new political movement called the Tea Party has emerged, following the elections of 2008. Supporters of this movement associate themselves with the colonists who objected to British policies in the colonies. In particular they identify themselves with colonists linked to the Boston Tea Party of 1773. Tea, as you may recall, was an important consumer good in the years leading up to the American Revolution. On December 16, 1773, several colonists, including Samuel Adams, boarded ships docked in Boston Harbor and dumped tea overboard. This action was intended as a protest against the Tea Act of 1773, which had established a tax on tea that many colonists regarded as unfair because it was imposed on them even though they had no representation in the British Parliament.

The Tea Party members of 2010 are not much interested in tea, but they are interested in taxes and related issues. Among the Tea Party's goals are the following:

- Reduce the size of government.
- Balance the national budget.
- Reduce income taxes on businesses and individuals.

The ideas favored by today's Tea Party appear to have been influential in turning out voters in the Congressional elections of 2010. Several politicians who supported Tea Party goals were elected to the U.S. Senate, including Marco Rubio of Florida, Rand Paul of Kentucky, and Ron Johnson of Wisconsin.

As you might expect, the new Tea Party movement has been controversial. Some critics have accused the movement of operating on the fringes of mainstream politics. They contend that the desire of Tea Party members to reduce the size of government runs counter to the interests and values of many voters. They ask: "Do American voters really wish to see cuts in popular government programs such as Social Security and Medicare?"

Other critics suggest that the comparison of the new Tea Party to the Boston Tea Party of 1773 is not plausible. Throughout most of the colonial period, the tax burden on Americans was quite low, much lower than the burden on taxpayers in Britain. Reliable estimates are hard to come by, but most colonists probably paid less than a dollar per year for taxes. (Here it is also important to remember that per capita annual income in the colonies probably ranged between $60 and $100.) Soon after they adopted the Constitution, which gave voters a voice in taxation policy, Americans in the new republic taxed themselves at higher rates than the rates imposed by the British prior to the Revolution. Over the past century, this upward movement in taxation has continued. According to the Tax Foundation, Americans paid 5.9 percent of their income for all taxes in 1900. The rate increased to 24 percent in 1950. It reached a high (to date) of 33 percent in 2000. And in 2010 Americans paid 26.9

percent of their income for all taxes (www. taxfoundation.org).

Colonists were British citizens who had no voice in the British Parliament. They protested against "taxation without representation." But American citizens today elect their representatives to Congress and to state legislatures, and these elected officials make decisions about taxes. It might be said, then, that voters today are getting the tax levels and regulations they have chosen, through the votes they have cast. Today's Tea Partiers might disagree. They might claim that American voters have lost control of tax policy because their representatives in Congress are no longer following the wishes of voters back home. Thus a Tea Party battle cry: "Toss them out!"

THEN & NOW — QUESTIONS for DISCUSSION

1. What is the new Tea Party movement?
2. Has the Tea Party movement been successful? Explain your answer.
3. How does the Tea Party of 2010 compare to the Tea Party of 1773? Explain your answer.

Web Resources

Digital History
http://www.digitalhistory.uh.edu/database/article_display.cfm?HHID=268

This site presents an interactive, multimedia history of the United States from the Revolution to the present.

Archiving Early America:
http://www.earlyamerica.com

This site provides primary sources that enable users to learn about the Revolutionary War through the eyes of those who lived it. It includes directions on how to read 200-year-old documents, along with portraits, maps, and contemporary media.

Then & Now: Party Like It's 1773
http://www.southfloridateaparty.net

This site provides an introduction to the tea party movement.

How Did the U.S. Constitution Provide a Road Map to Economic Prosperity?

The U.S. Constitution as it looked in 1789.

A Chance to Reset the Government

The Constitutional Convention convened in Independence Hall in Philadelphia on May 14, 1787. The stated goal was to revise the Articles of Confederation. As the meetings progressed, however, the delegates decided to draft an entirely new framework for a new government. The result was the U.S. Constitution, which was eventually ratified by all 13 states and took effect in 1789.

Without the efforts of one key person, it never would have happened. He had retired from public life to run his farm and spend time with his wife and two adopted children. Because his business had declined during the Revolutionary War, there was much for him to do. He typically rose at dawn and caught up with his letters. After breakfast, he mounted his horse and rode out into his estate to inspect work being done, to give directions, and to plan improvements. In the evening, he relaxed with family and friends, read, played cards, or maybe enjoyed a dance. From his quiet retreat, however, he was slowly drawn back into public affairs. He knew things were going badly. He wrote, "We have errors to correct. We have probably had too good an opinion of human nature in forming our confederation." [1]

KEY ECONOMIC CONCEPTS

Market economy
Rules of the game
Free trade zone

Gross Domestic Product (GDP)
Command economy

He was approached by state leaders who asked him to head up Virginia's delegation to the Constitutional Convention. At first he declined, but they persisted, arguing that his presence was critical to dignify the Convention and to show that there was no secret plan among the delegates to establish a monarchy. He finally agreed to serve as a delegate, and on May 25, 1787, he was chosen by a unanimous vote to serve as president of the Convention. His name was George Washington. [2]

Rarely do people get a chance to "reset" their government. But that is exactly what Washington and the other Founders did. They wrote new rules for how the central government of the new nation would operate. The Constitution they wrote established a framework for the central government, describing the powers of the President, Congress, the Supreme Court, and the

The signing of the United States Constitution.

states. It also has proved to be the basis for the world's most successful and enduring democracy. But the Constitution is an economic document. It has contributed to the development of the world's most prosperous economy. We know how the U.S Constitution provided for political freedom through the Bill of Rights. In what ways did the Constitution establish economic freedom as well?

The Historical Context
Economic Conditions under the Articles of Confederation

The Articles of Confederation had been adopted in 1781. They represented the first attempt by the Americans to establish a new government after the Revolution. Memories of British rule and the struggle to be rid of it were very fresh. As a result, many of the Founders then were reluctant to grant power to a central government. But the new nation later faced three severe economic problems that had to be addressed.

1. The Congress of the Confederation had incurred an enormous debt. Large amounts of money were owed to France and to people who held bonds sold during the war. Large commitments had been made to war veterans. And the government needed to pay its employees. But the Congress of the Confederation had no power to tax; only the states could do that. The Congress of the Confederation had to rely on revenue provided by the states. Not surprisingly, state legislatures were reluctant to make the payments requested by the Congress of the Confederation. They had their own financial problems.

2. Trade wars between the states loomed. States were free to impose tariffs—taxes—on imports from and exports to other states. Although in the short term these tariffs might help the states raise tax revenue to pay for their own operating expenses, in the long term tariffs would lower the standard of living in the new nation by making goods and services more expensive for consumers. Yet

the Congress of the Confederation had no power to stop the states from imposing tariffs on one another. It had no power to regulate trade between the states.

3. The military forces of the new nation were in tatters after having fought a long war. But the nation still faced threats on all sides, and this was no time to rest. The British occupied territories in the Great Lakes region, in clear violation of the Treaty of Paris. Spain denied Americans navigation rights on the Mississippi River. Barbary pirates were raiding American shipping in the Mediterranean Sea. But without the power to tax, the Congress of the Confederation had no way to establish and maintain an army or a navy.

The conveners of the Constitutional Convention were deeply worried about these problems. The Federalists among them, supporters of a strong central government, believed the new nation was in crisis and urgently needed a new constitution to hold it together. The Anti-Federalists opposed establishment of a stronger federal government and later argued against ratification of the new Constitution.

Adam Smith and the Economics of the U.S. Constitution

Ideas from two important documents published in 1776 helped to shape the new Constitution. One was the Declaration of Independence. The Declaration announced that the 13 colonies would no longer be part of Britain. It stated that "all men" are created equal and that they possess unalienable rights—rights that a legitimate government cannot take away. It explained that people establish governments to protect those rights. If a government fails to meet its responsibility, it is the right of the people to abolish that government and replace it. These principles have had a profound impact on modern history in the United States and elsewhere.

The other influential document published in 1776 was a book written by Adam Smith. It is known today by its shortened title, *The*

Wealth of Nations. This book also changed the course of history. It established the intellectual foundations of modern economics, and it dealt with the economic issues that the delegates to the Constitutional Convention in Philadelphia needed to address.

The Wealth of Nations explained basic concepts of a **market economy**, including the need to protect private property rights, the importance of the profit motive, and the benefits of free trade. The American Founders were familiar with *The Wealth of Nations*; some of them knew it well. Thomas Jefferson frequently quoted from Smith in his papers and letters. The ideals of economic freedom expressed by Smith appealed to the Founders, as they did to many other Americans—people accustomed to making their own economic choices with little intrusion from the government.

Economic Features of the New Constitution

Delegates to the Constitutional Convention sought to address economic weaknesses in the Articles of Confederation. How could widespread gains in productivity, and the prosperity these gains would bring about, be achieved in the new nation? And, as a practical matter, how could the powers of the new federal government be expanded and yet limited? To address the latter problem, the Founders adopted the Bill of Rights, which placed explicit limits on the exercise of governmental power. They also created an innovative constitutional structure—a system of checks and balances. The goal of the checks-and-balances system was to limit the central government's power by establishing separate governmental branches: a bi-cameral (that is, a two-chamber) legislative branch (the U.S. Congress), an executive branch (the presidency), and a judicial branch (the federal courts, including the U.S. Supreme Court). They designed this structure to make it impossible for the central government to get very much done unless it acted on the basis of broad agreement.

The Founders were highly suspicious of the powers of a central government. They knew all about the capacity of interest groups to use governmental power for their own benefit. James Madison in *Federalist Paper No. 15* called interest groups "factions." He and others wanted to make it difficult for any faction to use government for its own purposes—for example, by redistributing income from one group and giving it to another group.

Today, thousands of bills are considered by Congress each year, yet only a handful eventually are enacted into law. That outcome often comes in for criticism, but it is consistent with what the Founders intended. Critics complain when their favored bills are not enacted into law; other observers contend that checks and balances impede efforts to redistribute income from the rich to the poor or from the poor to the rich. The outcome is one that Adam Smith would have approved. He believed people should establish productive enterprises, earn an income by producing goods and services other people are willing to pay for, and rely on themselves and their families in times of need.

Certain specific features of the Constitution have played an especially important role in establishing a market economy in the United States. These features established the **rules of the game**; these rules, in turn, have acted as powerful incentives, influencing people's choices.

One example has to do with taxation. Under the Articles of Confederation, the central government could not collect taxes. But Article I, Section 8, of the U.S. Constitution—the Taxation clause—states that Congress shall have the power "to lay and collect taxes." This provision enabled the new nation to solve some serious problems. It provided the U.S. government with a reliable way to raise revenue, pay off its debts, and defend its interests. Paying off debts calmed fears that the new nation would be unable to obtain loans from banks in other nations in the future. It built trust, and the trust it built provided an incentive for bankers in Europe to lend money to the new nation, which had previously seemed liked a risky proposition. Taxation would also provide the revenue needed to finance an army and a navy to defend the nation's interests against Britain, Spain, France, and the Barbary pirates.

Even so, the Anti-Federalists worried about granting the power of direct taxation to the federal government. They feared that abuse of this power could result in the reestablishment of something resembling a monarchy. At the time, however, the Founders were searching for a balance between federal authority and economic freedom. A market economy depends on government to perform certain critical functions, among which is national defense. Without the power to tax, the new nation could not raise an army or a navy to defend its political and commercial interests. In a weak nation, businesses would suffer. The chance of earning profits in an insecure environment is greatly reduced.

The Constitution also enabled the new nation to deal with problems related to interstate commerce. In creating the European Union, late in the 20th century, several European countries gained an opportunity to conduct business in a free trade zone. A **free trade zone** is an area in which trade barriers such as tariffs (taxes on imports) and quotas (numerical restrictions on imports) are reduced or eliminated. The U.S. Constitution established a free trade zone in the United States 200 years earlier. It did so by means of Article I, Section 8, Clause 3, of the U.S. Constitution—the Commerce Clause— which states that Congress shall have power "To regulate Commerce with foreign Nations, and among the several States, and with the Indian Tribes." The Commerce Clause took the power to impose tariffs away from the states, thus preventing states from engaging in trade wars ("If you place a tariff on corn we Iowans export to Minnesota, we'll place a tariff on timber you Minnesotans export to Iowa"). Trade wars conducted with tariffs as weapons would reduce trade between the states and discourage specialization.

There was nothing imaginary about the problem of interstate trade wars. Memories were fresh of the time when New York had imposed a fee on vessels traveling to and from Connecticut and New Jersey. New Jersey then retaliated by imposing a tax on a New York lighthouse on New Jersey soil. If such trade wars became widespread, they would stifle economic growth and reduce prosperity in the new nation. In providing for the regulation of interstate commerce only at the federal level, the Commerce Clause did away with the threat of interstate trade wars.

Is it true that individuals could "walk away" from debts before the establishment of the Constitution?

Yes. Under the Articles of Confederation, each state could make its own decisions about how contracts would be handled. Farmers facing foreclosures, for example, sometimes pressured local and state governments to let them walk away from debts they owed according to contracts they had signed. Another debt-related issue had to do with loans from foreign sources. Some Americans argued that state legislators should not pay back foreign loans issued during the Revolution. The bonds in question were held after the Revolutionary War by "speculators" or foreigners, it was said, as if people answering to those descriptions should have no legal standing. But the Founders were concerned that if contracts were not enforced by the government, no one in the future would have confidence in the new U.S. financial system.

They drafted, accordingly, Article I, Section 10, Clause 1, of the new Constitution, called the Contract Clause. It states that "No state shall…pass any…law impairing the Obligation of Contracts," thus ensuring that contracts, including those dealing with debts, would be enforced. The Contract Clause helped to make day-to-day business transactions stable and predictable. It provided an incentive for business owners to expand their operations without fear that the government might intrude to help out one party to a contract (say, the debtor) to the detriment of the other party(say, the lender).

The Fifth Amendment to the U.S. Constitution focuses on protecting the rights of suspected criminals, right?

Not exactly. The Due Process Clause of the Fifth Amendment does indeed protect certain rights people have if they are questioned by police or arrested. But the Amendment does much more than that. In its Takings Clause, for example, it states that the government may not take private property for public uses without paying "just compensation."

The Takings Clause of the Fifth Amendment established the principle that the government itself is not above the law. Given the protection for private property it established, individuals could invest in their farms and businesses without fear that the federal government might some day, for some reason, confiscate their property. Today, in nations such as Zimbabwe and Venezuela, where economic freedom is not well protected, citizens do worry about the possibility that the government might confiscate their businesses or their savings, with little or no compensation. It is a threat that can generate crippling fear and stifle economic activity. Would you invest in a business or keep money in a savings account if you thought the government might take it away from you and leave you without compensation? Unlikely. The Founders prohibited governmental action of that sort by adopting the Fifth Amendment. In doing so, they created an incentive for Americans to save, invest, and start new enterprises.

How important was the Constitution to American prosperity?

The Constitution established rules that shaped the future development of the U.S. market system. The extraordinary success of the Constitution was in part a result of timing: it came into being at a critical period in American history. It was written by a group of men with immense ability and common interests. They were able to complete their task without significant obstruction from those who did not support the project. In the absence of these conditions, it is doubtful that anybody could have produced a document that would serve us as well.

The Constitution left many questions unanswered, however. Its economic elements, such as the Commerce Clause, still had to be tested in the courts. Several Supreme Court decisions, some issued by the Marshall Court (1801–1835), would be needed to transform the Constitution's general rules into more specific policies. For example, in *Gibbons v. Ogden* (1824), the Court overturned a monopoly granted by the state of New York to steamships operating between New York and New Jersey. This ruling confirmed the point that the federal government, rather than the states, held authority to regulate interstate commerce.

Has the Constitution been an economic success? While cause and effect relationships are difficult to establish, it is significant that the U.S. economy experienced rapid economic expansion from the period of 1790 to 1850. Figure 1 shows the change in Gross Domestic Product (GDP) during the period. **GDP** represents the dollar value of all the final goods and services produced within a nation during a specific period. Economists regard GDP as an important measure of the overall health of an economy. Although many factors were involved in the rapid growth the United States experienced after 1790, the upward trend must reflect positive effects of the rules of the game established by the Constitution.

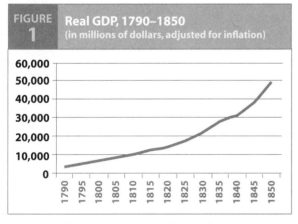

FIGURE 1 — **Real GDP, 1790–1850** (in millions of dollars, adjusted for inflation)

Source: Louis Johnston and Samuel H. Williamson, "What Was the U.S. GDP Then?" Measuring Worth, 2010. URL: http://www.measuringworth.org/usgdp

QUESTIONS for DISCUSSION

1. How did the ideas of Adam Smith influence the writing of the U.S. Constitution? Explain your answer.
2. How did the structure of the U.S. Constitution—its allocation of power to three separate branches of government—serve to limit the role the government would play in the new economy? Explain your answer.
3. Which elements of the U.S. Constitution might be regarded as the "Articles of the market economy"?
4. Which economic clause do you regard as the most important for protecting economic freedom? Explain your answer.
5. What evidence is there that the U.S. economy grew after the ratification of the Constitution?

Federalist No. 15

The *Federalist Papers* (also known as *The Federalist*) were written and published between 1787 and 1788. The authors of *The Federalist Papers* were Alexander Hamilton, James Madison, and John Jay. (However, they wrote under the pseudonym of *Publius*, which means "public" in Latin.) The authors' purpose was simple. They wished to persuade New Yorkers to ratify the Constitution that had been adopted in Philadelphia in September 1787. The following excerpt from *Federalist No. 15* is part of an essay by Alexander Hamilton titled "The Insufficiency of the Present Confederation to Preserve the Union."

There is scarcely anything that can wound the pride or degrade the character of an independent nation which we do not experience . . . . [W]e owe debts to foreigners and to our own citizens. . . .[T]hese remain without any proper or satisfactory provision for their discharge . . . .We have neither troops, nor treasury, nor government. . . . Are we entitled by nature and compact to a free participation in the navigation of the Mississippi? Spain excludes us from it. Is public credit an indispensable resource. . .? We seem to have abandoned its cause. . . . Is commerce of importance to national wealth? Ours is at the lowest point. . . . Is respectability in the eyes of foreign powers a safeguard against foreign encroachments? The imbecility of our government [under the Articles of Confederation] even forbids them to treat with us.[3]

Alexander Hamilton was the author of Federalist 15.

PRIMARY SOURCE QUESTIONS for DISCUSSION

1. What are the economic problems that Hamilton identifies?
2. How is Hamilton attempting to persuade his readers to his point of view?

In this chapter we have focused on how the U.S. Constitution helped shape the American economy. Throughout world history, however, many constitutions have been written, and some have had results that differ dramatically from those associated with the U.S. Constitution. Today, possible changes in the governance of Cuba are much in the news. Dissatisfaction within Cuba often focuses on the Cuban government's economic policies, which are based on Cuba's constitution. In what way has that constitution shaped Cuba's economy?

The Cuban Constitution and Cuba's Command Economy

Cuba is a contemporary example of a command economy. In a **command economy**, the government makes nearly all of the economic decisions. The Cuban government's authority over the economy is rooted in Cuba's constitution. Here are some excerpts from the most recent version of the Cuban Constitution. Let's compare these provisions to provisions in the U.S. Constitution that you have learned about.

ARTICLE 11. The state exercises its sovereignty:

a) over the entire national territory, which consists of the island of Cuba, the Isle of Youth and all other adjacent islands and keys; internal waters; the territorial waters in the extension prescribed by law; and the air space corresponding to the above;

b) over the environment and natural resources of the country;

c) over mineral, plant and animal resources on and under the ocean floor and those in waters comprised in the Republic's maritime economic area, as prescribed by law, in keeping with international practice…

ARTICLE 15. Socialist state property, which is the property of the entire people, comprises:

a) the lands that do not belong to small farmers or to cooperatives formed by them, the subsoil, mines, mineral, plant and animal resources in the Republic's maritime economic area, forests, waters and means of communications;

b) the sugar mills, factories, chief means of transportation and all those enterprises, banks and facilities that have been nationalized and expropriated from the imperialist, landholders and bourgeoisie, as well as the factories, enterprises and economic facilities and scientific, social, cultural and sports centers built, fostered or purchased by the state and those to be built, fostered or purchased by the state in the future.

Property ownership may not be transferred to natural persons or legal entities, save for exceptional cases. . . .

ARTICLE 19. The state recognizes the right of small farmers to legal ownership of their lands and other real estate and personal property necessary for the exploitation of their land, as prescribed by law.

Small farmers may only incorporate their lands to agricultural production cooperatives…

Land leases, sharecropping, mortgages and all other acts which entail a lien on the land or cession to private individuals of the rights to the land which is the property of the small farmers are all prohibited…

ARTICLE 21. The state guarantees the right to personal ownership of earnings and savings derived from one's own work, of the dwelling to which one has legal title and of the other possessions and objects which serve to satisfy one's material and cultural needs.

Likewise, the state guarantees the right of citizens to ownership of their personal or family work tools. These tools may not be used to obtain earning derived from the exploitation of the work of others. . . .

THEN & NOW — QUESTIONS for DISCUSSION

1. On a separate sheet of paper or in class discussion, complete the chart below.

Questions	U.S. Constitution	Cuban Constitution
1. Who owns the most productive resources?		
2. Who controls the contracts that determine how goods and services are exchanged?		
3. Is private ownership of property protected? How?		

2. Compare the economic views of Adam Smith and the writers of the U.S. Constitution to the economic view built into in the Cuban Constitution.

Web Resources

The United States Constitution
http://www.house.gov/house/Constitution/Constitution.html

This site provides the full text of the United States Constitution

The Federalist Papers
http://thomas.loc.gov/home/histdox/fedpapers.html

This site provides a full listing and text of the Federalist Papers, from the Library of Congress.

The Cuban Constitution
http://www.cubaverdad.net/cuban_constitution_english.htm

This site provides the full text of the Cuban Constitution, translated into English.

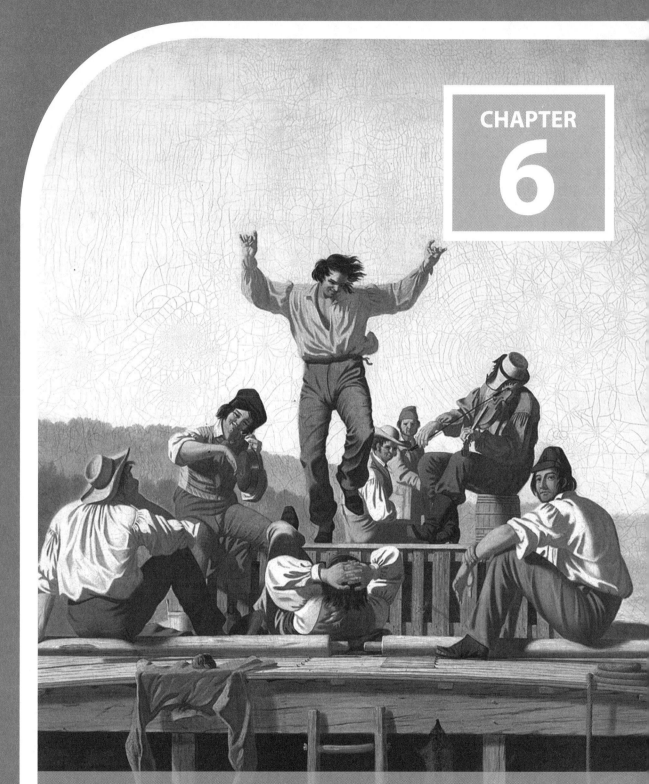

Turnpikes, Canals, and Railroads: What Did We Do Before We Had Interstate Highways?

The Jolly Flatboatman, an 1846 painting, depicts life on the river.

Abraham's River Journeys

In 1828, a 19-year-old farm boy named Abraham went on the adventure of his life: a flatboat trip downriver from Indiana to New Orleans. As a deck hand, he made some money and saw a place very unlike Indiana. New Orleans had a busy seaport, an active slave trade, and constant parties. Three years later Abraham made another trip to New Orleans, this time as a flatboat pilot. He then returned upriver to his new home in Illinois, traveling by the latest mode of transportation, a steamboat.[1]

If Abraham had stuck with life on the river, American history would have been far different. Instead, he turned to the study of law and public service. This Abraham was Abraham Lincoln, once a riverman and flatboater, who later became the president who held the nation together through its darkest years and a civil war.

Abraham Lincoln and other Midwesterners spent a lot of time and effort going up and down rivers. Why would they do that? In fact, it was not unusual. Moving about by one means or another has been a common practice throughout our history. Many Americans have worked hard to transport themselves and their goods from one place to another, often over considerable distances. Many continue to do so today. One reason is that we have become accustomed to having access to goods from all over the country: peaches from California, cars from Michigan, maple syrup from Vermont, and so on. Most of these products travel in trucks over a highly developed highway system. But before we had cars and trucks, travelers used a network of turnpikes, canals, and railroads.

In this chapter we look at the critical role played by **transportation**—the movement of people, goods, and services from one location to another—in the early 1800s. We will see how improvements in transportation provided access to distant markets, expanding opportunities

KEY ECONOMIC CONCEPTS

Cost	Profit
Law of One Price	Transportation

for trade and commerce even in areas that had previously seemed remote and isolated. How did local and regional markets, formerly isolated from one another, come to be included in the national economy? What did we do before we had interstate highways?

The Historical Context
Distance, Cost, and Transportation

One major attraction for settlers in the New World was land. In Europe, land was a major component of wealth that only the rich could afford. In the United States, plenty of land was available, and it was relatively cheap. Much of the land was remote, however; thus, transportation over long distances quickly became a part of the American way of life.

Water played a vital role in transportation. An Ohio farmer's wheat might eventually make its way to a table in Philadelphia, in the form of bread, after a long journey mostly by water. Ohio wheat would be ground into flour and shipped downriver to New Orleans, about a thousand miles away. From there, seagoing vessels might carry the flour up the Atlantic coast to consumers in Philadelphia and other cities. That voyage would add another two thousand miles to the shipment. Despite the great distance involved, however, the roundabout water route was considerably less expensive than the alternative—a 500-mile overland route from Ohio to Philadelphia.[2] As we will see, the economics of transportation motivated many decisions early in our history.

A flatboatman on the Ohio River.

The Economics of Transportation

Location matters. That simple insight says a great deal about transportation economics. There may be cheap and abundant apples in an orchard region, but they have little economic value unless they can be sold to consumers who may not live nearby. A basket of apples harvested is much less valuable than a basket of apples harvested and delivered to paying customers. That is why it makes sense for people to spend time and money on transportation.

Our national transportation system arises from public and private decisions. The Constitution gave Congress the authority "To establish Post Offices and Post Roads."[3] Once roads are built, people make their own decisions on where and when to travel. Business transportation is guided by an interest in **profit**— the money a business has left after it pays for all its costs of operation. Transportation often helps businesses generate profits because of customers' willingness to pay—sometimes a lot—for getting goods to or from the right place at the right time.

Many goods sell for similar prices in different places, once you account for the cost of transportation. The reason has to do with supply and demand. Suppose corn sells for $4 per bushel in Chicago, but $3 in St. Louis. A smart corn trader could buy corn for $3 in St. Louis, ship it to Chicago, and resell it for $4. The corn trader would make a profit if the shipping cost was less than $1. As corn traders buy more in St. Louis, however, the greater demand drives up the price there. As corn becomes more abundant in Chicago, its price falls there. Eventually the price is about the same in both places.

Economists call the tendency of goods to sell for the same price everywhere the **Law of One Price**. The Law of One Price works when transportation is easy and inexpensive. Under such conditions, traders look for big differences in price and try to make profits. They do this by buying goods for low prices and selling them at high prices, like the corn trader in our example. A byproduct of profit-seeking is that people move goods from where they are plentiful to where they are rare. It was profit that motivated the river flatboaters, the early railroad pioneers, and the users of inland canals.

Why was water transportation so important early in U.S. history?

Water transportation was important because its **cost** per mile was much lower than the cost of overland transportation. That is one reason why many settlements, and then cities, grew up close to waterways. Because decisions about transportation depended more on cost than on the total number of miles to be traveled, longer water routes were frequently favored over shorter overland routes. This explains why, in the 1800s, Ohio wheat might travel through the port of New Orleans, as flour on its way to Philadelphia, instead of traveling directly overland.

The cost differences were dramatic. Table 1 shows the cost of transporting freight in New York State before and after the opening of the Erie Canal from Albany to Buffalo. Rates are quoted in ton-miles, or tons of cargo times miles moved. In 1817, before the canal opened, the cost was 19.12 cents per ton-mile. After the canal opened, the cost dropped to 1.68 cents per ton-mile, a 91 percent reduction.

Water transportation enabled people to do business in some markets that would otherwise have been out of reach. Before water transportation became available in upstate New York, the cost of shipping wheat overland to New York City amounted to three times the wheat's value. It would have been hard for an upstate wheat farmer to make a profit by selling to buyers in New York City, given the high transportation cost. Costs were even higher for overland transportation of corn (six times its value) and oats (12 times its value). But after the canal

TABLE 1	Cost of Transporting Freight in New York State, per Ton-Mile, Selected Years						
1817	19.12	1853	1.1	1858	0.8	1860	0.99
1840	1.68	1857	0.8	1859	0.67		

Source: George Rogers Taylor, *The Transportation Revolution,* 1815–1860 (New York: Holt, Rinehart and Winston, 1951).

opened, there was a booming in-state grain trade in New York.[4]

Map 1 shows the canal system of the United States as it existed in about 1850. Notice that the Erie Canal links the Great Lakes with upstate New York, thus opening up a water transportation route to the port of New York by way of the Hudson River.

Were crops processed to reduce transportation costs?

Yes, in some cases. Unlike materials such as timber, coal, and iron ore—which were typically transported in raw form—crops such as wheat from Ohio could be transported more economically after being processed into flour because the unwanted waste of wheat (chaff) stayed behind. For similar reasons, Pennsylvania corn farmers distilled their corn into a more valuable and more easily transportable product: whiskey. Whiskey took up less space than corn in transit, and farmers received a higher price for whiskey than for corn.

Why would anyone build a boat for just one trip, only to destroy it at the end of the trip?

Boat owners today are justifiably proud of their crafts, so the idea of building a boat for only one trip seems odd. But that is what flatboaters on the Ohio and Mississippi Rivers did. Using timber from nearby sources, they made boats and loaded them with farm products. They floated their products downstream to New Orleans, where crops could be sold and offloaded to seagoing vessels.

It would have been very expensive, however, to get those boats back up the river, against the current, because they had no power. The flatboats then had little value except as timber. They could be broken up and sold as timber for a gain.

Robert Fulton introduced the steamboat in 1807. The early steamboats made upriver travel more feasible. They did not initially threaten to take over downriver agricultural traffic; there were not enough of them, and they were relatively expensive to use. But they did sometimes help flatboaters by providing them with a much quicker way to get back home from New Orleans. Before steamboats appeared on the scene, flatboaters had walked home, taking several months to do so. Steamboats cut that time to a mere week or two.[5]

Why did railroads and then highways replace water transportation?

Early in our nation's history, water transportation offered a huge cost advantage, as overland transportation was slow and expensive. Where natural waterways did not exist, canals provided superior transportation. On rivers, the advantages increased with the success of the steamboat.

But the advantage shifted as railroads came into use. Trains ran faster than boats, and they could move people and freight even when waterways were frozen. The first trains were horse-drawn, running on wooden or iron rails, usually at speeds under 10 miles per hour. The first steam locomotives, introduced in the 1830s, reached speeds of only 10 to 15 miles per hour. Speeds increased throughout the 1800s, reaching 50 to 70 miles per hour by 1900. Railroads became increasingly important throughout the 1800s; after the Civil War, they dominated transportation in the United States.[6]

Early highways had crude surfaces and were impassable in bad weather. Before highway travel could assume a major role in transportation, better highways had to be financed somehow. One way to finance them was by charging tolls—fees paid by the people who used the highways.

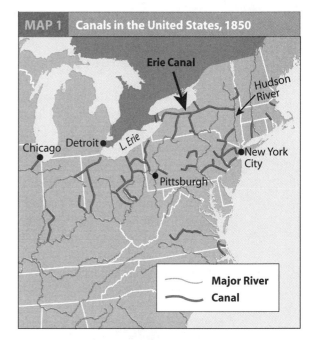

This map shows canals in the United States as of about 1850. Notice that the Erie Canal links the Great Lakes with upstate New York, thus opening up a water transportation route to the port of New York by way of the Hudson River.

Revenue from fees could go to pay for the building and upkeep of roads. (Today's word "turnpike" comes from the toll roads of the past. A large bar or "pike" would be placed across toll roads. Only after a traveler had paid the toll would the operator "turn the pike" and permit travel.) Through a mix of toll and tax financing, roads were gradually improved. Still, highway transportation for goods and people came to dominate travel only after motor vehicles became common in the 20th century.

QUESTIONS for DISCUSSION

1. Why was long-distance transportation important for the United States economy in the 1800s?
2. Why did Midwestern farmers ship their products over thousands of miles by water instead of shipping them several hundred miles by land to East Coast markets?
3. Suppose that, temporarily, the Law of One Price does not come into effect, and the same good sells for very different prices in different places—places connected by good transportation. How might a profit-seeking trader make money in this situation?
4. Why might Western Pennsylvania farmers sell their corn crop in the form of distilled whiskey, rather than simply shipping and selling unprocessed corn?
5. Why would a Mississippi River flatboater break his boat up at New Orleans after its first trip downriver?
6. What advantages did railroads offer, compared to water transportation?

Turnpikes, Canals, and Railroads

Clinton's Folly Becomes Clinton's Victory

How would you like to do something so foolish that you had a "folly" named after you? That's what happened to DeWitt Clinton, governor of New York in the early 1800s. He was a champion of "Clinton's Folly" and "the Big Ditch"—names applied to a canal that many people believed could not be built. The so-called "folly" was the Erie Canal, which would run from Albany to Buffalo. Clinton was voted out of office in 1822 in part because of his folly. But was it folly? Clinton was reelected in 1824, and the Erie Canal was completed in 1825. "Clinton's Folly" turned into Clinton's victory as the canal opened to universal acclaim. Revenue from the canal easily repaid its construction costs and earned profits for the state of New York, year after year.

New York Governor DeWitt Clinton pours water from Lake Erie into a harbor in New York City to celebrate the opening of the Erie Canal in 1825. The ceremony was called "the Marriage of the Waters," referring to Lake Erie and the Atlantic Ocean.

The famous author Nathaniel Hawthorne took a trip on the Erie Canal in the 1830s and published his report in *New-England Magazine*.

This simple and mighty conception [The Erie Canal] had conferred inestimable value on spots which Nature seemed to have thrown carelessly into the great body of the earth, without foreseeing that they could ever attain importance. I pictured the surprise of the sleepy Dutchmen when the new river first glittered by their doors, bringing them hard cash or foreign commodities, in exchange for their hitherto unmarketable produce. Surely, the water of this canal must be the most fertilizing of all fluids; for it causes towns—with their masses of brick and stone, their churches and theatres, their business and hubbub, their luxury and refinement, their gay dames and polished citizens—to spring up, till, in time, the wondrous stream may flow between two continuous lines of buildings, through one thronged street, from Buffalo to Albany. I embarked about thirty miles below Utica, determining to voyage along the whole extent of the canal, at least twice in the course of the summer.

Behold us, then, fairly afloat, with three horses harnessed to our vessel, like the steeds of Neptune to a huge scallop-shell, in mythological pictures. Bound to a distant port, we had neither chart nor compass, nor cared about the wind, nor felt the heaving of a billow, nor dreaded shipwreck, however fierce the tempest, in our adventurous navigation of an interminable mud-puddle—for a mud-puddle it seemed, and as dark and turbid as if every kennel in the land paid contribution to it. . . .

Sometimes we met a black and rusty-looking vessel, laden with lumber, salt from Syracuse, or Genesee flour, and shaped at both ends like a square-toed boot; as if it had two sterns, and were fated always to advance backward. On its deck would be a square hut, and a woman seen through the window at her household work, with a little tribe of children, who perhaps had been born in this strange dwelling and knew no other home.[7]

PRIMARY SOURCE QUESTIONS for DISCUSSION

1. Hawthorne writes that the canal "conferred inestimable value on spots which Nature seemed to have thrown carelessly into the great body of the earth." How did the Erie Canal do that?
2. How did Hawthorne think the canal would affect city growth on its banks?
3. How does Hawthorne contrast the canal trip with the difficulty of ocean navigation?
4. Why would cargoes mentioned by Hawthorne (salt, flour, and lumber) be especially suited to transport by canal?

The Trains Roll On, with Warren Buffet at the Controls

It was a surprising move when noted investor Warren Buffet spent $26.3 billion to acquire the Burlington Northern Santa Fe Railroad. Buffet had been known for shrewd investments in underappreciated companies—but a stodgy old railroad? To Buffet's keen eye for appraising value, rail transportation was ready for a comeback.[8]

It had not been an easy time for railroads in the 20th century. They struggled to remain competitive for freight and passenger transportation. Trucks took over much of the traffic in freight because of their flexibility, speed, and point-to-point service. For light cargo that needed super-fast delivery over long distances, air service soon became dominant. In passenger service, airlines replaced trains for lengthy trips, while most people chose to use their cars for shorter trips.

Rail passenger service has continued to languish. Rail freight service is a different story. It experienced strong growth throughout the second half of the 20th century. In 2007, railroads carried about 43 percent of freight traffic, compared with about 31 percent for trucks. These statistics are based on ton-miles (tons of cargo times miles moved). The ton-mile measure favors long-distance hauling of heavy cargoes, and therefore favors railroads, but it does highlight the continuing importance and steady growth of freight transport by rail.

Table 2 provides summary figures on freight and passengers transported by railroads

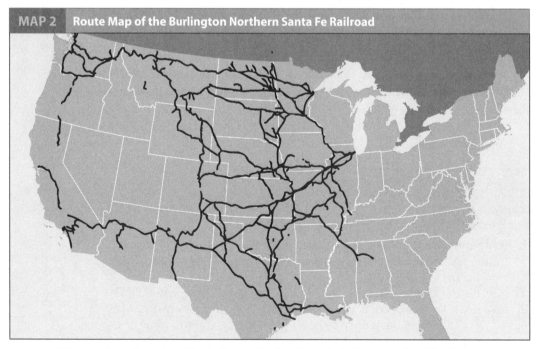

MAP 2   Route Map of the Burlington Northern Santa Fe Railroad

This map shows the routes of the Burlington Northern Santa Fe Railroad, purchased by Warren Buffet's investment company in 2010. The routes are predominantly west of the Mississippi River.

TABLE 2	Rail Passengers and Freight, 1960–2007	
Year	**Railroad Passengers** (millions of passenger-miles)	**Railroad Freight** (billions of ton-miles)
1960	17,064	575
1970	6,179	771
1980	4,503	932
1990	6,057	1064
2000	5,498	1546
2007	5,784	1820

Source: Research and Innovative Technology Administration, Bureau of Transportation Statistics, "U.S. Passenger-Miles."

in the second half of the 20th century.

Fuel efficiency and environmental advantages are two main reasons why the future of rail transport looks encouraging. The CSX railroad reports that its trains can move a ton of freight nearly 500 miles on a gallon of fuel, a figure three times as fuel-efficient as truck transport.[9] Less fuel burned means a lower environmental impact. Further, trains can relieve highway congestion by carrying freight that would otherwise move by truck.

Just as was true in the 1800s, the bottom line for shippers is how they can transport goods at the lowest overall cost. In the 1800s, that might have meant a long round-about journey to take advantage of cheap water transportation—more miles, but at a lower cost. Today that means a mix of rail, truck, and air transportation. Table 3 shows approximate costs of moving goods by different means of transportation.

For heavy cargoes traveling long distances, transportation increasingly calls for today's updated version of the 19th century's star technology, the railroad. With billions of dollars at stake, Warren Buffet certainly hopes so.

TABLE 3	Ton-mile Costs of Alternative Means of Transportation[a]
Method	**Cost per ton-mile, cents**
Air	80.4
Truck	26.6
Rail	2.24
Water (barge)	0.72
Oil pipeline	1.47

[a]Most recent figures as of 2001.

Source: U.S. Department of Transportation, Research and Innovative Technology Administration, National Transportation Statistics.

THEN & NOW   QUESTIONS for DISCUSSION

1. For railroads, what trend can you see in freight versus passenger traffic?
2. What current advantages does rail transport have over truck transport?
3. Why might a freight shipper avoid rail transport and choose trucks even if the cost per mile were higher?
4. Given the high cost for weight shipped, what cargoes would you expect to be shipped by air?

American History
http://americanhistory.si.edu/onthemove/

A brief history of transportation with videos included. Links to artifacts at the Smithsonian. Explore how transportation shaped our lives, landscapes, culture, and communities.

Transportation History at the Smithsonian
http://www.si.edu/encyclopedia_SI/Science_and_Technology/Transportation_Technology.htm

History with pictures and links to exhibits on the many forms of transportations that have been used in the United States.

History of Railroads and Maps at the Library of Congress
http://memory.loc.gov/ammem/gmdhtml/rrhtml/rrintro.html

Shows the joint history of railroads and mapping. These activities flourished in the United States as people began moving inland over the inadequately mapped continent.

Then & Now: National Transportation Statistics
http://www.bts.gov/publications/national_transportation_statistics

A wealth of statistics and content on the U.S. transportation system, including its physical components, safety record, economic performance, the human and natural environment, and national security; updated quarterly.

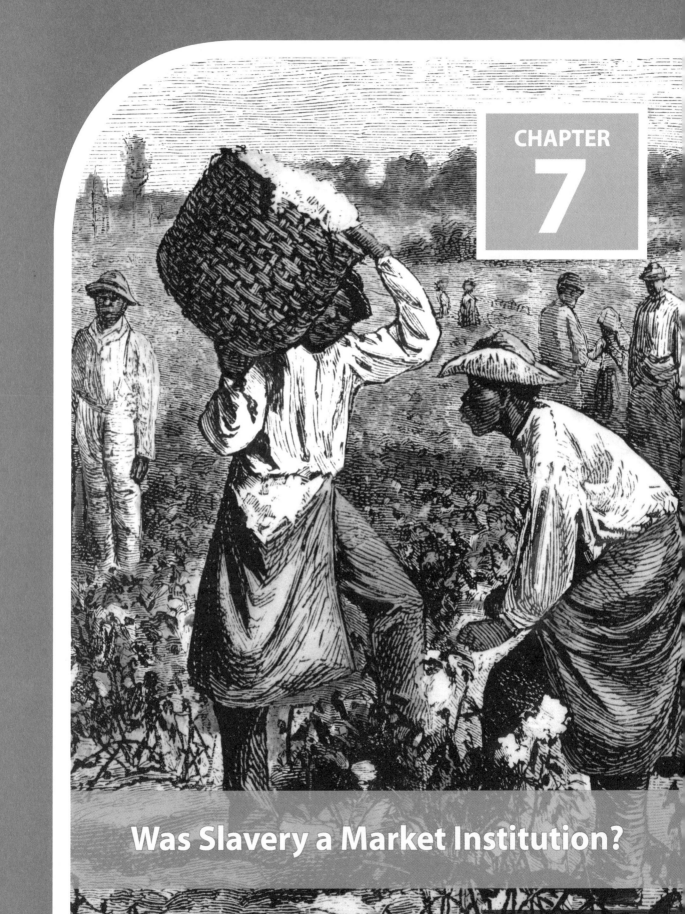

Was Slavery a Market Institution?

Enslaved workers on a cotton plantation.

Louis Hughes was born near Charlottesville, Virginia, in 1832. By the summer of 1870, he was managing the coatroom in Milwaukee's new Plankinton House Hotel. To the people around him, Hughes probably seemed like an ordinary man, married with three children. But Hughes's life was anything but ordinary. It had changed completely between 1832 and 1870. Hughes had been born into slavery. In his autobiography, he wrote about the emotional pain of being sold and separated from his mother at about the age of 11. While he recalled that his old master had been more humane than some others, he wrote extensively about the cruelties of slavery and life on plantations.

After the Civil War, life changed for African Americans. Many decided to remain in the South to work in an economy no longer dependent on the labor of enslaved individuals. Hughes, however, headed north, seeking other economic opportunities. He worked in Memphis, driving carriages. He did odd jobs in Cincinnati, and he worked as a hotel porter in Windsor, Canada. In 1867, he took a job as a sailor on the steamer *Saginaw*. He and his family eventually settled

Louis Hughes is the author of an autobiography in which he describes his life from bondage to freedom.

KEY ECONOMIC CONCEPTS

Competition	Productivity
Economic freedom	Profit
Market economy	Profit motive
Per capita income	Voluntary exchange
Private property	

in Milwaukee, Wisconsin, where he worked at the Plankinton House Hotel and ran his own business, a laundry. He had a lifelong interest in folk medicines, and he spent the last several years of his work-life as a nurse. He wrote, "My duties as nurse have taken me to different parts of the state, to Chicago, to California and to Florida; and I have thus gained no little experience, not only in my business, but in many other directions."[1]

Slavery was an institution that dominated the economy of the South from the mid-1600s to 1865. It ended only as the result of a long and destructive Civil War.

From the kidnapping of Africans, the conditions on board ships that carried them across the Atlantic, the slave markets in the South, and the lives of enslaved people on plantations, slavery operated as a morally abhorrent institution. Various explanations have been offered for its persistence in a country that was, as President Lincoln stated, conceived in liberty and dedicated to the proposition that all men are created equal. One line of inquiry and explanation has to do with economics. Was slavery profitable? Did it provide an efficient system of production? Was slavery economically viable immediately prior to the Civil War, or was it fading away? We will address these and related questions in this chapter.

We will also address another, more controversial economic question regarding slavery. The system of slavery operated, in some ways, like a modern market. It involved buyers, sellers, prices, trade, production, distribution, and investments. Was slavery, then, a market institution? Or was it the opposite: a blatant violation of the principles of a free-market economy?

The Historical Context
A Lost Chance to Abolish Slavery

In the early days of the new nation, there were hopes that slavery would fade away. Many Americans regarded slavery as morally repugnant. Others defended it. Many thought that its inefficiencies and immoral nature would cause it to collapse.

The best early opportunity to abolish slavery almost certainly occurred at the Constitutional Convention of 1787, where the delegates debated the issue. George Mason of Virginia argued eloquently against slavery. He warned that bad things were in store for the new nation if the delegates failed to act:

> Every master of slaves is born a petty tyrant. [These masters] bring the judgment of heaven on a country. As nations cannot be rewarded or punished in the next world, they must be in this. By an inevitable chain of causes and effects, providence punishes national sins by national calamities.[2]

Other delegates from the South argued that the new government should not be allowed to interfere with the institution of slavery. Delegates who supported slavery wished to count all people, free and enslaved, for purposes of Congressional representation. They hoped that this approach to allocating representatives would strengthen the power of the slave states in Congress and thus make emancipation less likely. Delegates who opposed slavery wished to count only free citizens. They hoped that this approach would weaken the power of the slave states in Congress and thus make emancipation more likely. In order to come up with the votes needed for ratification of the Constitution, the Founders chose to make compromises. They decided that, for determining representation in Congress, an enslaved individual would be counted as three-fifths of a person. The delegates also voted to eliminate the external slave trade—that is, the bringing of new slaves into the country. That practice would have to end, they determined, in 1808 (it did). After that date, the only slaves in the country would be those already there, and later their descendants. The delegates failed, however, to abolish the institution of slavery outright.

Several states made efforts of their own to abolish slavery. In 1777, the Constitution of Vermont prohibited slavery. In 1780, the Constitution of Massachusetts stated that all men are free and equal by birth. This proclamation eventually resulted in a judicial decision to abolish slavery there. In 1780, Pennsylvania adopted a plan for gradual emancipation, providing that newborn African Americans would be declared free when they reached adulthood. Several other states—including Rhode Island in 1784, Connecticut in 1784, New York in 1799, and New Jersey in 1804—passed similar laws.

These forms of gradual emancipation put the cost of freedom wholly on formerly enslaved individuals. Once freed, they typically would have no money, employment, shelter, or medical care, and taxpayers would have no responsibility to pay for their needs. This lack of responsibility built into plans for gradual emancipation helped to make those plans tolerable among legislators and their white constituents. The plans would impose no new costs on slave owners or on taxpayers generally.

Why couldn't plans for gradual emancipation have been enacted in the South as well? The labor market in the South was quite different from the one in the North. The economy in the North was becoming increasingly diversified. Northern factories attracted immigrants looking for jobs. In the South, agriculture and slavery persisted, making it less appealing for immigrants. The economic stakes in slavery were high, and resistance to emancipation occurred at every turn. In 1860, there were nearly four million slaves in the United States. Nearly all (see Table 1) were in the South.

TABLE 1	The White Population and the Slave Population in the South, 1790–1860	
Year	White	Slave
1790	1,240,454	654,121
1800	1,691,892	851,532
1810	2,118,144	1,103,700
1820	2,867,454	1,509,904
1830	3,614,600	1,983,860
1840	4,601,873	2,481,390
1850	6,184,477	3,200,364
1860	8,036,700	3,950,511

Source: Historical Statistics of the United States, Colonial Times to 1970 (Washington D.C.: U.S. Department of Commerce: U.S. Census Bureau).

The Economics of Slavery

Eli Whitney's invention of the cotton gin in 1793 changed the economy of the South. Before its invention, a worker could clean about one pound of cotton per day. With Whitney's invention, a worker could clean 50 pounds per day—a huge increase in productivity. **Productivity** refers to efficiency in industry, measured by the amount of goods and services that can be produced with a unit of input, such as labor, in a certain period of time. An increase in productivity means that more goods or services can be produced using the same quantity of resources, or fewer resources. When productivity increases, profits usually increase.

Before the cotton gin, many people believed that slavery would fade away. Tobacco was on the decline. Farms producing more than one crop were beginning to increase. But the cotton gin changed everything. Cotton quickly became King Cotton in the South, increasing the capacity of Southern plantations to supply fast-growing textile industries in Britain and the United States. Instead of dying out, slavery became more productive and profitable.

The Relationship between Slavery and a Market Economy

A **market economy** relies on individual choices and voluntary exchange to determine which goods and services will be produced. Market economies have certain characteristics, including the following.

- **Private property**: Markets depend on individuals' ability to own and sell property. In market transactions, people can choose to sell property to others and transfer the right of ownership with the sale. The transactions are voluntary. No one can force you to purchase a hamburger from McDonalds or an iPad from Apple.

- **Competition**: Markets foster competition because they allow many producers to enter market sectors and strive to meet the demands of consumers. Competition puts pressure on businesses to satisfy consumers. Businesses that fail to satisfy consumers are eventually forced out of business, making room for others to try to do better.

- **Profit motive**: Profits are the money that is left after a business has paid all its expenses. Profits act as incentives for businesses to produce the goods and services consumers want. Those businesses that satisfy consumers and produce efficiently are rewarded with profits.

- **Voluntary exchange**: Producers and consumers participate voluntarily in market transactions. Nobody is required to produce particular products; nobody is required to buy particular products. Producers can focus their efforts on what they do best and trade their surplus production to others. Markets encourage trade and thus create wealth.

Was Slavery a Market System?

Taken together, these four characteristics go a long way toward describing a market economy. And it might seem, at first glance, that the institution of slavery fits neatly into that profile. Enslaved people were, indeed, regarded as private property. Courts enforced that principle. Markets for enslaved people involved competition, exchange, and profit seeking. Prices for individuals on sale in these markets depended on certain distinguishing characteristics (age, gender, physical condition, skills, and so on), just as prices for other goods depended on their characteristics.

What Makes a Free Market Free?

Still, slavery was not a market institution. It operated in flagrant violation of a central principle of market economies. To explain this point, we turn now to a quick review of two sorts of freedom: political freedom and economic freedom.

You are familiar with the concept of political freedoms. In the American tradition, they include the "unalienable rights" identified in the Declaration of Independence and also the protections listed in the U.S. Constitution's Bill of Rights—freedom of speech, freedom of assembly, the right to due process of law, and so on.

The concept of **economic freedom** has been defined as follows in an influential study by Gwartney, Lawson, and Block:

> Individuals have economic freedom when property they acquire without the use of force, fraud, or theft is protected from physical invasions by others and they are free to use, exchange, or give their property as long as their actions do not violate the identical rights of others.[3]

This definition closely matches key provisions for economic freedom identified in America's most important founding document, the U.S. Constitution. The Fifth Amendment to the Constitution protects the right of individuals to own property. The government may not take property from individuals without due process of law. If it does take property, by legal means, it must offer "just compensation" for what it takes. The Copyright Clause of the Constitution protects ownership rights for inventors and authors. The Contract Clause protects the right of individuals to enter into private contracts, knowing that their contractual agreements will be enforced. These protections—and the elaborations of them that have been developed since 1789—enable Americans to exercise economic freedom within America's market economy.

The key characteristic of economic freedom, as highlighted in the definition by Gwartney, Lawson, and Block, is that all exchanges must be voluntary. You might decide that it's time to fill your car's gas tank. You determine that the gas you pump into the tank is worth more to you than the money you pay the gas station owner. The owner, on the other hand, views the money he or she receives in payment as worth more than the gas you pumped. You are both better off from this exchange—provided that no force, theft, or deception has been used. In any voluntary or free exchange, both parties expect to benefit. If one side does not expect to benefit, the exchange does not go forward. An exchange in which one of the parties knew he or she would be a loser—she hands over her purse, for example, because a mugger threatens to kill her if she holds back—would not be an exercise of economic freedom.

This brings us back to the issue of slavery and markets. Adam Smith, introduced in Chapter 1 as the founder of economics, opposed slavery on moral and economic grounds. He regarded slavery as economically unsustainable: "I believe," he wrote in *The Wealth of Nations*, "that the work done by free men comes cheaper in the end than the work performed by slaves. Whatever work he [a slave] does . . . can be squeezed out of him by violence only, and not by any interest of his own."[4]

Smith would agree that private ownership of property is the fundamental economic freedom. And from that point of view, the right to own oneself is surely the fundamental property right. If this right is not protected by the government, then the system is one of exploitation, not market exchange. Coercion—or the threat of force—must be used to induce individuals to make transactions to which they do not voluntarily agree, such as getting abducted and being forced to pick cotton in another man's field, for no pay. It is here that slavery fundamentally fails the test of being a market institution. At its root, it depended on coerced, involuntary exchanges. Enslaved people never gave their consent to be involved in any transaction with slave holders. They complied only because threats of dire consequences for non-compliance forced them to do so.

Was the economy in the South growing in the period before the Civil War?

Yes. Although economic growth across the region was not even, growth did occur, from 1840 to 1860, in the area in the South where "Cotton was King." In fact, **per capita income** (that is, average per person income) for the free population in the South was increasing faster than per capita income in the North.

Was slavery profitable in the period before the Civil War?

Yes, according to most economic historians. Enslaved workers were productive. Economic historians Fogel and Engerman compared Southern farms that were identical in terms of land, livestock, machinery, and labor. The only difference was that some farms used free labor—workers who were paid—and the other farms (plantations) used the labor of enslaved workers. Fogel and Engerman concluded that investments in slaves were highly profitable for the owners. Their findings more or less settled the debate among economic historians. Most now believe that, on the eve of the Civil War, slavery was becoming economically stronger, not weaker.[5] This economic success concentrated the Southern economy on agriculture dependent on slavery.

Did owners of enslaved people have an incentive to provide them with basic necessities for survival such as food, shelter, and medical care?

Yes. Slaves were expensive. By 1860, the total value of slaves in the United States was more than $3 billion. It would not make economic sense for owners to deny them food, clothing, and shelter. To do so would mean that the slaves would be too weak to work productively. Despite these incentives, however, many accounts of slavery report mistreatment of enslaved people, including whippings and beatings such as those described by Louis Hughes.[6]

Was the Southern economy heavily industrialized?

No. Given its economic success in producing cotton, the South had little incentive to shift from agriculture to industrialization, the path taken by the North. Unlike the North, it was slow to industrialize. It also was unattractive to immigrants. Free workers almost certainly believed that it would be difficult to compete for jobs in a labor market dominated by slavery. Immigrants preferred locations in the North. Thus, while the economy of the South was successful under slavery, the perpetuation of slavery weakened long-term economic growth of the South by delaying the development of a more diversified economy, one with more industrial might.

QUESTIONS for DISCUSSION

1. What are the characteristics of a market economy?
2. What does "economic freedom" mean? Give an example of an incident that illustrates economic freedom.
3. In the United States before the Civil War, there were slave markets. Does this mean that slavery was a market institution? Explain your answer.
4. What was the economic status of slavery as an institution in the years leading up to the Civil War?
5. How did the perpetuation of slavery reduce prospects for long-term economic growth in the South?

Technology and Slavery

The following is an excerpt from a letter written by Eli Whitney, the inventor of the cotton gin, to his family.

Eli Whitney, Senr., Sept. 11th, 1793.

Dear Parent,

I received your letter of the 16th of August with peculiar satisfaction and delight. It gave me no small pleasure to hear of your health and [I] was very happy to be informed that your health and that of the family has been so good since I saw you. . . . I will give you a summary account of my southern expedition.

I went from N. York with the family of the late Major General Greene to Georgia. I went immediately with the family to their Plantation about twelve miles from Savannah. . . . During this time I heard much said of the extreme difficulty of ginning Cotton that is, separating it from its seeds. [A] number of very respectable Gentlemen at Mrs. Greene's who all agreed that if a machine could be invented which would clean the cotton [quickly and easily] it would be a great thing both to the Country and to the inventor. I involuntarily happened to be thinking on the subject and struck out a plan of a Machine in my mind, which I communicated to [a Mr.] Miller,

[who] was pleased with the Plan and said if I would pursue it and try an experiment to see if it would answer, he would be at the whole expense, I should loose nothing but my time, and if I succeeded we would share the profits. . . . I concluded to . . . turn my attention to perfecting the Machine. I made one . . . which required the labor of one man to turn it and with which one man will clean ten times as much cotton as he can in any other way before known and also cleanse it much better than in the Usual mode. [With this] machine . . . one man and horse will do more than fifty men with the old machines. It makes the labor fifty times less, without throwing any class of People out of business.

I returned to the Northward for the purpose of having a machine made on a large scale and obtaining a Patent for the invention. . . .

With respects to Mama I am, kind Parent, your most obt. Son Mr. Eli Whitney.

Eli Whitney

Eli Whitney

Cotton Gin

Available at http://www.chroniclesofamerica.com/invention/eli_whitney_and_the_cotton_gin.htm

PRIMARY SOURCE QUESTIONS for DISCUSSION

1. What is productivity? According to Whitney, how much was the cotton gin likely to increase productivity?
2. How did Whitney learn of the problem of cleaning cotton?
3. How did the cotton gin change the economy of the South?

Some Consequences of Economic Freedom

The main point of this chapter has been that slavery was not a free-market economic institution. Economists dating back to Adam Smith have observed that slavery depends on coercion or force rather than voluntary exchange. This obviously involves a denial of economic freedom to those who are enslaved.

Despite the period of slavery that marked U.S. history until after the Civil War, the U.S. economy has been marked otherwise by a high level of economic freedom. The U.S. Constitution was designed to limit the power of the federal government to intervene in the economy. Private property rights, the profit motive, competition and voluntary exchange were widely understood and applied in the young nation.

The concept of economic freedom has recently gained national and international attention as a factor associated with economic well-being. Numerous studies have found that economic freedom is closely associated with the level of prosperity nations achieve, and that growth in economic freedom spurs economic growth. Given the importance of economic freedom to any country's economic success, the *Economic Freedom of the World Report* produces an annual index that ranks nations with regard to economic freedom. The authors of the report state that the key ingredients of economic freedom are these:

- personal choice,
- voluntary exchange coordinated by markets,
- freedom to enter and compete in markets, and protection of persons and their property from aggression by others.

The authors of the report observe that:

In order to achieve a high Economic Freedom of the World rating, a country must provide secure protection of privately owned property, even-handed enforcement of contracts, and a stable monetary environment. It also must keep taxes low, refrain from creating barriers to both domestic and international trade, and rely more fully on markets rather than the political process to allocate goods and resources.[3]

Evidence shows that economic freedom matters. Nations with more economic freedom grow more rapidly and achieve higher levels of per capita income than those that are less free. Countries with more economic freedom:

- Have substantially higher per capital incomes.
- Tend to have economies that grow more rapidly.
- Have a much greater amount of per capita income going to the poorest 10 percent of the population.
- Have a life expectancy rate over 20 years longer than the rate in less economically free countries.
- Have stronger political freedoms, including free elections and freedom of speech.
- Have fewer opportunities for political corruption.

Table 2 shows the 10 nations of the world that are most economically free and the 10 nations that are least economically free.

Figure 1 illustrates the relationship between economic freedom and per capita income. As you can see, the nations that rank high in economic freedom have several times more per capita income than the nations that are least free, economically.

TABLE 2	Economically Free and Unfree Nations[a]	
10 Most-Economically-Free Nations	**10 Least-Economically-Free Nations**	
Hong Kong	Algeria	
Singapore	Burundi	
New Zealand	Guinea-Bissau	
Switzerland	Central African Republic	
Chile	Congo, Democratic Republic	
United States	Congo, Republic of	
Canada	Venezuela	
Australia	Angola	
Mauritius	Myanmar	
United Kingdom	Zimbabwe	

[a]Listings are in descending order (Hong Kong, most-free; Zimbabwe, least-free). Economically unfree nations such as Cuba and North Korea are not included in the *Economic Freedom of the World Report 2010* due to lack of reliable data about their conditions.

FIGURE 1 Economic Freedom and Per Capita Income

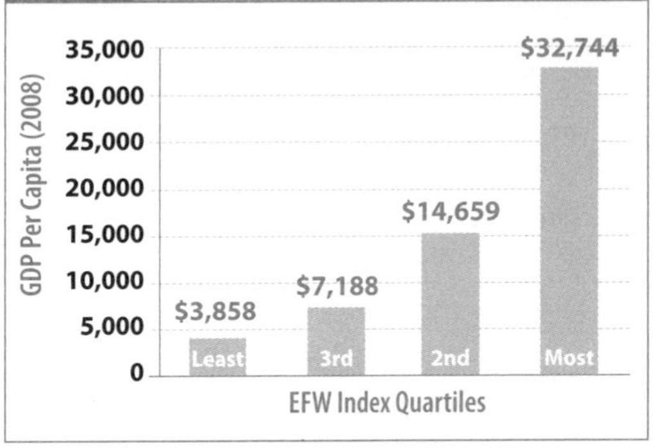

Source: http://www.freetheworld.com/2010/reports/world/EFW2010

THEN & NOW QUESTIONS for DISCUSSION

1. How is economic freedom related to a nation's well being?
2. Why do you think economic freedom is associated with higher incomes and economic growth?

The Cotton Economy of the Old South
http://www.history.iastate.edu/agprimer/Page28.html

This article provides an in-depth look at the role cotton played in the Southern economy; includes pictures.

Colonial Economy and Slavery
http://www.teachersdomain.org/browse/?fq_hierarchy=k12.socst.ush.col.econ

Resources for teachers, including videos on the economic effects of slavery.

Eli Whitney and the Cotton Gin
http://www.learnnc.org/lp/editions/nchist-newnation/5031

Detailed information about the invention of the cotton gin; includes Eli Whitney's original drawing of the first cotton gin.

Economic Freedom of the World
http://www.freetheworld.com

Defines "economic freedom"; ranks nations of the world according to their levels of economic freedom.

The Civil War and Lee's Dilemma: Why Fight a War When the North's Economy Was So Much Stronger?

The Battle of Chickamauga, 1863.

In 1861, U.S. Army Colonel Robert E. Lee (later, General Robert E. Lee) faced a life-changing decision. A West Point graduate and son of a Revolutionary War hero, he was perhaps the best military officer of his time. He had been offered command of his nation's army. It would be the pinnacle of a distinguished military career. His quandary was that the army's next big mission would be an internal one: a civil war pitting the Confederate States of America (CSA, or the Confederacy) against the Union. Lee was reluctant to fight against his beloved native state, Virginia.

At first it seemed Lee might not have to fight. Early in the year, a vote in Virginia to secede from the Union failed. But Virginia did secede later, and Lee faced the toughest choice of his lifetime: to lead the Union Army in an invasion of Virginia, or to lead Confederate forces against the Union. Lee was later to write, "I have been unable to make up my mind to raise my hand against my native state, my relations, my children & my home. . . ." [1]

As Lee was making his decision, others in the South wondered whether they could win a war against the Union. The Union would be a formidable foe, economically, and the war would

Colonel Robert E. Lee, before the Civil War.

KEY ECONOMIC CONCEPTS

Benefits	Gross Domestic
Costs	Product (GDP)
	Opportunity cost

be a bloody struggle. Today we know that the Civil War took more American lives than the American Revolution, World War I, World War II, and the Vietnam War combined. One estimate is that 620,000 Americans lost their lives at the hands of other Americans in the Civil War. [2]

Economists say that individuals act irrationally if they deliberately act against their own interests. Using this definition, was Lee's decision irrational? Was the Confederacy's decision to secede irrational? Or did each of these decisions represent a miscalculation of costs and benefits—on a personal scale for Lee and on a large, public scale for the Confederacy?

The Historical Context
Economic Balance Shifts to the North

At the outset of the Civil War, President Lincoln's primary goal was to preserve the Union. But this goal was related to the goal of ending slavery. Slavery had for a long time been America's problem that had no solution. Among the Founders, it was the subject of uneasy compromises. One of these, written into the Constitution, provided that three-fifths of the population of enslaved individuals would be counted for representation and taxes. The "three-fifths compromise" enabled the Founders to ratify the Constitution without resolving the slavery question. Other compromises followed, each maintaining a balance of pro-slavery and anti-slavery interests in the political arena.

While political power was balanced, economic power shifted overwhelmingly, after

TABLE 1	Comparing the Union and the Confederate States of America, 1861	
Feature	Union	Confederate States of America
Population	22,100,000	9,100,000
Free population	21,700,000	5,600,000
Soldiers	2,100,000	1,064,000
Manufactured items	90 percent	10 percent

Source: Historical Statistics of the United States, 1790–1970,
Washington D.C.: U.S. Department of Commerce, Bureau of the Census.

1789, in favor of the Union states (see Table 1). By 1861, the Union's population had grown to over 22 million, and it was more urban than the South's population. The CSA had a total population of 9 million, about 3.5 million of whom were slaves.

The Union held more than 90 percent of the nation's industries. It produced 97 percent of the nation's firearms. It out-produced the CSA in iron by a ratio of 20 to 1, in coal by a ratio of 38 to 1, and in textiles by a ratio of 17 to 1. It had over 20,000 miles of railroad track compared to about 9,000 miles for the CSA. Long wars are won by economics as well as military strength. But the Union also looked strong militarily. It had a larger army than the CSA, and it controlled the U.S. Navy. The Union would have an overwhelming advantage if the Civil War turned out to be a long war—as it did.

The Economics of War
The Costs and Benefits

Decisions to go to war involve a combination of logical and emotional considerations. According to cold logic, a nation would go to war only if it expected the benefits of war to exceed the costs. The **benefits** are all the positive consequences, whether they are measurable in dollars or not. The **costs** are all the negative consequences, thought of in terms of **opportunity cost**. That is, resources devoted to war are not available for their next-best use; the next-best use is what must be given up to fight the war. In real cases, of course, these considerations of cold logic compete with other considerations, including passionate ideals or simple hatred of the enemy.

As the threat of war grew, the Union and the CSA faced three possible courses of action, given the related issues of secession and slavery at stake:

1. *Continue to compromise, refusing to fight a war.*

Resolving the slavery question had been postponed for almost 100 years. Additional compromises would delay the resolution further, perhaps keeping hope alive that war could be avoided. After all, support for slavery had been eroding around the world. Optimists might have supposed that all Americans would soon see that the end of slavery was inevitable and that a peaceful solution was therefore warranted.

On the eve of war, however, a different view prevailed. It seemed to many observers that there could be no more compromises. The Missouri Compromise of 1820, which prohibited slavery in northern states, was no longer in effect. The Kansas-Nebraska Act of 1854 authorized people in the territories of Kansas and Nebraska to decide whether or not to allow slavery within their borders. Taken together, these developments meant that slavery could be extended to new areas. Abolitionists were shocked at this prospect, while many in the South were encouraged by it. The U.S. Supreme Court's decision in *Dred Scott v. Sanford* (1857) further heightened tensions. It held that people moving from one place to another were legally entitled to take their property—material or human—with them, throughout the country. This ruling meant that slave holders could take their slaves into the free states and territories and retain control of them. The ruling seemed to force the issue: take action to end slavery now, abolitionists argued, or it will be too late.

2. *Free the slaves, but provide taxpayer-financed compensation to slave owners.*

To avoid war, according to this alternative, the U.S. government would raise money from its tax base to pay slave owners for emancipating enslaved individuals throughout the nation. In other words, slave owners would be compensated for the loss imposed on them by abolition.

How much would this have cost? Slaves were

very valuable, and the required payouts would have been unprecedented in size. In 1805 there were about one million slaves in the United States, worth about $300 million. In 1860, there were four million slaves, worth close to $3 billion, a daunting amount at the time.[3]

Further, the cost would have been borne largely by Union states. They were more prosperous, overall, than other states, and they paid a larger share of total tax revenue. Would northerners, even those who opposed slavery, be willing to pay higher taxes to preserve the Union, abolish slavery, and avoid war?

Or consider the other side of the problem. Would slave owners have given up on slavery in exchange for a payment of the market value for their slaves? It seems unlikely. Slaves were gaining in value each year. Surely slave owners would want to be compensated not only for the present value of slaves but for the future value as well. It was extremely unlikely that either northern taxpayers or southern slave owners would agree to such a financial sacrifice.

3. *Go to war.*

Like the other alternatives, war would come with benefits and costs. The benefits (for a Union victory) would include preserving the Union and ending slavery without paying compensation. In addition to being expensive, paying compensation was morally objectionable to many who opposed slavery; it would simply reward those who had engaged in the deeply immoral act of holding slaves. Moreover, both sides imagined that the cost of war, even counting deaths and injuries, would be small *in the event of a short and decisive campaign*. Why did they imagine that the war would be short? We turn to that question next.

HISTORICAL QUESTIONS & ECONOMIC ANSWERS

Why did each side think it could win the war quickly?

Each side's decision to fight depended crucially on the assumption that the war would be short. It turned out that both sides miscalculated.

The Union was right to assume that it had overwhelming economic advantages in population and industrial might. President Lincoln hoped for a quick capture of the confederate capital of Richmond, Virginia, less than 100 miles south of Washington, D.C. Optimism ran so high that the initial battle at Bull Run was attended by Washington residents, carrying picnic baskets, looking on from convenient vantage points. After an unexpectedly fierce battle, however, the Union Army was defeated and fell back to Washington in disarray.

People in the CSA were also confident that the war would be short. The South had a strong tradition of providing military leaders for the United States. Many of these men were highly trained officers like General Robert E. Lee.[4] Now these men would lead the military forces of the CSA.

The CSA would also have the advantage of fighting a defensive war in its own territory. The CSA would not have to defeat the Union. It would only have to drive the Union forces out of the South. It had no plan to occupy Boston, New York, or Philadelphia. Perhaps only a few key CSA victories would be needed to demonstrate to President Lincoln and the citizens of the Union the futility of waging a war.

Panic among soldiers and civilians at the first battle at Bull Run.

Did the CSA miscalculate the costs and benefits when it chose to fight?

Yes. Leaders in the CSA miscalculated. They decided that war was the only feasible way to preserve slavery and defend the rights of the states to secede from the Union. They expected the benefits to exceed the costs of a short and decisive war. They were not irrational, but they were mistaken. There was no quick victory, and the costs were very high.

Did the Union miscalculate the costs and benefits when it chose to fight?

Yes. The leaders of the Union decided that war was the only feasible way to end slavery and preserve the Union. The preservation of the Union was crucial for President Lincoln. He said, famously, that without the end of slavery the issue was whether a nation "conceived in Liberty, and dedicated to the proposition that all men are created equal" could endure. Union leaders expected to win the war quickly, just as their Confederate counterparts did. Thus, although both sides were badly mistaken about the costs and length of the war, neither side was intentionally self-destructive or "irrational."

What was the ultimate cost of the war?

Economic historians Claudia D. Goldin and Frank D. Lewis estimated the costs of the Civil War. The direct costs were government war spending, losses from destruction of property, and the loss of human capital caused by deaths and injuries. Goldin and Lewis combined these costs with other variables, including destruction in the South. They concluded that the Civil War

TABLE 2	Direct Costs[a] of the Civil War (in 1860 dollars)
Direct Union costs	$3,365,846,000
Direct CSA costs	$3,285,900,000
TOTAL	$6,651,746,000

[a]Direct costs include war-related government spending, loss of human capital caused by death and injuries, and loss of physical capital.

Source: Claudia D. Goldin and Frank D. Lewis, "The Economic Cost of the Civil War: Estimates and Implications," *The Journal of Economic History* (June 1975), pp. 299–326

had a total cost of $6.6 billion, more or less evenly divided between the two regions.[5] To gauge the magnitude of this cost, consider that in 1860, on the eve of the Civil War, the actual **Gross Domestic Product** (the value of all the goods produced within the borders of the United States) was $4.345 billion.

In summary, continued efforts to find a peaceful solution, yielding an end to slavery and preservation of the Union, would have been the best economic choice if all the costs and benefits had been clearly identified at the time. Economic historians Jeremy Atack and Peter Passell explain that the $6.6 billion cost of the war would have been enough to buy the freedom of all the enslaved individuals (at 1860 market value), to give each former slave family a 40-acre farm and a mule, and still have $3.5 billion left over to offer to former enslaved individuals as partial compensation for wages that were never paid.[5] Unfortunately, lacking information about the actual costs of the war, neither side analyzed its decision in this manner. And neither side knew in advance who was going to win.

QUESTIONS for DISCUSSION

1. After 1857, why was additional compromise over the slavery question unlikely?
2. Why was it unlikely that war could have been avoided by freeing the slaves and compensating slave owners for their loss?
3. What was the estimated cost of the war to both sides?
4. Before a nation fights a war, can it use a definite procedure for determining whether the benefits will exceed the costs?

The Republican Platform of 1860

PRIMARY SOURCE

Much of the wealth of the CSA was tied to the value of enslaved people. Southerners feared losing this wealth. They could easily observe that attitudes in other parts of the nation were changing. Support for the abolition of slavery was growing. The following are excerpts from the platform of the Republican Party in 1860. As you read the platform, consider whether Southerners' fears about the abolition of slavery were justified, according to the content of this document.

Resolved

That we, the delegated representatives of the republican electors of the United States, in convention assembled, in discharge of the duty we owe to our constituents and our country, unite in the following declarations:

- [W]e hold in abhorrence all schemes for disunion, come from whatever source they may . . . .

- [It is] the right of each state, to order and control its own domestic institutions according to its own judgment exclusively. . . . we denounce the lawless invasion by armed force of the soil of any state or territory, no matter under what pretext, as among the gravest of crimes.

- [The idea] that the constitution of its own force carries slavery into any or all of the territories of the United States, is a dangerous political heresy . . . and subversive of the peace and harmony of the country.

- [T]he normal condition of all the territory of the United States is that of freedom . . . we deny the authority of congress, of a territorial legislature, or of any individuals, to give legal existence to slavery in any territory of the United States.

Source: National Republican platform adopted by the National Republican Convention, held in Chicago, May 17, 1860. Chicago, Press & Tribune office [1860]. Library of Congress: Washington D.C.

PRIMARY SOURCE QUESTIONS for DISCUSSION

1. What was the Republican Party's stand on secession from the Union?
2. What was the Republican Party's position on slavery in the South?
3. What was the Republican Party's position on slavery in the territories?
4. Should Southerners who wanted to maintain slavery have felt threatened by the Republican Platform of 1860?

This chapter has stressed the point that the North and the South miscalculated the costs and the benefits of fighting the Civil War. If the nation had possessed more accurate forecasts about the costs and benefits of fighting, both sides might have been willing to work out a peaceful solution.

The United States and its allies entered into a war in Iraq beginning in 2003. In the run-up to the war there was widespread debate, in the United States and elsewhere, about the likely costs and benefits it might yield. Is this another case in which a different decision would have been made if better estimates of the costs had existed before the fighting began?

In the period before the war, there was widespread concern about the capability of Saddam Hussein, then the leader of Iraq, to develop and eventually use weapons of mass destruction—nuclear, chemical, and biological weapons. There were also concerns that such weapons might be shared with terrorist organizations who threatened the United States and other nations. Weapons of mass destruction were never found. However, Saddam Hussein, a brutal dictator and threat to other nations in the region, was removed as Iraq's leader, charged with war crimes, and executed by a new Iraqi government.

Estimated Costs of the War in Iraq

One of the first cost estimates was provided in 2003 by University of Chicago economists Steven T. Davis, Kevin M. Murphy, and Robert H. Topel. They compared the costs of continuing to keep Saddam Hussein contained in Iraq, through such actions as military pressure and inspections, to the cost of an actual invasion. They concluded that the cost of the war would be $125 billion. They considered this a low estimate. They viewed containment of Saddam Hussein to be a more expensive alternative ($380 billion). [7]

A 2007 report from the Congressional Budget Office estimated that, from 2003 to 2007, the United States had spent $412 billion on the war. This estimate included $368 for military operations, $19 billion for support of Iraqi security forces, and $25 billion for diplomatic operations and foreign aid.[8]

More recently, Linda J. Bilmes of Harvard University and Joseph E. Stigler of Columbia University estimated that the war will ultimately cost $3 trillion. Blimes and Stigler take account of the cost of military operations and much more. They explain, for example, that the cost has increased greatly over time as costs have risen for military personnel, fuel, and the restocking of military equipment that has worn out due to the length of the war.[9]

These cost estimates span a wide range, from $125 billion to $3 trillion. Perhaps the actual cost lies somewhere in between. Most observers now believe that the actual costs have turned out to be much greater than people expected them to be.

The benefits in question are even more difficult to assess. One way to approach the task is by posing certain questions. For example:

- As a result of the war, will the Middle East be a more stable region, less likely to draw nations into armed conflicts?

- Will Iraq succeed in establishing a peaceful democracy with a market economy, leading to increased prosperity and independence for the Iraqi people?

- Will terrorist organizations like Al Qaeda have been dealt a serious blow by the War in Iraq and thus become a diminished threat?

Observers will continue to formulate answers to these questions and to discuss the answers in light of ongoing information about costs. These deliberations will inform American citizens as they continue to debate the underlying question: Would the United States and its allies have invaded Iraq if the true cost of the war could have been accurately identified in advance?

THEN & NOW QUESTIONS for DISCUSSION

1. What are the estimated dollar costs of the Iraq War?
2. What are some potential benefits of the war?
3. Do you think the United States and its allies would have invaded Iraq if the cost of the war had been accurately identified in advance?

Web Resources

Three Sources on the Civil War

http://www.nps.gov/archive/gett/gettkidz/cause.htm

A National Park Service page from Gettysburg on why the Civil War conflict arose.

http://civilwarcauses.org

Primary source documents: speeches, party platforms, and succession.

http://www.greatamericanhistory.net/causes.htm

An analysis of the reasons for the Civil War, with links to other sites, lesson plans, and quizzes.

Arlington House: The Robert E. Lee Memorial Virtual Museum Exhibit

http://www.nps.gov/history/museum/exhibits/arho

This exhibit, maintained by the National Park Service, includes a broad range of information on Robert E. Lee and his times.

Then & Now: The War in Iraq

http://www.becker-posner-blog.com/2007/07/index.html

Prominent economist Gary Becker and renowed judge and legal scholar Richard Posoner analyze the costs of the war in Iraq.

How Did the Civil War Change the U.S. Economy?

Atlanta, Georgia, shortly after the end of the Civil War. The city's railroad roundhouse is in ruins.

How Did the Civil War Change the U.S. Economy?

After the Civil War, who was the richest person in the United States? Perhaps a Northern manufacturer or banker? By one account, the wealthiest citizen at the end of the war was George A. Trenholm, a Confederate smuggler. Trenholm made his fortune by running blockades during the war. He smuggled cotton and gold out of the South and traded it in Europe for war materials and medicines. His steamships ran out of Charleston, Savannah, and Wilmington. He even succeeded in buying guns in New York and smuggling them back to the South to help arm the Confederate forces.

At the Civil War's end, Trenholm had earned the equivalent of more than a billion dollars in gold. This swashbuckling smuggler is said to be the inspiration for the character Rhett Butler in the novel and movie *Gone with the Wind* (the number-one movie of all time in the number of tickets sold). Like his real-life counterpart, Rhett Butler was unashamed of profiting in wartime. "What most people don't seem to realize," he said, "is that there is just as much money to be made out of the wreckage of a civilization as from the upbuilding of one."[1]

George Alfred Trenholm

KEY ECONOMIC CONCEPTS

Demand
Gross Domestic
    Product (GDP)
Human capital

Opportunity cost
Physical capital
Supply

Undoubtedly some people make fortunes out of war. Others lose all they have. The individual stories can be colorful and wrenching. But wars also have general effects on economic growth and living standards. In the case of the Civil War, what were the general effects? Did the war foster economic growth, as Northern industries increased production? How was the economy different in the aftermath of the Civil War? Of course, the biggest change produced by the Civil War was the elimination of slavery. How did the defeat of the South change the economic circumstances of African Americans?

The Historical Context
The Aftermath of the Civil War

The Union's victory in the Civil War prevented secession by the Confederacy. This was the outcome President Lincoln had sought. "From Sumter to Appomattox, it was for him a war to preserve the Union."[2] Preserving the Union also meant that enslaved people in the South would be freed. "The moment came," Lincoln said, "when I felt that slavery must die [so] that the nation might live." The Union cause had been fused with the cause of human liberty.[3]

Preserving the Union and ending slavery came at a high cost. Casualties were high on both sides. About 620,000 Americans—about 2 percent of the population at the time—were killed. (By comparison, the United States suffered about 116,000 war deaths in World War I, 405,000 in World War II, and 58,000 in the Vietnam War.[4]) While the Union suffered more wartime deaths, the losses were proportionally higher in the CSA, as a percentage of the South's smaller population.

Southerners bore most of the destruction wrought by the war. Major cities like Atlanta and Richmond were badly damaged. The railroad yards in Atlanta, a rail hub for the entire South, were ruined. Southerners lost barns, farm equipment, houses, shops, and factories. In the aftermath of battles, horses and mules were nowhere to be found. Many plantations were left to decay. Fences in the countryside were destroyed, bridges were down, and roads had fallen into disrepair. Effects of wartime destruction would mark the South for years to come.

Industrial production increased in the North after the war. Production in the South continued to focus on agriculture, with cotton as a staple crop. But plantation agriculture as Southerners had known it would never recover. The elimination of slavery meant that a new labor system would have to be worked out. Plantation owners would have to find new ways to produce their crops—or turn to other work. Newly freed African Americans also had new choices to make for themselves and their families. Recovery from the turmoil generated by war turned out to be a much larger task than anyone had imagined.

The Economic Effects of the Civil War

In economic terms, the wartime casualties—deaths and injuries—amounted to an enormous loss of human capital. **Human capital** is the knowledge, education, experience, and skills individuals possess. It is the "stuff" that enables people to work and earn a living. Nations rich in human capital are able to produce the goods and services needed to satisfy the desires of consumers. Losses of human capital—brain power, muscle power, energy—decrease the ability of a nation or a region to produce goods and services. That happened, in some measure, in the South. The after-effects of deaths and injuries,

of workers drained from the economy by war, diminished the supply of goods and services.

Similarly, the South suffered a loss of physical capital. **Physical capital** is buildings, machines, tools, and equipment. Investments in physical capital stimulate growth of production; inadequate physical capital retards growth. Even though the South's investment in farm equipment and factories was relatively small, wartime destruction of physical capital contributed to a post-war reduction in income flows.[5] Property owners of all sorts also faced losses resulting from the severe decline in the value of their land after the war, and from the neglect of property that occurred when workers left their jobs to fight.

Economic Winners and Losers

The Civil War brought costs and benefits. Surely those who benefited the most were the previously enslaved people of the South. The Civil War liberated nearly four million African Americans. Without the war, their freedom would have been delayed indefinitely.

People who were willing to take advantage of economic opportunities presented by the war certainly benefitted. These included people like George A. Trenholm, who exported and imported goods across battle lines. Producers of war-related goods also benefited. Manufacturers who supplied war material and products to the military saw an increase in their incomes.

Plantation owners and other owners of slaves lost heavily. Before the Civil War, enslaved people were regarded as private property. The end of slavery produced an uncompensated loss to the former owners. This was no small matter. Slavery had been a flourishing institution at the outset of the Civil War, especially for the cotton market. The total market value of enslaved people was estimated to be more than $3 billion. The slave holders' losses, of course, amounted to a compensating gain for the freed slaves.

The Economics of Wages

Workers in most U.S. labor markets are paid wages. The amount paid is determined in large

part by the laws of supply and demand. The **supply** is the number of workers who are willing and able to work at specific rates of pay. In the case of farm labor, the supply is how many farm workers are willing and able to work for farm owners at specific wage rates. The **demand** is the number of workers employers are willing and able to hire at specific wage rates. In the case of farming, the demand is how many farm workers farm owners are willing and able to hire at specific wage rates.

The emancipation of African Americans eliminated the plantation system. It required a restructuring of the South's agricultural system, which would no longer depend on slavery. Instead it would employ free workers, many of whom were African American. Free African Americans had several economic alternatives. Perhaps their most important problem was that most of them did not own land. (Most laborers in the North and West also were landless.) Many African Americas therefore chose to work as farm laborers, hoping to save enough money to be able eventually to purchase farmland. By saving and borrowing money, some African Americans were eventually able to buy land. By 1880, however, only 20 percent of African American farmers had managed to purchase a farm. Others—about 26 percent—decided to rent farm land. A relatively small group of African Americans choose to become homesteaders and moved to the Midwest and West. Others found jobs working land that they neither owned nor rented.

After the war, Southern planters tried at first to preserve the structure of the plantation system by hiring newly freed African Americans on annual wage contracts. This system involved using gangs of workers to work the land, supervised by overseers who could fire or impose fines on workers. In many ways, the gang labor system resembled production methods used on plantations under slavery. The new system proved to be unworkable. Planters cooperated among themselves to keep wages for African American farm workers below competitive rates. Understandably, African Americans refused to go along, and by and large the system of annual wage contracts was abandoned.

The Economics of Sharecropping

One result of these trial-and-error efforts was a compromise arrangement called sharecropping. In sharecropping, a tenant farmer (and perhaps his whole family) lived and worked on a landlord's farmland and split (or *shared*) the crop—usually 50/50—with the landlord after the harvest. Details of the system varied from place to place. Typically the landlord provided farming equipment, food, and housing. The sharecropper paid no rent. About 54 percent of freed African Americans eventually participated in sharecropping. Many white farmers also worked as sharecroppers.

Sharecroppers found advantages and disadvantages in the arrangement. On the positive side, sharecropping provided farm workers with basic necessities for productive farming—land, equipment, housing. It also provided a steady source of employment that hired laborers—workers who could be easily fired—did not enjoy.

Sharecropping also came with disadvantages. It prolonged landlords' and workers' dependence on certain cash crops such as cotton, tobacco, and rice. Merchants generally had confidence in these crops and so were willing to issue credit to landlords who produced them. Sharecropping also prolonged the dependence of sharecroppers on landlords and merchants. Sharecroppers typically had little or no cash. They purchased things they needed—seed, tools, fertilizer, food, and clothing—from a local merchant, usually a white merchant. Without cash, sharecroppers would pay for these purchases with revenue from their crops—often cotton—after the harvest, at high repayment rates. They would harvest their crops and sell them to the merchants who had extended credit. Merchants then would deduct the amounts sharecroppers owed them, and amounts for the landlords' shares, from the price they paid for the crops; the sharecroppers would keep the difference. The value of the crops was not always sufficient to cover the money sharecroppers owed. In these cases, the deficit would be added to sharecroppers' debts.

Because sharecropping depended heavily on cashless transactions, sharecroppers found it difficult to leave and seek other economic opportunities. You can't buy a railroad ticket to Detroit with a bale of cotton. The cycle of dependence was hard to break.

Landlords also faced advantages and disadvantages in sharecropping. On the positive side, the landlord received a steady source of labor to work the land. Hired farmhands might take their earnings and leave at any time; workers with a place to live, but not much cash, had an incentive to stay. Sharecropping also provided a way of sharing the risk of crop failure. If a crop failed, the landlord did not bear the entire loss; he at least had not paid wages for the effort that went into producing a crop that failed.

But there was a negative side. Landlords were locked into producing cotton and a few other cash crops as much as the sharecroppers were. The system discouraged sharecroppers and landlords from innovating by experimenting with other cash crops such as peanuts.

Freed African-American workers collect pay after a harvest in Virginia, 1870s.

HISTORICAL QUESTIONS
& ECONOMIC ANSWERS

What was the Beard-Hacker Thesis? Why was it historically important?

Charles Beard was a well-known scholar who taught history at Columbia University in New York City, beginning in 1904. Another respected scholar, Louis M. Hacker, was an economic historian who joined the faculty of Columbia's economics department in 1935. Together, Beard and Hacker developed what was known as the "Beard-Hacker Thesis." They called the Civil War the "Second American Revolution." By this they meant that the Civil War had shifted the balance of power away from Southern planters, in favor of Northern manufacturers. They contended that the Civil War changed the direction of the U.S. economy and propelled it down the path toward industrialization.

Was the Beard-Hacker Thesis widely accepted?

Yes. The Beard-Hacker Thesis became the most widely accepted interpretation of the economic impact of the Civil War. It is still influential among some scholars.

Did the Civil War change the direction of the economy? Was there an opportunity cost?

Stanley Lebergott, an economic historian, disagrees with the Beard-Hacker Thesis, as do most other economic historians today. Lebergott argues that the Civil War slowed American economic growth. He provides three reasons for this contention.[6]

- The war caused a tremendous loss of human capital. If there had been no war, many of the dead and wounded would have contributed as entrepreneurs and workers to the U.S. civilian economy, in the North and the South.

- Without the war, most of the people who served in the military would otherwise have been employed in the civilian labor force. They would have produced goods and services that, because of the war, were never produced.

- Without the Civil War, investment would not have been diverted from the civilian economy into military production. For example, productive resources would have been used to manufacture clothing and invest in private physical capital rather than armaments and uniforms—important military goods, but goods with limited value otherwise.

These three reasons describe the war's huge opportunity cost. **Opportunity cost** is the next-best alternative people give up in any decision they make. In choosing to go to war, the Union and the CSA sacrificed the productive capacity of those who were killed and disabled, the productive capacity of those who performed military service for years rather than engaging in civilian employment, and the value of the resources that were invested in military production rather than projects in the civilian economy. This opportunity cost implies that, in many ways, most American producers and consumers would have been better off without the war. That is not, however, a decisive argument against the war. The war also preserved the Union and put an end to slavery. Giving up on those outcomes would have meant, from the Union's point of view, another huge opportunity cost.

A trend of economic expansion in industry and agriculture was well underway prior to the onset of the Civil War. Had there been no war, the momentum for economic growth that emerged after 1870 would have been there anyway,

TABLE 1	Real Growth in Gross Domestic Product Before and After the Civil War	
Decades Before, During, and After the Civil War	**Real Annualized GDP Growth**
1850–1859	5.64 percent
1860–1869	3.20 percent
1870–1879	5.20 percent

Source: Lawrence H. Officer and Samuel H. Williamson, "Annualized Growth Rate and Graphs of Various Historical Economic Series," Measuring Worth, 2009.

TABLE 2	Mining, Agriculture, and Manufacturing Production per Decade, 1860–1880, by Region		
Year	Total Percent Increase	Percent Increase in Mining and Agriculture	Percent Increase in Manufacturing
North and West			
1860–1870	40	46	33
1870–1880	66	49	84
1860–1880	232	218	245
South			
1860–1870	-25	-25	-20
1870–1880	57	53	76
1860–1880	118	115	141

Source: Percentages calculated from Robert W. Fogel and Stanley Engerman, "The Economic Impact of the Civil War," reprinted in Fogel and Engerman, eds., *The Reinterpretation of American Economic History* (New York: Harper & Row, 1971), p. 37.

developing at a more rapid pace. Information summarized in Table 1 suggests that this is the case at the national level. As you can see, real growth in **Gross Domestic Product** (**GDP**)—the total value of all the goods and services produced in the United States—grew more slowly in the 1860s than in surrounding decades.

Why has there been confusion among respected historians regarding the economic impact of the Civil War?

Economic historian Roger L. Ranson emphasizes the fact that the Civil War involved a huge effort to mobilize resources.[7] This effort made it *appear* that the economy was growing, when in fact resources were being shifted from one sector (the production of consumer goods) to another (the production of military goods). Historians may have mistaken this increase in military production for an increase in overall economic activity.

Did the economies of the North and South grow at different rates?

Yes. While the national economy grew overall after the war, the South took much longer to recover. Production declined in the South following the war, while it expanded in the North and the West. Information summarized in Table 2 describes this initial decline, and the slower expansion of the South in comparison to the North, in terms of production in manufacturing. Table 2 suggests that the system of sharecropping, with its emphasis on the production of cotton, was one of the culprits, slowing down industrialization and economic expansion in the South.

QUESTIONS for DISCUSSION

1. Explain, in economic terms, the losses caused by the Civil War.
2. Who were the economic winners and losers?
3. What was the opportunity cost of the Civil War?
4. What is the Beard-Hacker Thesis?
5. Does Lebergott agree or disagree with Beard and Hacker? Explain your answer.
6. Which thesis—Lebergott's or Beard's and Hacker's—do you agree with? Why?

The Debate on the Economic Future of African Americans

PRIMARY SOURCE

What economic course of action should African Americans have pursued after the Civil War? This was a hotly debated topic among African Americans and other Americans. The leading spokesmen for African Americans were Booker T. Washington and W.E.B. Du Bois.

Booker T. Washington, a former Southern slave, sought economic progress for African Americans by stressing the importance of education and self-improvement, to be accomplished in a way that would be acceptable to the white Southerners with whom they lived. He believed that economic progress within Southern society would lead eventually to social progress and political equality for African Americans.

W.E.B. Du Bois, a New Englander, was the first African American to receive a Doctor of Philosophy (Ph.D.) degree from Harvard University (the Ph.D. is the highest degree granted by universities). While initially in agreement with Washington, he soon argued that African Americans should follow a different path. He believed that political and social equality must be fought for directly and immediately through social action and changes in the law. He also emphasized the importance of providing advanced college and university education for an academically elite group (the top 10 percent) of African Americans. Excellent education for those African Americans, he contended, would benefit the African American cause more than education of the masses.

Here is a quotation from Booker T. Washington's 1895 Atlanta Exposition Address, later known as the Atlanta Compromise Speech, delivered to white Southerners:

Nearly sixteen millions of hands will aid you in pulling the load upward, or they will pull against you the load downward. We shall constitute one-third and more of the ignorance and crime of the South, or one-third [of] its intelligence and progress; we shall contribute one-third to the business and industrial prosperity of the South, or we shall prove a veritable body of death, stagnating, depressing, retarding every effort to advance the body politic.

Booker T. Washington

Here is a quotation from *The Souls of Black Folk*, by W.E.B. Du Bois, in which Du Bois discusses Booker T. Washington:

So far as Mr. Washington preaches Thrift, Patience, and Industrial Training for the masses, we must hold up his hands and strive with him, rejoicing in his honors .... But so far as Mr. Washington apologizes for injustice, North or South, does not rightly value the privilege and duty of voting, belittles the emasculating effects of caste distinctions [separation or discrimination based on race], and opposes the higher training and ambition of our brighter minds—so far as he, the South, or the Nation, does this—we must unceasingly and firmly oppose them.

W.E.B. Du Bois

PRIMARY SOURCE — QUESTIONS for DISCUSSION

1. What is the main idea Booker T. Washington advocates in this excerpt from his Atlanta Exposition Address?
2. What is the main idea advocated by W.E.B. Du Bois in this excerpt from *The Souls of Black Folk?*
3. Who do you think has the stronger argument: Du Bois or Washington? Explain your answer.

The Economy of the New South

The "New South" is a term used to describe the economic transformation of the South. Today the economy of the South closely resembles that of the rest of the nation. It has developed several hub cities for banking, manufacturing, construction, and services. For example, the corporate headquarters of Bank of America—the nation's largest bank— is located in Charlotte, North Carolina. In addition, BMW, Toyota, Mercedes, Honda, Nissan, and Volkswagen all have built plants in the South—in Georgia, Alabama, South Carolina, Kentucky, Texas, and Mississippi. The editor of *Black Enterprise* magazine has stated that "This New South is a marvel to behold. It is what the young people who participated in the civil rights movement had in mind when they said if the South ever changed, it would be the place to be."[8]

Changes in Agriculture, Manufacturing, and Service Industries

The economy of the South today is diversified. While agricultural production remains important, the percentage of workers who earn their living on farms is lower in the South than it is for the nation as a whole. This marks a complete reversal from the South's previous farm-dominated economy.

Manufacturing is a vital part of today's Southern economy, especially in today's higher-technology, higher-skilled industries. Manufacturing production has increased largely due to automobile manufacturing. In 2006, for example, there were 119,000 auto manufacturing jobs in the South.

The factories of the South have for some time manufactured more products with fewer workers. As the number of manufacturing jobs declined, the services sector expanded. The services sector involves a wide range of jobs, from high-skill jobs in accounting, advertising, communications, computer software, and law to lower-skill jobs in retail sales, hospitality, pest control, security services, building maintenance, and telemarketing. Service-sector jobs jumped from 67 percent of the Southeast's total employment in 1970 to just short of 84 percent by 2007. The shift to growth in service jobs reflects similar trends in the national economy.

Economic changes in the South have attracted people to the region. The population of the South has recently grown faster than the population of the country as a whole. For example, between 1960 and 2007, Florida's population nearly quadrupled, and Georgia's population more than doubled (see Table 3 for regional summaries).

This trend has been affected by recent migration decisions of African Americans. African Americans have reversed the pattern established during World War I of leaving the South for better jobs in the North. Beginning around 1970, African Americans

TABLE 3	Regional Population Growth, in Percentages: 1990, 2000, and 2010		
Regions	**1990**	**2000**	**2010**
Northeast	3.4	5.5	3.2
South	13.4	17.3	14.3
Midwest	1.4	7.9	3.9
West	22.1	19.7	13.8

Source: http://2010.census.gov/2010census/data

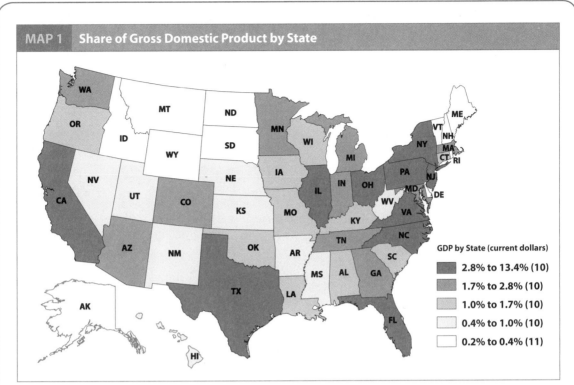

MAP 1 Share of Gross Domestic Product by State

GDP by State (current dollars)

- 2.8% to 13.4% (10)
- 1.7% to 2.8% (10)
- 1.0% to 1.7% (10)
- 0.4% to 1.0% (10)
- 0.2% to 0.4% (11)

Source: U.S. Bureau of Economic Analysis.

increasingly migrated to the South from the West, Northeast, and Midwest. Many have chosen to settle in such cities as Atlanta, Dallas, Charlotte, and Orlando.[9]

The arrival of new people and industries has increased total state GDP in the South. State GDP is the total value of all the goods and services produced within the borders of a state. It is the state's contribution to national GDP. Today, GDP in Southern states represents a significant share of the production of the nation. Map 1 shows each state's share of total GDP. Texas, Florida, North Carolina, and Virginia rank near the top, nationally, followed by Georgia.

Personal incomes in the South now approach those of people in other states. Average per capita (per person) income for the United States as a whole in 2009 was $39,626. Virginia ranked seventh in the nation with a per capita income of $44,129; Florida ranked twenty-third with a per capita income of $40,054. Louisiana was not far behind, ranking twenty-eighth with a per capita income of $37,520. Other Southern states lagged, however. South Carolina ranked forty-fifth with a per capita income of $32,338, and Mississippi ranked fiftieth with a per capita income of $30,426.[10]

THEN & NOW QUESTIONS for DISCUSSION

1. What is new about the New South?
2. What evidence do you see of positive changes in the Southern economy?
3. Why do you think African Americans increasingly began moving to the South after 1970?

The Civil War
http://www.civilwar.com

In-depth information on the Civil War, including a section for Teacher's Resources.

Slavery and Emancipation
http://www.archives.gov/northeast

Information from the National Archives on the state of African Americans after the Civil War; includes primary documents.

Slave to Sharecropper
http://www.pbs.org/wgbh/amex/reconstruction/sharecrop/ps_adams.html

Primary sources and information about the practice of sharecropping after the Civil War.

African Americans Migrate Back to the South
http://www.brookings.edu/reports/2004/05demographics_frey.aspx

Read a report which traces the return of African Americans to the South.

The Homestead Act of 1862: Was Free Land Really Free?

Daniel Freeman, first homesteader in Beatrice, Nebraska.

Daniel Freeman, a soldier in the Union Army, had a problem. He planned to leave Gage County, Nebraska Territory, on January 1, 1863, to report for duty in St. Louis on January 2. But there was something Freeman wanted to do before he left. He had long wanted to be the first person to file for a homestead under a new government program. He had traveled to Nebraska to find property to homestead, and he found the property he wanted in Gage County. But Freeman's timing was bad. The Homestead Act of 1862 was scheduled to go into effect on January 1, 1863, and the local land office was scheduled to be closed on January 1 for the New Year's Day holiday.

How could Freeman file a homestead claim and still make it to St. Louis by January 2? At a New Year's Eve party, Freeman worked out a solution. He met some local land office agents at the party and convinced one of them to open the office 10 minutes after midnight on January 1 to enable him to file a land claim. In doing so, Freeman became one of the first of many Americans to take advantage of the opportunities provided by the Homestead Act.[1]

President Abraham Lincoln signed the Homestead Act on May 20, 1862. The Act was intended to help people like Daniel Freeman. It opened up 270 million acres of publicly owned western land for settlement. Eventually, 10 percent of U.S. land was given away under the Homestead Act.

Distributing land in this way was out of the ordinary. Ordinarily, land is distributed on the basis of price. The U.S. government could have held land auctions in which public land would have sold to the highest bidders. Revenue from auctions of this sort might have helped the U.S. Treasury pay off Civil War debts; it might also have helped to pay for new roads and canals. But no such auctions took place. Instead, the government gave land away to homesteaders—to people like Daniel Freeman, who were willing to settle on the land they received. Was free land a good deal for homesteaders? Was it a good deal for U.S. taxpayers?

KEY ECONOMIC CONCEPTS

Demand	Market economy
Gross Domestic Product (GDP)	Market price
	Opportunity cost
Market	Supply

The Historical Context
Homesteading Was No Picnic

The Homestead Act of 1862 offered a homesteader ownership of 160 acres of land. The law required the prospective owner to file an application, to file for deed of title (proving ownership), and then to improve the land. The homesteader was to build a home on the property and occupy it for five years. Homesteaders had to pay a small filing fee, or they could take title by paying a fee of $1.25 an acre after six months.

Who was eligible? Anyone could file for a homestead if he or she met these criteria:

- 21 years old,
- the head of a family, or a single woman, and
- had never taken up arms against the U.S. government.

"Anyone" here included African Americans—those freed by the Emancipation Proclamation of 1862 and those who were eventually freed with the passage of the 13th Amendment to the U.S. Constitution in 1865.

What was homesteading like? It was certainly not for the faint of heart. We can get a glimpse from the homesteader H. B. Thomas, who was

A family and their homestead on the prairie.

interviewed by George Hartman as part of the Federal Writers Project of 1936–1940. Born in Knox County, Illinois, in 1856, Thomas claimed a homestead in Nebraska in 1882. Here is an excerpt from his story in his own words:

> I homesteaded in southwestern Nebraska about 53 years ago. We went to [the] land office in North Platte, Nebraska, and got the papers filed. There was 5 of us looking for claims and sent to North Platte to see what land was free. We located on the prairies . . . .
>
> Our homestead was in Lincoln County. After we got the homestead we went back to Gosper where I was working there. . . . We drove yolk cattle down to our claims and put up a sod home.
>
> We broke prairie, made our homes and settled. We found that we plowed on some land that wasn't ours. A good many old Union soldiers… settled on these homesteads. We had to live on our claims 5 years to get the land. One of the soldiers claimed that he had a harder time homesteading than he did when he served in the army.
>
> We built our houses out of sod. We built churches out of sod as well as schoolhouses. I gave one corner of my land to the authorities for a schoolhouse. . . .
>
> There was one winter in 1886 that we had 3 blizzards, one came the 16th of November and the drifts of snow laid on the ground until April. We left this territory and moved to Madison County. I had lost all of my crops on my homestead and [went through] a depression and drought which ruined me.[2]

The Economics of Public Land Policy

Decades before the passage of the Homestead Act, elected officials had to make choices about how to distribute public land. It was serious business. Substantial resources were at stake. Many Americans paid close attention to opportunities to obtain land. The possibility of owning farm land was a powerful incentive.

The public land opened up by the Homestead Act was a valuable resource. Although it was abundant, Homestead land was nonetheless scarce. Why? Because it had alterative uses. Choices about how to use land always involve **opportunity cost**—that is, the next-best alternative use of it. President Lincoln understood that although the United States claimed many large land holdings, American Indians still controlled much of this public land, and they might have preferred to use land they controlled for hunting, fishing, or agriculture. Settlers might have chosen to buy public land for farming and ranching. Some public land was rich in timber, water, and minerals. Business people might have chosen to buy that public land for logging, irrigation, and mining. The railroads were interested, too. They were eager to obtain lands in the West to build new rail lines and encourage settlement along those rail lines.

Obviously, there was a market for these vast tracts of public land. A **market** is any place or situation in which people buy and sell goods and services. Normally, the laws of supply and demand set market prices for land.

A key feature of a **market economy** is that goods and services are distributed on the basis of price. In the United States before 1862, the federal government often sold public land at market prices. The prices apparently looked attractive. By the mid-1830s, land sales accounted for more than 40 percent of federal revenues. By 1860, 10 million people lived west of the Mississippi River. The price charged for land in these land sales was a market price. A **market price**—the price at which the quantity demanded by consumers and the quantity supplied by suppliers is the same—is determined by the interaction of supply and demand. The **supply** in early sales of public land was the quantity of land the federal government was willing and able to sell at specific prices. At high prices, suppliers are typically willing to sell more; at lower prices, they are typically willing to sell less. The **demand** in early sales of public land was the quantity of land that buyers were willing and able to purchase at each price. At high prices,

buyers are typically willing to buy less; at lower prices, they are typically willing to buy more.

Despite this history of selling land, the idea of giving land away for homesteading had been gaining support among elected officials in the years prior to 1862. It might seem like a strange idea. Why give land away rather than sell it? But the Homestead Act of 1862 made good political sense. By May 1862, 11 states had seceded from the Union. Southern states opposed to homestead legislation were no longer represented in Congress. And the outcome of the Civil War was uncertain. Might the Confederacy win? The early successes of General Robert E. Lee and early failures of Union generals made that appear to be a real possibility. With the war going poorly for the Union, President Lincoln saw clear reasons to encourage settlement of the West. He wanted to make sure the West would be dominated by pro-Union settlers opposed to slavery.

Also, giving land away was popular with several groups including Civil War veterans, formerly enslaved African Americans, laborers from eastern cities, and newly-arrived immigrants from Europe. Officials from western states pushed hard for homesteading because an influx of homesteaders would foster development in their areas.

Was Free Land a Good Deal for Homesteaders?

The prospect of free land was highly attractive to some American settlers. Fifteen thousand homesteads, comprising 25 million acres, were given away during the Civil War years. Still, homestead land was not exactly free. It came with predictable monetary costs. Some of these were costs settlers would have faced whether they had bought new land or obtained it by homesteading. In either case, settlers would need to travel to their new lands, thus incurring transportation costs. And in either case they would face costs related to putting the land into production—buying tools and other resources needed to clear timber, move boulders, dig wells, build shelters, plow thick prairie grass, plant seeds, and kill game to put food on the table. Once crops were harvested, moreover, settlers would need to ship their crops to a market, incurring freight charges. In addition to these costs, homesteaders faced the specific cost of being required to live on their property for five years.

There were also nonmonetary costs, in the form of things homesteaders (and some other settlers) would need to live without. Homesteads were often located in isolated areas, far from family members and friends who had been left behind. Schools, churches, stores, doctors, and lawyers were most likely miles away. Roads were poor or nonexistent.

Because homestead land came with costs of this sort, many settlers passed it over, preferring to buy land. Economic historian Stanley Lebergott provides some details:

> From 1863 to 1872, ten times as many acres were sold for cash as were homesteaded. In the next decade three and a half times as many were sold. Farmers continued to pay cash far oftener than they took up homestead land. And they bought land at $4.50 from railroads while good U.S. land could be had for $1.25. [3]

Why would farmers pay for land rather than accept homestead land? Homestead land, it turned out, was not always such a good deal. Purchased land—often land sold by railroad companies—might be better. First, it was more likely to be well suited for agriculture. The fertile lands in western Minnesota, Iowa, and the Dakotas were settled rapidly. Land on the Great Plains, which had less rainfall, posed higher risks of crop failure. Second, moving crops to markets over large distances was expensive. Owning land close to rail lines substantially reduced the cost of transporting crops to market.

Railroad companies obtained land from the federal government. They sold a great deal of their land to settlers for farming. After the Civil War, settlers had many choices about where to locate; millions of acres were available for settlement. Under pressure to sell their land in a competitive market, railroads sometimes offered farmers incentives such as low-interest loans or even 40 acres of land at no charge. The railroads took these steps to encourage settlers to buy land from them and build farms near their railroad lines. Farms located near rail lines provided a stable source of revenue, from the shipment of agricultural products, for the railroads.

Settlers build fences around a homestead on the frontier.

Did the Homestead Act have unintended consequences?

Yes. Giving away land to individuals stirred debates about the precedent it set. The government was choosing to provide important economic benefits to some groups but not to others. If the federal government could give away land, why not give away other resources? Why not give away money? Using government power to transfer wealth from one group (all taxpayers) to another group (those taxpayers willing and able to homestead) might set a bad precedent, encouraging other groups to seek similar favors. Lobbying the government for favors has now become standard practice for interest groups of all sorts.

Unfortunately, too, the Homestead Act created incentives that invited corruption. Mining and logging companies with strong interests at stake paid close attention to land development in the West. Since these companies were prevented from acquiring homestead land from the government, one of them might approach a homesteader directly, persuading him to make a claim or purchase and then transfer it to the company. Also, officials who administered land policies were sometimes corrupt. They sometimes entered claims for fictitious people and later transferred these titles to mining companies and timber companies. As a result, public lands frequently wound up in the hands of owners who were not homesteaders. Such owners obtained land at well below market rates, thus harming the interests of taxpayers.

In what way might the Homestead Act be regarded as an economic success?

The Homestead Act succeeded in opening up millions of acres of western land for private business and family settlement. Land was homesteaded in 30 of what are today's states, primarily those in the central part of the nation including Minnesota, North Dakota, South Dakota, and Kansas. Nebraska was the largest participant; 45 percent of its land was homesteaded. All the western states, including California and Alaska, were available for homesteading. A few states in the Southeast, including Alabama, Mississippi, and Florida, were also involved. Eventually two million claims, which included 10 percent of the entire area of the United States, were filed under the Homestead Act.

In what way might the Homestead Act be regarded as an economic failure?

Figure 1 shows the number of claims that were settled between 1871 and 1960. These settled claims were called "patents." The peak homesteading years were 1911 to 1920. These large numbers, however, might be misleading. For the two million claims made under the Homestead Act, only 40 percent of homesteaders "proved up" (built a home, farmed, and remained on the land for five years) on their claims and earned the deed from the federal government. Thus, less than half of the claims were *successfully* homesteaded.

This high failure rate suggests that the cost of "free" land was indeed high. Variables contributing to homestead failures include the high start-up and transportation costs described previously. In addition, homestead land further west presented special problems. Much public land in western Nebraska, for example, was treeless grassland. Settlers there often lived in primitive conditions. They used sod to build homes; they used dried buffalo dung ("chips") for fuel. They were vulnerable to the limited rainfall and dry winds that destroyed their crops and blew away the thin layer of topsoil exposed after prairie grass had been plowed. Between 1888 and 1892, half the population of western Nebraska gave up their claims and moved back east, leaving dusty fields and ghost towns behind them.

In creating an incentive to bring marginal agricultural land of this sort into production long before "dry farming" techniques had been developed, the Homestead Act helped to set the

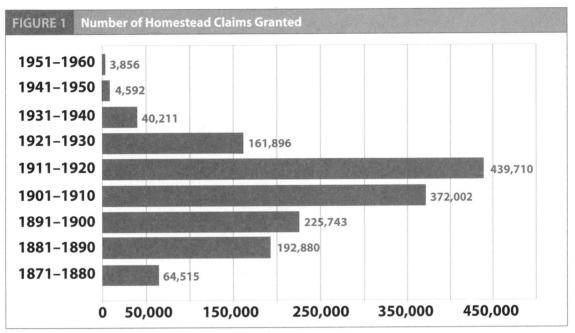

FIGURE 1 **Number of Homestead Claims Granted**

Source: http://www.nps.gov/home/historyculture/upload/Final%20Patents.pdf

stage for the Dust Bowl of the Great Depression and widespread environmental damage.

Was the Homestead Act a good deal for taxpayers?

Not likely. It is impossible to know for sure how much revenue taxpayers lost because of the Homestead Act. Much of the public land at the time had not been surveyed. No auctions had been held. We will never know what the prices for that land might have been.

Congress distributed 270 million acres of public land under the Homestead Act. It was, according to Gary M. Anderson and Dolores T. Martin, the largest spending program of the 19th century. But the cost was hidden because the value of public land was not included in the federal budget. Anderson and Martin estimate that the land the federal government gave away had an average per-acre value of at least $7.53 in 1870. This suggests that the Homestead Act cost tax payers in excess of $20 billion during the time of the program (1862–1986).[4] The relative size of that loss can be gauged by a comparison. In 1870, near the beginning of the Homestead program, the U.S. **Gross Domestic Product (GDP)**—the

final value of all the goods and services produced in the nation—was almost $8 billion, and in 1920, near the peak of the program, GDP was almost $90 billion. In light of GDP in 1870 and 1920, the estimated loss of $20 billion over the years of the program appears to be substantial.

Was there a more efficient way to distribute land?

Different choices for the distribution of land would have yielded different results. Perhaps the government could have used its military forces to close off the Homestead lands to early settlement, allowing time for teams to survey the public lands. Then the government could have held auctions in which public land would have sold to the highest bidders. The best land would have commanded the highest prices; poor land would have sold for lower prices. As a result, the risk of widespread fraud would have been reduced, and the U.S. Treasury would have been enhanced.

This process would also have offered other advantages. The authors of the Homestead Act lacked detailed information about lands in the far West. Almost certainly, they imagined that homesteaders would find fertile soil with adequate rainfall and plentiful timber to be used to build homes, barns, fences, schools, and other necessities. Surveys, had they been done, would have described the wide variety in climate and terrain actually found in the public lands. Individuals and businesses would have benefitted from the time lag needed to prepare for auctions. Those with limited means would have had time to save money or obtain lines of credit to help them in the bidding process. People unskilled in farming might have taken note of the survey information and been discouraged by it. People possessed of the skills, knowledge, and attitudes needed for farming would have been more likely to bid and more likely to focus their bidding on land that looked suitable. This process of self-selection among prospective bidders probably would have reduced homestead failure rates.

What were the chances that such an auction system would have worked in the real world of 1862?

Realistically, no chance. President Lincoln was focused on fighting the Civil War. It is unlikely that he could have allocated resources to keep settlers out of millions of acres of land in the vast Western territories. It had always been difficult, in fact, for the government to keep high-risk explorers and settlers off public lands. And once an adventuresome farmer or miner settled on public land, he was inclined to believe he had earned a right to keep it, and inclined to

resist such niceties as competitive bidding. As you might expect, some of these frontiersmen were tough, well-armed characters. They might not simply disappear into the woods if a judge told them to give up their land because what they were doing was illegal.

There was also a question about how American Indians—the people who had direct control over many public lands— would have viewed a governmental takeover, to be followed by surveys and auctions. The U.S. military would not only need to keep white settlers out, it would need to establish control over the lands in question. Given the reluctance of American Indians to give up the lands they occupied, establishing control would have come only at a high cost.

Was Congress aware of problems with the Homestead Act? Did it attempt to make changes in the Act?

Yes and yes. Congress passed the Enlarged Homestead Act in 1909. The original provision of 160 acres of land was not suitable for arid lands far to the west. The 1909 Act attempted to make dry-land farming more feasible by increasing the number of acres for a homestead to 320. Later, the Stock Raising Homestead Act of 1916 opened homesteads of 640 acres to settlers interested in ranching. In 1976, homesteading was discontinued on federal land, except in Alaska, where it continued until 1986.

QUESTIONS for DISCUSSION

1. How does a market economy typically distribute goods and services?
2. Why did President Lincoln and members of Congress decide to give away land to people who were willing to settle it?
3. For settlers who homesteaded, what were the expected and unexpected consequences of the Homestead Act of 1862?
4. In what way was the nation helped and hurt by the Homestead Act of 1862?
5. Suppose you were distributing land today. What method of land distribution, other than giving it away, might you use?

How the Railroads Promoted Land Sales

M any more farmers paid cash for land than were willing to accept "free" land offered by the Homestead Act of 1862. Land in Iowa and Nebraska promised to be good agricultural land, and railroad companies provided incentives for settlers to buy such land. Below is an 1872 poster advertising land for sale from the Burlington & Missouri River Railroad Company. Study the poster; then respond to the questions that follow.

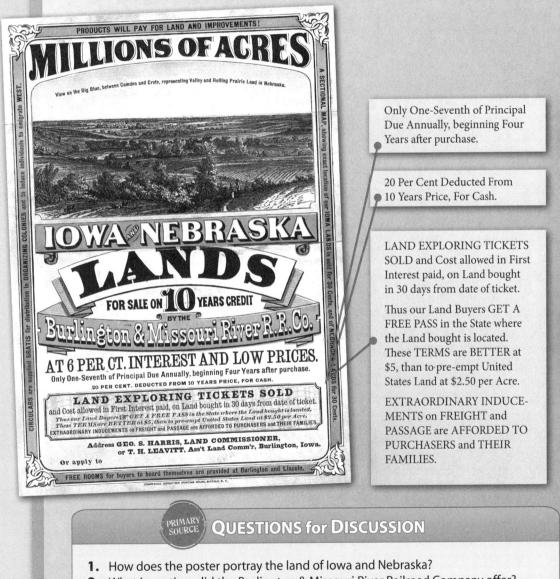

Only One-Seventh of Principal Due Annually, beginning Four Years after purchase.

20 Per Cent Deducted From 10 Years Price, For Cash.

LAND EXPLORING TICKETS SOLD and Cost allowed in First Interest paid, on Land bought in 30 days from date of ticket.

Thus our Land Buyers GET A FREE PASS in the State where the Land bought is located. These TERMS are BETTER at $5, than to pre-empt United States Land at $2.50 per Acre.

EXTRAORDINARY INDUCEMENTS on FREIGHT and PASSAGE are AFFORDED TO PURCHASERS and THEIR FAMILIES.

PRIMARY SOURCE QUESTIONS for DISCUSSION

1. How does the poster portray the land of Iowa and Nebraska?
2. What incentives did the Burlington & Missouri River Railroad Company offer?
3. Why would railroads want to encourage settlement?

The Homestead Act of 1862 distributed public land to settlers without charging market prices. Settlers could acquire a homestead by paying some small fees and occupying and working the land. Although the Homestead Act succeeded in rapidly moving land into private hands, it had some unintended consequences. The costs to settlers were often higher than expected. There was evidence of widespread corruption. Taxpayers did not receive the full dollar value of the public land that the government gave away.

Fast-forward to 2007. The U.S. economy took a nose dive entering into the worst recession Americans had seen since the Great Depression of the 1930s. In response, elected officials searched for ways to encourage consumer spending and thus shorten the recession. They came up with the idea of offering "Cash for Clunkers." Like the Homestead Act of 1862, Cash for Clunkers was a program for distributing goods at a cost below the market price—but this time the goods were cars, not farms.

In 2009, Congress allotted $3 billion for the Car Allowance Rebate System (CARS), which was quickly dubbed Cash for Clunkers. The program offered financial incentives for Americans to purchase new, fuel-efficient cars when trading cars that were less fuel-efficient. The program was promoted as a way to boost auto sales while at the same time improving the environment by putting cleaner, fuel-efficient vehicles on the roadways. Automobile manufactures, auto workers, and many environmentalists thought that it was a great idea.

Here is how the program worked. The federal government provided an incentive to encourage people to purchase new cars. The incentive was a reduction in the cost buyers would pay for new cars. The reduction came in the form of a rebate. Car buyers would be eligible for a rebate ranging from $3,500 to $4,500 for trading in a gas-guzzler and purchasing a new fuel-efficient vehicle. The exact amount of the rebate would depend on the type of car purchased and the difference in fuel economy between the new car and the trade-in. To qualify for the rebate, the trade-in vehicle had to be less than 25 years old, get 18 miles to the gallon or less, and be registered and insured continuously for the full year preceding the trade-in. The program required that the car dealer would disable the engine of the eligible trade-in vehicle. Then the vehicle would be scrapped.

Cash for Clunkers: A Government Success?

A 2010 report by the Government Accounting office suggests that Cash for Clunkers was successful in some respects. The goals of the program were to help stimulate a lagging economy and to put fuel-efficient vehicles on the road. The report concluded that the program achieved these broad objectives. For example, nearly 680,000 consumers purchased or leased vehicles using the program's credit plan. And the average fuel economy of new vehicles purchased or leased under the program was 24.9 miles per gallon, compared with 15.7 miles per gallon for vehicles traded in. Figure 2 shows numbers for vehicle sales during the Cash for Clunkers program. You can see the spike in sales in the summer of 2009.

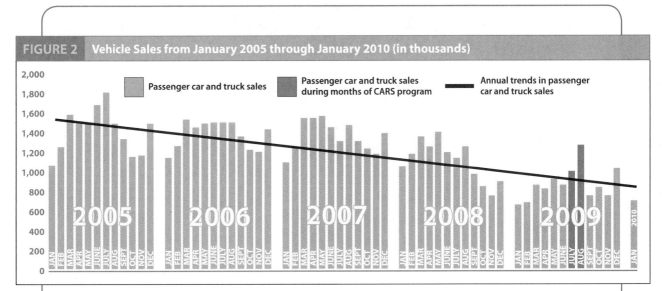

FIGURE 2 Vehicle Sales from January 2005 through January 2010 (in thousands)

Passenger car and truck sales

Passenger car and truck sales during months of CARS program

Annual trends in passenger car and truck sales

Source: U.S. Government Accountability Office, Auto Industry: *Lessons Learned from Cash for Clunkers* Program, April 2010.

Cash for Clunkers: A Government Failure?

Did sales of automobiles increase? According to economists Atif Mian of the University of California at Berkeley and Amir Sufi of the University of Chicago, sales did increase, but only in the short term. The Cash for Clunkers program did result in an increase in car sales It turned out, however, that the program only attracted people who were going to buy new cars anyway. The early increase in sales was followed by a decrease in sales of about the same amount.[4] Note the drop off in sales (shown in Figure 2) after the program was over.

Did Cash for Clunkers improve the environment? Not likely. The scale of the program was too small to have any meaningful environmental impact. The Department of Transportation estimates that there are more than 250 million registered passenger vehicles in the United States. The Cash for Clunkers program took 680,000 automobiles off the road. Thus, the program replaced less than 1 percent of existing automobiles that would otherwise have been on the road. It seems unlikely that retiring so few clunkers would produce any measurable improvement in air quality.

THEN & NOW **QUESTIONS for DISCUSSION**

1. What was the Cash for Clunkers Program?
2. In what ways was the Car Allowance Rebate System of 2009 like the Homestead Act of 1862?
3. Do you regard Cash for Clunkers as an economic success or failure? Why?

Homestead Act of 1862

http://www.nathankramer.com/settle/article/homestead.htm

The Congressional Act of 1862.

Teaching with Documents: The Homestead Act of 1862

http://www.archives.gov/education/lessons/homestead-act

A view of the Homestead Act by reference to Daniel Freedman, including his Homestead application, proof of improvements, and certificate of eligibility.

About the Homestead Act

http://www.nps.gov/home/historyculture/abouthomesteadactlaw.htm

General information about the Act, including age requirements, filing fees, and the process of claiming land.

Then & Now: Cash for Clunkers

http://www.gao.gov/new.items/d10486.pdf

This report explains lessons to be learned from the Cash for Clunkers program.

Did the Comanche and Other American Indians Favor Communal Ownership?

Comanche brave on horseback.

Communal Ownership among American Indians

American Indians are often thought to be people who favored communal ownership of resources. Books and movies about American Indians frequently suggest that private ownership was little known among them, and that communal or common ownership was widespread.

Sitting Bull (1831–1890) was the principal chief of the Dakota Sioux. He is best known for having defeated General George A. Custer at the battle of the Little Big Horn River in 1876. Here is what Sitting Bull is reported to have said regarding the relationship of the Native American peoples to the environment and land ownership:

> Behold, my brothers, the spring has come. The earth has received the embraces of the sun and we shall soon see the results of that love! Every seed is awakened and so has all animal life. It is through this mysterious power that we too have our being and we therefore yield to our neighbors, even our animal neighbors, the same right as ourselves to inhabit this land. My love of our native soil is wholly mystical.[1]
>
> —Chief Sitting Bull (Tatanka Iyotaka), Hunkpapa Sioux

Chief Sitting Bull

KEY ECONOMIC CONCEPTS

Market Economy	Rules of the game
Profit	Scarcity
Property rights	

Here Sitting Bull speaks warmly about the earth, suggesting that it belongs to humans and animals alike. Its resources should be shared by all. One neighbor should yield to another an equal right to inhabit the land.

Sitting Bull's statement captures the Plains Indians' attitude of reverence for the land. But the statement does not include any general argument against all private ownership of property. This is not surprising. All societies face choices regarding what will be owned by the group and what will be owned by individuals. The choices vary from one culture to another. Outsiders commenting on those choices sometimes oversimplify or misrepresent them, in the way that tourists visiting foreign countries may give inaccurate accounts of the cultures they briefly observe. Giving an accurate account, of course, is not always easy. Here we turn to a case in point. Did American Indians reject private ownership of property, preferring communal ownership? Or is this view oversimplified—perhaps a romantic myth?

The Historical Context
Talk or Fight?

Land ownership rights have often been a source of conflict between white settlers and American Indians. The conflict evolved over time. Early contacts between white settlers and American Indians often involved peaceful negotiation of treaties rather than warfare. During the colonial period, Britain, Spain, and France claimed many North American lands occupied by American

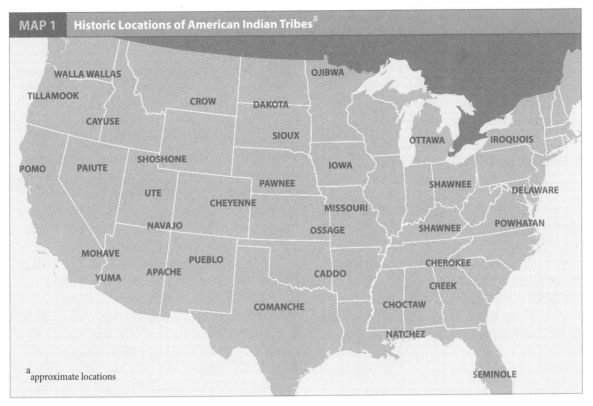

MAP 1   Historic Locations of American Indian Tribes[a]

WALLA WALLAS
TILLAMOOK
CAYUSE
CROW
OJIBWA
DAKOTA
SIOUX
OTTAWA
IROQUOIS
POMO
PAIUTE
SHOSHONE
IOWA
SHAWNEE
DELAWARE
UTE
PAWNEE
CHEYENNE
MISSOURI
NAVAJO
OSSAGE
SHAWNEE
POWHATAN
MOHAVE
PUEBLO
YUMA
APACHE
CADDO
CHEROKEE
CREEK
COMANCHE
CHOCTAW
NATCHEZ
SEMINOLE

[a] approximate locations

Indians. The colonists recognized, however, that they could not enforce their governments' land claims without coming to an accommodation with American Indians who claimed their own rights to use the land.

In the late 18th and early 19th centuries, U.S. policy regarding land occupied by American Indians also emphasized negotiation and accommodation. It recognized that the U.S. government had an obligation to compensate Indian tribes when it removed them from land over which it wished to establish property ownership rights. From 1778 until the Civil War, the U.S. government tried to resolve ownership rights by negotiating treaties. The treaties were officially regarded as formal agreements between sovereign nations. Indians would give up their rights to hunt and live on huge parcels of land that they had inhabited in exchange for trade goods, yearly cash annuity payments, and assurances that no further demands would be made on them. Some treaties provided for the Indians to continue to use land they ceded to the government. The extent to which Indians actually agreed to these treaties has been called into question. The Indians

often agreed in name only, according to one respected historian: "federal commissioners bribed important chiefs and, if necessary, got them drunk enough to sign anything."[2]

The emphasis on removing Indians to remote, undesirable locations lessened during the presidency of John Quincy Adams (1825–1829); it resumed under the presidency of Andrew Jackson (1829–1837). The Indian Removal Act of 1830 authorized the U.S. government to take ownership of Indian lands in the East, with compensation, and to resettle Indians west of the Missouri River. Many Shawnee, Delaware, Wyandot, Choctaw and other Indians suffered greatly, from disease and starvation, in their resettlement journeys.[3]

After the Civil War, U.S. policy became increasingly harsh, intensifying the approach exemplified in the Indian Removal Act of 1830. No treaties were negotiated from 1870 to 1900. Warfare, not negotiation, became the preferred option of the U.S. government in resolving land issues with American Indians. Up until 1860, white settlers and American Indians had fought about 300 battles; from 1860 to 1897, they fought nearly 1,500 battles.[4] The upsurge in conflicts may be explained in part by the fact that westward expansion after the Civil War brought many more settlers into areas occupied by American Indians. Also, the U.S. government had a strong standing army at the end of the Civil War. Its military strength may have encouraged an inclination to turn away from negotiation and toward fighting.

American Indian Economic Traditions

Ownership rights among American Indians were influenced by the Indians' environment and by the resources available to them. Indians developed customs and traditions—**the rules of the game**—that enabled them to live successful lives within their environments. For example, as illustrated in Map 1, the Comanche people settled across parts of the present-day states of Arizona, Colorado, Kansas, Texas, and Oklahoma. They were hunter-gatherers—they hunted game and foraged for food—and these environments suited them well. The horse became a key element of their culture, enhancing their capacity to use resources provided by their environment.

Other Indian groups developed forms of agriculture. The Choctaw people lived in what is today Mississippi, western Alabama, and eastern Louisiana. Choctaw farmers raised a variety of crops including corn, beans, squash, melons, and sweet potatoes. At the time of early contact with white settlers, the Iroquois people lived in what is today the northeastern United States and southeastern Canada. They made their living by farming, fishing, hunting, and gathering. The women raised the "three sisters" of highly complementary agricultural products—corn, beans, and squash.

The Pueblo people occupied what is today north central New Mexico. They raised corn, beans, and squash; they grew cotton and kept domesticated turkeys. And, like most American Indian groups, the Pueblo participated in trade with their neighbors. They exchanged agricultural products with the Comanche, who offered buffalo hides, buckskins, jerked meat, and horses in exchange.

The Economics of Property Rights

Property rights are rights to use, control, and benefit from the possession of a good or resource. An automobile owner can drive her car, or leave it parked in her garage, or sell it for cash, depending on her preferences; her ownership rights give her those options. **Market economies**—economies that stress the importance of individual choices and voluntary exchange—emphasize the importance of rights for individuals to own land, businesses, homes, and so forth. The key assumption is that when property ownership rights are clearly defined and enforced, people have an incentive to manage their resources responsibly and productively.

Perhaps you have noticed that people tend to take better care of things they own. You might take better care of your smart phone than you would care for a phone owned by your brother or sister. People generally care for cars they own better than cars they rent. (Have you ever heard of anyone washing a rented car?) The reason in these cases is not merely a mysterious sort of pride in ownership, though that may be part of it. The underlying reason is that if you don't care for a phone or a car, it may get dinged up and deteriorate in value. And then, if it is *your* phone or car, the loss will be yours, too.

Given the importance of property rights, modern societies have established elaborate sets of rules to identify and protect ownership. When you buy a car, you receive a title of ownership that is registered with the state. The Vehicle Identification Number (VIN) is clearly imprinted on the car, much like the brand or tag on cattle that ranchers use to mark ownership. When you buy a home or a condo, the process is even more elaborate. You receive a deed signifying ownership, and the deed is registered with the state. The deed is conferred only after a careful legal search has been conducted to confirm the property's history of ownership.

American Indian groups did not develop formal rules of this sort to specify property rights. They did have rules, however; their rules were matters of common knowledge in their communities, and they were carefully enforced.

Property Rights among the Comanche

Traditional American Indian culture was highly decentralized. Because rules and customs varied from tribe to tribe, the following discussion focuses on one group of Plains Indians, the Comanche, as an example. The Comanche of the 1800s were a loosely organized group of small bands. They had no strong central government. Even band leaders had little formal authority. Although leaders made decisions regarding the affairs of the band, individual members of the group were free to ignore the decisions of the leaders. The power of leaders depended on gaining the voluntary cooperation of members of the group.

While the Comanche had a decentralized system of government, they nonetheless had clear rules regarding property rights. But their rules differed from the rules of the American legal system. Like other Plains Indians, the Comanche did not recognize private ownership of land. This fact alone may have encouraged onlookers to assume that the Comanche and other Plains Indians recognized no property rights whatsoever. After all, the right to own land was fundamental in American law. Lacking that property right, one might have assumed, the traditional Comanche culture had been one in which all property was communally owned.

The decision by the Comanche to allow for communal ownership of land was not based on a general disapproval of private ownership. It was based more specifically on reasons related to the environment and culture of the Comanche, and these reasons made economic sense. Land in the Great Plains was abundant, and the Comanche did not use it for farming. They had no reason, therefore, to fence off pieces of property, in order to establish individually owned fields. They were hunters, however, and they did care about establishing rights to their hunting grounds. They developed a form of enforceable group property rights related to hunting grounds. They knew that, without control over access to hunting grounds, those grounds would soon be overrun by other groups. Overhunting would reduce food

A buffalo hunt on horseback.

supplies, and the survival of the band would be threatened. The hunting grounds established among Plains Indians—often marked by natural features such as mountains, ridges, and streams—were known by other groups. The Comanche were known for their ability to defend their hunting grounds from trespass by others.

While individual ownership of land meant nothing to the Comanche, the horse meant a great deal. The Comanche developed individual ownership rights to buffalo horses—horses used in the buffalo hunts—because these horses were critical for survival. In the early days of buffalo hunting on the Great Plains, before the arrival of the horse, acquiring food came at a high cost. Hunters on foot faced severe limitations. They could track buffalo only as far as they could walk. Hunts typically involved stalking buffalo on foot and then surrounding them. Once surrounded, the buffalo would run about in a circle; hunters then killed them with arrows and lances. Another approach was to drive buffalo toward some natural or man-made barrier, trapping them so that they could be killed. These approaches took days of planning, and they involved most members in a Comanche band. While a hunt was on, there was little time for doing other things.

The arrival of the horse eliminated these challenges. Horses could carry heavy loads, and on horseback Plains Indians could travel fast and far. Horses reduced transportation costs and enabled Indians to increase their food supplies. On horseback, a lone hunter could bring down a buffalo by himself. By following buffalo across the plains, Indians coped more easily with the problem of scarcity, obtaining an abundant supply of meat. (**Scarcity** is the condition of wanting more than one can have, given the available resources.) Their diets changed accordingly. They ate fewer seeds, roots, and corn, and more meat. And as hunting required less expenditure of time and effort, the Plains Indians gained more time for arts, crafts, and spirituality.

The Comanche also established private ownership for tools, food, weapons, clothing, jewelry, and other personal possessions. How were the the ownership rules enforced? Economist Bruce L. Benson says that ownership rules among American Indians were enforced by the threat of ostracism. To be ostracized was to be banished from the group—a serious form of punishment. Ridicule was another powerful tool used to encourage people to follow the rules.[5]

HISTORICAL QUESTIONS
& ECONOMIC ANSWERS

Did individuals benefit from ownership of horses?

Yes. Riding on horseback, individuals could hunt buffalo and other game more successfully than they otherwise could have. And horses had monetary value; they could be bought and sold. A "millionaire" among the Plains Indians was a man who owned several strong hunting horses.

Were the best hunters rewarded in some fashion?

Yes. Plains Indians developed ownership rules and incentives to reward the best hunters. For example, individual hunters used arrows with distinctive marks. These arrows identified which hunter killed which buffalo. The hunter who killed the buffalo was given the best portions of the meat. Other portions were divided among the helpers who followed the hunters.

Horses required care. They had to be fed, groomed, exercised, and protected from theft. By allowing individuals to own horses, the Comanche created an incentive for individuals to take good care of horses. The benefits spilled over to others in the group, since horses well cared for enhanced Comanche success in hunting for buffalo and other game.

Did private ownership exist among American Indians?

Yes. Plains Indians developed ownership rules and incentives to preserve critically important resources—horses, tools, weapons, jewelry, clothing, and so on. This is how most human societies have adapted to their environmental circumstances. The popular view that American Indians recognized no rights to private ownership may be based on an inference from one aspect of Comanche culture—communal ownership of land.

QUESTIONS for DISCUSSION

1. In what ways did American Indians adjust to their environment in order to survive?
2. Did the Comanche establish any private ownership rights? Provide an example.
3. How were ownership rights enforced by the Comanche?
4. Why would individual property rights be established in some instances but not in others? Explain your answer.

Thomas Jefferson's
Confidential Letter to Congress

As early as 1803, Thomas Jefferson recognized that Americans wanted to own land. At that time, however, claiming a piece of land was no guarantee of being able to use that land. It might be land occupied by American Indians. In that case, the right actually to use the land would be difficult to obtain without negotiation or conflict. This problem concerned Jefferson. In a confidential letter to Congress requesting funds for the Lewis and Clark expedition, he wrote as follows:

The Indian tribes residing within the limits of the U.S. have for a considerable time been growing more & more uneasy at the constant diminution of the territory they occupy, altho' effected by their own voluntary sales.... In order peaceably to counteract this policy of theirs, and to provide an extension of territory which the rapid increase of our numbers will call for, two measures are deemed expedient. First, to encourage them to abandon hunting, to apply to the raising stock, to agriculture and domestic manufacture . . . . Secondly to multiply trading houses among them & place within their reach those things which will contribute more to their domestic comfort than the profession of extensive, but uncultivated wilds. . . .[6]

Thomas Jefferson

PRIMARY SOURCE QUESTIONS for DISCUSSION

1. What approaches did Jefferson recommend for dealing with the concerns American Indians faced?
2. Why do you suppose that Jefferson stressed peaceful interaction rather than other approaches such as war?
3. Do you agree with Jefferson's overall approach toward American Indians, as illustrated in this letter? Explain your answer.

A theme of this chapter has been that all societies make choices about what is owned individually and what is owned by the community. We have focused on how property ownership rights were established among some American Indians. We identified cases in which group ownership was preferred and cases in which private ownership was preferred.

Today, a new controversy has sprung up regarding U.S. airports. Should airports be owned publicly, as they currently are? Or should they be owned privately? The question has arisen recently in part because people around the globe have begun to experiment with private ownership of airports. Dissatisfaction among air travelers is relevant here. They often complain about long delays in airport security lines and late take-offs. Travelers wonder if there might be a more efficient way to run an airport.

How might private ownership of airports come about? There are several possibilities, ranging from partial to full privatization. Partial privatization might involve the government owner entering into contracts with private providers to manage specific airport services such as restaurants, parking, and baggage handling. Under this arrangement, the government would maintain full ownership rights. Another approach would be for the government owner to enter into a contract with a private company to manage the whole airport. The government then would retain ownership of the airport, while a private operator managed the airport for a specific period of time. To bring about full privatization, the government would sell shares of ownership to a private company. The company then would be responsible for running the airport, in hopes of earning a profit. (**Profit** is the money left over after a business has paid for all its costs.)

Advantages and Disadvantages

Airport privatization is controversial in the United States. Supporters argue that privately managed airports have generally been able to reduce costs, improve the quality of services offered, and increase innovation. By way of analogy, they point to successful privatization efforts such as the lease, recently, of the Chicago Skyway (a toll road). Within months of assuming control of the Chicago Skyway, the new operator instituted electronic tolling and other improvements. How did Chicago benefit? It earned nearly $2 billion (a payment in exchange for future revenue Chicago would no longer receive).

Proponents of privatization of airports point to several possible advantages:

- Sales of airports to private firms can help local governments raise revenue.

- Privatization reduces the responsibility of government for managing the airport. This shift of responsibility might enable government to concentrate selectively on functions such as improving airport security.

- Privatization might foster economic growth by unleashing entrepreneurial activity and innovation.

Opponents are less confident. They contend that certain shared resources, including airports, must be available to all citizens and managed on behalf of all citizens.

They note that operating an airport differs greatly from running a tollway. They point to several possible disadvantages:

- Privatization might increase costs to air travelers. Private owners, for example, might charge higher landing fees to airlines, and airlines might pass those costs on to customers.

- When airports are run well, local governments earn revenue by charging customers for the services they provide.

- Airports have special safety concerns, such as air-traffic control and security, that the private sector cannot be trusted to address. Private firms might cut corners on security measures, for example, in order to enhance their profits.

Whether the proponents of airport privatization are right or wrong, one thing is sure. The idea has become very popular in several nations. Table 1 lists major airports that are completely or partially privatized.

The *New York Times* recently reported on a new airport—the only privately financed airport in the United States.[7] It is located in Branson, Missouri. Branson is known for its family-friendly shows featuring magicians, rock 'n' roll, country music, comedy, variety shows, dinner shows, and well-known performers that play limited engagements. It is also known for its lakes, fishing, and golf. It attracts 8.5 million visitors a year.

Until the new airport was built, Branson's nearest airport had been 44 miles out of town,

TABLE 1	Major Private or Partially Private Airports
Airport	**Country**
Athens	Greece
Auckland	New Zealand
Brussels	Belgium
Copenhagen	Denmark
Frankfurt	Germany
Hamburg	Germany
London (Gatwick and Heathrow)	Britain
Melbourne	Australia
Naples	Italy
Rome	Italy
Sydney	Australia
Vienna	Austria

Source: Tae H. Ouma, Nicole Adlerb, and Chunyan Yu, "Privatization, Corporatization, Ownership Forms and their Effects on the Performance of the World's Major Airports," *Journal of Air Transport Management* (2006), pp. 109–121.

in Springfield, Missouri. Entrepreneurs saw an opportunity. Private airports typically earn revenue by charging landing fees to airlines and offering services such as food and parking to travelers. Investors thought they had a chance to earn a profit and provide Branson with an important new service. These investors spent $155 million to buy 925 acres of land. They built a runway, a control tower, and a 58,000 square-foot terminal all in less than two years.

THEN & NOW QUESTIONS for DISCUSSION

1. What are some possible advantages of privatized airports?
2. What are some possible disadvantages of privatized airports?
3. Do you think airports in the United States should be privatized? Explain your answer.

Communal vs. Private Property Rights
http://www.thefreemanonline.org/columns/communal-vs-private-property-rights

Detailed information on Native American communal property rights and European private property rights.

Colonial American Culture
http://www.history.com/topics/colonial-culture

Information on Colonial America, including relations with Native Americans.

Property Rights
http://www.econlib.org/library/Enc/PropertyRights.html

Detailed explanation and analysis of private property rights.

Property Rights and Current Issues on Indian Reservations
http://www.perc.org/articles/article802.php

Information on the development of private property rights among American Indians, and a discussion of ways to increase private ownership on today's Indian reservations.

Then & Now: Airports and Private Property Rights
http://www.brookings.edu/articles/2008/05_aviation_winston.aspx

This article provides a brief overview of issues related to airport privatization.

Why Did Frank H. Mayer and His Fellow Hunters Kill Buffalo, Almost to Extinction?

Hunters shoot buffalo from a train, 1871.

The American Buffalo Nears Extinction

Before white settlers arrived on the North American continent, millions of buffalo roamed the plains. Early explorers were astonished at their numbers. On April 25, 1805, Meriwether Lewis and William Clark recorded in their journal, "The whole face of the country was covered with herds of buffalo, elk, & antelopes."[1]

The buffalo was a vital resource to the Plains Indians. It was the source of hides for their shelters, their beds, and their coats; it was also an important source of food. John Fire Lame Deer, an American Indian author, was later to write, "The buffalo gave us everything we needed. Without it we were nothing. His flesh strengthened us, became flesh of our flesh..."[2]

By 1890 those millions of buffalo had been reduced nearly to extinction by white hunters. Fewer than a thousand buffalo survived. Hunters had slaughtered buffalo for their hides, often leaving the meat to rot on the plains. Because the buffalo hides were sold to markets back East, it would be easy to blame over-hunting of the buffalo on the market system. A **market** is a place or a situation in which people can come together to buy and sell goods or services. After all, hunters killed buffalo "for sport and profit," and the profit motive is central to market economies.[3]

KEY ECONOMIC CONCEPTS

Markets	**Opportunity cost**
Ocean resources	**Property rights**

Still, that cannot be the entire story. Other animals, such as deer, have been hunted for sport but not brought close to extinction. Other outdoor ventures, such as producing honey, have been conducted for profit without killing off honeybees or degrading the environment. How was the buffalo's case different? Why did hunters kill so many buffalo that they nearly killed off the species?

The Historical Context
Adventurers Go West

In the post-Civil War period, Frank H. Mayer was among thousands of young men restless for adventure. Mayer was born in 1850. He was too young to fight in the Civil War, but he did serve as a bugler. Of that period, he wrote, "At the close of any war there are bound to be thousands of young men who find peacetime pursuits too dull for their adventure-stirred lives. Maybe that was truer after the Civil War than at any other time."[4] Mayer and many of his fellow adventurers became buffalo hunters.

Whenever people make a choice, they incur an opportunity cost. The **opportunity cost** is whatever they might have chosen as their next-best alternative. According to his account, Mayer's opportunity cost for becoming a buffalo hunter was uncertain and low. "I had nothing to look forward to in civilization," he wrote; "I didn't know exactly what I wanted."[5] Mayer was not sure what his next-best choice would have been if he had not decided to become a buffalo hunter. Whatever that alternative was, it was back in civilization and not on the frontier, which is where Mayer felt he belonged.

The Economics of Property Rights

A **property right** is the owner's right to determine how his or her property will be used. Property rights may be held by individuals, groups, or governments.[6] About property rights, as we will see, the most important point in some cases is not *who owns* the property rights to a given resource but rather *that someone does own* the property rights to that resource.

Before white hunters arrived and began killing buffalo, property rights to buffalo effectively belonged to the Plains Indians. They could determine how buffalo would be used. Their authority, however, was not formally backed up by the U.S. government. There was, at the time, no legal means for establishing and protecting property rights in live buffalo. The free-ranging nature of the buffalo made property rights difficult to claim and manage. It was through informal agreements among tribes and within tribes that the Plains Indians managed access to buffalo herds. They saw themselves, in fact, as more than herd managers, particularly the Sioux. "We Sioux have a close relationship to the buffalo. He is our brother," wrote John Fire Lame Deer.[7]

This relationship was disrupted by the arrival of Mayer and his fellow hunters armed with powerful rifles. They had superior firepower, and that was important; but it was not their most important advantage. The absence of property rights was more important. White hunters could kill buffalo without regard for the Plains Indians' claims because, according to U.S. law, the Indians had no enforceable claims. The buffalo could not be taken from them because they did not own the buffalo in the first place.

For the hunters, the stakes were high. U.S. gold pieces were the most valuable coins in use at the time. In the West, buffalo were so valuable that people referred to them as "walking gold pieces." Hunters could sell buffalo hides at prices ranging from $1 to $3 each, a large amount of money in those days. And the buffalo seemed to be free for the taking. Mayer put his finger on this point: "They didn't belong to anybody. If you could kill them, what they brought was yours."[8] Notice the sharp contrast: for Mayer and the other hunters,

there were no property rights to free-ranging buffalo. Nobody owned them. But there were property rights to a killed buffalo. The hunter who killed a buffalo owned the buffalo he killed, with its valuable hide, and he was free to keep the money he collected from its sale.

The property rights problem in buffalo was accentuated by the animals' size and herding characteristics. Buffalo were large, and they gathered in large herds. Buffalo hunters who came upon a herd could easily kill all the buffalo in it. The technique was to mortally wound, but not instantly kill, the herd leader. The leader was often an older cow buffalo. "Buffalo society, you see, was a matriarchy," Mayer said, "and the cow was queen. When she stampeded, [the rest of the herd] stampeded. When she got into trouble, they didn't know what to do."[9] With the herd leader disabled by early rifle shots, the other buffalo would gather around and the hunters would pick them off one by one.

In the absence of property rights, it did not make sense for a buffalo hunter to conserve any portion of a herd. Any buffalo left unharmed today might be killed by another hunter tomorrow. If the Plains Indians had been able to enforce their property rights, the situation would have been different. They could have refused access to the herds entirely, or sold limited access to them. If the U.S. government had assumed property rights, it could have regulated buffalo hunting. But in the absence of any enforceable property rights in live buffalo, the slaughter continued until the buffalo were nearly wiped out. Table 1 shows the dimensions of the killing; a population of 40 million was reduced to fewer than 1,000 by 1895.

TABLE 1	Buffalo Population, Selected Years, 1800–2010		
1800	40,000,000	1885	20,000
1850	20,000,000	1889	1,091
1865	15,000,000	1895	<1,000
1870	14,000,000	1902	1,940
1875	1,000,000	1983	50,000
1880	395,000	2010	450,000

Source: Russell Thornton, *American Indians: Holocaust and Survival* (Norman, Oklahoma: University of Oklahoma Press, 1987).

Did the U.S. government support the buffalo slaughter?

The government did support the slaughter, even though it never issued a decree to kill buffalo. Instead, Frank Mayer reported, "[what] did happen was that army officers in charge of plains operations encouraged the slaughter of buffalo in every possible way."[10] The army provided free ammunition to buffalo hunters, far more than they could use. The hunters traded the excess for other supplies. In this way, the free ammunition was very much like a grant of money.

Were the buffalo killed to control the Plains Indians?

Although it was not official policy to kill buffalo in order to control the Indians, government-supported killing of buffalo had that effect. It deprived the Plains Indians of resources they needed, including food. Wiping out the buffalo might have the effect of starving Indians into submission. General Philip Sheridan told a legislative body that buffalo hunting had done more to defeat the Plains Indians than all the efforts of the Army. "For the sake of lasting peace," he said, "let them kill, skin and sell until the buffaloes are exterminated."[11]

Government-supported buffalo killing fit with overall government policy toward American Indians, incorporated in a series of treaties. More than 400 treaties came into effect between 1778 and the Civil War era. Under these agreements, Indians left their land and were moved to areas known as reservations, where they had limited rights of self-government. Indians negotiated early treaties from a position of strength until the early 1800s. Later treaties were much less favorable for the Indians, effectively amounting to forced surrenders.[12]

Table 2 shows the population decline of the Plains Indian tribes from their first contact with white Americans until 1990. By 1907, the population of southern Plains Indians had declined to only 7 percent of the population at first contact. The population of northern Plains Indians had declined to about half of the population at first contact. By 1990, the population of southern Plains Indians had recovered from a near-extinction level to almost half the population at first contact. The northern tribes, by 1990, had doubled their populations. By then, however, the traditional way of life of the Plains Indians was long gone.

How did the buffalo escape extinction?

If the last surviving buffalo had remained concentrated in easily located herds, all of them might have been killed. But, as their numbers dwindled, it became harder for hunters to locate herds. As hunters had to spend more time and other resources to find herds—as their opportunity cost went up—the financial rewards they could gain from killing buffalo decreased. Fewer hunters then made the choice to continue killing them.

The remaining buffalo population began to thrive only when the U.S. government established property rights for ownership of buffalo. Remember, property rights can be held by

	At First Contact with White Americans		1907		1990	
	Population	Tribes	Population	Tribes	Popluation	Tribes
Northern Plains Indians	100,800	20	50,477	19	217,183	16
Southern Plains Indians	41,000	12	2,861	7	20,157	6

TABLE 2 — Plains Indian Tribes: Selected Population Statistics from First Contact with White Americans to 1990

Source: Russell Thornton, We Shall Live Again: The 1870 and 1890 Ghost Dance Movements as Demographic Revitalization (Cambridge: Cambridge University Press, 1986).

individuals, groups, or a government. Yellowstone National Park was established in 1872, and today it is the home of a large herd of buffalo, owned and legally protected by the U.S. government. Federal protection measures for other buffalo herds were established later.

Private ownership also helped the buffalo to survive. Some ranchers took to ranching buffalo in the second half of the 20th century. On private ranches, property rights to buffalo can be established, and buffalo ranchers have a clear incentive to protect and enlarge the herds of buffalo they own. Once property rights are established, markets can arise. No one could sell the rights to a free-ranging buffalo in 1850 or 1880, but such sales are commonplace now that people own buffalo. Today there is a thriving market in buffalo, in breeding stock, and in buffalo products. There are about 450,000 buffalo in North America today.[13]

If property rights for ownership of buffalo had been established earlier by the U.S. government, many buffalo could have been saved. People or public agencies holding ownership rights to a resource have a reason to take care of their property, but resources owned by nobody are often wasted.

Two men pose on a pile of buffalo skulls in the 1870s.

Were the buffalo hunters bloodthirsty?

The easy answer is yes, the buffalo hunters were bloodthirsty. They slaughtered millions of animals. The deeper answer to the question lies in property rights. No incentives encouraged hunters to conserve buffalo, and so they killed them. But if their motivation had been simply a bloodthirsty desire to kill, they would have killed other animals, such as ranchers' cattle. Yet they did not, and it is important to consider why they didn't. Property rights in cattle were well defined and well enforced in the Old West, even on the open range. Though Western movies may exaggerate the point, there were strong penalties against stealing or "rustling" cattle.

QUESTIONS for DISCUSSION

1. Suppose Frank Mayer and other would-be buffalo hunters had received offers for interesting, high-paying jobs before they headed West. How would this option have affected their opportunity cost in the choice to become buffalo hunters?
2. How did the buffalo's value and herding behavior affect the attractiveness of buffalo hunting?
3. Why would it have not made sense for a buffalo hunter to avoid killing a small buffalo, with the intent of coming back to kill him next year, when the buffalo had grown larger?
4. What was the U.S. government's policy toward the buffalo slaughter? What happened to the population of the Plains Indians as the slaughter of buffalo continued?
5. How did the absence of property rights lead to the buffalo's near-extinction? How did the establishment of property rights lead to its comeback?

Protesting the Slaughter of a "Noble and Harmless Animal"

Here is an 1872 letter from Col. W. B. Hazen, of Fort Hays, Kansas, about the evils of buffalo hunting as then practiced on the American plains. The letter was published in the *New York Times* and later entered into the official record of Congress.[14]

WANTON BUTCHERY

The Evils of Buffalo Hunting—Letter to Mr. Henry Bergh, from Kansas

Yesterday Mr. Bergh received the following letter from Col. W.B. Hazen of Fort Hays:

Head-quarters, Fort Hays, Kansas, Jan. 20, 1872

H. Bergh, Esq. —Dear Sir: Hoping to interest you, and through you the people of the country and Congress, would respectfully state that the extraordinary introduction of railroads into and across the wilds of our country has made the vast herds of wild buffalo of the plains accessible to all classes of people, and each year vast numbers are slaughtered for so-called sport, and a greater number by hunters for their hides, which net about $1 each. I have seen numbers of men this Winter who have during the past season killed 1,000 each for the paltry sum of $1 apiece, the carcasses being left to rot on the plains. The buffalo is a noble and harmless animal, timid, and as easily taken as a cow, and very valuable as food for man. It lives upon a short grass which grows luxuriously upon the high arid plains of this middle region, that is from dryness unfit for agriculture. The theory that the buffalo should be killed to deprive the Indians of food is a fallacy, as these people are becoming harmless under a rule of justice. In view of these facts I would most respectfully and earnestly request that you use such proper influence as may be at your disposal to bring this subject before Congress, with the intention of having such steps taken as will prevent this wicked and wanton waste both of the lives of God's creatures and the valuable food they furnish.

I am, very respectfully, your obedient servant
W.B. Hazen, Colonel Sixth Infantry
Brevet Major-General United States Army

PRIMARY SOURCE QUESTIONS for DISCUSSION

1. According to Col. Hazen, what made the buffalo herds accessible to all classes of people (and not just professional hunters)?
2. Did Col. Hazen believe the buffalo provided a suitable challenge for sporting hunters? Explain your answer.
3. Did Col. Hazen support the killing of buffalo as a means of pacifying the Plains Indians? Explain your answer.
4. How would American Indians operating under treaties view Col. Hazen's observation that they were "becoming harmless under a rule of justice"? Explain your answer.

Ocean resources include fish and shellfish, minerals, and oil. Efforts to harvest some of these resources—whales, for example—provide a present-day economic parallel to the endangered buffalo of the American plains. Some species of whales have been hunted nearly to extinction, in an absence of enforceable property rights. Whalers have had little incentive to conserve the stock of whales. Any whale left unharmed by one whaler might be killed by a competing whaler. Only with international agreements to limit the harvest have whale populations stabilized.

The underlying problem here, as in the case of the buffalo, is an absence of property rights. Nobody owns whales, until a whale is killed. Then property rights come into play. The same situation holds for other ocean life. Once an ocean fish is caught and placed in the hold of a fishing boat, it is subject to property rights. Stealing at sea is punishable by anti-piracy measures. Before the catch, a freely swimming fish is not subject to property rights. It will belong to the fishing-boat captain who catches it.

A United Nations report in 2010 warned that fish populations are in great danger. Without new conservation measures, the report said, important fish species will become extinct. Based on estimates, "we are in the situation where 40 years down the line we, effectively, are out of fish," said Pavan Sukhdev, a UN official.[15] The UN report calls for setting up protected areas that will allow female fish to grow to full size, rather than being harvested too early. International cooperation—always difficult to arrange—is necessary because there are no clearly enforceable property rights for fish.

When common property resources are exploited—when whales are over-hunted, for example—prices send the wrong signals. A low price might be set because the resource is being quickly exploited, artificially increasing the supply. Just as buffalo hides became cheap in the late 1800s, given the absence of property rights, ocean resources may be underpriced today. For example, Maine yellowtail flounder are a valuable food fish, but they are over-fished. Yet they continue to sell for well under $2 per pound.[16] Policy solutions to this problem are not easy to devise. Any solution, however, would involve someone—individuals, groups, or governments—gaining property rights to enable them to manage the resource.

THEN & NOW — QUESTIONS for DISCUSSION

1. What is the difference, in respect to property rights, between a fish swimming in international waters and a fish caught and brought on board a fishing boat?
2. When many fishermen harvest fish from the same fishing areas, and property rights to fish are poorly defined or non-existent, will the fishermen be likely to harvest fish quickly, or slowly and carefully? Explain your answer.
3. How could protected areas enabling female fish to reach maturity help to overcome the problem of undefined property rights? Explain your answer.

The Buffalo

http://www.americanwest.com/critters/buffindx.htm

History of the buffalo, including links to other sites on the buffalo.

The Bison

http://www.defenders.org/wildlife_and_habitat/wildlife/bison.php#

Basic facts about the bison/buffalo.

Buffalo Field Campaign

http://www.buffalofieldcampaign.org/aboutbuffalo/bisonnativeamericans.html

Resources on the buffalo from a group that favors additional protections for the Yellowstone buffalo herd.

Archives of the West, 1868–187: The Buffalo Harvest

http://www.pbs.org/weta/thewest/resources/archives/five/buffalo.htm

This is the Public Broadcasting System's companion page to the documentary series The West, *with links to primary source materials and lesson plans.*

Then & Now: Ocean Resources and Property Rights

http://www.unep.org/greeneconomy/GreenEconomyReport/tabid/1375/Default.aspx

From the United Nations Environment Program, a report with information on ocean resources and other environmental issues linked to the economy.

Did Railroads Cause the Economy of the Late 1800s to Grow?

California's Governor Stanford takes a mighty swing to drive in the golden spike that joined the Union Pacific and Central Pacific railways.

"Crazy Judah's" Dream

"Crazy Judah" was the nickname applied to Theodore Judah for his impossible dream of the 1850s: a railroad that would run all the way across the United States. Judah studied civil engineering and went to work as a railroad surveyor at the age of 18. He was not yet 30 years old when he got the idea of completing a railroad link from the Atlantic Ocean to the Pacific Ocean.

By 1860, railroads linking Eastern states to one another had pushed as far west as the Missouri River. Taking the next step—completing a transcontinental rail line—would involve crossing large unpopulated plains and the Sierra Nevada Mountains. Mountain altitude coupled with unforgiving climate conditions would make the work difficult and dangerous. Many lives might be lost.

Crazy Judah nevertheless believed in the project. He became the chief engineer of the Central Pacific Railroad. He wrote plans, recruited financiers, and lobbied Congress. Not only was it possible to build a transcontinental railroad, he claimed, but the job could be done within ten years. Skeptics doubted the estimate, but government authorization for the project was granted in 1862, and the project was completed

Theodore Judah, also known as "Crazy Judah" for his vision of a transcontinental railroad.

KEY ECONOMIC CONCEPTS

Creative class	**Land grants**
Direct benefits	**Opportunity costs**
Economic growth	**Subsidy**
External benefits	

in less than seven years. The Union Pacific railroad moved westward through Nebraska and Wyoming; the Central Pacific railway moved eastward from California through the Sierra Nevadas and the deserts of Nevada. They joined rails, with a symbolic golden spike, near the Great Salt Lake on May 10, 1869. Crazy Judah was not present to see it happen, but his dream had come true.[1]

In the history of American railroads there are many similar can-do stories. Railroads expanded rapidly after the Civil War as the U.S. economy grew. At first glance, it might appear that the railroads *caused* the economy to grow. After all, they fostered settlement and trade in areas that had previously seemed remote and isolated. Anything to promote the expansion of railroads, including government money and grants of land, therefore seemed appropriate. But were the railroads indispensable? Has our sentimental attraction to heroic railway stories and bold images of the "iron horse" caused us to overestimate the importance of railroads?

The Historical Context
Railroads and the Economy Grow

From 1870 to 1900, the U.S. economy grew. Production (as measured by GDP per person—the value of all goods and services produced, divided by the population) almost doubled. At the same time, railroads more than tripled their mileage of track (Table 1). Highways and waterways were also improving. Transportation played a key role in this period of economic growth. (**Economic growth**

TABLE 1	Production per Person and Railroad Track Mileage, 1870–1900[a]	
Year	Production per person	Railroad Track mileage
1870	$2,375	53,000
1880	$3,431	93,000
1890	$3,656	167,000
1900	$4,204	207,000

[a]Production per person measured by real GDP in 1996 dollars
Source: From *Historical Statistics of the United States*, "Table Ca9-19—Gross Domestic Product: 1790–2002.

is an increase in the production of goods and services.) The United States and its territories had expanded enormously, and people increasingly demanded means for moving themselves and their goods from place to place within its huge expanse.[2]

When early modes of transportation were slow and costly, markets were relatively small. A farmer would buy tools from local sources; a store owner would hire help from people who lived nearby. As improved transportation enabled people and goods to move around quickly and at lower costs, markets became larger. Consumers could look well beyond a few local merchants for choosing what to buy. Producers could count on selling into distant markets. This effect was especially important for farm production, which typically occurred some distance from urban markets. Railroads thus were associated with growth and prosperity, leading to proposals for government subsidy of railroads to generate even more prosperity.

The Economics of Subsidies

An old economic proverb says, "If you want less of something, tax it; if you want more of something, subsidize it." That proverb has been attributed to several economists and a former U.S. president.[3] A tax discourages people from producing or buying the taxed item. A **subsidy** has the opposite effect; it uses government funds to encourage people to produce or consume something. For example, a city government might use revenue from taxes to build a new office

park and then offer reduced rent to businesses that move into the new facility. The reduced rent would amount to a subsidy to businesses that accepted the offer.

Subsidies have been used to promote everything from growing certain farm products to vaccinating people against the flu. These subsidies provide benefits. The benefits come when a subsidized economic activity results, for example, in new jobs created in the community.

Subsidies provide **direct benefits**—that is, advantages to those who receive the subsidies. The direct benefits of a program providing free flu shots, for example, go to the people who get the shots without charge.

Subsidies may also provide **external benefits**—that is, advantages that go to people other than those who benefit directly. Because recipients of free flu shots are less likely to become ill (the direct benefit), they are also less likely to spread an illness to others (the external benefit). Flu shots and other public health programs have provided large external benefits to the economy. The external benefits constitute a justification for government support. If people made their own choices about getting flu shots in the absence of public support—in the way they might make choices about entertainment— perhaps fewer of them would get vaccinated. Some cases of flu that could have been prevented then might occur, causing children to miss days at school, workers to miss days at work, and so on.

While subsidies provide benefits, they also come with costs. The costs are not always obvious. Imagine a subsidy provided by an outside party— Santa Claus, perhaps, or your rich Aunt Maggie. Such a subsidy would come at no cost to you, and you might think of it as free. If Aunt Maggie said, "Here are two tickets to the concert—go, take your friend, and have a good time," you would be likely to accept her offer. And Aunt Maggie might be pleased by your acceptance. If her goal is getting nieces and nephews to concerts, a subsidy serves the purpose well.

But real-world government subsidies do not come from outside parties. There is no Santa Claus or Aunt Maggie who bestows subsidies on the economy at no cost. Instead, governments must finance subsidies through taxation or borrowing. Citizens then pay for the subsidies, including the cost of borrowing, by paying their taxes. The analysis of a subsidy is incomplete if it treats the subsidy as a simple gift.

As logical as this principle is, it is often overlooked in discussions of government subsidies. The party seeking the subsidy typically points only to the advantages of the proposed government spending, ignoring the opportunity cost of using funds to pay for the subsidy. The **opportunity cost** of any decision is the second-best choice. It is what you give up when you make a decision. If a state legislature decides to spend $10 million subsidizing railroad construction, it gives up the chance to use that $10 million for other purposes. The legislature could spend the $10 million on health care clinics instead, or public swimming pools, or state parks. Or it might allow the $10 million to stay with taxpayers, for them to save or spend as they see fit. The value of the subsidized project cannot be determined unless it is weighed against the alternative possibilities.

For these reasons, not all tax-and-subsidy policies are desirable; instead, we must consider each one individually. The most effective subsidies are those that provide large external benefits, supporting projects unlikely to occur in the absence of a subsidy. People who seek subsidies understand this point. When they make their case for a subsidy, to be granted through the political system, they typically claim that the subsidy will produce important external benefits. They are also very likely to downplay any direct benefits they may gain from the subsidy, and to downplay or ignore the subsidy's costs. Producers of ethanol (to be used as a fuel additive), say little about the government money that will go to them when they get subsidies. Instead they emphasize gains for the farmers who grow the corn used for ethanol, or they claim that adding ethanol to gasoline will yield environmental benefits.

Railroads in the post-Civil War period received many government subsidies. Some came in the form of cash grants and loans, but the most well-known subsidies were land grants provided by the U.S. Congress. A **land grant** is a grant of public land by the government. A railroad company would be given (granted) land along a proposed railway route, with rights to build on the land and to sell unused portions of it. After constructing rail tracks, the company would sell left-over land, which would have increased in value because of its nearness to the new rail line. Farmers especially attached a high value to such

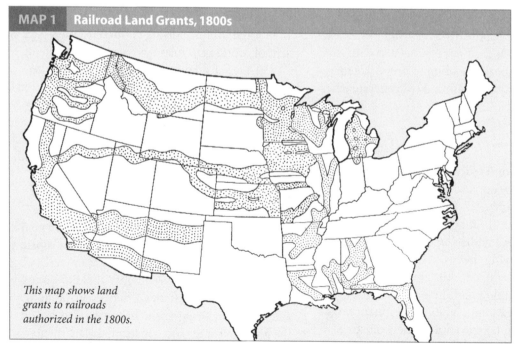

MAP 1   Railroad Land Grants, 1800s

This map shows land grants to railroads authorized in the 1800s.

Source: "Rise of Industrial America, 1876-1900," Library of Congress.

This 1863 image shows a locomotive with a crowd posing for famed photographer Matthew Brady at Hanover Junction, Pennsylvania.

land; nearness to rail lines reduced their costs for transporting farm products to markets. Railroad companies made large gains from these sales, and buyers benefitted by acquiring valuable land.

In many cases subsidies help to change the timing or location of economic activity that would have occurred anyway. Subsidies may also promote new economic activity. However, subsidies have not shown a consistent record of causing new economic activity with significant external benefits. Think about subsidies to small businesses—for example, low-interest loans from the Small Business Administration or preferential treatment on government contracts. These subsidies help the recipient businesses, but they do not always provide significant external benefits.

For a more specific example, consider a subsidized loan that helps to start up a small company that makes signs for stores. The benefit of the loan goes to the new business. But its sales come at the expense of other sign-making businesses. The community does not get *more* signs as a result of the subsidized loan. Most gains to subsidized small businesses come at the expense of other small businesses; they are usually not new benefits sending ripple effects throughout the economy.[4]

HISTORICAL QUESTIONS & ECONOMIC ANSWERS

Were land grants an effective form of subsidy?

Yes. The U.S. government's grants of land to railroads along their proposed western routes were effective. Land grants promoted results that the government wanted to encourage. The government wanted to see railroads expand quickly into unsettled areas, where their presence would encourage new settlement, investment, and trade. Land grants encouraged railroad companies to go ahead and build new rail lines. If railroad companies had simply held onto the land granted to them, its value would not have increased rapidly; but if they built a rail line and then sold unused land near the rail line, they were likely to make big gains on those sales.

Did Railroads Cause the Economy of the Late 1800s to Grow?

Did the railroads foster westward expansion, or did westward expansion increase the demand for railroads?

One thing is sure: railroads *accompanied* westward expansion. But determining cause and effect here is difficult. New railroads promoted development as more and more people moved into newly served areas, to settle and to do business. On the other hand, many areas had been settled, often with minimal government aid, before the railroads came through. Even in these cases, however, the railroads may have been influential. They may have encouraged something known as "anticipatory settlement."[5] New territories set for railroad construction often became the scene of accelerated farm and business development. Farmers might increase their production of wheat, and businessmen might build new hotels and stores, in anticipation of boom times that would follow as the new railroad came through. Either way, by jumping ahead of development or following it, the railroads played an important role in westward expansion.

Is the reluctance of private investors to fund a project a valid justification for subsidies?

Not always. The reluctance of private investors to fund a project may mean simply that it looks like an unprofitable, ill-considered project. Therefore, not every project rejected by private investors should be on the fast track for government subsidy. Rather, the important question is whether the project will provide important external benefits—benefits that people other than the investors will receive. In such a case, private investors might decline to fund a project that would, overall, benefit the economy. A subsidy then might be very appropriate.

In the case of subsidies for the transcontinental railroad, proponents claimed that many benefits would follow railroad construction. Some of the benefits they emphasized had to do with symbolism, unity, and national pride. A long, devastating civil war had intensified the belief voiced by President Lincoln that "a house divided against itself cannot stand." That belief in turn intensified the feeling that a national transport system was needed to bind the nation together.[6] But linking both coasts by a new rail line, while seemingly good for national pride, would not necessarily translate into dollars for the participating railroads. Initial subsidies alone cannot guarantee a successful venture. In fact, the Union Pacific and Central Pacific railroads went bankrupt soon after they made the connection that established the transcontinental line. Looking back, then, if the U.S. government believed that linking the coasts was an important objective, a subsidy in support of that objective was appropriate. The government could ensure that a new symbol of unity and national pride would become a reality, whereas the project might have stalled if it depended entirely on funding from private investors; they would expect to earn a profit on their investments.

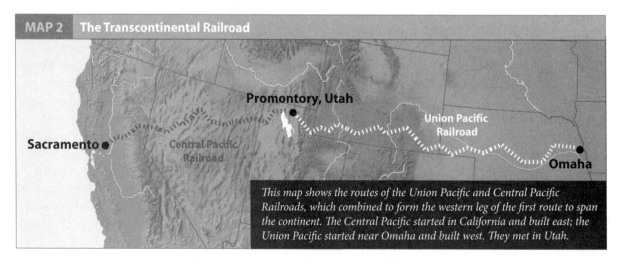

MAP 2   The Transcontinental Railroad

This map shows the routes of the Union Pacific and Central Pacific Railroads, which combined to form the western leg of the first route to span the continent. The Central Pacific started in California and built east; the Union Pacific started near Omaha and built west. They met in Utah.

Historically, have transportation subsidies arisen from national transportation planning conducted by Congress?

No. As appealing as it might sound to assume that transportation subsidies have arisen from a coordinated national plan, the reality is different. Subsidies are granted by legislation enacted by Congress and signed by the president. The success of would-be subsidy recipients has depended far more on political influence than on any plans or studies carried out to demonstrate the benefits in question. In the late 1800s, economic theory did not emphasize the importance of external benefits as a justification for subsidies. Later, the importance of external benefits became known. The U.S. Army Corps of Engineers, which built railroad bridges in Civil War times, turned to canals and other water projects in the 20th century. The Corps became known for overstating external benefits in its water projects to justify subsidies.[7] Today the Corps has reformed its methods to generate more realistic estimates of external benefits.

Why has Congress not made its own calculation of external benefits in weighing the value of proposed subsidies?

Calculating external benefits is difficult and time-consuming. People not specially trained for the task would find it difficult to know who will use new transportation facilities, how many passengers will use them, and what quantity of goods they will carry. That is why, since 1974, Congress has used the Congressional Budget Office to provide nonpartisan analyses of such questions. In the days of the railroad land grants Congress had no such agency to provide assistance. Even with information provided by expert analyses, however, Congressional action may depend more on the political influence of those seeking subsidies than on nonpartisan calculations of external benefits. The history of this activity shows clearly that interest groups seeking subsidies claim larger external benefits for their projects than the evidence from neutral analysis would suggest.

Were the railroads indispensable for economic growth?

Without railroads, the U.S. economy would have grown more slowly. In 1870-1900, however, the issue was never all or nothing. It was not whether the West would have railroads or have no railroads. Instead, decisions on subsidies determined whether there would be somewhat more rail activity or somewhat less. And, as always, alternatives mattered.

Would a nationwide transportation network have remained undeveloped if the federal and state governments had not subsidized railroads? No. There were alternatives. Roads and canals would surely have been improved and expanded if railroads had not been developed on a large scale. Well-documented statistical models have allowed economists to estimate the impact of railroads at the time. Separate estimates indicate that in 1859 (and even in 1890), national output would have been cut by less than 5 percent in the absence of railroad expansion. Five percent of a national economy is a large amount, but it is not large enough to warrant the conclusion that the railroads were indispensible.[8]

QUESTIONS for DISCUSSION

1. Why should a government subsidy to railroads not be regarded as money from an outside source? Where does the money for subsidies come from?
2. For railroads in the late 1800s, why would a land grant be a more effective subsidy than a simple grant of cash? Explain your answer.
3. Were the railroads indispensable to economic growth in the United States in the late 1800s? If the economy and the railroads grew larger at the same time, does that mean that the expansion of the railroads caused the economic growth? Explain your answer.

"Crazy Judah's" Railroad Plan

We have already met Theodore Judah, "Crazy Judah," who was instrumental in the construction of the first transcontinental railroad. Although Judah advocated for the transcontinental railroad and surveyed key parts of the route, his life was cut short at age 37 by yellow fever he contracted in Panama. He never lived to see his dream come true.

Below are excerpts from Judah's 1857 proposal for the transcontinental railroad (available online at http://www.sfmuseum.org/hist4/practical.html).

PACIFIC RAILROAD

The project for construction of a great Railroad through the United States of America, connecting the Atlantic with the Pacific Ocean, has been in agitation for over fifteen years. It is the most magnificent project ever conceived. It is an enterprise more important in its bearings and results to the people of the United States, than any other project involving an expenditure of an equal amount of capital.

It connects these two great oceans. It is an [unbreakable] bond of union between the populous States of the East, and the undeveloped regions of the fruitful West. It is a highway which leads to peace and future prosperity. An iron bond for the perpetuation of the Union and independence which we now enjoy. . . .

This road is but two thousand miles in length, and its cost not over, say, $150,000,000. As many as eight or ten great avenues of transit between the present East and West (three of which, in the State of New York alone, cost one hundred million of dollars) have been constructed.

This highway, the greatest and most important of them all, remains unbuilt, it may be said unsurveyed....

Why is this? Its popularity is universal. Its importance admitted. Its practicability believed in. Its profitableness unquestioned.

1st. It is because these projects have been speculative in their nature; and the people are disposed to look with distrust upon grand speculations.

2ndly. There are different routes, advocated by diverse interests, each eager that the road be built to subserve its own particular interest, but unwilling to make common cause upon a common route.

3dly. From the lack of confidence in private capitalists, dissuading them from investing in any project, through which they cannot see their way clear.

This plan assumes to [avoid] these objections; and,

1st. To build the Pacific Railroad.

2ndly. To accomplish the same in ten years.

3dly. To raise the capital therefore.

PRIMARY SOURCE QUESTIONS for DISCUSSION

1. Writing in 1857, Judah maintained that a transcontinental railroad would promote unity. How? If it had been built in the 1850s, would it have reduced the likelihood of the Civil War? Explain your answer.
2. In his time, Judah wrote that people were "disposed to look with distrust upon grand speculations." Is that sort of distrust widespread today? Why or why not? Use an example to support your answer.
3. Judah said the "profitableness" of the transcontinental railroad was unquestioned. If the profits were truly certain, could the railroad have been built without government subsidy? Why or why not?

The Quest for Growth

In the late 1800s, promoting railroad expansion seemed to be the way to generate economic growth. A direct descendant of that strategy in the 20th century was "smokestack chasing," or trying to attract heavy industry by offering subsidies for companies to build new plants. Because the symbol of this strategy, the smokestack, became associated with poor environmental quality, the term "smokestack chasing" died out. Even so, the strategy today is little changed, but competition has shifted from attracting factories to attracting high-technology employers. Everyone wants to build "the next Silicon Valley"—California's highly successful technology region, home to companies such as Apple, Google, and Hewlett Packard.

In efforts to attract industries and encourage business expansion, subsidies such as tax reductions remain the policy of choice. But a different approach to fostering growth has been proposed by business professor Richard Florida. What's important today, Florida claims, is attracting the **creative class,** or people whose job is primarily to create. These individuals can include engineers, designers, and entrepreneurs. They differ from other workers who are paid primarily to do their jobs according to plans created by the creative class. Florida sees attracting the creative class as a primary means of fostering the growth of a city or region. Cities vary widely in their attractiveness to the creative class, according to Florida (see Table 2).

What attracts the creative class? According to Florida, lifestyle issues

TABLE 2	Top and Bottom Creative Cities (among 49 Metropolitan Areas Over 1 Million Population)	
	TOP 5	**BOTTOM 5**
	1. Austin, Texas	45. Jacksonville, Florida
	2. San Francisco, California	46. Greensboro, North Carolina
	3. Seattle, Washington	47. New Orleans, Louisiana
	4. Boston, Massachusetts	48. Buffalo, New York
	5. Raleigh-Durham, North Carolina	49. Louisville, Kentucky

Source: Richard Florida, *The Rise of the Creative Class* (New York: Basic Books, 2003), p. xxii.

matter a great deal, with the edge going to communities that are rich in diversity and cultural attractions. Thus, the prescription for promoting growth is to make a community more pleasant, more interesting, and more "livable." Then high-quality employers will naturally seek to locate there. If the strategy does not work, at least the community will have been improved.

Florida's ideas generate spirited debate. For one thing, his emphasis on attracting the creative class suggests that the "subsidy wars" fought by state and local governments may be misguided. "Whereas companies—or sports teams—that get financial incentives can pull up and leave at virtually a moment's notice, investments in amenities like urban parks, for example, last for generations," Florida writes.[9]

In opposition to Florida's ideas, economists such as Steven Malanga point out that attracting the creative class has its opportunity costs as well. You cannot build museums and theaters for free. Also, it is difficult to say in advance exactly what will make any given city more attractive to the creative class. Finally, detailed studies have revealed little or no connection between the creative class and economic growth.[10] Today as in the late 1800s, there is no easy formula for promoting the growth of a region or a nation.

THEN & NOW QUESTIONS for DISCUSSION

1. If a government subsidizes a technology park in a city and new businesses move there, does the presence of the new businesses alone indicate that the subsidy was a success? Why or why not?
2. How might the strategy of "attracting the creative class" result in new businesses getting established in an area? What are the arguments for and against trying to attract the creative class?
3. Which do you think would be more effective in your area: offering subsidies or attracting the creative class?

Web Resources

A Practical Museum Plan for Building the Pacific Railroad
http://www.sfmuseum.org/hist4/practical.html

Full text of Theodore Judah's A Practical Plan for Building the Pacific Railroad; provided by the City of San Francisco.

Chronology of the Northern Pacific and Related Land Grant Railroads
http://www.landgrant.org/history.html

Detailed timeline of many land-granted railroads including the Northern Pacific.

Railroad Land Grants
http://www.coxrail.com/land-grants.htm

In-depth discussion of the theory and history behind railroad land grants.

The Creative Class
http://www.creativeclass.com

Resources, news and updates on "creative class" ideas for how our society lives, works and plays.

CROWN OF THORNS
USED
BY BRYAN,
IN CAMPAIGN SPEECHES.

SPEECH TORN FROM
BIBLE

FROM THE
BIBLE

USED IN BRYAN'S
CHICAGO SPEECH

CROSS OF GOLD.

SPEECH PLAGIARIZED
FROM
THE BIBLE

Hard Currency:
Sound Money or a Cross of Gold?

*An 1896 political cartoon of William
Jennings Bryan's "Cross of Gold" speech.*

Why a "Cross of Gold"?

A bright young political candidate concludes a convention speech and crowds rush the stage, applauding and shouting for 20 minutes. Flag bearers dance in the aisles and two bands play. The disturbance is a "tumult almost beyond the power of the Chairman to restrain," a newspaper reports.[1] What is the issue that has so electrified the convention? It is a dispute about whether to make silver coins and how to set the value of the dollar.

Today, this monetary dispute may seem dry and technical, but the issue dominated the 1896 Democratic National Convention in Chicago. It was William Jennings Bryan who delivered the electrifying speech. At the time, Bryan was 36, barely old enough to run for president. Bryan opposed the **gold standard**, which tied the value of the U.S. dollar to gold. We will see how, to

William Jennings Bryan at age 36, photographed in the year in which he gave the "Cross of Gold" speech. Most photographs of Bryan were taken when he was considerably older. There were no recordings of the original speech, though a much older Bryan re-created the speech after recording technology became available.

KEY ECONOMIC CONCEPTS

Deflation	Loose money
Gold standard	Money
Inflation	Tight money

the people of that time, the debate about the gold standard was serious business. Bryan thundered, possibly poetically, that the gold standard had killed tens of thousands of people. His conclusion invoked religious imagery: "You shall not crucify mankind upon a cross of gold."[2]

The convention nominated Bryan to run for president on the Democratic ticket. Although Bryan was defeated by William McKinley in the general election, his "Cross of Gold" speech is considered among the finest speeches in American history. But was the economic policy regarding the gold standard that harsh? Were the government's policies so punishing that they deserved the symbolic label "Cross of Gold"?

The Historical Context
What Could Be Bad about Falling Prices?

During the Civil War, the U.S. government had paid for a large portion of its wartime expenses simply by printing and spending paper money. This new flow of paper money enlarged the supply of money in circulation. (People also used coins at the time.) Prices went up rapidly during the war. After the war, the government withdrew the extra paper money. Then, between 1873 and 1896, the United States experienced a 30 percent reduction in overall prices.[3] By definition, a sustained decrease in average prices is known as **deflation**. Falling prices would seem to be a good thing, if you had plenty of money. But incomes also fall in a time of deflation. Severe deflation can hurt an economy badly.

Deflation late in the 1800s created a special problem for farmers. A farmer's prosperity then was most affected by two factors: (1) the prices the farmer could charge for the crops he raised and sold; and (2) the amount of money he would need to make payments on farm loans he had taken out. Farmers experienced hardship during the time of deflation because declining crop prices cut their incomes. A farmer who sold 500 bushels of wheat for $1 per bushel would receive $500. But if wheat fell to 80 cents per bushel, his income would be only $400 (that is, 500 x $0.80).

Also, farmers typically were in debt. They borrowed money frequently to purchase land and supplies, and they had to make payments on their debts every year. Think about a farmer who had to repay $500 every year. In our example, at $1 per bushel, selling 500 bushels of wheat would bring in enough money to make the repayment. But if wheat fell to 80 cents per bushel, selling that same amount of wheat would no longer be enough. The farmer might be unable to repay his debt and might face financial ruin.

Each year during the time of deflation it became harder for farmers to make payments on their debts. It was against this backdrop of deflation and struggling farmers that the Democrats met in 1896 and nominated Bryan to run for president.

The Economics of Money

In economics, **money** is anything commonly accepted in exchange for goods and services. Dollar bills and coins are obvious examples of money, but dollars transferred by checks or bank cards are also money. The U.S. government has always had the authority to create new money, even during the time of the Continental Congress.

We can understand the effects of changes in the supply of money if we consider a tiny economy— one so tiny that its only product is cereal. The producers in this economy make four boxes of cereal per time period. The economy has money that totals $4, and people spend that money once per time period. In such a simple economy, the price of cereal will be $1. Given that people are spending $4 to purchase four boxes of cereal, the price of each box has to be $1.

If the amount of money doubled, to $8, the effects would be simple. Now people in this tiny economy would have $8 to use for purchasing four boxes of cereal, and the price of cereal would double, to $2 per box.

Although the example is simple, the insight is a solid one: overall prices go up when money grows faster than production. In this example, money doubled (from $4 to $8) while production (four boxes of cereal) stayed the same—so prices doubled. This is an example of **inflation,** or a rise in overall prices.

As long as our tiny economy is making four boxes of cereal, there is an easy formula for avoiding inflation and keeping prices steady: keep the amount of money constant at $4.

The U.S. government has always had a much harder problem in dealing with these matters than our tiny economy had. The real economy produces a vast array of goods and services, not just four boxes of cereal. The real economy's production does not remain constant; instead, it grows (in most years) and falls (in a few bad years). Money is held by banks, other financial institutions, and government agencies. Even with these complexities, though, the goal of regulating money is easy to state: keep the value of money relatively stable, with little inflation or deflation.

In real economies, bad things happen when the value of money changes unexpectedly. This is easy to see in the case of severe inflation, which occurs when money becomes worthless because too much of it is created. In our example of the cereal-box economy, printing $400 to be spent on the four boxes of cereal would bring the price of cereal up to $100 per box. This sort of thing does sometimes happen in the real economy. During the Revolutionary War the Continental Congress created so many paper dollars that their value fell to 1 percent of their former value. During the Civil War, the Confederacy created so many Confederate dollars that they, too, became worthless. Within the 20th century, Germany, some Latin American nations, and Zimbabwe all have been hurt by inflation so severe that the money in each country became useless.

Why would governments get themselves into this sort of trouble? The answer has to do with an eagerness to spend money. Governments that are desperate to spend money—in wartime, for example—sometimes print money as a last resort, particularly when they do not have good sources of tax revenue. Printing money enables governments to spend quickly—but inflation soon catches up.

When the value of money is stable, people can make plans and enter into contracts without worrying that money will soon have a very different value. In the U.S. economy, just as in the cereal-box economy, the value of money depends on a race between (1) production and (2) the total amount of money in circulation. If money keeps pace with production—and does not run much faster or slower—prices are stable and money retains its value. Think about a cereal-box economy that goes from producing four cereal boxes to producing five. If that economy lets its money grow from $4 to $5, it will still take only one dollar to buy each box of cereal. The price will remain stable at $1.

For U.S. farmers in the late 1800s, stable money would have been far better than deflation. They would not have faced increasing burdens imposed by falling prices for crops. They would have been even better off in a period of mild inflation. Mild inflation would have boosted crop prices slightly each year. Think again about the wheat farmer who started out growing 500 bushels, selling his crop for $1 per bushel, and paying out $500 on his debt. If the price of wheat increased from $1 to $1.10 per bushel, then 500 bushels of wheat would sell for $550 (500 x $1.10). The farmer then could make a $500 payment on his loan and have $50 left over. In the late 1800s, farmers and their allies favored this kind of inflation. As a general rule, inflation helps anyone who owes a fixed money payment.

Table 1 illustrates the effects of inflation and deflation from 1860 to 1910. For the five years surrounding the Civil War, 1860 to 1865, the inflation rate was 78.4 percent. That meant prices were 78.4 percent higher in 1865 than they had been in 1860. The U.S. government had printed a large quantity of paper money, known as "greenbacks," and prices rose sharply.

The opposite effect occurred after the war. The government withdrew the greenbacks. In our

TABLE 1	Inflation in the United States, Five-Year Averages, 1860–1910		
Year	Inflation Rate	Year	Inflation Rate
1860	-7.8%	1890	0.5%
1865	78.4%	1895	-7.8%
1870	-26.3%	1900	3.8%
1875	-11.3%	1905	5.6%
1880	-9.3%	1910	10.1%
1885	-8.5%		

Source: Historical Statistics of the United States, "Price Deflator," Series Ca13.

cereal-box economy, this would be like reducing the supply of money to $3 even as four boxes of cereal were still being produced. A box of cereal then would sell for 75 cents ($3 ÷ 4 = $0.75). That outcome would be fine if you had a lot of money and wanted to buy cereal. But if you were the producer of the cereal—the role corresponding to a farmer late in the 1800s—you would be hurt. Since you earn your money by selling cereal, you would suffer a large loss of income if the price fell from $1 per box to $0.75 per box.

Simply put, the monetary debate after the Civil War was loose money versus tight money. Printing of large amounts of paper money would mean rapid growth in the supply of money—that is, **loose money**. Loose money would relieve pressure on debtors and promote economic activity. Farmers, farm-supply stores, and other rural interests favored loose money.

The opposite policy involved keeping the supply of money from growing, to ensure that money would keep its value. This policy, aimed at avoiding any threat of inflation, was known as **tight money**. Lenders preferred to be repaid with the valuable money that a tight money policy would create. East Coast banks and urban interests favored tight money.

In 1896, the debate was not cast in terms of tight and loose money. Instead, these were the terms:

- *The Greenback Movement*, a coalition of interests favoring loose money, issuance of paper currency ("greenbacks"), and inflation to reverse the persistent deflation.

- *Bimetallism* ("two metals"), a method for increasing the money supply by recognizing both gold and silver in the system of money. Silver was plentiful compared to gold. If silver held a formal place in the money system, its status could prompt the government to buy large amounts of silver, make it into coins, and issue it. The result would be loose money, which farmers and their allies favored.

- *The Free Silver Movement*, a movement favoring mining interests, with a loose money policy. Supporters of this movement wanted the government to increase the money supply by buying up silver and making it into silver coins to be issued.

- *The gold standard*, a system under which the government would keep the U.S. dollar constant in value relative to gold. A gold standard meant tight money in the late 1800s because of the limited supply of gold at the time.

All of these movements were important at the time, but the most important economic variable was the *size* of the money supply, not its composition. Loose money, whether created by issuing paper currency, recognizing silver, or issuing large numbers of silver coins, would push prices upward and relieve pressure on farmers owing debts. On the other hand, money so tight that it caused deflation would hurt farmers who owed debts, whether gold was involved or not.

The key issue in Bryan's time was what would happen to the overall quantity of money. However, gold provided a powerful symbol. The "Cross of Gold" debate illustrates how real lives and fortunes can be changed by technical features of the monetary system. Millions of people have been affected by tight money versus loose money. With the knowledge we have today, we can see that stable money would have prevented deflation and greatly eased the hardship of farmers and their allies in the late 1800s. Although Bryan's "Cross of Gold" may be an excessive image, the hardship it referred to was real, and it was preventable.

HISTORICAL QUESTIONS & ECONOMIC ANSWERS

Did Bryan win the election after his famous speech?

No, he did not. Despite his eloquence, Bryan lost the 1896 election to Republican William McKinley. Those who wanted a greater role for silver had been defeated, but they ultimately got their wish for a loose money policy. Increases in the supply of money under President McKinley and his successors led to inflation and reduced the pressure on farmers and other debtors.

Did McKinley intentionally pursue a loose money policy?

No, he did not. He held to the gold standard. However, the gold standard has an important quirk as a monetary system: money responds to gold mining activity, independently of the government's policies. If a fixed relationship is maintained between the dollar and gold, money becomes looser and less valuable when gold becomes more abundant. That is exactly what happened after McKinley's election. There were new discoveries of gold in Colorado, Alaska, Australia, and South Africa, making gold more plentiful. The increased supply of gold increased the money supply, which then pushed prices up. That overall increase in prices, by definition, was inflation. It decisively reversed the deflation of the late 1800s.

Does a tight money policy necessarily follow from having a gold standard?

No. A tight money policy occurs any time that growth in the supply of money is slow. Tight money is reversed when growth in the supply of money speeds up, regardless of the details of silver and gold components in the system of money. In William Jennings Bryan's time, the gold standard meant tight money because gold then was especially scarce. Under McKinley, a gold standard actually meant loose money, as gold became more plentiful.

Was the tight money–loose money debate regional?

It certainly had regional overtones. Farmers, who favored loose money, were far more numerous in the South, West, and Midwest. Money lenders and suppliers of capital, who favored tight money, were far more likely to be located in the East, especially in the U.S. financial capital, New York City.

Is the United States on the gold standard, or a partial gold standard, today?

No. The United States today has a system in which money is not backed by gold, silver, or any other physical asset. The value of money in the United States comes from its acceptance as money by the public. Confidence in its value is enhanced by the fact that it is always acceptable for payment of taxes.

Many people believe that U.S. currency has some official relationship today to silver or gold. They believe that the government must hold certain amounts of silver or gold to support the currency it issues. That belief is not correct. The government does own a huge gold depository at Fort Knox, Kentucky, but gold is held there only for such uses as production of the American Eagle commemorative coin. It has no significant monetary role.[4]

Was *The Wizard of Oz* a story about money?

Among old movies, *The Wizard of Oz* remains a favorite. It is the story of a girl named Dorothy. She is from Kansas, and she is thrown by a tornado to a magical place called Oz. There she meets fanciful companions and follows a yellow brick road to try to find her way home. The film is based on the 1900 children's novel *The Wonderful Wizard of Oz*, by L. Frank Baum. In addition to telling a good story, Baum may have been making a statement about the monetary debate then raging. Economic historian Hugh Rockoff documented the following correspondences:

- Dorothy perhaps represented traditional American values. She wanted to get back to Kansas, and she was told that the answer lay in Emerald City—perhaps representing Washington, D.C. Returning to Kansas would symbolize returning the nation to traditional values of fairness, thought by some to have been corrupted by the tight money policy of the late 1800s.

- The Scarecrow, the first of Dorothy's companions in Oz, perhaps represented farmers. The Scarecrow thought he had no brains, since his head was stuffed with straw, but he actually was clever and resourceful.

This cartoon from Denver's Rocky Mountain News *depicts Bryan as a lion among dogs. Some economic historians believe that images such as this may have inspired L. Frank Baum to cast Bryan as a lion in his book* The Wonderful Wizard of Oz.

He represented the idea that farmers of the late 1800s—thought by some to be too unintelligent to understand money—were fully capable of comprehending the debate about gold, silver, and currency.

- The Tin Woodman perhaps represented industrial workers. The Tin Woodman was rusting away from unemployment, a victim of tight money policies that caused many industrial workers to lose their jobs.

- The Cowardly Lion may have represented William Jennings Bryan himself. He was a lion because of his roaring oratory, but he was cowardly, in the author's opinion, because he did not press the attack against the gold standard after 1896.

And the yellow brick road? Perhaps it represented the gold standard, which led Dorothy to disappointment early on, before she was able to get back to Kansas.[5]

The first edition of The Wonderful Wizard of Oz.

QUESTIONS for DISCUSSION

1. Think about a farmer who has borrowed large amounts of money for land and must repay fixed amounts of his debt every year. What would this farmer's attitude toward deflation be? Explain your answer.

2. Since deflation would reduce the prices farmers paid for goods that they bought, why would farmers be hurt by deflation? Explain your answer.

3. How could deflation benefit a money lender receiving fixed payments?

4. If the government had greatly changed the proportion of gold and silver coins it issued in the late 1800s but still followed a tight money policy, would that have helped farmers? Why or why not?

5. The money you receive and spend today has no official link to gold. Does that fact make you less confident about the future value of money? Explain your answer.

The "Cross of Gold" Speech

Here are some key passages from William Jennings Bryan's "Cross of Gold" speech.[6]

There are two ideas of government. There are those who believe that if you just legislate to make the well-to-do prosperous, that their prosperity will leak through on those below. The Democratic idea has been that if you legislate to make the masses prosperous their prosperity will find its way up and through every class that rests upon it.

You come to us and tell us that the great cities are in favor of the gold standard. I tell you that the great cities rest upon these broad and fertile prairies. Burn down your cities and leave our farms, and your cities will spring up again as if by magic. But destroy our farms and the grass will grow in the streets of every city in the country.

My friends, we shall declare that this nation is able to legislate for its own people on every question without waiting for the aid or consent of any other nation on earth, and upon that issue we expect to carry every single state in the Union.

. . .

If they dare to come out in the open field and defend the gold standard as a good thing, we shall fight them to the uttermost, having behind us the producing masses of the nation and the world. Having behind us the commercial interests and the laboring interests and all the toiling masses, we shall answer their demands for a gold standard by saying to them, you shall not press down upon the brow of labor this crown of thorns. You shall not crucify mankind upon a cross of gold.

An older William Jennings Bryan giving a speech in 1908.

PRIMARY SOURCE QUESTIONS for DISCUSSION

1. Bryan argues that his party "should legislate to make the masses prosperous." What monetary outcome is Bryan arguing for, and how would it help?
2. Bryan acknowledges that "the great cities are in favor of the gold standard." How does Bryan argue against favoring the cities over the rural areas?
3. Bryan predicts that his party will win every state in the upcoming presidential election. What actually happened in that election?
4. Bryan cites the support of "commercial interests and the laboring interests and all the toiling masses" for his platform. What attitude did all of these interests have toward loose money?

Could a Little Inflation Be Good for the Economy?

The U.S. government authorities who regulate money surprised some observers late in 2010 by suggesting that they might engineer a small amount of inflation. This would involve increasing the amount of money in the economy. If they were to succeed, prices would rise by a few more percentage points than had been expected.[7] This would be a modern version of the loose money policy favored by rural interests in the late 1800s.

Although critics were quick to pounce on the 2010 announcement, others defended the strategy as a reasonable reaction to the distress many homeowners felt at the time. Recall that the farmers of the late 1800s had two main concerns: the prices they could get for their crops and the fixed debts they had to repay. In a manner that echoes their concerns, the distressed homeowners of 2010 also had two main concerns: (1) the market value of their houses and (2) the mortgages they had to repay. Some homeowners faced fixed payments, but for others it was still worse because the terms of their loans caused monthly payments to go up.

Homeowners are best off if the market value of their homes exceeds (by a large amount) the money they owe. Homeowners in 2010 wanted the market value of their homes to go up. But housing prices had fallen in the ongoing financial distress that began in 2007.

Some people who fell behind on their mortgage payments wanted to be able to sell their homes and pay off their loans. If housing prices had been on the rise, they might even have come out ahead in this way. However, low housing prices meant that, for many sellers, home sales brought in too little money. Millions of homeowners were stuck, unable to make their mortgage payments but unable to sell their homes and get out.

These homeowners had reason to hope for a modest amount of inflation. If overall prices were to rise by a few extra percentage points, that rise would also translate into higher housing prices. Seeing the prospect of higher future prices, more home buyers might jump into the market. This would make home prices go up, helping the homeowners specifically. More housing sales would also increase economic activity as people moved in—and perhaps did some remodeling, bought new furniture, and so on.

A common worry in the late 1800s also was echoed in 2010. Critics worried that if slight inflation set in, it might snowball, eventually producing a high rate of inflation. Engineering a slight rate of inflation, they thought, was like playing with fire. On one point there was no disagreement, then or now: a spell of very high inflation would be bad all around.

THEN & NOW QUESTIONS for DISCUSSION

1. How were distressed homeowners of 2010 like distressed farmers of the late 1800s? Explain your answer.
2. How could higher inflation benefit someone hoping to sell a house and move to a new community?
3. What is the danger involved in trying to engineer a small amount of inflation?

Why a "Cross of Gold"?
http://historymatters.gmu.edu/d/5354

Audio of William Jennings Bryan's "Cross of Gold" speech

The Economics of Money
http://www.britannica.com/presidents/article-9037961

Detailed information on the Greenback Movement

The Wonderful Wizard of Oz—a Monetary Reform Parable?
http://prosperityuk.com/2001/01/a-wonderful-wizard-of-oz-a-monetary-reform-parable

An account of monetary allusions in the The Wonderful Wizard of Oz, with links to scholarly articles on the subject.

Then & Now: Could a Little Inflation Be Good for the Economy?
http://www.federalreserve.gov/boarddocs/speeches/2004/200401032/default.htm

A classic statement about what can and cannot be said when government authorities seek to engineer additional inflation or other monetary policies.

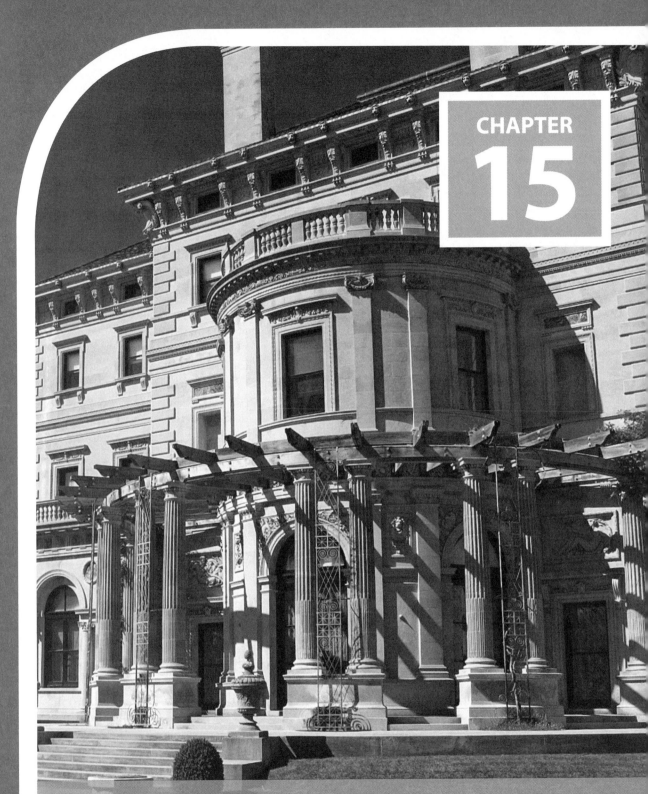

Were the Robber Barons Robbers or Barons?

The Breakers, a mansion in Newport, Rhode Island built by the wealthy Vanderbilt family.

Robber Barons or Captains of Industry?

Cornelius Vanderbilt was born into a poor family on Staten Island, New York, on May 27, 1794. He went to work at age 11 on his father's ferry boat. When he was 16, he bought a sailboat and began operating a passenger and freight service between Staten Island and New York City. Offering low fares, he competed successfully with other ferry services and was able to expand his fleet. In 1818 he sold all his sailing vessels and became a steamboat captain, operating a ferry service, with a partner, between New Brunswick, New Jersey, and New York City. Again, he charged low fares. He soon added new routes, and his ferry service became the dominant service between Philadelphia and New York City. By the 1840s Vanderbilt owned a fleet of 100 steamships. He continued to offer his customers low fares as well as speed and luxury. He became the nation's largest employer. In the 1860s Vanderbilt moved in a new direction, setting his sights on railroads. Eventually he acquired half a dozen railroads, operating from New York to Chicago, again offering low fares and improved service.

Cornelius Vanderbilt, businessman and philanthropist.

KEY ECONOMIC CONCEPTS

Consolidation	Productivity
Economies of scale	Profit
Fixed cost	Variable cost
Invisible hand	

Vanderbilt died in 1877. Although he is not well known today as a philanthropist, he donated $1 million to Nashville's Central University. In today's terms, $1 million would equal $17 million. The University would become known as Vanderbilt University in Nashville, Tennessee.

Vanderbilt and others like him helped to shape today's economy. Industrialization and the emergence of big business had profound effects on American life. These changes, however, did not occur without controversy. One such controversy focused on business consolidation—as practiced by industrialists like Cornelius Vanderbilt.

Journalists often described the 19th-century industrialists as "Robber Barons." The term was meant to be derogatory. It implied that these men had special privileges, as if they were members of a noble or royal family, and that they acted ruthlessly to achieve their economic success. The term is still used today, in some history books, to describe business leaders including Andrew Carnegie of Carnegie Steel, John D. Rockefeller of Standard Oil, and Henry Ford of the Ford Motor Company.

Journalists, historians, and other observers often use colorful language to enliven their accounts of the past and emphasize particular interpretations of it. Sometimes a vivid image or metaphor serves well to represent important aspects of the issue in question. But colorful language can be misleading when it serves as a substitute for careful analysis. With this in mind, we turn to an analysis of the business people who have been described as Robber Barons. Were these men Robber Barons, in any legitimate sense of that term—stealing from their customers and their employees, and making society worse off? Or were they entrepreneurs, serving their customers, and society overall, by providing better and cheaper products?

The Historical Context
Business Consolidation: Three Snapshots

Between 1860 and 1920, the U.S. economy evolved from its early agricultural base to a new base in industry. By the 1890s, the United States had emerged as the world's leading industrial power. This period of industrial growth was marked by frequent consolidation of businesses. **Consolidation** of businesses often meant the merging or combining of firms into large corporations. The trend toward consolidation can be illustrated by changes in three large and important industries—steel, petroleum, and automobiles—and the roles played by their leading businessmen, Andrew Carnegie, John D. Rockefeller, and Henry Ford.

In 1872, Andrew Carnegie established Carnegie Steel Limited, near Pittsburgh, to manufacture steel rails. Over time, he acquired other steel companies and built new ones. Managing by the motto "watch costs and the profits take care of themselves," Carnegie was relentless in driving down costs. By 1900 Carnegie Steel produced more steel than all the steel firms in Great Britain. In 1901, J.P. Morgan was able to purchase Carnegie's many properties and combine them with other steel firms to form the United States Steel Corporation.

The story of consolidation in oil was different. Railroad firms, manufacturers, and builders demanded steel. Who wanted oil? When oil first oozed out of the ground in western Pennsylvania, it was regarded as a nuisance. But by the 1880s, oil had found a new use, as a source of kerosene. Kerosene had been known since the 1850s as a good fuel for lighting; soon after 1880, it replaced whale and coal oil as consumers' indoor lighting fuel of choice. By the early 1900s, kerosene was

Andrew Carnegie at his desk in 1913.

used to power the internal combustion engines of that new phenomenon, the automobile.

Enter John D. Rockefeller, who led the way in consolidation of the oil industry. Substituting tanker cars for barrels, Rockefeller cut costs in the transportation of oil. A big customer of railroads, he pressured rail companies into giving him better rates ("sweetheart deals") than his competitors could get. After establishing oil pipelines, Rockefeller greatly expanded Standard Oil, making it the dominant oil company in the country.

The automobile industry emerged at the end of the 19th century. People had been experimenting with building automobiles since the 1870s, but it was Henry Ford who launched the manufacture of the modern automobile. He combined using interchangeable parts and mass production to develop an assembly line for making cars, which allowed more cars to be produced in less time and at lower costs.

Ford's "break-out" year occurred in 1908–1909 when he developed the Model T car, which was produced until 1927. The Model T was the first mass-produced, affordable car in America. With Ford's innovations, owning an automobile became something all Americans, not just rich Americans, could do. The automobile industry also provided new jobs. Spreading throughout the Great Lakes region, it employed thousands and attracted workers to such cities as Detroit, Chicago, and Milwaukee. Detroit became the "Motor City" because of Henry Ford.

Then and now, many critics have charged that people like Carnegie, Rockefeller, and Ford achieved their wealth and power illegitimately—exploiting workers, running roughshod over other businesses, and disregarding the harmful effects of their business practices on society overall. This general accusation is represented in the derogatory term "Robber Barons." We turn now to an examination of the criticisms implied by that term.

The Economics of Scale

Large companies are able to take advantage of **economies of scale**—that is, the ability to reduce the cost for each unit of the things they produce by increasing the number of units produced over a period of time. In ordinary language: bigger is better. As output increases, the average cost of each unit produced falls. If you produce cell phones or toasters or chain saws, you probably can cut your costs per item by producing *many* cell phones or toasters or chain saws. Large firms can produce on a large scale because they sell their goods to many, many customers. In producing on a large scale and selling to large pools of customers, large firms benefit from a cost structure that differs from the cost structure of small firms.

Firms have two sorts of costs, variable and fixed. **Variable costs** change with the number of items produced. In the case of building an automobile, the cost of steel, rubber, and fabrics from which the car is manufactured, as well as the

hourly wages of the workers assembling the car, all are variable costs. That is because as more cars are built, more costs are incurred—for more steel, more workers' pay, and so on.

Fixed Costs, on the other hand, are the same no matter how many (or how few) products are manufactured. Using the example of cars again: the cost of building or heating the factory in which the car is built, the cost of designing the car prior to manufacturing it, the cost of advertising it in magazines—these costs do not change with the number of cars produced. They are fixed costs. Understanding fixed costs helps to explain why businesses often benefit from large-scale production.

Henry Ford was an entrepreneur who understood the advantages of economies of scale. He recognized that his company could spread its fixed costs over many units. By spreading fixed costs over many units of production, the company could realize a profit even when the price of a car declined. **Profit** is the amount of money left over after all of a business's costs are paid. Economies of scale thus benefit customers and large-scale

TABLE 1	Production of Ford's Model T	
YEARS	Model T Fords Produced	Average Price
1908–1909	14,161	$837.50
1910	20,173	$925.00
1911	53,998	$730.00
1912	94,662	$640.00
1913	224,783	$562.50
1914	247,715	$465.00
1915	372,249	$415.00
1916	586,202	$352.50
1917	834,662	$352.50
1918	382,246	$512.50
1919	828,544	$512.50
1920	1,038,447	$485.00
1921	869,651	$340.00
1922	1,384,999	$333.50

Source: David L. Lewis, *The Public image of Henry Ford: An American Folk Hero and His Company* (Detroit: Wayne State University Press, 1976), p. 44.

producers: customers benefit from lower prices; large-scale producers benefit by earning profits.

Table 1 shows production numbers and prices for the first 14 years of Ford's production of the Model T. Notice the relationship between increased production and declining average price from 1908 to 1922. As production increased, prices decreased steadily (except in 1910 and 1918).

Ford Motor Company was not an isolated case. Breakouts were occurring in several industries, from sewing machines (Singer Sewing Machine Company) to meat packing (Armour and Company, Swift Bros. and Company) to matches (Diamond Match). Consider refrigerators, something most of us take for granted, as an example of the benefits of economies of scale. In 1920, the cost of a Frigidaire refrigerator was $1,000. In today's prices, $1,000 is the same as $10,940! By 1925 the price for Frigidaire refrigerators had dropped to about $500. Prices of refrigerators continued to decline in subsequent years. Before long, millions of Americans could afford to buy refrigerators.

HISTORICAL QUESTIONS & ECONOMIC ANSWERS

Were the Robber Barons barons?

The term "Robber Baron" is rich in connotations. It implies that the likes of Carnegie, Rockefeller, and Ford were people born into noble families—people who inherited their wealth and power, then idled away their adult lives extorting money from powerless victims. But our so-called Robber Barons were nothing of the sort. Young Andrew Carnegie was a penniless Scottish immigrant who began his work career as a bobbin boy in a textile factory. Rockefeller was the son of a vagabond who sold questionable "elixirs" (magical or medicinal potions) door to door and was rarely around to care for his family. Henry Ford was born on a farm in what is today Dearborn, Michigan. His father was an immigrant from County Cork, Ireland, and his mother was the daughter of Belgian immigrants.

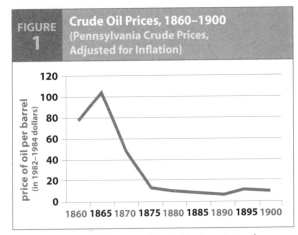

FIGURE 1 **Crude Oil Prices, 1860–1900**
(Pennsylvania Crude Prices, Adjusted for Inflation)

Source: Department of Commerce, *Report of the Commission of Corporation in the Petroleum Industry: Part II Prices and Profits* (Washington, D.C.: Government Printing Office, 1907).

Were the Robber Barons robbers?

No. They did not steal from their employees or customers, literally or figuratively. Rockefeller serves as an excellent example. He was a tough-minded, cutthroat competitor because of his ability to undercut the prices charged by his competitors. Because of his many innovations, including the use of tank cars and pipelines, together with economies of scale, Rockefeller found ways to reduce his costs and reduce the prices his customers paid. He did not sell oil below *his* costs. But he did set his prices below the prices his rivals charged—and, much to their chagrin, he could still earn a profit. While other producers complained, consumers benefitted from lower prices. Examine the graph in Figure 1. It shows the price of a barrel of Pennsylvania crude oil from 1860 to 1900, adjusted for inflation. The price increased from 1860 to 1865. Although the price cycled up and down thereafter, much as prices do today, the trend after 1865 was toward flat or lower prices. Robbers do not confer benefits of this sort on the people with whom they interact.

What happened to employees' wages during the time of the Robber Barons?

From the perspective of the 21st century, working conditions for people in the late 19th and early 20th centuries were tough indeed. Life was often "nasty, brutish, and short." Many Americans worked on farms, where accidents were common. In fact, agriculture had one of the highest injury rates of any industry. Revulsion against life on the farm is what prompted many rural Americans to seek jobs in industry. But working conditions in factories presented risks, too, often leading to accidents, injuries, and even death. Wages were a matter of controversy. For Carnegie, Rockefeller, and other industrialists, the focus on keeping costs low meant that they also tried to keep tight control over the wages of their employees.

However, while prices for many goods and services declined from 1900 to 1920, employees' earnings did not decline during that period. Rather, beginning in 1900, there was a relatively steady increase in the annual earnings of nonfarm employees. Figure 2 shows the changes in earnings from 1900 to 1920, adjusted for inflation. One reason for these wage increases is that economies of scale enabled industrial employers to profit and thus offer improved wages over time.

Did workers have to work longer hours during this time period?

Unskilled workers put in long hours in the early 1900s—often working six days a week, nine hours a day, and more in some industries. But the overall number of hours worked during the period declined. Table 2 shows that the average number of hours of work per week declined from about 62 in 1870 to 51.2 by 1920. Here again, one reason for the decline in working hours is that economies

TABLE 2	Estimated Average Weekly Hours Worked in Manufacturing, 1870–1920
Year	Hours Worked
1870	About 62
1890	60.1
1900	59.6
1910	57.3
1920	51.2

Source: Robert Whaples, "Hours of Work in U.S. History." EH.Net Encyclopedia, edited by Robert Whaples. August 14, 2001. Data for 1880 not available.

of scale enabled industrial employers to reduce the amount of labor required for production.

Why did Ford double the wages of his employees in 1914?

In 1914, Henry Ford surprised his competitors and everyone else by introducing the $5 work day. That is, he began paying his workers a minimum wage of $5 per day. This might not seem like much today, but back then it was more than twice the going wage rate. Many observers at the time praised Ford for this wage increase and characterized it as an act of human kindness. After all, the $5 per day wage rate represented a $10 million increase in the company's 1914 costs. Others wondered if Ford did it to gain publicity. Economists, however, argue that the pay raise was another example of Ford acting as a savvy entrepreneur.

Here is the economic story. [1] Ford had trouble keeping his employees. He had a high worker turnover rate. In 1913, Ford had to hire 50,448 workers in order to maintain the average number of workers at 13,623. At the same time, Ford also had problems with absenteeism—workers not coming to work. In 1913, Ford faced a daily absenteeism rate of 10 percent. Taken together, these numbers mean that Ford had to hire an average of about 1,360 replacement workers each day—workers who were not very familiar with the requirements of their jobs.

Ford made extensive use of the assembly line. Workers in an assembly line depend on one another to do their jobs well. If a worker is absent

FIGURE 2 Nonfarm Employees' Real Annual Earnings in 1914 Dollars

Source: Stanley Lebergott, "Wages and Working Conditions," in David Henderson, ed., *Concise Encyclopedia of Economics.* (Indianapolis, Indiana: Liberty Fund, 1993).

or works slowly, the whole process slows down. With slowdowns, the assembly line works less efficiently. It produces less even though it uses the same number of workers and machines.

Ford's $5 a day wage plan solved many of his labor problems. After it was implemented, the turnover in workers fell from 50,448 in 1913 to 2,931 by 1915. Absenteeism fell from 10 percent to 2.5 percent in the same period. With less turnover and absenteeism, Ford was able to keeping his experienced workers on the job. This led, in turn, to an increase in productivity. **Productivity** is the amount of goods that a worker can produce in a given time. An increase in productivity means that the same amount of labor is producing more goods. Ford's productivity increase reduced the cost of producing automobiles. Cost reductions can be passed along to consumers in the form of lower prices. At the new wage rate of $5 per day, moreover, many Ford employees found themselves able to buy a Ford car.

Is the growth of big business in the late 19th century an example of Adam Smith's invisible hand at work?

Adam Smith claimed in *The Wealth of Nations* that free markets operate as if an invisible hand is at work, promoting positive social outcomes from everyday business transactions, even though these outcomes are not intended by the people involved in the transactions. The metaphor of the invisible hand has been controversial. It seems to defy common sense. Every consumer knows that business owners wish to charge as much as possible for their goods and services. Every business owner knows that consumers look for low prices. Yet Smith explains that allowing people to act in their own self-interest produces unintended social benefits. It is not as strange as it seems. After all, business people need customers to buy their goods and services if they are to earn a profit, and consumers need businesses if they are to obtain the goods and services they desire.

Were the Robber Barons Robbers or Barons?

Did the invisible hand produce positive results during the era of industrialization, as Smith would have predicted? Let's examine the case. Did Carnegie Steel, Standard Oil, and the Ford Motor Company benefit from the business practices of Carnegie, Rockefeller, and Ford? Yes. They earned profits, and their shareholders were better off. Did consumers benefit? Yes. Over time, people who bought petroleum products, steel, and automobiles paid lower prices, thanks to industrial innovations and economies of scale. Finally, did employees benefit? Yes. While it may or may not have been the intention of Carnegie or Rockefeller to improve workers' pay and working conditions, economic gains over the decades lifted wages and reduced the number of hours workers worked.

What did the Robber Barons do with their tremendous wealth?

Carnegie, Rockefeller, and Ford worked almost as hard at giving their fortunes away as they did at earning them. Rockefeller gave away hundreds of millions of dollars. His gifts created the University of Chicago, Rockefeller University, and the Rockefeller Foundation. In 1909 Rockefeller established the Rockefeller Sanitary Commission, which was largely responsible for eradicating hookworm disease in the American South by 1927. At the time of his death in 1937, he had given away most of his money.

Andrew Carnegie spent much of his fortune establishing more than 2,500 public libraries throughout the United States. He also made contributions to colleges and universities, including the Carnegie Institute of Technology, which he established in 1900. By the time of his death in 1919, he had given away $350 million.

Henry Ford also had a legacy of giving. He and his son Edsel Ford founded the Ford Foundation in 1936. It operates nationally and internationally as an independent, nonprofit, nongovernmental organization. It has provided nearly $13 billion for grants, projects, and loans since 1980.

QUESTIONS for DISCUSSION

1. What sectors of the U.S. economy experienced large changes late in the 19th century? Which industrialists were most closely associated with each?
2. What are economies of scale, and how did 19th-century industrialists achieve them?
3. Was Ford's implementation of the $5 work day an act of humanity or just good business? Explain your answer.
4. How do productivity gains help consumers?
5. Do you think the term "Robber Baron" should be applied to people such as Vanderbilt, Carnegie, Rockefeller, and Ford? Or did the industrial consolidations and innovations of the late 19th century show that the invisible hand was at work? Explain your answer.
6. What were the most important achievements of John D. Rockefeller and Andrew Carnegie? Explain your answer.

How Did Standard Oil Succeed?
Two Perspectives

Standard Oil was controversial early in the 20th century. In 1904, Ida Tarbell (1857–1954) wrote *The History of Standard Oil*, in which she accused Rockefeller of engaging in many unsavory business practices. Tarbell's work was regarded as a breakthrough piece of investigative reporting. For his part, Rockefeller wrote his own book in which he defended his actions. Read the following quotations and then respond to the questions that follow.

PRIMARY SOURCE

Ida Tarbell in 1904.

In the fall of 1871…certain Pennsylvania refiners… brought [to Mr. Rockefeller and his friends] a remarkable scheme…to bring together secretly a large enough body of refiners and shippers and to [force] all the railroads handling oil to give the company formed special rates [discounts] on its oil and [to charge higher rates to others]. If they could get such rates it was clear that those outside the combination could not compete with them long, and that they would become eventually the only refiners. They could limit their output to actual demand and so keep prices up."[2]

—Ida Tarbell

John D. Rockefeller in 1909.

I ascribe the success of Standard Oil Company to its consistent policy of making the volume of its business large through the merit and cheapness of its products.

. . . .

It has spared no expense in utilizing the best and most efficient methods of manufacture.[3]

—John D. Rockefeller

PRIMARY SOURCE **QUESTIONS for DISCUSSION**

1. How does Ida Tarbell characterize Rockefeller's business practices?
2. How do you think Rockefeller would respond to Tarbell's remarks about his business practices?

This chapter has focused on the changing economy in the 19th century, with special attention paid to the role of Andrew Carnegie, John D. Rockefeller, and Henry Ford. There are some interesting parallels between the development of large 19th-century businesses and today's well-known retailer Walmart.

Like the big businesses of the 19th century, Walmart was founded by a formidable competitor with a modest background. Sam Walton was born in Kingfisher, Oklahoma, where his family owned a farm. His father eventually gave up farming and returned to work as a mortgage banker. In 1945, after he graduated from college and served in the military, Sam Walton took over the management of a Ben Franklin variety store in Newport, Arkansas. Here he developed many of the business practices that would prove to be important in his future. These included providing a wide range of goods at low prices and keeping his store open for long hours. Walton hoped to earn a large profit by selling a lot of merchandise.

Of course, Walton is best known for establishing Walmart stores, the first of which opened in 1962 in Bentonville, Arkansas. Today, Walmart is the world's largest retailer, with more than 8,000 stores in 15 countries, employing more than 2 million employees.

Walmart has many critics, and their criticisms are similar to the ones leveled against Rockefeller about 100 years ago. Walmart is accused of being a monopoly—a business with huge market power. And, like Rockefeller's Standard Oil, Walmart is accused of driving its rivals out of business. In the case of Walmart, however, it is "mom and pop" stores—dime stores, clothing stores, bakeries, and drug stores operating on the main streets of small towns—that are sometimes unable to compete.

Critics say that when Walmart builds a big store on the edge of a small town, its low prices, vast selection, and convenient store hours drive the main-street retailers out of business. President Clinton's former secretary of labor, Robert B. Reich, wrote in a 2005 *New York Times* article that Walmart turns "main streets into ghost towns by sucking business away from small retailers."[3]

Are the critics right? There is certainly evidence from many small towns that Walmart has had an adverse effect on small retailers. Antigo is a small town in northern Wisconsin, with a population of about 9,000 people. Soon after a Walmart Super Center opened on the edge of Antigo, the downtown clothing and small department stores simply vanished.

But does Walmart hurt consumers? Walmart can't force shoppers to walk into its stores and fill up shopping carts. Yet more than 100 million Americans choose to shop at Walmart every week. They must prefer Walmart to their alternative possibilities. Even consumers in small towns have shopping alternatives, including buying online or driving to larger communities to shop.

Several studies show that Walmart charges lower prices than its competitors and puts pressure on competitors to reduce their prices. Consider, the findings of Emek Basker of the University of Missouri. She looked at prices for 10 widely-used consumer products (aspirin, cigarettes, Coke, detergent, Kleenex, shampoo, toothpaste, men's dress shirts, pants, and underwear) in 65 cities. She found that the opening of a new Walmart store results in city-wide price reductions on these 10 items—price reductions of two to three percent in the short term and approximately 10 percent in the long run.[5]

In their study of Walmart, Richard Vedder and Wendell Cox identified ways in which Walmart benefits the poor. While people of all income levels shop at Walmart, Figure 3 shows that most Walmart shoppers are people earning moderate or low incomes. Vedder and Cox explain that this pattern is primarily the result of Walmart's emphasis on low prices and good quality.[6] Walmart successfully attracts customers of modest means.

Low prices benefit particular consumers and the overall economy. Every dollar consumers save on their purchases permits them to buy other items, or to save more or invest more. More consumers' desires can be fulfilled when prices are

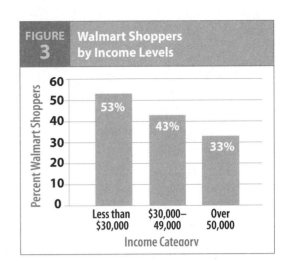

Source: Richard Vedder and Wendell Cox, *The Walmart Revolution* (Washington D.C.: AEI Press, 2006). Percentages shown in the three columns are derived independently and do not total 100 percent.

lower than when prices are higher. Because a consumer's dollars go further at lower prices, more merchandise can be manufactured and sold. This benefits consumers and producers alike. All this is little consolation, of course, to a small retailer driven out of business by Walmart.

THEN & NOW — QUESTIONS for DISCUSSION

1. What are some similarities between the 19th-century business practices described in this chapter and the practices associated with Walmart?

2. In what ways does Walmart benefit consumers?

3. In what way does Walmart hurt its competitors?

4. Why do you think Walmart is controversial? Explain your answer.

The Steel Business
http://www.pbs.org/wgbh/amex/carnegie/sfeature/mf_flames.html

Additional information, including pictures, related to Andrew Carnegie and Carnegie Steel.

The Life of Henry Ford
http://www.hfmgv.org/exhibits/hf

Extensive information on the life of Henry Ford and the origins of the Ford Motor Company.

John D. and Standard Oil
http://www.bgsu.edu/departments/acs/1890s/rockefeller/bio2.htm

Biographical information on John D. Rockefeller, as well as in-depth information on Standard Oil.

The Life of Ida Tarbell
http://www.pbs.org/wgbh/amex/rockefellers/peopleevents/p_tarbell.html

Biographical information on Ida Tarbell, her father and her book, The History of the Standard Oil Company.

Walmart
http://www.aei.org/book/867

Walmart's impact on workers' wages, labor issues, health insurance, and land-use policies.

Why Did the 19th-Century Monopolies Disappear?

An 1881 cartoon of a snake, representing monopolies, threatening Lady Liberty.

What Happened to the Trusts?

Theodore Roosevelt was born into a wealthy New York family in 1858. He was an unhealthy child. At the age of 18 he entered Harvard College, where he excelled as a student and became a skillful boxer. Soon after leaving Harvard he was elected to the Assembly of New York State, where he was regarded as an up-and-coming young reformer. In 1884, after a bout of ill health and the death of his first wife, he left New York. He bought a cattle ranch in the Badlands of Dakota Territory, intending to remain there. But his ranching business did not go well, and in 1886 he returned to New York. He remarried and plunged into politics again. In 1900, as William McKinley's running mate, he was elected Vice President of the United States. When President McKinley was assassinated in 1901, Roosevelt became the youngest United States president.

It was not Roosevelt's first major accomplishment. He had served previously as assistant secretary of the U.S. Navy, as a Rough Rider (a volunteer soldier) in the Spanish-American War, as a police commissioner, and as a state governor. He was a man of action, and he harbored deep suspicions of big business.

Theodore Roosevelt in 1901.

KEY ECONOMIC CONCEPTS

Corporation
Competition
Horizontal
  integration

Monopoly
Natural monopoly
Trusts
Vertical integration

At the turn of the 20th century, American business was characterized by expansion and combination. Many businesses merged with others in efforts to dominate their industries. The investment bank of J.P. Morgan, for example, organized the consolidation that established the United States Steel Corporation. When it was founded in 1901, U.S. Steel was the largest business enterprise ever launched, with a value of $1.4 billion. In its first year of operation, U.S. Steel made 67 percent of all the steel produced in the United States. Business consolidations also took place in other industries, including petroleum, cotton seed, whiskey, sugar refining, and tobacco.

It is relatively easy to account for the increase in business mergers during this period. Mass markets—markets with many customers—were emerging at the time. Entrepreneurs were learning how to be highly productive. They used the division of labor and interchangeable parts to accomplish mass production. And a firm could make large profits if it dominated its market.

That is what worried critics of big business: market domination might enable a few producers to gain great wealth by squelching competition and keeping prices high, to the disadvantage of ordinary consumers. Congress responded to this fear by enacting antitrust legislation aimed at breaking up big business consolidations, particularly those known as trusts. (As a name for a certain kind of business organization, the term trust is now dated; in Roosevelt's time **trust** referred to a large business formed by the merger of several businesses in a given industry, with controlling power given over to a single board of directors.) The Roosevelt administration launched 44 antitrust lawsuits against large firms including Northern Securities (the merged railroads of the Great Northern and Great Pacific Railroads), Standard Oil, and the American Tobacco Company. It was this legal campaign that earned President Roosevelt his reputation as a "trust buster." Despite the lawsuits, however, the courts succeeded in breaking up only a few consolidations. What happened to all the others?

The Historical Context
Fears Regarding Business Consolidation

Efforts by business leaders to consolidate were immensely unpopular among many Americans. They feared that power consolidated in big businesses would prevent competition from doing its job—prevent it, that is, from putting pressure on businesses to hold prices in line and maintain quality in the goods and services they supplied. Farmers were especially vocal opponents of big business. They had been hurt by economic downturns in the periods 1873–1879 and 1883–1886. They believed that the rates railroads charged to transport their products to urban areas had been set above market rates. Mary Lease, a lawyer and popular speaker, told farmers in Halstead, Kansas, they should take action against the business practices that had hurt them. They should, she said, "raise less corn and more hell."

Others expressed similar grievances. The American teacher, author, and journalist Ida Tarbell (1857–1954), for example, was a leading "muckraker." Her 1904 blockbuster book, *The History of Standard Oil*, severely criticized the business practices of the Standard Oil firm and damaged the reputation of John D. Rockefeller. Tarbell had firsthand experience with the oil business. Her father was among the refiners who had been forced out of the oil business by Rockefeller's South Improvement Company.

Elected officials eventually reacted to the criticisms. Theodore Roosevelt campaigned for public office as a "trust buster." John Sherman,

In this political cartoon, Theodore Roosevelt aims a rifle at three creatures representing hard coal, beef, and Standard Oil trusts.

brother of the American Civil War general William Tecumseh Sherman, was the chief author of the Sherman Antitrust Act of 1890. The Act states, in part, that

> Every contract, combination in the form of trust or otherwise, or conspiracy, in restraint of trade or commerce among the several states or with foreign nations is hereby declared to be illegal….

The Sherman Act authorized the U.S. attorney general to initiate lawsuits against firms regarded as acting in restraint of trade by establishing or attempting to establish illegal trusts. Some of these lawsuits were eventually settled by the U.S. Supreme Court. But in 1911 the Supreme Court broke up only two big businesses—Standard Oil and American Tobacco. Over time, other trusts also disappeared, but not as a result of government action. Something else must have been at work to undo the trusts. That something was competition.

The Economics of Monopolies

Consumers benefit from **competition**, the rivalry between businesses striving to earn income by offering the goods and services consumers wish to have. Market economies depend on competition to control prices and encourage the production of better quality in goods and services. But lower prices can be a problem for business owners seeking large profits, which may be increased if prices can be kept high.

Even though most industries in the United States are competitive, some are more competitive than others. The degree of competition affects the decisions firms make. Firms in a purely competitive industry are so small relative to their industry that they can have no influence over prices charged. Purely competitive industries are ones in which there are many suppliers, each holding a relatively small share of market sales, each selling the same product. The market for corn or soy beans is an example.

Firms that gain a measure of monopoly power, on the other hand, face less competition, and they can have success in keeping prices high. **Monopoly** power is the power to dominate an industry. An extreme case would be a pure monopoly—an industry with only one supplier, selling a unique product in a market that is difficult to enter, often because of high start-up costs. A pharmaceutical company with a patent on a unique type of cancer medication might be an example.

Angry farmers and muckraking journalists aren't the only opponents of monopolies. Economists also object to monopolies in the private sector. Why? First, monopolies may hurt consumers. Successful monopolies can charge prices higher than the prices that would be charged in a competitive market. Thus, consumers pay more. Second, monopolies hurt society as a whole. At the higher prices monopolists charge, consumers buy less. The result is a decrease in what otherwise would be produced for sale, which also makes society less well off.

Big Businesses Seek to Form Monopolies

In the late 19th century, most industries in the U.S. economy were fiercely competitive. Some industrialists reacted to the competition they faced by trying to control their markets and gain monopoly power. They experimented with various forms of collusion, or "gentlemen's agreements," in which they agreed to set prices and not engage in underselling one another. They also experimented with "pools," according to which they agreed not to compete in one another's territories. However, these schemes rarely worked, and industrialists were seldom able to hold prices at uncompetitive rates.[1]

Business owners therefore sought other ways to consolidate so that they could limit production and keep prices high. One way to do that was to put pressure on all or most producers in a given industry to combine. From 1895 to 1900, hundreds of firms "disappeared" as they combined or merged with other firms. These combinations involved vertical integration and horizontal integration.

Vertical integration occurs when a firm acquires resources all along the chain of production. Carnegie Steel Company used vertical integration to control not only the mills where its steel was manufactured but also the mines that supplied the iron ore for that steel, the coal mines that supplied the coal for energy, the ships that transported the iron ore, and the railroads that transported coal to the factories.

Horizontal integration occurs when firms in an industry merge. It is the widening of a business at a given point in the supply chain. For example, a grocery store chain might wish to expand its business by acquiring other grocery store companies, or a fast food chain that sells fried chicken might wish to acquire another fast food provider that sells tacos. Horizontal integration enables firms to increase their sales among a larger pool of the same type of potential customers. In the1880s, Standard Oil expanded horizontally by acquiring oil refineries in cities in the Northeast.

The Rise of Trusts

In the 1880s, some owners of big businesses used horizontal integration to form trusts as a way to gain monopoly power. This occurred among meatpackers, railroads, and producers of sugar, lead, whiskey, salt, oil, cottonseed oil, and steel. A **trust** is a type of business merger. It worked this way: business owners in the sugar industry, for example, would agree to place control of their firms in the hands of a single board of directors. They also would agree—and they would *trust* one another to follow the agreement—that no individual company would diverge from the practices established by the directors of the trust. The goal of trust arrangements was to make it difficult for one business to reduce its prices in order to out-compete the others.

Beginning early in the 20th century, giant enterprises dominated the American economy. The big enterprises were usually corporations. A **corporation** is a business owned by shareholders who possess ownership rights to the firm's profits. Ownership rights are represented by stocks. Corporations are legal entities separate from their owners. A corporation is liable for its debts; it may earn profits; and it pays taxes.

The development of the corporation provided a convenient approach to establishing trusts. Stockholders in several corporations would transfer their shares to a single board of directors. In the case of Standard Oil, all its properties were given to a board of trustees in 1882. In exchange, the stockholders would receive a certificate entitling them to a specified share of the consolidated earnings of the companies in the trust. In the case of Standard Oil, each stockholder received 20 trust shares for each share of Standard Oil stock he or she owned. Finally, all profits from the consolidated companies were sent to the trustees, who set the dividends (payments to stock holders) and selected the directors and officers of all the participating companies. In the case of Standard Oil, nine trustees made these decisions. These arrangements allowed Standard Oil to function as a near monopoly. Trusts of this sort dominated several industries

It's Hard to Hold a Trust Together

Economic historian Naomi Lamoreaux studied the merging or consolidation of American business in the late 19th century and early 20th centuries. She calculated that 157 consolidations took place in the manufacturing sector of the economy between 1895 and 1904. During the same period, more than 1,800 businesses disappeared.[2] Businesses close down for various reasons, of course, but the consolidations must have played a part in some of the 1,800 closures. Even in such a business climate, however, it proved to be difficult for a dominant producer to maintain monopoly power. Market economies offer incentives that, over time, make it difficult for any firm to maintain control over a particular sector of the market. To see how this works, let's do a "thought experiment." Imagine the following classroom scene:

Mr. Morgan's History Class

Mr. Morgan: "Good morning. In today's history class, I'd like to try a little experiment. I am holding a $100 bill. I will give it to the member of the class who offers me the highest individual bid for it. Now I am going to step out of the room so that you can discuss my offer."

Andrew: "Hey, everyone. I might not be the best history student, but I sure can tell a great opportunity when I see one. I say that you all agree to give Mr. Morgan a bid of $0. I'll bid a penny. We'll come out with $99.99. We can use the money for a class party."

Alexis: "Sounds like a great idea to me."

Maria: "Count me in!"

John: "Let the fun begin!"

Other heads nod. Everyone appears to agree with Andrew's idea. Mr. Morgan returns to the classroom.

Mr. Morgan: "Okay, now let me explain how the bidding process will work. Each of you may submit a bid for the $100. Just write the amount of your bid and your name on a small piece of paper, seal it in the envelope I am providing, and turn it in to me. I will open the bids after class. All bids will remain confidential. Don't even write your name on the outside of the envelope. I will give the $100 bill to the highest bidder after school, in secret."

Mr. Morgan then allows the students to write down their bids, and he collects them.

Here is the question for the thought experiment: What do you think will happen? You can see the problem. Some students, protected by Mr. Morgan's confidential bidding procedure, will be tempted to "cheat." To out-fox Andrew, someone might offer two pennies. Or someone might offer $99.00—content to make just one dollar.

This situation is much like the one that faced 19th-century business leaders who tried to hold their trusts together. As long as trust members cooperated, the trust could hold. But competition was always a possibility. Competitors always had an incentive to break away and undersell others holding to the trust.

What Destroyed the Trusts: Competition or Government?

Competition, it turned out, was the biggest trust buster of them all. There are many tales from this period about failed attempts at consolidation, undone by competition. Economic historian Stanley Lebergott tells of one effort by Rockefeller and other oil producers to establish domination of their market in 1872. Their agreement was called the Treaty of Titusville. The plan was that all the producers of oil would stop drilling for an agreed-upon time. If they all stopped, they believed, they could force the price of oil to rise. It seemed like a good plan, and prices did begin to rise. But not all producers agreed with the plan. Producers in Clarion County, Pennsylvania, kept on drilling despite the agreement. As you can imagine, they were despised by the other producers. They were accused of being narrow minded and acting stubbornly. But they broke the trust, and prices of oil began to fall.[3]

Economic historians Werner Troesken and Karen Clay describe how the Whiskey Trust dominated the market for producers of alcoholic spirits from 1887 to 1895. As the trust gained control over its market during those years, it raised its prices. But higher prices acted as incentives, attracting new producers to the market. The new producers "cheated" by undercutting the price established by the trust, and the trust fell apart in 1895. Although the trust reorganized later, it never regained its former market power.[4]

A trust known as the Sugar Trust provides another example. It became, according to economic historian Gerald Gunderson, "a comedy of errors." Gunderson explains that when members of the trust raised their prices, competitors from outside the trust would appear almost overnight. Farmers from the West began growing sugar beets to compete with cane sugar. Other farmers began producing sugar cane in Louisiana. Importers began purchasing sugar cane from other nations. As new suppliers came on the scene, sugar prices fell.[5]

HISTORICAL QUESTIONS & ECONOMIC ANSWERS

Why did Standard Oil not control oil prices when it held monopoly power?

Rockefeller was a monopolist in the sense that his company, Standard Oil, was the dominant producer in the oil industry. One might think, then, that Standard Oil could have been effective in efforts to keep prices high.

The mere fact of Standard Oil's dominance, however, did not mean that there was no competition in the oil industry. No law prevented new firms from entering the oil industry. Other business people noticed that Standard Oil was earning impressive profits. They began to jump into the market, imitating Standard Oil's innovations and searching for ways to reduce their costs while offering quality products. New enterprises, established even while Standard Oil dominated the market, included the J. M. Guffey Petroleum Company (later known as Gulf Oil). It began operations in 1901. The Texas Company (later known as Texaco) was formed in 1902. Competition from new firms entering the market prevented Standard Oil from controlling prices.

Is it essential to have many sellers to ensure competition?

No. Economic historian Gerald Gunderson suggests that the traditional definition of a monopoly—an industry where there is only one seller—is misleading.[6] The sole producer in a market usually lasts only as long as it takes for competitors to catch up, destroying it or cutting it down to size. The leading seller is usually the industry innovator. Andrew Carnegie is a good example. He drove his competitors crazy by continuing to improve his methods of steel production while reducing his costs and his prices. He did this because he feared that—if he didn't—another company might find a way to produce steel at a lower cost than his cost of production; in that case he would lose his customers to that other company.

If having many sellers is not the hallmark of a competitive market, what is?

A better indicator of competition is not how many producers there are, but the ease with which new competitors can enter the industry. Questions to ask are: Is there any law or regulation preventing entry? Can the market be contested by new arrivals in the industry? Governments, perhaps acting in response to pressure from existing businesses, sometimes bar new businesses from entering a market. For example, the City of Chicago prohibits street vendors from selling flowers. The City of Los Angeles goes further and prohibits all sidewalk vending. (The fact that stores pay property taxes, and street vendors do not, may help to explain such prohibitions.) The City of Milwaukee allows only 50 cabs to serve its main airport. If you wish to be the 51st taxi driver to provide cab service to air travelers, you are out of luck. Except when governmental restrictions make it illegal, however, new competitors almost always find ways to enter into markets that look promising.

William C. Durant, and his wife, in the 1920s.

Where do competitors come from?

Competitors can emerge from nearly anywhere, but often they come from within an industry or a related industry. In the early 1900s, for example, the Ford Motor company dominated the automobile market. An entrepreneur named William C. Durant, however, saw an opportunity. In the 1890s, Durant had led the Durant-Dort Carriage Company, a manufacturer of horse-drawn carriages. Durant reasoned that his long-term interests might not be well served if he stuck to manufacturing carriages, so he made a change. He founded General Motors (GM) and used it to produce Buick automobiles. Soon he acquired Oldsmobile and Cadillac. General Motors took off in the 1920s. While Ford clung stubbornly to a basic design for its automobiles, GM offered stylish colors, new designs, and new features like heaters and better tires. For a while, competition pushed Ford to the side of the road.

Today, many American companies face stiff competition from businesses headquartered in other countries. Ford and GM, for example, compete with international rivals such as Toyota, Honda, and Hyundai.

QUESTIONS for DISCUSSION

1. Why do economists object to monopolies?
2. How could competition have acted as a "trust buster"?
3. One definition of "monopoly" is an industry in which there is only one seller. What is another definition of the term?
4. Apart from counting how many sellers there are in a market, is there a better way of knowing if a market is competitive? Explain your answer.
5. What do you think is the more effective form of trust busting: competition or government action authorized by the Sherman Antitrust Act? Explain your answer.

"Fighting Bob" and the Railroads

Railroads in the United States were built with governmental assistance in the form of subsidies and land grants. Railroad owners resisted the construction of parallel rail lines that would enable one railroad to compete with another. Railroad owners tended to establish regional monopolies, which drew strong complaints from farmers.

Robert "Fighting Bob" La Follette was a Wisconsin politician who served as a governor, and as a U.S. senator. In 1924, he ran for the presidency on the Progressive Party ticket. He got approximately one-sixth of the popular vote.

Examine the cartoon below, read La Follette's statement regarding railroads, and answer the questions that follow.

PRIMARY SOURCE

La Follette's Message on Railroad Regulation, 1904: Wages and Rates

Whenever the public complains that [freight hauling] rates are unjustly increased, we are at once told in a sweeping, though somewhat indefinite way that [rates] . . . have been . . . increased [to meet] expenses and higher wages paid to employees. The corporations well understand the public regard for all the men employed in this hazardous calling, and that such an explanation will go a long way to quiet criticism.

It is true that [the cost of] material is somewhat higher. It is likewise true that companies are paying higher wages or rather higher salaries. The total wages paid by the roads of late years have increased, owing mostly to the increase in the number of men employed to handle the traffic or business. But the total wages per mile of road from 1897 to 1902 did not increase over 32 cent which is a much lower ratio of increase than the increase in both gross and net earnings.[7]

PRIMARY SOURCE · QUESTIONS for DISCUSSION

1. How does this 1906 cartoon depict Senator La Follette?
2. What is Senator La Follette's view of the railroads? Explain your answer.
3. Today we hear few complaints about railroad monopolies. What brought competition to the railroad industry? To respond to this question, think about vehicles you see every day.

The most well-known antitrust case in recent times was *United States v. Microsoft*. Beginning in the spring of 1998, the U.S. Department of Justice (DOJ) charged that Microsoft used monopoly power when it added an Internet browser (Internet Explorer) to its Windows operating system. This might seem surprising. After all, today's computer industry is home to many competitors including Apple, Linux, Google, and Facebook.

After a lengthy trial, at which Bill Gates testified in person—and an appeal, and millions of dollars in legal fees—the DOJ announced in 2001 that it would no longer seek to break up Microsoft. Later in 2001, the DOJ reached a legal settlement with Microsoft, according to which Microsoft would be subject to ongoing scrutiny of its practices. However, Microsoft was not prevented from bundling future software to its Windows operating system. To critics of Microsoft, this "slap on the wrist" was a huge disappointment.

Antitrust prosecutions today seem to be problematic. In the Microsoft case, teams of lawyers worked for a long time in an effort that led, from the prosecutors' point of view, to very little. Similar antitrust prosecutions in the future may also be problematic, for three main reasons.

First, nobody has clearly defined what constitutes a monopoly. Economists, legislators, and lawyers have argued for various definitions of the term, without succeeding in settling the question. Is the key issue whether, in a given industry, there is only one producer? If so, there will not be many successful prosecutions, since nearly every industry in the United States is served by many producers, each holding market shares. In fact, in a market economy, we are likely to find sole-producer industries only when the government declares that it is illegal for competitors to enter that market. This situation is called, somewhat curiously, a natural monopoly.

A natural monopoly exists when a single producer can supply the entire market more efficiently than multiple producers could. One example is local providers of cable television. Providing cable television requires a large initial investment to cover the cost of wiring homes and businesses. These fixed costs are high, while the variable costs of providing television programming are relatively low. Cable companies have often been granted exclusive contracts by local governments to wire various cities and counties. That is, some local governments have established rules to prevent competitors from entering the cable market.

Recent technological developments now threaten even natural monopolies. Cable television today competes with providers of satellite television; online innovators today offer more and more entertainment to homes at low cost, or no cost. Competitive forces make it hard for a monopoly, even a natural monopoly, to survive.

Second, nobody has clearly and conclusively defined what constitutes a competitive market. How many competitors are enough? If the market in question is narrowly defined, there may be few competitors. In the Microsoft case, the market was defined as computer operating systems for stand-alone personal computers using microchips of the kind manufactured by Intel. This definition left out the operating systems running Apple computers, and Sun Microsystems. Given the narrow definition, Microsoft clearly dominated the market. But a broader definition would have revealed many competitors.

Third, there is the problem of monopoly pricing. The traditional defense of antitrust regulations, calling for breaking up dominant producers, is that monopolies will charge low prices initially, gain control of the market, and then charge high prices as soon they can get away with doing so. But Microsoft was never accused of charging higher prices in this manner. In fact, Microsoft offered its Internet browser free of charge, undermining rival browser Netscape. In reality, most of the well-known antitrust cases in the United States have involved businesses that charged lower prices than their competitors. Often it is complaints from unsuccessful competitors that have caused the government to act. It is nearly impossible to find a case where harm is done to consumers by a leading producer increasing prices.

THEN & NOW QUESTIONS for DISCUSSION

1. Why was Microsoft thought to be a monopoly by the Department of Justice?
2. What are some problems that make antitrust prosecutions problematic today?
3. What is a natural monopoly?
4. What destroys natural monopolies? Can you provide a new example?

Web Resources

Monopoly
http://www.econlib.org/library/Enc/Monopoly.html

An article that explains monopolies and their economic effects.

Trusts and Monopolies
http://projects.vassar.edu/1896/trusts.html

A short introduction to trusts and monopolies. The site includes links to political cartoons.

History of Monopolies in the United States
http://www.econedlink.org/lessons/index.php?lid=628&type=educator

Activities, resources, and lesson plans on monopolies.

U.S. v. Microsoft
http://www.justice.gov/atr/cases/f3800/msjudgex.htm

Read the actual case against Microsoft.

How Did Financial Panics Lead to the Establishment of an Independent Central Bank?

This magazine illustration shows a stock exchange closing its door to keep panicked members out during the Panic of 1873.

Imagine someone who controlled five banks, a railroad, and factories employing 10,000 people in 1872. Would that person have been considered rich? Undoubtedly! Yet that person, Senator William Sprague IV (1830–1915), lost most of his fortune by 1874. The event that caused most of his fortune to evaporate was called the Panic of 1873.

Sprague's biography reads like a soap opera or movie script, complete with high triumphs and stunning setbacks. His father was murdered when young William was only 13. As a young adult he seemed to have much better luck, inheriting a fortune at age 26 and serving with distinction in the Union Army at the battle of Bull Run. He was elected governor of Rhode Island and then U.S. senator for Rhode Island. He married Washington D.C.'s most eligible bachelorette, Kate Chase. She was the daughter of Secretary of the Treasury Salmon P. Chase, who later became Chief Justice of the U.S. Supreme Court.

But then came the Panic of 1873. Sprague lost his fortune as his banks and businesses faltered. His marriage to Kate ended amid allegations of her infidelity. After a long career in business and public service, Sprague had planned to live out his years at the family estate in Rhode Island—but it burned to the ground.[1]

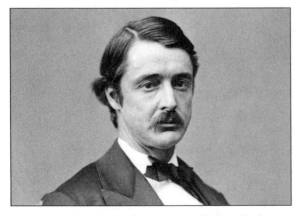

William Sprague IV, the political and business leader whose family fortune was lost in the Panic of 1873.

KEY ECONOMIC CONCEPTS

Federal Reserve System   Money supply
Financial panic   Reserves
Monetary policy

Economic events shape personal stories. No one knows whether Sprague's good luck as an adult would have continued if the Panic of 1873 had never happened. But for rich and poor alike, the financial panics of the 1800s were life-changing. Bank failures hurt not only the banks' owners and customers, but also farmers and manufacturers with minimal ties to the financial system. How did these financial panics lead to creation of a powerful central bank, the Federal Reserve System? And why was the Federal Reserve set up with a high degree of independence from the political system?

The Historical Context
Financial Panics in the 1800s

A **financial panic** occurs when banks suddenly lose a large amount of their value, causing fear and widespread losses among their customers. Several panics occurred between 1819 and 1893. The financial system was free-wheeling in those days, with money being issued not only by the federal government but also by states, cities, and even private banks. Privately issued bank money was referred to as "wildcat money," after a Michigan bank that issued a currency that became worthless in a panic. That bank's money bore a picture of a wildcat.[2]

The federal government could do little to intervene in financial panics in the 1800s. Because money could be issued from many different sources, including banks, there was no centralized control over the economy's money. In a panic, financial losses led to widespread economic weakness, including losses of production and jobs. Eventually the economy would right itself after a panic, but in the meantime the distress was real.

The Economics of Money and Banking

Many people use self-storage warehouses. They rent a space there, put items into storage, and return when they want to use the items again. Banks, however, are not "money warehouses." They do not just keep money in storage until a depositor comes to reclaim it. Instead, they group, or "pool," money that might otherwise be idle; then they lend money from the pool to customers who are likely to repay it. Individual customers can buy goods and services with the money they borrow, and business customers can use loans to expand their operations. In this way, the money banks lend produces additional goods and services. The money can also produce a profit for the bank, which charges interest for loans.

Historically, what made banks useful also made them vulnerable. If a bank had lent out some of its deposits, it literally did not have all of its customers' money at hand. Ordinarily, lending out deposits was not a problem. Customers preferred to keep most of their money in the bank. But when a panic occurred and a bank's customers all tried to withdraw their money at the same time, the bank would be unable to meet their demands.

Because banks lend out customers' money, they have always had some **reserves**—that is, funds set aside for emergency use. If a bank faced an abnormally high number of customers seeking to withdraw cash, it could use its reserves. Before the Federal Reserve System was established in 1913, banks kept their reserves at other banks for security. The chain stretched from small-town agricultural banks to the financial center of New York City. The small-town banks kept their reserves at larger banks in nearby cities, geographic nearness being important in a day before rapid communications became possible. The city banks in turn kept their reserves in New York City banks. A bank that kept its emergency funds at another bank (experiencing a panic)

might find its money to be unavailable, too, when it was most needed.

A financial panic could start with the failure of a single large industrial firm with money on deposit in major banks, perhaps in New York. By pulling out its money, that company could endanger the New York bank's health. To come up with enough reserves in the face of such a failure, the banks might try to sell their holdings. In addition to the loans banks made, they also purchased and held *stocks*, certificates of partial ownership in corporations, as well as *bonds*, or certificates promising to repay borrowed money. Banks could sell these certificates if they needed to raise money quickly. Yet when large amounts of bank holdings came onto the market at the same time, the prices of stocks and bonds fell. Then the problem worsened, as banks realized they had to sell *more* stocks and bonds to replenish reserves. The result would be a full-blown panic among the banks trying to raise cash.

A banking panic would spread fear from the New York City banks to large city banks to small-town banks serving rural areas. Depositors anywhere in the country could wake up one morning to learn that their money—all their personal savings deposited in banks—was gone. For that reason, when bank failures seemed likely, people rushed to banks to withdraw all their money before others got there first. People were panicked about getting to the bank too late.

As we saw earlier, an important function of banks is to lend money. When banks lend, the loans they make become part of the **money supply**, the total quantity of money in the economy. Money resulting from loans is part of the money supply, along with the money in your pockets, your savings account, and your checking account. Bank lending affects how much money there is in the economy overall.

By the late 1800s, the United States had developed an important banking system, but it was a system that operated without central direction. This banking system was subject to financial panics of the sort that wiped out William Sprague's fortune. In the wake of these panics, support grew for a more stable banking system. A National Monetary Commission created by Congress in

1908 studied the problem and issued reports that became the basis for the Federal Reserve Act of 1913. The act was signed into law by President Woodrow Wilson, and the Federal Reserve System went into operation in 1914.

The **Federal Reserve System** is our nation's central bank, an institution designed to coordinate and serve the entire banking system. It is often called the Fed. The Fed provides a government-backed way for banks to hold reserves. With the Fed in place, a country bank could keep its reserves at the Fed instead of relying on the health of a nearby city bank, which in turn would be dependent on the health of a New York City bank.

The Fed was also set up as "lender of last resort"—that is, a bank in trouble could turn to the Fed if all else failed. With this new system in place, if a sound bank faces a cash crisis, it does not need permanent assistance. Rather, it only needs an opportunity to meet cash demands and to continue collecting loan payments so that it can replenish its reserves. Beyond its role in holding banks' reserves and in being a lender of last resort, however, the Fed came to have a major influence on national economic policy.

Before the Fed was established, the total amount of money in the economy—the money supply—was not controlled at the national level. Instead the money supply was determined by lending choices made by individual banks. The creation of the Fed meant that national control of the money supply would be possible.

Economists now know that changes in the money supply can have far-reaching effects on an economy. For example, an economy that begins to slow down might be aided by an increase in the money supply. A carefully applied injection of money into the banking system can keep the economy from slowing down too much. Or, if an economy threatens to expand too fast for stability, it can be slowed by reductions in the amount of money in the system.

Monetary policy is the control of the money supply and the banking system, exercised to influence the economy. In the United States, monetary policy is conducted by the Federal Reserve System.

HISTORICAL QUESTIONS & ECONOMIC ANSWERS

How could a panic's results spread so far through the economy?

If a panic caused all depositors to try to withdraw their money at the same time, their bank's cash holdings would not be enough. With reserves depleted, the bank might have to close. But then the problems would spread to nonbanking firms. First, these firms could lose access to their money as a direct effect of the panic (when their banks closed). Second, nonbanking firms could lose access to bank loans they needed to finance their operations. Third, the customers of nonbanking firms could lose access to their money.

As a result, the panic could depress activity throughout the economy. A farm equipment dealer in Kansas, for example, could find its customers unable to pay for equipment they purchased on credit because the customers' Topeka bank had its Chicago reserves wiped out. A mine in Colorado might find itself unable to pay its employees' wages because its Denver bank had closed. A farmer in Pennsylvania might be unable to borrow money for spring planting.

Why is the Fed politically independent?

The Federal Reserve was set up with a high degree of political independence. It is run by seven governors who have unusually long terms—14 years. Other government appointees automatically change when a new presidential administration comes into power, but not the Fed's governors. The Fed's governors may not be removed for policy differences in the way that a Secretary of Defense might be. Fed supporters say that its independence is crucial because it may have to make politically unpopular decisions that are nonetheless necessary for the economy's long-term health. If the economy is running too fast, the Fed might decide to cut back on the money supply. This "tighter" money supply will slow things down and, typically, cause interest rates to rise. The cost of buying on credit throughout

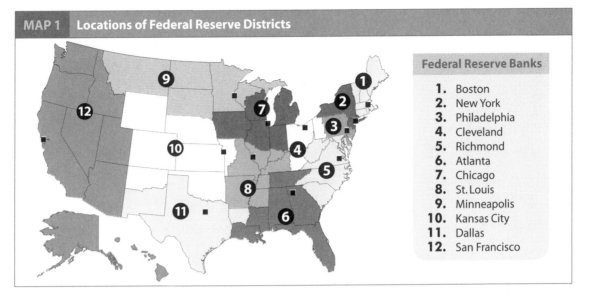

MAP 1 | Locations of Federal Reserve Districts

Federal Reserve Banks

1. Boston
2. New York
3. Philadelphia
4. Cleveland
5. Richmond
6. Atlanta
7. Chicago
8. St. Louis
9. Minneapolis
10. Kansas City
11. Dallas
12. San Francisco

the economy will then be higher. Car dealers, homebuilders, and farmers will be hit hard.

When those hurt by tighter money complain to the president and Congress, it is important that the Fed be able to hold the line. Abandoning the fight against inflation could make matters worse for everyone. Although the president and members of Congress may criticize the Fed's policy in cases of this sort, they can also say that they have no ability to control the Fed. Describing just such a possibility, a former Fed governor said the Fed's job is "to take away the punch bowl just as the party gets going."[3]

There have been attempts to assert greater political control over the Fed. Critics believe that the Fed should be accountable to public opinion. But taking power away from the unelected Fed governors would mean giving it to someone else. The alternative would most likely be the president or Congress; either one might be susceptible to political pressures to create too much (or too little) money in a short time.

Why was the Federal Reserve partly centralized and partly decentralized?

When the Fed was created in 1913, there were many disputes about how it should be structured and what powers it should have. Although rural interests saw the benefit of having a central bank and more flexibility in the money supply, they were also wary of a powerful governmental body that would run the banking system. They wanted to be sure that voices from around the nation would be heard within the central bank's governing body. Urban interests wanted a central bank with enough power to stop the panics.

A compromise was embodied in the Federal Reserve Act of 1913. The Act centralized power in a national Board of Governors appointed by the president and confirmed by the Senate. However, it also divided the country into 12 districts, each with its own Federal Reserve Bank (see Map 1). Federal Reserve power was to be shared across this complex structure.[4]

QUESTIONS for DISCUSSION

1. Before 1913, how could the failure of a New York bank hurt a country bank that had no direct ties to New York?
2. Would the economy be better off if banks served only as money warehouses, keeping individuals' deposits and not lending them? Explain your answer.
3. What would be the effect of shortening Federal Reserve governors' terms to four years, expiring in presidential-election years, so that the governors could be replaced by an incoming new president?

Report on the Panic of 1907

Here are some paragraphs from the report of the Comptroller of the Currency, a federal official. The report concerns the last financial panic before the establishment of the Federal Reserve System.

Central Bank of Issue and Reserve

The conditions which led to the panic of October and November, 1907, were not due to the failure of a few individual banks. They were not due to the lack of confidence of the people in the banks, but more to a lack of confidence of the banks in themselves and their reserves. Banks have been fearful that the reserve system would break down, and in consequence it has broken down, and the reserve deposits have been only partially available. They were also fearful that not sufficent currency could be supplied to meet the demand, and as they all made the demand at once, there has not been sufficient currency. The result has been currency famine.

The remedy for this state of affairs is to improve the reserve system so that the reserve deposits of the banks can be kept in a bank where they are surely and certainly available.

[The] most desirable changes can be best accomplished—in fact, they can only be satisfactorily acomplished—through the establishment by the Government of a central bank of issue and reserve. This is the system which has been adopted and found to work most satisfactorily in the great commerical countries of Europe and is the one that gives the surest promise of satisfactory operation in this country.

Source: Senate Committee on Banking and Currency, "Annual Report of the Comptroller of the Currency, 1907," *Federal Banking Laws and Reports: A Compilation of Major Federal Banking Documents, 1780–1912* (Washington: U.S. Government Printing Office, 1963), pp. 453–463.

PRIMARY SOURCE — QUESTIONS for DISCUSSION

1. The Comptroller says the Panic of 1907 was not caused by a few individual bank failures or even by customers' loss of faith in banks. What was the cause?
2. According to the Comptroller's report, what is the cure for this reserve problem?
3. If banks began selling stocks and bonds in a financial panic, what would happen to the prices of those stocks and bonds? How could the very act of responding to a panic make the panic worse?

THEN & NOW

The Modern Equivalent of 1800s Financial Panics

The 21st-century banking system of the United States does not experience financial panics exactly like those of the 1800s, but from time to time there is still panic. Bank runs, however, are no longer the problem. Operating in conjunction with the Fed, the Federal Deposit Insurance Corporation (FDIC) guarantees that customers will not lose insured deposits (up to $250,000 in a single bank). The closing of an insolvent bank has become essentially routine and trouble-free. Often the old bank will close on a Friday; teams will take over during the weekend; and the bank will reopen Monday, possibly under a new name, but its customers will lose no money.

Today the main concern is not the loss of depositors' money but the larger economic effects of financial failures. The 2008–2010 crisis tested regulators' abilities because of its size and scope. In today's economy, banks lend large amounts of money back and forth for short time periods. Ordinarily there is no concern about banks' being able to pay each other back. But in 2008, many banks were holding loans of questionable value. The loans had been made to people who might not be able to repay. Would banks in turn be able to repay their loans to one another? Because of that doubt, there was a financial panic—not of individuals worrying about their money, but of banks worried about other banks. The Federal Reserve provided large amounts of money to eliminate the panic.

Figure 1 shows how large the Fed's intervention was. Notice that the Fed's response to the terrorist attacks of September 11, 2001, considered large at the time, is a tiny blip on the graph compared to what happened when the financial system began to fail in fall 2008. The recent response dwarfs the size of the entire banking system of the 1800s.

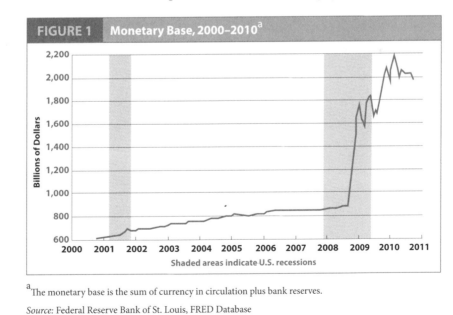

FIGURE 1   Monetary Base, 2000–2010[a]

Shaded areas indicate U.S. recessions

[a]The monetary base is the sum of currency in circulation plus bank reserves.

Source: Federal Reserve Bank of St. Louis, FRED Database

QUESTIONS for DISCUSSION

1. If the Federal Reserve has solved the problem of loss of reserves by banks, why is a financial panic still possible?
2. Should large financial firms facing heavy losses simply be allowed to fail? Why or why not?
3. Is your deposited money safer today in a struggling bank, or safer kept at your home? Explain your answer.

Web Resources

New York and the Panic of 1873
http://cityroom.blogs.nytimes.com/2008/10/14/learning-lessons-from-the-panic-of-1873

Additional historical information on the Panic of 1873.

The Financial Panic of 1907: Running from History
http://www.smithsonianmag.com/history-archaeology/1907_Panic.html

An overview of the Panic of 1907 and how it relates to current economic problems.

The Founding of the Fed
http://www.ny.frb.org/aboutthefed/history_article.html

Chronological history of the establishment of the Federal Reserve System.

Federal Reserve Economic Education
http://www.federalreserveeducation.org

A comprehensive teacher resource from the Federal Reserve, including videos and lesson plans.

Who Was the *Titanic* Baby and Where Was He Going?

Passengers flee on lifeboats as the Titanic goes down.

Tragedy at Sea amid a Flood of Immigrants

When the steamship *Titanic* sank on April 15, 1912, many passengers housed in the lower part of the ship (third class) did not make it out alive. One who did survive was the "*Titanic* baby," 10-month-old Frank Aks.

In the confusion after the *Titanic* struck an iceberg and began filling with water, Frank was separated from his mother, Leah. One account even suggested that Frank was dropped or thrown into a lifeboat. Leah survived on a separate lifeboat. Mother and child were reunited on board the *Carpathia*, a passenger ship that picked up *Titanic* survivors.

When the *Titanic* went down, Leah and Frank were traveling on their way from Poland to the United States, where they would join husband and father, Samuel Aks. It might seem surprising that a Polish family would voluntarily undergo as much hardship and separation as the Aks family did when the father traveled to the United States. He left behind his wife, who was expecting a child. Reuniting the family would depend on job prospects that he could not find in Poland.

The Aks family story is similar to that of many other immigrants to the United States. Many individuals left home, knowing that they might never see their friends, family, or homeland again. Many immigrants arriving from 1880 to 1920 did not speak English and did not understand American traditions. Why did these

Leah and Samuel Aks, with their son, Frank.

KEY ECONOMIC CONCEPTS

Immigration
Opportunity cost

immigrants risk so much to come to the United States? And what was the economic effect of this large influx—on the immigrants and on their new home economy?

The Historical Context
A Wave of Immigrants

A huge wave of immigrants came to the United States between 1880 and 1920, many seeking better jobs than they could find in Europe. This was the story for the Aks family. Samuel became a successful tailor in Norfolk, Virginia. He quickly saved enough money to send for his wife Leah and 10-month-old Frank, who had been born in his absence. The third-class fare for two was almost 19 British pounds (about $1,600 in today's money)— an enormous amount at that time.

The plight of immigrants sailing to America was difficult and harsh by today's standards. Today we would consider conditions aboard the *Titanic* for third-class passengers to be crude. For 700 third-class passengers there were only two bathtubs. After immigrants arrived in America, success was not instantaneous or guaranteed. In time, however, most immigrants improved both their home and work conditions.

The Aks family story illustrates a common pattern, with the father coming to the United States first. If the father succeeded, he could send for the rest of the family. After being reunited in the United States, the family would enjoy a higher standard of living. For most of those in the 1880–1920 wave of immigration, the risky decision to move to America would be vindicated by favorable results.

This photo shows the last lifeboat from the Titanic *just before survivors are picked up by the* Carpathia.

The Economics of Immigration

Immigration is the act of moving to a new country. We can think about immigration and its effects in at least three ways: (1) as an individual choice; (2) as an influence on particular locations or occupations affected by immigrants; and (3) as an influence that affects the whole economy of a country receiving immigrants. Economics helps us to understand all three views.

1. Immigration as an individual choice.

Potential immigrants always have at least two choices: stay or go. "Stay" may be a comfortable choice, since it involves:

- remaining close to family and friends and homeland,
- continuing to get along with a familiar job and language,
- experiencing less uncertainty about life in general, and
- avoiding the hazards of travel.

Given strong reasons to stay, it is no surprise that many of Samuel Ak's friends and neighbors made that choice.

"Go" is a more adventurous and risky choice. The immigrant gives up familiar things. Remember that in any decision you make, the **opportunity cost** is what you give up—that is the next-best alternative you did not choose. Giving up familiar surroundings can amount to a high opportunity cost. In return, however, the immigrant might gain important benefits:

- better career opportunities, and
- a chance to attain a higher standard of living, for the individual immigrant and for the entire family.

In the case of Samuel Aks, there was another powerful force at work. As a Polish Jew, he faced the possibility of deadly religious persecution if he stayed home. Pogroms (riots directed against Jews) killed hundreds of Jewish people in Russian-occupied parts of Poland during the years leading up to Aks's decision.[1]

Although the Aks family's decision was "go" rather than "stay," the *Titanic's* fate certainly affected their plans. Samuel Aks would not have booked passage on the *Titanic* for his wife and child if he had known the ship would sink. Still, with the knowledge he had at the time of his decision, the *Titanic* was a reasonable choice. It was operated by the respected White Star Line. A White Star brochure about the *Titanic* and sister ship *Olympic* stated that "as far as it is possible to do so, these two wonderful vessels are designed to be unsinkable."[2]

Completing the picture of expected benefits and costs, immigrants knew that labor incomes were relatively high in the United States, with its growing economy and scarce supply of labor. The high demand for labor, together with the limited supply, made wages high. Based on the knowledge the Aks family had at the time, moving to the United States was a reasonable choice.

2. Immigration's influence on particular locations and occupations.

As immigrants arrive in a new country and begin working, they increase the supply of labor in specific occupations and places. Taken by itself, this increase makes wages lower. Tailoring in Norfolk, Virginia, became somewhat less profitable in 1912 because of the competition provided by Samuel Aks. It is not an isolated example. Day labor in the American West would have been more highly paid without the competition of Asian immigrants.

Immigrants' effects in particular labor markets are only part of the story, however. In addition to supplying labor, immigrants earn money and purchase goods and services. Their economic activity increases the demand for the output of all businesses, both native- and immigrant-owned, and therefore increases profits. Further, both native and immigrant consumers benefit from the greater variety of goods and services that become available when an economy grows. In Norfolk in 1912, customers in search of tailors benefited from having an additional provider of tailoring service, Samuel Aks. Over time, areas affected by immigration have not only absorbed immigrants, but have thrived because of the labor and entrepreneurial skill contributed by the immigrants.

3. Immigration's influence on the national economy.

Economists have closely studied the effects of immigration on the national economy. There are many effects to account for:

- Immigrants engage in invention, discovery, and entrepreneurship. In carrying out these activities they benefit themselves and the larger economy.

- Immigrants increase the total supply and demand for goods and services, making the entire economy larger. Because of the advantages of large-scale production, the entire economy benefits.

- Immigrants tend to come to this country after their basic schooling has been paid for, and they tend to begin working soon after arrival. The economy gets the benefit of their labor without having to bear all the costs of basic education.

- Immigrants receive government services, but they also pay taxes, depending on their work situation and legal status. Sales taxes in particular are paid by everyone who buys things in ordinary retail markets.

- Immigrants are less likely to come to the United States during periods of high unemployment. In this way they buffer the labor market against shocks. They provide additional labor when times are good; they offer less competition for jobs in times when jobs are scarce.[3]

According to economists who specialize in the issue, immigration has been positive overall for the U.S. economy.

HISTORICAL QUESTIONS & ECONOMIC ANSWERS

On average, are immigrants people just like the people who stay behind?

No. By the very fact that they are willing to leave their homelands behind, immigrants are self-selected to be more ambitious and more inclined toward risk-taking. They are also more likely to be in their prime earning years, as opposed to being very young or (especially) very old. Older people are less likely to move.

Can immigrants know that the place they're heading for will be better than the place they're leaving?

Immigrants cannot know with certainty that they will have better opportunity in a new place. They have to make their decisions based on incomplete information. This problem is not unique. People make many decisions, even big decisions, on the basis of incomplete information. In the case of immigration, incomplete information provided one reason for families to send the primary wage-earner of the family ahead. He or she could acquire first-hand knowledge of life in the United States and send information to family members back home. The family then could decide whether to reunite in the new country or back in the old country.

TABLE 1	Labor Force and Wage Statistics, 1880–1920						
Year	Total Labor Force	Total Immigration	Agricultural Labor Force	Manufacturing Labor Force	Service Labor Force	All Other Labor Force	Annual Nonfarm Wage
1880	17,390,000	457,257	8,920,000	3,290,000	1,360,000	3,820,000	$317
1890	23,320,000	455,302	9,960,000	4,390,000	1,930,000	7,040,000	$440
1900	29,070,000	448,572	11,680,000	5,895,000	2,236,000	9,259,000	$483
1910	37,480,000	1,041,570	11,770,000	8,332,000	2,685,000	14,693,000	$562
1920	41,610,000	430,001	10,790,000	11,190,000	2,412,000	17,218,000	$599

Source: Historical Statistics of the United States, wages in constant 1900 dollars. "All other" category includes fishing, mining, trade, and transportation.

Do the statistics show that the 1880–1920 wave of immigration drove down wages?

No. It is theoretically possible that a large increase in the size of the labor force, caused by immigration, could cause wages to fall. However, that is not what happened in the United States between 1880 and 1920.

Table 1 shows that the total labor force grew throughout the period. Among the years shown, the peak year for immigration was 1910, when more than a million immigrants arrived. The growing U.S. economy easily absorbed the newcomers. Annual wages were higher in each decade, starting at $317 and ending at $599.

Historically, have immigrants adapted well to the U.S. economy?

Yes. A classic study by labor economist Barry Chiswick provided impressive evidence of an "earnings crossover" among men who came to the United States. About 15 years after immigrants'

arrival, their earnings "crossed over" (exceeded) those of the native born—after having started at much lower levels than natives' earnings. Although immigrants typically began their new lives with a lack of local knowledge, and they sometimes faced discrimination, their earnings grew over time because of their ability, motivation to work, and their investments in training.[4]

Was There a Happy Ending for Frank Aks?

As a society rich in natural resources but short on labor, the United States offered high incomes to those who could immigrate and begin working. Frank Aks, the *Titanic* baby, grew up to become the successful owner of his own business, Eastern Salvage Company. He was a pillar of the community in Norfolk and a long-time member of the Congregation Beth El, the Khedive Shrine Temple, and the Jewish Community Center. After a long and successful life, he died in 1991.

QUESTIONS for DISCUSSION

1. Before the *Titanic* sailed, was it considered a safe ship? Explain your answer.
2. Why would a family endure hardship and separation to send its primary earner to the United States in the early 1900s?
3. In an immigrant family, why is it easier for the second and third generation to earn higher incomes than incomes earned by the original immigrants?
4. Prospective immigrants to the United States face a "stay or go" decision. Consider the internal movement of African Americans in large numbers early in the 20th Century from the South to the urban North (the Great Migration). How were these internal migration decisions similar to international immigration decisions? How were they different?

Was There Discrimination By Age, Gender, and Class When the *Titanic* sank?

Opportunity cost is seldom a matter of life and death, but it was exactly that on board the *Titanic* the night the *Titanic* sank. Philosophy students sometimes study "lifeboat cases": On a sinking ship with not enough lifeboats to save everyone, whose life should be spared? On board the *Titanic*, this was no idle philosophical problem.

The ethic of the time was that women and children should be given preference for survival. An adult male who boarded a lifeboat ahead of women and children would suffer a loss of honor. If he survived, he would not be known as a true gentleman. On that night in 1912, some men would calculate that an honorable death was better than the next-best alternative—life without honor. In other words: the choice of boarding a lifeboat ahead of women and children had a high opportunity cost, that of living without honor. The alternative was death in the icy North Atlantic.

What actually happened? Table 2, assembled from information collected in the inquiry that followed the sinking, shows survival rates by passenger category.

TABLE 2	Survival rates on the *Titanic*				
Passenger category	Number saved	Number lost	Percentage saved	Percentage lost	Total category percentage saved
First-class children	6	0	100%	0%	Children 52%
Second-class children	24	0	100%	0%	
Third-class children	27	52	34%	66%	
First-class women	140	4	97%	3%	Women 74%
Second-class women	80	13	86%	14%	
Third-class women	76	89	46%	54%	
Crew women	20	3	87%	13%	
First-class men	57	118	33%	67%	Men 20%
Second-class men	14	154	8%	92%	
Third-class men	75	387	16%	84%	
Crew men	192	693	22%	78%	
Total	**711**	**1513**	**32%**	**68%**	

Source: Chuck Anesi, "The *Titanic* Casualty Figures."

A group of survivors of the Titanic *disaster aboard the* Carpathia *after being rescued.*

One more factor seems to be important in such life-and-death decisions: time. Researchers have done careful statistical studies of the sinking of the *Titanic* and of the *Lusitania*, an ocean liner sunk by a German submarine in 1915. The *Lusitania* sank in just 18 minutes after it was hit, while the *Titanic* took nearly three hours to go down. On the *Lusitania*, women and children were far less likely to survive than women and children on the *Titanic*. "When you have to react very, very fast, human instincts are much faster than internalized social norms," said researcher Benno Torgler, one of the authors of the study.[6] With more time to consider, even the opportunity cost of one's own death apparently becomes thinkable.

PRIMARY SOURCE **QUESTIONS for DISCUSSION**

1. Does Table 2 suggest that the *Titanic's* crew loaded the lifeboats with "women and children first," as traditional protocol would require?
2. Compare the survival rate of third-class women with that of first-class men. Does this comparison suggest that class or gender was the more important factor in determining survival?
3. Do these survival rates prove that there was life-and-death discrimination against third-class passengers? Why or why not?

The Changing Face of Immigration

By the time the *Titanic* sailed the Atlantic, immigration had already changed a great deal. Early in the history of the United States, immigrants came mainly from Great Britain, Germany, and the Scandinavian countries. After the 1890s, however, more immigrants began arriving from central, eastern, and southern Europe. There were substantial differences between their native cultures and the emerging American culture. Still, the newly arrived immigrants followed a pattern similar to that of their predecessors. Although many started off working as unskilled laborers, the next generation—with greater skills in English and more local knowledge—moved up the economic ladder.

Today, the United States faces complex immigration policy choices. They include choices about the number and characteristics of immigrants that should be admitted, the degree of preference for immigration that reunites families, and problems of border security.

In recent years, immigration has become an important issue for the high-technology industries. To compete successfully, firms in these industries often seek to employ immigrants that are highly educated and already speak English. Many recent immigrants with technology and management skills have been highly successful in U.S. firms. Table 3 illustrates some of the biggest successes, in the form of noted companies founded by immigrants.

Technology companies report that it is difficult to get permission for their immigrant workers to remain and work in the United States. Google alone spends $4.5 million annually on administration of visas,

TABLE 3	Major U.S. Firms Founded by Immigrants
Company	**Founder**
Intel Corp.	Andy Grove, Hungary
Solectron Corp.	Winston Chen, Taiwan
Sanmina-SCI Corp.	Jule Sola, Bosnia; Milan Mandaric, Croatia
Sun Micro-systems, Inc.	Adreas Bechtolsheim, Germany; Vinod Khosla, India
eBay Inc.	Pierre Omidyar, France
Yahoo Inc.	Jerry Yang, Taiwan
Life Time Fitness Inc.	Bahram Akradi, Iran
Tetra Tech Inc.	Henri Hodara, France
UTStarcom Inc.	Ying Wu, China
Google Inc.	Sergey Brin (cofounder), Russia

Source: ZDNet Research, "Top US companies founded by immigrants: Intel, Solectron, Sanmina-SCI, Sun," November 16, 2006.

the documents that grant its immigrant employees permission to work.[7]

The national origin of immigrants has continued to change, with the largest numbers today coming from Latin America. Mexico sends more immigrants than any other country, followed by China (see Table 4).

Many first-generation immigrants do not speak English well, and they typically have little formal education. The second generation narrows the gap, often speaking fluent English. Among the third generation, most will have no gap at all in English-speaking ability or education. Rand Corporation researcher James P. Smith reported, after extensive study, "the concern that educational generational progress among Latino immigrants has

TABLE 4	Top Ten Countries of Origin for U.S. Immigrants, 2009
Nation	**New Permanent Residents**
Mexico	164,920
China	64,238
Philippines	60,029
India	57,304
Dominican Republic	49,414
Cuba	38,954
Vietnam	29,234
Colombia	27,849
South Korea	25,859
Haiti	24,280

Source: U.S. Department of Homeland Security, *2009 Yearbook of Immigration Statistics*, Washington: Office of Immigration Statistics, August 2010, p. 6.

lagged behind other immigrant groups is largely unfounded."[8] Research indicates that Latin American immigrants generally follow a pattern similar to the one followed by earlier immigrants.

Still, not all Latin American immigrants, especially those who enter the United States without permission, follow the pattern. Smith found that Hispanic male immigrants entering under U.S. immigration laws had 10.12 years of education, on average, while those entering without permission had 6.90 years (see Table 5). Immigrants with only a temporary attachment to the United States and poor English-speaking skills often find that their opportunities are limited. Yet, because they have no clear path to citizenship, they may decide it would not be worthwhile to make a large investment in learning English and gaining further education. How can immigration policy provide the right incentives in this case? The answers are not easy. Immigration is a notoriously difficult issue for the U.S. political system.

TABLE 5	Education Levels of Recent Male Immigrants, by Category	
Category	**Years of Education for All**	**Years of Education Among Hispanics**
Native born	12.99	11.52
Immigrants entering with permission	12.64	10.12
Immigrants entering without permission	10.79	6.90

Source: James P. Smith, "Immigrants and the Labor Market," *Journal of Labor Economics*, (April 2006), p. 215.

THEN & NOW — QUESTIONS for DISCUSSION

1. Early in U.S. history, where did most immigrants come from?
2. Why was there concern about the ability of post-1890s immigrants from central, eastern, and southern Europe to assimilate into the economy of the United States? Did they assimilate well?
3. What part of the world currently provides the greatest number of immigrants to the United States? Have these immigrants closed gaps in English-speaking skills and educational attainment?
4. Statistically, how do Latin American immigrants entering the United States under the immigration laws differ from those entering without permission?
5. Why is immigration such a difficult issue for the U.S. political system?

Titanic Facts

http://www.titanic-facts.com

Information about the Titanic, including pictures, passenger information, facts, and the history of the vessel.

Titanic

http://www.history.com/topics/titanic

History.com's view of the Titanic, including an analysis of the catastrophe.

The Sinking of the *Titanic*, 1912

http://www.eyewitnesstohistory.com/titanic.htm

A first-hand perspective on the sinking of the Titanic.

Then & Now: The Changing Face of Immigration

http://www.dhs.gov/files/statistics/immigration.shtm

Analytical papers and updated statistics on immigration from the Office of Immigration Statistics, part of the U.S. Department of Homeland Security.

What Made the Roaring Twenties Roar, Economically: Real Growth or a Stock Market Bubble?

Two women dance the Charleston on a railing near the U.S. Capitol Building, prompting a passer-by to join in the fun.

Most teenagers have occasional disputes with their parents as they try out their freedom, but few find that their family disagreements become the subject of newspaper articles. That was what happened to 19-year-old Eugenia Kelly of New York City in 1915. And what had caused the rift between Eugenia and her parents? The teenager was going to dance halls, smoking, and drinking. She was wearing wild fashions and behaving in an unladylike manner. Her mother said Eugenia "was likely to become depraved."

The mother-daughter dispute went to court when Eugenia's mother asked that the police arrest Eugenia for disobedience. There was a lot at stake, because Eugenia was set to inherit $10 million, a huge fortune at the time, if she could stay out of trouble. After much wrangling and a widely publicized trial, Eugenia said what her mother was hoping to hear: "I realize now that I was dazzled by the glamour of the white lights and the music and the dancing of Broadway." She promised to behave. Unfortunately, Eugenia was unable to keep her promise. She eloped with a man her family didn't like, and she never gave up her partying.

Actress Norma Talmadge as a young flapper.

KEY ECONOMIC CONCEPTS

Economic growth	Physical capital
Financial economy	Real economy
Human capital	Speculative bubble
Investor	Speculator
Natural resources	Stock

Eugenia Kelly was ahead of the curve, as a rebellious and independent young woman, or "flapper," in 1915.[1] Flappers would become a symbol of the 1920s, a time of rapid social change in the United States.

In the 1920s the American economy experienced enormous growth. The economy's total output of goods and services rose from $62 billion in 1920 to $90 billion by 1929.[2] People found themselves with money to spend, on necessities and on luxuries. The automobile, once a luxury, became a mass-purchased item.

The stock market rose so fast that, in retrospect, its heights were clearly unsustainable. At the time, things were not so certain. As in any such boom, observers offered a mix of exaggerated claims and also a core of sound economic reasons to explain why the economy would continue growing. To many analysts, it seemed a reasonable bet that stock prices would remain high forever. Investors heard no less an authority than noted Yale professor Irving Fisher tell them that "Stock prices have reached what looks like a permanently high plateau."[3]

Fisher was wrong, as the 1929 crash of stock prices was to prove. Although Fisher was wrong, the larger issue raised in the Roaring Twenties remains unsettled today. How can we tell when prosperity is real? When the economy seems to be booming, how much of that boom is real and how much cannot last?

Norwegian pole vault champion, Charles Hoff, dances with Tempest Stevens in a Charleston contest, 1926.

The Historical Context
Social Change after World War I

The United States and its economy emerged from World War I ready for change. In 1920 the Eighteenth Amendment to the Constitution imposed a nationwide prohibition, later repealed, on the manufacture and sale of alcoholic beverages, and the Nineteenth Amendment granted women the right to vote. Motion pictures, a black-and-white silent medium at the beginning of the decade, became available with sound. The 1920s seemed to generate larger-than-life figures, such as the notorious gangster Al Capone, baseball star Babe Ruth, and escape artist Harry Houdini.

The decade of rapid social change was symbolized by "flappers" like Eugenia. The Charleston became a popular dance, featuring moves considered uninhibited and provocative at the time. A rapidly growing economy seemed a natural accompaniment to the social and technological changes that were occurring.

The Economics of Growth and Stock Speculation

Economic growth is an increase in the production of goods and services over time. There are four major sources of economic growth:

1. Human capital.

Human capital refers to the knowledge, skills, and abilities of an individual or a given set of people. As a society's individuals develop their human capital through education, training and experience, they become more productive.

2. Natural resources.

Natural resources are the productive elements available from the environment, including land, water resources, wildlife, timber, and climate. As an economy's access to natural resources improves, it becomes capable of producing more output.

---

3. Physical capital.

As more **physical capital**—factories, offices, and laboratories—becomes available, an economy becomes capable of producing more output.

4. Technological advances.

As technological knowledge improves, people discover ways to increase productivity. Assembly lines and team production are two examples of techniques that are more productive than individual craft work. In a similar way, electric motors are more productive than steam power, and computers are more productive than the adding machines and typewriters they replaced.

Together, all of a society's human capital, physical capital, natural resources, and technological knowledge make up its **real economy**. Living standards depend directly on what the real economy can produce.

The banks and other money-handling institutions of a society, together with its money and financial assets, make up its **financial economy**. Think of the distinction between the real and the financial economy with the example of housing: The real economy builds a house, whereas the financial economy arranges for the home loan that allows someone to buy the house. People can only have good housing if the real economy first builds it—but the real economy will not build it unless somebody can arrange financing.

When these institutions are working well, the real economy and the financial economy support each other. The real economy produces a growing total of goods and services. The financial economy, through a combination of government policy and normal demand for financial services, helps money flow smoothly in a set of continuous loops between households, firms, and governments. People in households earn money and spend it; businesses accept that spending and produce goods and services; governments impose taxes and spend money for public purposes.

The distinction between the real and financial economies becomes obvious only when they are not in "sync." If the financial economy is unable to supply sufficient loans to qualified borrowers,

the real economy suffers. At that point the real economy cannot produce the goods and services people wish to have. For example, when the financial economy does not provide adequate car loans, individuals suffer—and the automobile industry suffers too.

Just as the financial economy can hurt the real economy, the real economy can hurt the financial economy. When the real economy produces the wrong kinds of cars or housing, this error can cause problems for the financial economy. For example, making unwanted gas-guzzling autos in a time of high fuel prices will mean unsold cars accumulating on dealers' lots. Building more mansions than people want to buy will result in unsold houses and slow times for real estate agents. The resulting distress in the automobile and housing industries then ripples through the bank accounts of people who depend on these industries for their living.

Figure 1 shows how the financial economy ran far ahead of the real economy during the Roaring Twenties. The lower line represents the value of the economy's production, as measured by the Gross Domestic Product (GDP), or total value of goods and services produced. The upper line is an average of stock prices. GDP increased by about 19 percent between 1920 and 1929, but stock prices shot up much faster, only to crash at the decade's end. Although the two lines cannot be expected always to track closely, the graph

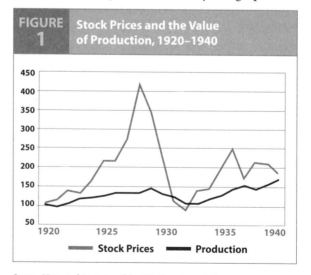

FIGURE 1 Stock Prices and the Value of Production, 1920–1940

Source: Historical Statistics of the U.S., Dow Jones Industrial Average and Real GDP in millions of dollars, both standardized to 1920 = 100.

Operators at the New York Stock Exchange, 1928.

suggests how the stock market overshot the economy's real growth before the crash. The lower line shows sustained growth in production across the period, even as the upper line measuring stock prices shot upward. By 1929 the financial economy had run far ahead of the real economy, before collapsing to more realistic levels in the 1930s.

One key role played by the financial economy involves investors. **Investors** are people who buy financial assets such as stocks and bonds in hope of making future gains. When they invest their funds, they commit money to the financial economy. The most common form of investment begins when a company issues shares of **stock** that signify part ownership in the company. Investors buy the stock, giving up money now in return for a stake in the company's future value. The ownership share will become more valuable and go up in price if the company's prospects improve.

A **speculator** is a type of investor interested in making money by betting on short-term movements of prices. Stock speculators attempt to buy low and sell high, using their specific information or insight.

We may not approve of speculators' goals, but speculators and stock traders, seeking only to get rich, sometimes end up helping the economy. We saw in Chapter 1 that unintended consequences frequently occur in an economy. Sometimes those consequences hurt the economy, as when regulations on rental rates have side effects that hurt renters. In the case of stock speculation, however, people seeking their own fortunes may unintentionally help the economy. How does this work?

The short answer is that speculation in stocks is part of a process that allocates money to promising businesses. On any given day, some people who own stock are ready to sell. Some other people are ready to buy. Will the seller of stock get a good price? The answer is "yes" if competitive speculators are actively trading the stock. These speculators look for places where stock is selling for unusually low prices. Then they move quickly buy up the stock, planning to resell for a profit—but their actions in buying stock make its price go up. In financial markets, as elsewhere in the economy, prices go up when people jump in, seeking to buy.

Speculators also function in the economy by sending signals about promising investment opportunities. When they receive or develop information that a particular company is going to do well, they quickly buy that company's stock and send its price higher. For example, automobile companies had promising prospects in the early 20th century, and speculators sent automobile stock prices up. The high stock prices accompanied an inflow of investment in that industry. Speculation can even give an early warning that a corporation is not doing a good job with its resources. Even before bad news is officially announced, speculators selling a stock sometimes signal the problem to the public.

If the chapter up to this point provided the whole story about speculation, there would be little to fault in stock speculators' behavior. The problems with speculation arise from other considerations.

First, in any given case, the speculators may simply be wrong. In good times, there is always a combination of growth in the real economy along with some guessing about how strong future growth will be. If the guesses are excessive, the financial economy can run ahead of the real economy, pushing stock prices beyond what would be justified by the real economy. When that happens, speculators may incorrectly predict high prices for stocks and start buying on that incorrect belief. When high stock prices do not materialize, the speculators will lose money. They will have caused a temporary false rise in stock prices, followed by a fall. If stocks are headed up, though, they make money—and they have every reason to try to be right.

Second, speculators may follow flawed, incorrect trading rules, thereby reducing or reversing their beneficial effects. What if speculators do not accurately forecast the market but simply "buy where stock prices are rising" and "sell where stock prices are falling"? This approach to speculating has sometimes been called the *greater fool theory*, as in: "I'm a fool to buy stocks at high prices now, but I'll resell at even higher prices to a greater fool." Some speculators operating under the "greater fool" theory will, of course, find the hoped-for greater fool and make money. Their actions will change a small upturn in stocks into a more pronounced upturn. At some point, stock prices get so high that they must crash, but only after speculation has made stock prices temporarily higher. Eventually the supply of greater fools is exhausted and many speculators sell at a loss. Speculators operating under the "greater fool" theory add to the ups and downs of a stock market.

Third, consider the case of a speculator who expects to make and keep a lot of money by being right—but does not need to face the consequences of wrong decisions. It might be a speculator who expects a government bailout if things go sour. That speculator will clearly be motivated to gamble.

HISTORICAL QUESTIONS & ECONOMIC ANSWERS

Was the stock speculation of the 1920s excessive?

Stock speculation in the 1920s reflected a variety of strategies. Some of them came from careful analysts identifying promising new opportunities in the real economy. The rising prices of those stocks signaled productive ventures where companies could usefully employ funding.

Equally true, some speculation in the 1920s had no basis in the real economy; instead, it was of the "greater fool" variety. At the height of the speculation, large amounts of stock were being purchased "on margin"—that is, with much of the cost covered by borrowed money. This practice increased the speculator's return if stocks kept going up, but it would make the crash even more pronounced if a crash occurred—and it did.

Clearly the speculation of the 1920s pushed stocks to unrealistically high values. But it is difficult to be exact here about how high was too high. Noted economists J. Bradford DeLong and Andre Shleifer estimate that, at its peak, the stock market's excess valuation was about 30 percent—not 200 percent, not 300 percent, but only 30 percent.[4] Although a 30 percent correction of stock values (that is, a 30 percent drop in stock prices) cannot be painless for investors, neither is it obvious proof of excessive speculation.

What is a "speculative bubble," and does that phrase describe the 1920s?

A **speculative bubble** is said to occur when prices go up in the absence of fundamental reasons suggested by the real economy. Such a bubble is possible if many people are operating under the "greater fool" theory—thinking of buying *only because prices are going up*. On the other hand, it is not a bubble if people are buying because of good growth prospects in the real economy. In retrospect, we now know that stock prices in the 1920s were driven higher by a mix of economic fundamentals and speculative forces—the real economy and the financial economy. The prosperity of the 1920s was not all real, but neither was it entirely an illusion.

What were the real factors that strengthened the 1920s economy?

Of the major factors driving real economic growth in the 1920s, the following stand out:

- **Mass production of automobiles and other consumer goods**. Old models of one-at-a-time craftsmanship gave way to mass production in factories, for automobiles and new appliances. Technological knowledge was increasing. The productivity of factory techniques led to gains for all parties, including workers, who now had income to spend on the products of the factory system.

- **Increasing access to credit.** In the 1920s, consumer credit became widely available, in combination with the availability of automobiles and other consumer durables. "Buy now, pay later" was a relatively new concept at the time, but it caught on quickly. The new buying spurred investments in physical capital (new factories, for example) to meet the demand.

- **Increasingly qualified labor.** There was substantial growth in the quality and quantity of labor as high school graduation rates more than tripled between 1910 and 1928.[5] Immigration brought thousands of new workers into the labor force. The economy's total stock of human capital grew markedly.

Was the Great Depression a payback for the 1920s?

It may make a satisfying story to say that the Great Depression, a sharp downturn beginning in 1929, was payback for the prosperity of the 1920s. However, there could be no person or institution capable of arranging for such a payback. Economic historians have concluded that the Great Depression might have been much milder if the government had employed appropriate policies—for example, stopping bank failures and keeping taxes low until the crisis was past. The boom of the 1920s did not make a severe depression inevitable. But the fact that the financial economy was not in sync with the real economy made some downward adjustment unavoidable.

QUESTIONS for DISCUSSION

1. If a real economy produces very little in goods and services, will living standards improve if the government increases the quantity of money flowing through the financial economy?
2. Why is the distinction between the real economy and the financial economy easier to identify when economic times are bad?
3. How can a speculator make money in the stock market?
4. What useful function does stock speculation serve when it drives up the price of a promising new company?
5. Would you support a rule to allow serious investors but not speculators to buy and sell stocks? Why or why not?

Stock Experts Everywhere

Bernard Baruch, a prominent financier and economic adviser of the 1920s, wrote the following about the widespread ownership of stocks at the time:

> Taxi drivers told you what to buy. The shoeshine boy could give you a summary of the day's financial news as he worked with rag and polish. An old beggar who regularly patrolled the street in front of my office now gave me tips and, I suppose, spent the money I and others gave him in the market. My cook had a brokerage account and followed the [stock market] ticker closely. Her paper profits were quickly blown away in the gale of 1929.[6]

Bernard Baruch in 1938.

PRIMARY SOURCE QUESTIONS for DISCUSSION

1. When a taxi driver gave customers recommendations on the stock market in the 1920s, do you think the driver had done extensive analysis of the real economy or the financial economy? What was the probable basis of the driver's recommendations?
2. Joseph Kennedy, patriarch of the Kennedy family in Massachusetts, was said to have sold out of the stock market before it fell because he had gotten tips from a shoeshine boy. His reasoning was that when uninformed investors such as the shoeshine boy thought they understood the market, it was ready for a fall. Can stocks become too popular for their own good? Explain your answer.
3. In the quoted passage, Bernard Baruch said his cook had "paper profits" that "were quickly blown away in the gale of 1929." What did Baruch mean by "paper profits," and what blew them away?

Should the Federal Reserve "Pop" a Bubble?

The Federal Reserve's main job is to maintain a sound currency through its regulation of the money supply and the banking system. From time to time, the Fed considers adding a new duty: keeping financial speculation from getting out of hand. The idea is to act ahead of time if prices in some sector of the economy, such as housing, begin to go up too fast. In such a case, part of the financial economy is getting out of sync with the real economy. Think about what happens when home prices are going up far faster than might be justified by real forces such as household formation, population growth, and scarcity of rental housing. Should the Fed pop the bubble?

The gains from stopping a speculative bubble are easy enough to see. If a particular class of investments never becomes overpriced, then it need not suffer a large crash. If U.S. real estate prices had never been allowed to grow as fast as they did after 2000, then the crash of prices that set off a recession in late 2007 would never have happened. Similar arguments could be made about technology stock prices, which soared in the late 1990s only to crash near the turn of the century.

But popping a bubble is not as easy as it sounds. First the Federal Reserve must identify the bubble—easy to do after the fact, but not so obvious before. Technology was blossoming in the late 1990s, and it could be argued that technology stocks would outperform the rest of the economy indefinitely. Housing prices after 2000 grew fast in certain hot markets, but much more slowly elsewhere. There were plausible arguments that prices, though rising rapidly, were justified by the real economy.

Even if the Fed had identified a speculative bubble, however, popping it would necessarily have some unwelcome side effects on the economy. The Fed's control over the money supply does not allow it to fine-tune markets. If it brought housing prices down by limiting the whole economy's money supply, it might choke off beneficial growth. It could not bring particular stocks down without making the whole stock market more uncertain. It is possible that the side effects of reining in speculation would be worse than simply allowing the market to overshoot the real economy and correct the imbalance on its own. As always, unintended consequences cannot be ignored.

The Federal Reserve officially expresses caution about taking on the role of popping speculative bubbles. So far, it has not actively tried to pop such bubbles. Instead, the Fed has limited itself to supporting the banking system and economy after bubbles have popped. Frederic Mishkin, a former Federal Reserve governor, points out that knowing where a bubble existed in the past does not help the Fed know what to do in the future. He concludes, "You don't want to be fighting the last war."[7]

QUESTIONS for DISCUSSION

1. What would be the gains from successful Federal Reserve intervention to prevent a bubble from happening?
2. Is it obvious when a speculative bubble has developed? Why or why not?
3. What are the risks of Federal Reserve action to rein in speculation when a speculative bubble seems to be forming in a particular market segment?
4. If investors are making foolish choices, should the Federal Reserve try to save them from their folly? Explain your answer.

Web Resources

The Roaring Twenties
http://www.u-s-history.com/pages/h1564.html

Historical background on the 1920s.

American Economics in the 1920s and 1930s
http://www.hyperhistory.net/apwh/essays/cot/t2w29roaring20depress.htm

Summary of historical economic information with a quiz to test your knowledge.

Stock Market Crash of 1929
http://www.money-zine.com/Investing/Stocks/Stock-Market-Crash-of-1929

Chronological information on the causes of the Stock Market Crash of 1929.

Annual Symposium on Monetary Policy
http://www.kansascityfed.org/publications/research/escp/archive.cfm

Competing views on annual topics, including well-researched exchanges on whether the Federal Reserve can pop a financial bubble (some papers technical, but with accessible opening remarks).

Why Did a Mild Recession in 1929 Become the Great Depression of the 1930s?

Florence Thompson, a destitute migrant worker, with some of her seven children, 1936.

When Americans Scavenged for Fruit Scraps

Young Stanley Blum was not yet eight years old when he learned firsthand how difficult hard economic times could be. He had taken an opportunity to earn a few cents unloading train cars at an Ohio rail yard in the 1930s. His assignment was passing watermelons from a rail car to a truck.

"In the distance, I noticed a group of about 25 people, standing patiently and watching, with baskets over their arms," Stanley later recalled. "Pretty soon, by accident, I dropped a watermelon and it split into numerous pieces. Four or five of the people rushed over and began to fill their baskets with the watermelon pieces."

Stanley noticed several train cars loaded with produce, with groups of scavengers waiting near each one. Stanley recalled telling his father, "Daddy, we're not poor. Now I know what poor really is: all those people pushing to get to the spilled beans and watermelons." His father replied, "Yes, there are a lot of hungry people with no jobs who have to get food any way they can. We're in a Depression and times are hard."[1]

Young children living in a "Hooverville", or shanty town, in Sacramento, California.

KEY ECONOMIC CONCEPTS

Business cycle
Depression
Economic expansion
Economic recovery
Fiscal policy
Great Contraction

Gross Domestic
 Product (GDP)
Monetary policy
Multiplier effect
Recession

How could economic times become so difficult that ordinary Americans had to scavenge for vegetable and fruit scraps? Every economy has its ups and downs, but from 1929 to 1939 the United States and several other nations experienced a downturn so long and deep that it is known as "the Great Depression." Today it is hard to imagine just how difficult a time this was. When politicians say that a modern downturn is the "worst since the Great Depression," that description may be correct in certain respects. But, in the degree of hardship people suffered, no recent downturn has been anything like the Great Depression. At the Depression's worst time, a fourth of the U.S. labor force was unemployed. Formerly prosperous people literally worried about having enough to eat. How did this happen? How did a mild recession in 1929 turn into the longest and deepest depression in American history?

The Historical Context
Earlier Downturns

At first, the recession of 1929 did not seem historic to the people experiencing it. Previous downturns were called "panics" because of the financial distress they caused, but the panics that occurred before 1929 had ended quickly. Figure 1 shows how the Gross Domestic Product (GDP) generally rose over time from 1860 to 1940,

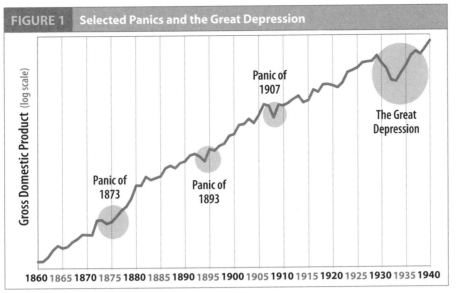

FIGURE 1   Selected Panics and the Great Depression

Gross Domestic Product (log scale)

Panic of 1907

The Great Depression

Panic of 1873

Panic of 1893

1860 1865 1870 1875 1880 1885 1890 1895 1900 1905 1910 1915 1920 1925 1930 1935 1940

Source: Historical Statistics of the United States, Millennial Edition Online, series Ca9.

but with significant setbacks in the panics of the 1800s. After an additional panic in 1907, the Great Depression dwarfed all the previous downturns.

The **Gross Domestic Product (GDP)** is the market value of all final goods and services produced within a nation during a year. The definition includes a number of key points:

- "market value" means the amount for which the goods and services were sold. For example, when a coffee shop sells four cups of coffee for $5 each, this transaction adds $20 ($5 x 4) to the GDP.

- "final" means ready for use by the consumer. A car transmission is not counted in the GDP, but the newly sold car with the transmission is counted.

- "goods and services" means that not only physical objects (goods) but also actions that people value (services) are included. A pair of running shoes is a good; a haircut is a service.

- "produced within a nation" means that the U.S. GDP counts only what is made in the United States. The production of other nations shows up in their GDP figures.

- "in a year" means that GDP counts this year's production. When a used car is sold, the value of the car doesn't enter GDP again. It was counted already in the year in which it was new.

Though each of the panics was unique, they shared some common features: an abrupt end to economic good times, failure of financial institutions, and reduced incomes. Figure 1 shows that GDP rose across time, barely affected by the early panics but more strongly affected by later panics. After a relatively large panic in 1907, Congress and the president established the Federal Reserve System in 1913. This was a new banking system intended to ensure financial stability. Despite the establishment of the Federal Reserve System, however, the economic downturn that began in 1929 proved to be far more severe than any previous panic. Before it was over, the nation would suffer through 10 years of unemployment and hardship.

The Economics of the Business Cycle

The **business cycle** is the pattern of up-and-down movements that occur in economic activity over time. The up period—that is, the period in which Gross Domestic Product is increasing—is called an **economic expansion** or an **economic recovery**. During this period people spend and receive more and more money. The economy's highest point before it decreases is called a peak because it looks, on a graph, something like a mountain peak. As you can see in Figure 1, there was a dramatic expansion of the U.S. economy in the 1920s. The pre-Depression peak occurred in 1929.

But downturns do occur, for reasons that are not always clear. When they occur, the economy tops out. After the peak has passed, the economy falls into a downturn. A short downturn is called a **recession**; a longer one is a **depression**. Figure 2 shows the ups and downs of a normal business cycle.

Since most recessions are relatively short and mild, people experiencing them usually do not think a depression is coming. Most of the time they will be right, but a downturn can continue long enough to become a full-blown depression, as it did during the Great Depression.

The economy's lowest point in Figure 2 is called a trough. After the trough has passed, the economy recovers—sometimes quickly and sometimes slowly. Since all economic expansions end eventually, we expect the pattern to be repeated. Business cycles occur in every economy. When the 1929 downturn became the Great Depression, however, something far worse had happened.

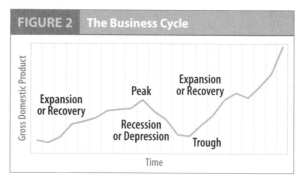

FIGURE 2   The Business Cycle

Unemployed workers in Minnesota, 1937.

The Economics of the Multiplier Effect

A common saying about winning streaks in sports is, "When you're hot you're hot." In a similar way, when the economy is growing, that very fact promotes more spending and growth. One person spends money and others receive the money as income. These new recipients pass it on. In a sense, the economy is hot because it's hot. Economists refer to the multiple waves of spending in an economic upturn as a **multiplier effect**.

Unfortunately, the multiplier effect also works in reverse when the economy slows down. If one person gets laid off and reduces his or her spending, that layoff cuts the income of others. The economy can spiral downward when large numbers of people are laid off.

A reverse multiplier effect was at work with a vengeance in the early years of the Depression. The trouble started with housing and automobiles, two industries whose expansion had led the growth of the 1920s. By the end of the 1920s, the people most likely to buy homes and cars had already bought them. When purchases of homes and cars slowed down, the stage was set for a mild recession in 1929. With sales for housing and cars falling, unemployment in those industries soon followed. The reduced spending from laid-off workers spread the damage beyond the housing and automotive industries. Even so, nothing unusual had yet happened.

For different reasons, agriculture had bad years in the late 1920s. Consumers were spending increasing portions of their income on things other than food. Profits on farm crops were low, and farmers' indebtedness was high. It would have taken an unlikely combination of good fortune in growing and high crop prices to make farming prosperous. The farming sector got neither bit of good fortune.

All this bad news made for a steep journey down to the trough, shown in Figure 2. Yet even with all this bad news, the Great Depression at first did not look so bad. The pattern of economic activity from 1929 through 1931 (see Figure 1) looked like one of the temporary pauses often experienced in the long upward march of prosperity. If the economy had turned back up in 1931, the whole episode would have seemed much like the Panic of 1907. Instead, it kept falling.

Some economists like to use a shorthand definition for "recession"—that is, the country is experiencing a recession when the GDP declines for two consecutive quarters (six months). The National Bureau of Economic Research (NBER) has a much broader definition. It defines "recession" as a "significant decline in economic activity spread across the country, lasting more than a few months, normally visible in real GDP growth, real personal income, employment, industrial production, and wholesale-retail sales." Most economists rely on the NBER definition to date the beginning and the end of recessions.

There is no universally accepted definition for a depression. One common standard is that a recession becomes a depression when GDP per person falls by 10 percent or more.[2] After the Great Depression hit that mark, the GDP continued to decline. At the trough, in 1933, GDP had fallen 27 percent from its 1929 high.

HISTORICAL QUESTIONS & ECONOMIC ANSWERS

Did the stock market crash cause the Great Depression?

The stock market had roared during the Roaring Twenties —that is, stock prices increased faster than growth in the real economy. But that rapid growth in stock prices ended with a crash in the fall of 1929. The Depression followed soon after this stock market crash, but that sequence of events does not mean that the crash *caused* the

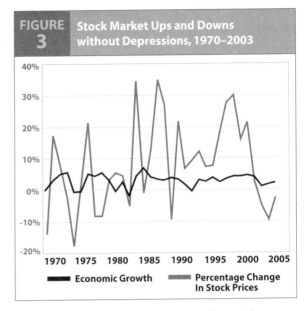

FIGURE 3 Stock Market Ups and Downs without Depressions, 1970–2003

Source: *Economic Report of the President 2010, Washington:* U.S. Government Printing Office, 2010.

Depression. Global and U.S. experience show that it is possible to have a stock market crash without a depression. The U.S. economy had stock market crashes in 1973–1974 and 2000–2002 that led only to mild recessions. It had a major stock market crash in 1987 with no recession at all. Figure 3 shows how these sharp downturns in stock prices were unaccompanied by depression.

A stock market crash is bad for an economy, to be sure. It causes people to be less wealthy and to get smaller incomes from stocks they own. Robert Barro and his colleagues studied 97 depressions worldwide. They concluded there is a 28 percent probability that a depression will follow a stock-market crash. Further, they found a 9 percent chance that a "major depression" (a fall in GDP of 25 percent or more) will follow a stock market crash.[3]

The direct damage is sometimes less important, however, than what the crash reveals about expectations for the future. Even if a crash does not immediately lead to a depression, it is a worrisome signal. When stock market investors are expecting continued prosperity, stock prices climb. A crash reveals a big change in what is expected for the economy's future. The crash does not pull the economy down as much as it signals that other forces are pulling the economy down.

Did U.S. trade policy make the Depression worse?

Yes, it did—to a limited degree. In 1930 Congress imposed high taxes—or tariffs—on imports. Although it was intended to protect certain U.S. industries from foreign competition, the Smoot-Hawley Tariff, named after its sponsors, had unintended effects. After it passed, U.S. trading partners retaliated; they raised their tariffs also. These higher taxes on internationally traded goods made the United States less able to sell its goods to other nations. U.S. consumers paid higher prices for goods from other nations because the tariffs caused prices to go up. World trade collapsed as the Depression spread around the globe.

Still, for two reasons, damage caused by the Smoot-Hawley Tariff was limited. Global trade at that time was not a major component of the U.S. economy. Goods and services sold to other countries (exports) in 1929 were only 3.9 percent of the U.S. GDP. Also, the new tariffs did not apply to all imports. At a time of uncertainty and pessimism, however, the controversial passage of the Smoot-Hawley Tariff gave the public one more reason to doubt the future of the economy. The counterpart of "when you're hot you're hot" in sports is "when you're cold you're freezing." The movement toward the trough shown in Figure 1 became even more pronounced as public pessimism mounted.

Why were banks vulnerable to failure early in the Depression era?

Waves of bank failures struck the economy between 1930 and 1933. More than 9,000 banks failed. The failures were caused in large measure by ill-considered monetary policy imposed by the Federal Reserve.

A properly run bank accepts deposits and makes loans. If it lends money wisely, only a few loans go bad. Even a perfectly run bank, however, is unable to withstand an extended bank run. In a bank run, all depositors seek to take their money out of their accounts at the same time. Of course, all of their money is not there to be withdrawn, because some of it has been lent out. That is why even though the bank may have made good loans that will return enough money to meet depositors' demands over time, it may have to stop meeting requests for withdrawals in the case of a bank run; not allowing those withdrawals could cause the bank to fail because of the immediate demand.

It is difficult to overstate how shocking a bank run followed by a bank failure can be. In the Great

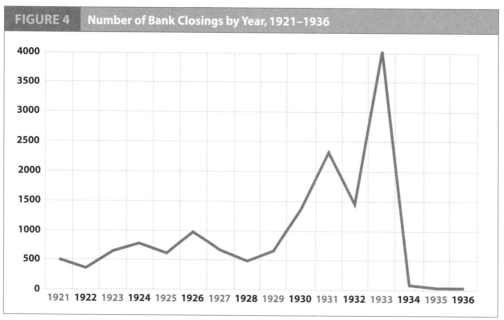

FIGURE 4 | **Number of Bank Closings by Year, 1921–1936**

Source: Historical Statistics of the United States, Series Cb70

Depression, people who lined up early during a bank run may have succeeded in withdrawing all their money, but those at the end of the line may have lost all their money. There was, at that time, no government insurance program for the protection of deposits in bank accounts.

Why did so many banks fail during the Great Depression?

The Federal Reserve System had been established in 1913 as a "lender of last resort." It was empowered to provide loans to prevent banks from failing. We now know that the Federal Reserve failed to act wisely as a lender of last resort in the early years of the Depression. It allowed banks to fail in large numbers, thereby allowing thousands of individual depositors to lose all their money.

The Federal Reserve's reasons for letting banks fail seemed plausible at the time. Some of the failing banks were badly managed. Letting them fail would rid the banking system of its weaker elements. However, letting them fail caused the fear of further failures to spread. Because people did not trust the banks, they held money in the form of cash instead of keeping money in bank accounts. As a result, banks limited their lending drastically. The supply of money, now known to be an important economic element, was allowed to shrink. Monetary historians Milton Friedman and Anna Schwartz called this specific reduction in money supply the **Great Contraction**.[3] They showed how the Great Contraction turned a mild recession in 1929 into the Great Depression of the 1930s.

The Federal Reserve's control of money and banking is known as **monetary policy**. We now know that the Federal Reserve's handling of monetary policy during the Depression was badly flawed.

Did President Hoover and Congress fight the Great Depression effectively?

No, they did not. In 1931, Congress and the Hoover administration saw that the tax revenue the government was collecting was not enough to pay for government spending. At Hoover's request, Congress approved tax increases in 1932, in an effort to balance the budget. With their focus on balancing the budget, Hoover and the Congress made a bad situation worse, adopting a budget that deepened the recession. The higher taxes cut household incomes, and spending fell in response. The use of taxing and spending to influence the economy is called **fiscal policy**.

With the benefit of hindsight, we now know that fiscal policy and monetary policy were used poorly during the Depression. These inappropriate policies helped to produce the steep decline toward the trough shown in Figure 1.

To summarize, what started as a mild recession became the Great Depression because of four main factors:

- a multiplier effect, operating in reverse,
- misguided trade policy (the Smoot-Hawley Tariff),
- bank failures allowed by the Federal Reserve, causing monetary contraction, and
- inappropriate fiscal policy.

QUESTIONS for DISCUSSION

1. Why were people unaware at first of how severe the Great Depression was?
2. How did the stock market crash of 1929 affect the U.S. economy? Did it cause the Depression? Explain your answer.
3. Why were bank runs so frightening during the Great Depression?
4. Does the record of the 1930s suggest that higher tariffs aid the economy? Why or why not?
5. Why do people say that the Federal Reserve's response to the Great Depression made a bad situation worse? Explain.

Bank Runs

PRIMARY SOURCE

Below are two images symbolic of economic downturns and worries about the financial health of our banking system. The first image depicts a run at the American Union Bank in 1931 in New York City. Customers are lined up outside the bank waiting to withdraw money from their accounts. The second image depicts a bank run in 2008. Customers are waiting under a tent to get their money from the failed IndyMac Bank.

Customers clamor for their money in a 1931 run on American Union Bank.

Customers wait in chairs under a tent for IndyMac bank in Encino, California, to open in 2008 so that they can withdraw their money.

PRIMARY SOURCE QUESTIONS for DISCUSSION

1. Examine the two images above. In what way are the two bank scenes similar?
2. In what ways are the two bank scenes different?
3. What might explain the differences you observe?

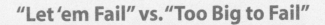

"Let 'em Fail" vs. "Too Big to Fail"

When the United States and world economies turned down in 2008–2010, people wondered: Was another Great Depression getting started? Although there are no guarantees in economic forecasting, the answer appeared to be "no."

The similarities between 1929 and 2008 were unsettling. In both years, the stock market seemed suddenly to come unglued. Confidence in the economy declined rapidly. Consumer spending fell, and businesses began laying people off. Layoffs in turn reduced consumer spending still more.

In 1929 and 2008, financial institutions began to fail. More than 9,000 banks failed nationwide between 1930 and 1933, with many depositors losing all their money. The regulatory authorities then took a stern view of bank failures that would seem unusual or perhaps irresponsible to us today. They believed that the failing banks were just badly managed. Their failure would make the remaining banks stronger. "Let 'em fail" was the attitude.

By contrast, in 2008-2010 the watchwords were "Too big to fail." This phrase did not mean financial institutions had gotten so big and powerful that their failure was impossible. Rather, it meant they were so big that the government was afraid to let them fail, for fear that the entire financial system would collapse.

As the crisis unfolded, it turned out that seemingly sound Wall Street firms such as Bear Stearns stood on the brink of failure. In the huge, interconnected financial system of the United States, the failure of one big firm would endanger other financial institutions. With the Great Depression as a backdrop, the U.S. government rejected "Let 'em fail."

Instead, the U.S. Treasury Department and the Federal Reserve engineered bailout plans that kept holders of some highly speculative assets from losing their money. The bailout used such mechanisms as TARP (the Troubled Asset Relief Program). Amid uncertainty about how it would work, TARP provided the banks with emergency funds. Within two years the crisis was over and financial institutions returned to profitability. The damage done by a financial crisis had been limited; it had not turned into another Great Depression. The political fallout, however, was large. Bailouts were the target of widespread anger. Critics complained that the bailouts favored Wall Street firms over Main Street Americans.

The bailouts left the nation with troubling questions. Now that some financial institutions had learned they were "too big to fail," what would keep them from taking on excessive risk in the future? Why would they not make risky bets again, counting on making money if the bets paid off and getting a bailout if they did not? Legislation to curtail "too big to fail" was adopted, but critics warned about the difficulty of making it apply in the future.

Policymakers face a tradeoff when they see a big institution that is about to fail. If they let it fail, they send a powerful warning to financial institutions not to expect bailouts. Nevertheless, if they let it fail, the effects of the failure may ripple through the system until they harm many innocent victims. For policymakers caught in this dilemma, it makes little difference whether the failing firm did or did not get into its shaky position by evading laws and regulations. Once large-scale financial failure has occured, policymakers face only bad choices.

---

1. What were the major similarities between the economic events of 1929 and 2008?
2. Were institutions labeled "too big to fail" in 2008 literally so large that failure was impossible? Explain your answer.
3. How might rescuing distressed financial institutions lead to greater risk-taking in the future?
4. Why are financial bailouts unpopular?

Web Resources

Modern American Poetry: The Great Depression
http://www.english.illinois.edu/maps/depression/depression.htm

Photographs, art gallery, and an overview of the Great Depression.

The Great Depression
http://www.nps.gov/archive/elro/glossary/great-depression.htm

This National Park Service website includes a brief outline of the Great Depression and links to photographs, historical documents, biographies, and lesson plans.

Great Depression
http://www.econlib.org/library/Enc/GreatDepression.html

An economic view of the Great Depression.

Then & Now: "Let 'em Fail" vs. "Too Big to Fail"
http://law.fordham.edu/corporate-law-center/16927.htm

Resources from a 2010 Forham Law School conference on "Too Big to Fail."

Was the New Deal
Good for the U.S. Economy?

*Members of the Kyle Canyon CCC camp
in Nevada raise the American flag.*

Why Did America Recover So Slowly from the Great Depression?

Harry Dallas had just graduated from high school, in the midst of the Great Depression. His chance of finding a job was slim if not zero. But he and thousands like him did find an opportunity. He signed up to work for the Civilian Conservation Corps (CCC) in southern Illinois. The CCC (1933–1942) was a government program designed to help young men from poor families by employing them to plant trees, construct parks, and work on other conservation-related projects on public land throughout the United States. CCC workers received meals, housing, and modest wages.

About signing up for the CCC, Dallas recalls, "times were very bleak. There wasn't anything to do, and I saw the sign on the courthouse wall where you could join the CCC, so I did." Dallas, now 87, was the oldest of three boys; his mother was single. According to Dallas, the CCC was crucial for his family. "We got paid a dollar a day, but most of that was sent home to our families and that money trickled through the economy." The CCC gave young men like Dallas a sense of hope in desperate times.[1]

KEY ECONOMIC CONCEPTS

Aggregate demand
Gross Domestic Product (GDP)

Primary effects
Secondary effects

Franklin D. Roosevelt (1882–1945) was elected president in 1932. He pledged himself to "a New Deal for the American people." The CCC was one of many New Deal programs Roosevelt introduced. Other New Deal programs provided new regulations for the banking, financial, and agricultural industries; created the Social Security system for old-age pensions; provided federal support for rural electrification, public water works, sewers, schools, slum clearance, and students' scholarships; and provided new regulations to govern employer-labor relations.

CCC workers reinforce a trench in Wisconsin, 1934.

The policies of the New Deal were intended to lift the United States out of the Great Depression, but the economy continued to struggle until about 1939. It is commonly believed that World War II provided the stimulus that eventually ended the Great Depression. It is also commonly believed that New Deal programs played an important role in the recovery. Although depression-era Americans lived through 10 years of economic hard times, perhaps hard times would have lasted even longer without the New Deal. Was the United States slow to recover from the Great Depression? Was the New Deal good for the U.S. economy?

The Historical Context
The Grim Economy of the Early 1930s

The Great Depression began late in 1929. By the end of 1932, conditions were grim. **Gross Domestic Product** (GDP)—the value of all final goods and services produced within the nation—declined by 30 percent from 1929 to 1932. Steel plants operated at 12 percent of capacity. Prices overall declined by 33 percent. Falling prices might sound like a good thing, from a consumer's point of view; but when prices fall, profits usually fall with them. Then producers are inclined to cut back on wages, hiring, and production, causing an economic downturn with widespread effects.

Jobs evaporated in the Great Depression. The unemployment rate was 9 percent in 1930. It subsequently reached levels exceeding 20 percent. It remained at 14 percent or worse from 1931 to 1939.

Many banks failed, and the public's trust in banks dropped sharply. In 1930, there were 23,679 banks in the United States. By 1932, there were 18,734; by 1933, the number had dropped to 14,207. Businesses could not get loans. Failing banks took people's savings with them into bankruptcies. Foreclosures forced many families out of their homes.

Life on the farm had been difficult since the end of World War I. During the Depression, it turned worse. Crop prices were low and credit was very scarce as banks failed. Most farms continued operating, but many could not. Unable to pay their mortgages or their taxes, many families lost their farms to foreclosures. Some packed their trucks, left their homes, and headed for California without waiting for the sheriff to evict them.

The Economics of New Deal Programs
The Bank Holiday

Economists and historians tend to agree that the New Deal brought a renewed sense of hope to people who were badly shaken by the economic downturn, and that this intangible effect contributed to eventual recovery. They are less certain, however, about the extent to which New Deal programs themselves fostered recovery. Some argue that the New Deal, by introducing frequent, wide-ranging, and irregular policy changes, stirred up uncertainty and doubts in the private sector, thus discouraging investment and slowing the pace of economic recovery.[2]

Apart from this general issue, most analysts agree that bold action was required to end the free fall of the banking system early in the Depression. In 1933, banks in 37 states had closed or were operating under state-imposed restrictions. President Roosevelt responded. On March 6, 1933, he issued a proclamation ordering the closing of all American banks, effective immediately. This action was quickly followed by passage of the Emergency Banking Act, which created rules for the reopening of the banks.

Under the terms of the Emergency Banking Act, federal authorities divided banks into three categories. Class A banks were solvent institutions in little or no danger of failing. They would be allowed to reopen first. Class B banks were in danger, but not insurmountable danger. They would reopen, but not until they were reorganized. Class C banks were bankrupt and were to remain closed. By March 15, many banks had reopened; however, people who had deposited money in class C banks lost their savings. Additional regulations addressed the range of assets banks were allowed to manage. The surviving banks would be more secure than banks had been before.

TABLE 1	Bank Failures by Year, 1921–1936		
Year	Bank Failures	Year	Bank Failures
1921	505	1929	659
1922	366	1930	1,350
1923	646	1931	2,293
1924	775	1932	1,453
1925	618	1933	4,000
1926	976	1934	57
1927	669	1935	34
1928	498	1936	44

Source: *Historical Statistics of the United States,* Series Cb70.

The Economics of the New Deal
The AAA and the NRA Programs

Early in the Depression, no one was quite sure why prices for goods and services were falling. President Roosevelt's advisers believed that competition, ordinarily good for an economy, had become excessive. They believed that excessive competition had led to the overproduction of goods and services. An oversupply of goods and services would cause prices to fall, resulting in deflation and then the Depression. Taking action intended to reduce competition and increase prices, the president and Congress established the centerpieces of the New Deal: the Agricultural Adjustment Administration (AAA) and the National Recovery Administration (NRA). To assess these programs, it is helpful to remember the distinction, introduced in Chapter 1, between primary and secondary effects.

The **primary effects** of an action are the immediate, visible effects. The **secondary effects** are indirectly related to the initial change; they influence events only with the passage of time. The classic statement about primary and secondary effects was written by Frédéric Bastiat, a French economist, in 1848:

There is only one difference between a bad economist and a good one: the bad economist confines himself to the *visible* effect; the good economist takes into account both the effect that can be seen and those effects that must be *foreseen.*

Yet this difference is tremendous; for it almost always happens that when the immediate consequence is favorable, the later consequences are disastrous, and vice versa. [Thus] it follows that the bad economist pursues a small present good that will be followed by a great evil to come, while the good economist pursues a great good to come, at the risk of a small present evil.[3]

The AAA provides an example of primary and secondary effects. The goal of the AAA was to increase farm prices by reducing farm production. Secretary of Agriculture Henry A. Wallace quickly went to work implementing the AAA. He ordered a governmental purchase and slaughter of six million hogs. The primary effect of this action was to reduce the supply of pork and raise prices for hog farmers. So far so good, one might say. But there were also secondary effects. The price of bacon and pork increased at a time when the nation faced widespread hunger and consumers struggled to pay for groceries. Most of the slaughtered hogs were converted into fertilizer. As a result, the price of fertilizer fell. Lower prices for fertilizer encouraged more use of fertilizer, and thus more production of crops, in the near future—the opposite of the AAA's production goal.

Cotton production was also thought to be too high. Under the AAA, cotton farmers were paid to plow under 10 million acres of cotton (the 1933 crop). The primary effect was to help cotton farmers by raising the prices they received for their crops. One secondary effect was to nearly wipe out poor tenant farmers who grew cotton, especially African Americans, because of a flaw in the program. Landowners were supposed to share their AAA payments with their tenants; because they were under no legal requirement to do so, however, few did. As a result, tenant farmers saw their incomes go down, and they grew less cotton even as cotton prices increased. There was an additional secondary effect. The increase in cotton

Eleanor Roosevelt and Nancy Cook put up a NRA Poster.

prices made it more difficult for poor people to buy clothing.

The goal of the National Industrial Recovery Act (the NRA) was to raise prices for industrial goods by reducing the supply of those goods. It would do so by encouraging firms to operate within government-sponsored cartels. A **cartel** is a group of manufacturers or suppliers acting together in efforts to restrict production and control the prices of their products. Firms participating in the NRA would accept production quotas. Fewer goods would then be produced, so there would be fewer goods to go around in the economy. When production did go down, competition among buyers for the reduced supply pushed prices up. For example, a timber mill operating within the NRA program was restricted as to how much lumber it could produce. This had the effect of increasing lumber prices, which in turn increased home-construction costs.

By 1934, for 507 industries, NRA codes regulated how many hours a day factories could operate. The codes also limited production and investment in new machinery. Producers in one region of the country were protected from the competition of producers in other regions. Industries were instructed not to sell below cost, although "cost" was never defined. Minimum prices were set for specific products.

Did these restrictions work? At first, they did. The primary effect was that reduced competition and production boosted prices. More money then came into firms, and, with their increased revenue, many firms paid higher wages for factory workers. In time, however, secondary effects began to appear. Restricting time for industrial production and setting production quotas limited the number of jobs available to the unemployed. Price increases fostered by NRA restrictions helped businesses but hurt consumers who were already hurting.

In 1935, three weeks before NRA's two-year expiration date, the U.S. Supreme Court unanimously declared it unconstitutional in *Schechter Poultry Corp. v. United States*. The Court held that legislation creating the NRA exceeded the powers granted to the federal government under the Commerce Clause of the U.S. Constitution.

HISTORICAL QUESTIONS & ECONOMIC ANSWERS

Which New Deal Programs worked as intended?

Although the AAA and NRA programs failed to work as intended, given their unintended consequences, other New Deal programs provided important relief to many Americans. The Works Progress Administration (WPA), the Civilian Conservation Corps (CCC), and the National Youth Administration (NYA) created programs for public-service employment. The largest of these efforts by far was the WPA, which employed millions of previously unemployed people. Even today, almost every community in the nation has a park, bridge, road, or school that was built by WPA workers back in the late 1930s.

Did the New Deal prolong the time needed to recover from the Great Depression?

Some observers believe that recovery in the United States was delayed by the unwillingness of business owners to expand their businesses and hire new employees. There had been 12.8 million unemployed in 1933; 9 million were still unemployed in 1936. According to this view, hesitation among business owners grew out of concern about new economic policies, especially new regulatory policies and taxes, that might emerge after Roosevelt's re-election, by a landslide vote, in 1936.

The extent to which business owners' concerns actually delayed recovery is unclear. Figure 1 shows changes in real GDP for the

WPA workers clear flood debris in Kentucky, 1937.

United States from 1929 to 1940. The information presented there suggests two generalizations. The overall trend in GDP from 1933 to 1940 was clearly upward. But the upward trend was interrupted by a dip in GDP from 1937 to 1938. While recovery was underway before the United States went to war in 1941, New Deal policies were unable to produce an unbroken line of recovery. The Great Depression thus turned out to be two recessions—one beginning early in 1929 and lasting until 1933, and another beginning in 1937.

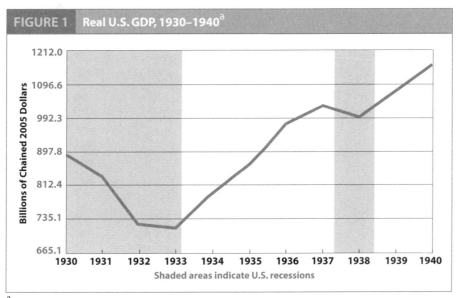

FIGURE 1 Real U.S. GDP, 1930–1940[a]

Billions of Chained 2005 Dollars

1212.0
1096.6
992.3
897.8
812.4
735.1
665.1

1930 1931 1932 1933 1934 1935 1936 1937 1938 1939 1940

Shaded areas indicate U.S. recessions

[a]"Chained dollars" in the vertical axis of Figure 1 means that the dollar amounts have been adjusted for inflation to equal the value of the dollar in 2005.

Source: Federal Reserve Bank of St. Louis.

QUESTIONS for DISCUSSION

1. What were the benefits of the AAA?
2. What were the costs of the AAA?
3. What were the benefits of the NRA?
4. What were the costs of the NRA?
5. Did the New Deal prolong the recovery from the Great Depression? Explain your answer.
6. Which aspects of the New Deal do you think were successes? Which do you classify as failures? Explain your answer.

A Cartoonist Looks at the AAA

The Agricultural Adjustment Act (AAA) was a controversial piece of legislation. The following cartoon was published at the time the Agricultural Adjustment Act was passed in 1933. The driver of the steamroller in the cartoon is supposed to be President Franklin Roosevelt. Examine the cartoon and respond to the questions that follow.

PRIMARY SOURCE QUESTIONS for DISCUSSION

1. Who is encouraging the driver?
2. According to the artist, who would be helped by the farm bill?
3. According to the artist, who would be hurt?

The deep recession of 2007–2009 focused American citizens on questions about what the government should do, if anything, to turn things around and reduce unemployment when the economy goes into a slump. It was the worst downturn since the Great Depression of the 1930s. Gross Domestic Product (GDP) declined in five of six quarters from 2008 to the first half of 2009. In January 2010, the unemployment rate peaked at 10 percent, with more than 14.8 million Americans unemployed.

The response of Congress was to approve an economic stimulus package: the $787 billion American Recovery and Reinvestment Act of 2009. This legislation was intended to put Americans back to work. It provided for federal tax cuts, an expansion of unemployment benefits, and new spending for education, health care, and infrastructure, including the energy sector.

Smith vs. Keynes

Economists will debate the American Recovery and Reinvestment Act for decades. What might they agree and disagree about? The following is a hypothetical debate between two well-known economists from the past.

Adam Smith (1723–1793), the Scottish moral philosopher, is well known for his explanations of how human nature leads people to buy and sell and seek profit. Influenced by the British economy of the 1700s, Smith approved of the way that governments were then able to set up basic legal frameworks for market activity and then stand back and let markets work.

John Maynard Keynes (1883–1946), a distinguished English economist, is best known for his writing during the Great Depression. Although he respected Smith's insights, he favored governmental intervention in the economy to tame wild market swings from boom to bust.

Adam Smith: John, do you think all this 21st-century intervention in the economy has been excessive? Remember what you taught your students at Cambridge—markets are resilient and self-correcting? After a downturn, the economy will eventually sort itself out. If people do not spend enough, prices will eventually fall to a level such that people will start spending again. The proper economic role of government in a market economy is to get the basic institutions right and then let the invisible hand do its work.

John Maynard Keynes: Adam, I agree with all that you say, as long as you are referring to the economy in the long run. I agree that the economy will likely cure itself if given enough time. Unfortunately, such time may simply cause too much suffering among those affected by an economic downturn. There are moments when economies do not correct themselves quickly enough, and people suffer in the meanwhile.

Adam Smith: What do you have in mind?

John Maynard Keynes: It's simple. Economic downturns happen when the people of a country don't buy enough goods and services. At that point there is not enough total demand in the economy to keep people employed, and government must provide the demand that businesses and consumers cannot provide. As you know, I am referring here to the idea of increasing **aggregate demand**—the total amount of production desired by all sectors of the economy put together. When aggregate demand goes into a deep slump, governments should increase their spending and cut taxes to counteract the decline in total spending. In other words, I think the 2009 stimulus plan was the right plan under the circumstances. And you, Adam? What would you suggest?

Adam Smith: I respectfully disagree. Instead, I suggest that under those circumstances the federal government should show by its actions that it remains committed to the principles of a free market economy. My advice would be to control federal spending and bring down the deficit. I regard the $787 billion stimulus package as too large and poorly targeted. I expect that there will be many unintended consequences.

THEN & NOW QUESTIONS for DISCUSSION

1. Compare the views of Adam Smith and John Maynard Keynes regarding the stimulus bill of 2009.
2. Whose arguments do you think are the more persuasive, Smith's or Keynes's? Explain your asnwer.

Web Resources

The Grim Economy of the Early 1930s
http://www.awesomestories.com/history/great-depression/story-preface

An overview of the Great Depression, with photos of conditions around the United States.

New Deal Relief
http://www.nisk.k12.ny.us/fdr/FDRcartoons.html

Political cartoons from FDR's presidency, with a section on the New Deal.

New Deal
http://www.youtube.com/watch?v=Aq5UiGdje8U

A video presentation on New Deal construction projects.

CCC Camps
http://www.flickr.com/photos/osucommons/sets/72157613061881243

Oregon State University's gallery of photographs from CCC camps.

Then & Now: American Recovery and the Reinvestment Act of 2009
http://www.recovery.gov/Pages/default.aspx

This site explains the stimulus legislation passed in 2009.

The Economics of Union Membership: Solidarity Forever?

A memorial to Samuel Gompers, founder of the American Federation of Labor.

The Ups and Downs of Union Membership

A **labor union** is an organization of employees, established for the purpose of improving wages, fringe benefits, and working conditions. (Fringe benefits are an indirect form of pay. They include things such as health care benefits and life insurance.) Employees form unions to negotiate with employers on behalf of all employees in a given company rather than having each employee negotiate an employment contract on his or her own behalf.

Most well-known leaders of U.S. labor unions had humble beginnings. Samuel Gompers (1850–1924) was no exception. In London, Gompers began making cigars at the age of 10, alongside his father. After his family came to New York, he joined Local 15 of the United Cigar Makers in 1863. In 1875, Gompers was elected president of Local 144 of the Cigar Makers' International Union in New York City. In 1886, he was elected to be the first president of the American Federation of Labor (AFL), a position he held for

Samuel Gompers in 1904.

KEY ECONOMIC CONCEPTS

Arbitration	Productivity
Boycott	Rules of the game
Collective bargaining	Supply
Demand	Strike
Labor union	Wages

nearly 40 years. Throughout his career, Gompers sought to build the labor movement into a powerful force.

Until about 1900, union membership was below 10 percent of the U.S. labor force. Union membership increased steadily from 1880 to 1920; it dropped in the 1920s, then increased again from 1930 to 1955. By 1955, over one-third of all U.S. workers were members of a labor union (see Figure 1). Most of these were workers in the private sector, employed by large manufacturers—for example, in steel and automobile manufacturing.

Since the mid-1950s, union membership has declined. In 2010, union members made up about 12 percent of the labor force.

Why did union membership increase in the 1930s? Why did it decrease beginning in the 1950s?

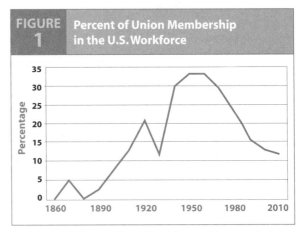

FIGURE 1 Percent of Union Membership in the U.S. Workforce

Source: Barry T. Hirsch and David A. Macpherson, "Union Membership and Coverage, Database from the Current Population Survey: Note," *Industrial and Labor Relations Review,* (January 2003), pp. 349–54.

The Historical Context
The Emergence of National Unions

Two large unions emerged in the United States between 1850 and 1900. They could not have been more different. One—the Noble Order of the Knights of Labor—accepted workers from all workplace backgrounds and had a large social agenda. The Knights wanted to influence national laws and policies that affected areas outside the work place. The other union—the American Federation of Labor—was more specialized, focusing on obtaining better pay and improved working conditions for its members.

The first significant labor organization with chapters in cities throughout the United States was the Noble Order of the Knights of Labor. It began meeting in 1869 as a secret social group— a fraternal organization—under the leadership of Uriah Stephens. Individuals joined the Knights voluntarily, seeking ways to improve conditions for workers. In 1878 the group went public, advocating a large social agenda. The Knights' principles called for no new public land for railroads (only for homesteaders); no employment of children under 15 in workshops, mines, and factories; and a progressive tax on income such that low-income people would pay lower taxes than high-income people. (The U.S. federal income tax is structured in this way today.) The Knights also sought to abolish individual wages and replace corporations with business enterprises owned by their members— that is, cooperatives. (Today's credit unions— nonprofit organizations whose members can borrow money from pooled deposits—are cooperatives.) They called for equal pay for men and women and for an eight-hour workday. Early on, they preferred arbitration to strikes. **Arbitration** is a way of settling a dispute by mutual agreement, outside the courts. A **strike** is an effort by a union to withhold its labor from an employer.

The Knights' membership grew. While leery of strikes at first, they did eventually support using strikes and boycotts. (To **boycott** a business is to refuse to buy or handle the goods it produces or sells.) They won victories with the Union

A Knights of Labor convention in 1886.

Pacific Strike of 1884 and the Wabash Railroad Strike in 1885. In 1886, the Knights had more than 700,000 members. After Knights leader Terrence V. Powderly launched a long and bitter strike against the Chicago meat packers, however, the organization began to fall apart. Powderly was accused of mismanaging the organization; this and other charges signaled the decline of the Knights of Labor.

The American Federation of Labor (AFL) was founded in 1886 as a rival to the Knights of Labor. The AFL was a national organization of trade unions. A trade or craft union restricts membership to workers with a particular trade or craft identification (plumbers or carpenters, for example). Whereas the Knights welcomed everyone, the AFL did not permit unskilled laborers to join. The AFL stressed workplace issues: better wages, shorter work days and weeks, and worker safety. It was less concerned with broad programs for reforming society. It was also unafraid to use strikes and boycotts to press for collective bargaining. **Collective bargaining** is a process of negotiation between representatives of a union and representatives of management, aimed at reaching an agreement on wages, working conditions, and related matters.

The Symbol of Unity between the AFL and the CIO.

The AFL dominated the organized labor movement in the United States until John L. Lewis and the coal miners' union came into prominence. Lewis, president of the United Mine Workers of American, led the founding of the Congress of Industrial organizations (CIO). The CIO at first had a strong social agenda. It merged with the AFL in 1955, however, and subsequently adopted the AFL's emphasis on improving wages and working conditions.

The Economics of Labor Markets

Wages are the market price employers pay workers—the money that goes into workers' pockets. Wage rates—how much workers get paid, by the hour or month, for example—are determined by the interaction of supply and demand. The **supply** is the number of workers who are willing and able to work at specific wage rates. Higher wages attract more workers into the market. Lower wages attract fewer workers. The **demand** is the number of workers that employers are willing and able to hire at specific wage rates. When wages are high, employers generally hire fewer people. When wages are low, employers generally are willing to hire more.

Labor unions are dedicated to improving the pay and working conditions of their members. They bargain to set wages at higher levels than those that would otherwise be established by the forces of supply and demand. This goal helps to explain why tensions are sometimes high when union representatives sit at the bargaining table with management to negotiate a collective bargaining agreement establishing wages, working conditions, and fringe benefits for union members.

Labor supply and labor demand interact in a framework set by government. As we saw in Chapter 1, the **rules of the game** act as incentives and influence the choices people make. When government policy encourages workers to organize into unions, those unions are more likely to succeed. Thus, rules that restrict the anti-union efforts of businesses, and make it easier for union organizers to sign up workers, pave the way for increased union membership. The opposite is also true. When government policy discourages unions, unions find it harder to maintain their influence. Thus, rules that enhance the anti-union efforts of businesses, and make it harder for union organizers to sign up workers, often result in decreased union membership.

Working Conditions and Earnings

Unions arose in response to workers' grievances over pay and working conditions. Life was not easy for workers in the late 19th and early 20th centuries. Two-week vacations, multiple holidays, sick days, personal days, health insurance, and early retirements were unknown. Work often meant hard physical labor. Common laborers stood, lifted, carried, shoveled, sweat, and froze. Working conditions in mills and mines were often hazardous. Injuries from malfunctioning machinery and suffering from exposure to extreme heat or cold were common. If an injured worker missed a day of work, he lost that day's pay. Mining and timber cutting were particularly dangerous occupations, with high injury and fatality rates.

Men and women usually worked ten-hour days, six days a week. Some worked from dawn to dusk—or longer than that, as indoor lighting came into use. Some children also worked, typically on their families' farms or in family stores. But the percentage of children aged 10–15 who were

TABLE 1	Annual Average Earnings for Nonfarm Workers (in 1914 dollars)	
Year	Money Earnings (dollars)	Percent Change
1901	597	24 percent
1905	550	-8 percent
1910	634	13 percent
1915	692	9 percent
1920	1,426	106 percent
1925	1,420	-1 percent
1930	1,495	5 percent

Source: Adapted from Stanley Lebergott, *The Americans: An Economic Record* (New York: W.W. Norton & Company, Inc., 1984), p. 380.

TABLE 2	Estimated Hours Worked per Week in Manufacturing, 1900–1929
Year	Estimated Average Weekly Hours
1900	55.0
1904	53.6
1909	53.1
1914	50.1
1919	46.1
1924	48.8
1929	48.0

Source: Robert Whaples, *Hours of Work in U.S. History* (2010).

"gainfully occupied" was relatively small, ranging between 13 percent and 18 percent from 1870 to 1910, and falling to less than 5 percent by 1930.[1]

Wages were meager by today's standards. In 1890, it was common for a worker to earn 10 cents an hour, a dollar a day. In today's dollars, that amounts to a daily wage of about $25.

For many workers, the period between 1890 and 1930 brought large-scale improvements in working conditions and wages. The improvements were made possible in large part by increases in productivity. **Productivity** is efficiency in industry, measured by the amount of goods that can be produced in a given time with a given amount of resources. As workers become more productive—as steam-shovel operators replace ditch diggers, for example—wages and working conditions tend to improve. Increases in productivity provide incentives for owners to try to retain their workers; more productive workers are more valuable to their employers. Other factors—including negotiations by unions, improved health care, and technology that replaced dangerous machines with safer ones—also contributed to improved conditions and wages. (Minimum-wage legislation would play a role later, beginning in 1938.)

Table 1 shows that average earnings of workers mostly increased from 1900 to 1930. Table 2 shows changes in the estimated number of hours worked in manufacturing over approximately the same period.

Do Unions Influence Wages?

Yes. According to the Bureau of Labor Statistics (see Figure 2), unionized workers in blue-collar occupations earned an average wage of $18.88 per hour in 2001, compared with $12.95 for nonunion blue-collar workers. The highest paid blue-collar workers among the major occupational groups were mechanics, craft, and repair workers. In these groups, union workers had average hourly earnings of $23.05, compared with $16.33 for nonunion workers. In service occupations such as health care, personal service, or food preparation, union workers had average hourly earnings of $16.22, compared with $8.98 for nonunion workers.

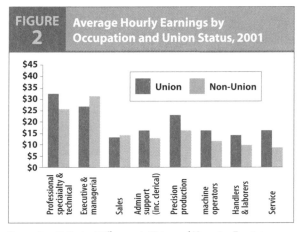

FIGURE 2 Average Hourly Earnings by Occupation and Union Status, 2001

Source: Ann C. Foster, *Differences in Union and Nonunion Earnings in Blue-collar and Service Occupations* (Washington D.C.: Bureau of Labor Statistics, June 25, 2003).

Legal Tools That Hurt Unions

Historically, U.S. employers have resisted unionization of their employees, regarding unionization as a costly interference in their businesses. In early efforts to resist unionization, employers had some success using injunctions and antitrust legislation.

An injunction is a legal order prohibiting a person or a group from doing something that threatens the legal right of another. Beginning in the 1880s and continuing into the early 20th century, employers frequently obtained injunctions to prevent labor unions from going on strike. The legal theory in these cases was that strikes threatened business owners' property rights. A strike, or the threat of calling a strike, is the primary tool unions use to negotiate better wages, fringe benefits, and working conditions. Strikes can be costly for firms, sometimes forcing them to reduce production or close down. The 1959 steel strike by the United Steel Workers of America is an example. The strike reduced steel production throughout the steel industry by more than 85 percent over a period of almost four months.

Employers have also used the Sherman Antitrust Act of 1890 to resist unionization. The Sherman Act was designed to break up monopolies or companies that attempt to form monopolies. The intended target was big business, but the Sherman Act's language is very broad. Section 1 states: "Every contract, combination in the form of trust or otherwise, or conspiracy, in restraint of trade … is hereby declared to be illegal." By reference to this language, employers have argued that strikes and boycotts amount to illegal conspiracies in restraint of trade.

The first major use of the Sherman Act against labor came in response to the Pullman Palace Car Company strike, which began on May 11, 1894.[2] The strike halted production of train cars manufactured in the Pullman factories. In support of workers in the Pullman factories, the American Railway Union launched a boycott—a withholding of services—stating that its members would no longer switch Pullman cars onto trains. Railroad workers across the nation honored the boycott, refusing to switch Pullman cars onto their trains. Railroad traffic was crippled nationwide.

The federal government took action. A federal court issued an injunction stating that the strike was illegal, according to the Sherman Act. When the strikers did not return to work the next day, President Grover Cleveland sent federal troops to Chicago to move the mail; he pointed to the stoppage of mail delivery as the reason for the federal government's interest in the strike. After considerable vandalism and violence, the boycott ended and the workers returned to work.

A later case involved a more explicit, far-reaching use of the Sherman Act. In 1902, the United Hatters Union began a nationwide boycott of non-union hat manufacturers. The much larger American Federation of Labor joined in support of the boycott. A Danbury, Connecticut, hat manufacturer, Dietrich Loewe, supported by the American Anti-Boycott Association, brought a suit in a U.S. Circuit Court on charges that the boycott amounted to a restraint of interstate commerce, in violation of the Sherman Act. In the lawsuit, Lowe obtained an injunction to stop the boycott. The decision in the case, *Loewe v. Lawlor* (1908), included this statement from the Supreme Court:

> The combination [the union] described in the declaration is a combination "in restraint of trade or commerce among the several states" in the sense in which those words are used in the [Sherman] Act.

The Supreme Court here declared that the Sherman Act applied to every action in restraint of trade. Labor unions as well as large corporations like Standard Oil were, for a time, subject to the Sherman Act's prohibition on combinations or conspiracies that restrained trade.

Legal Tools That Helped Unions

Following the Supreme Court decision in *Loewe v. Lawler*, the American Federation of Labor campaigned for modifications in antitrust laws. Congress responded by enacting the Clayton Antitrust Act in 1914. The act included a section declaring that unions could not be considered unlawful "combinations," except upon proof of certain prohibited conduct. It also stated that strikes, boycotting, and picketing were not violations of federal law. The Clayton Act was a major victory for organized labor. Samuel Gompers referred to it as "labor's charter of freedom."[3]

The Great Depression and the election of Franklin D. Roosevelt led to further Congressional action favorable to labor, providing new incentives for workers to organize.

The Norris-La Guardia Act of 1932 declared "yellow dog contracts" to be unenforceable in any U.S. court. A yellow dog contract is one in which an employee promises not to become a member of any labor organization. The Norris-La Guardia Act also limited the ability of federal courts to issue injunctions in labor disputes. For example, injunctions were not to be issued when workers were on strike peacefully or were involved in other nonviolent labor disputes.

The National Labor Relations Act of 1935, also known as the Wagner Act, gave workers new legal protection to organize unions for the purpose of collective bargaining. The Wagner Act prevented businesses from interfering with union activity; businesses were not permitted to discharge, question, or threaten potential union members. It also established the National Labor Relations Board (NRLB), which enforces the rights of employees to organize and bargain. The NLRB supervises union elections and may arbitrate deadlocked labor-management disputes. It may also penalize employers for unfair labor practices by employers.

Political support for union goals also was evident in the Fair Labor Standards Act of 1938. This legislation had as its objective the elimination of labor conditions harmful to standards of living necessary for the health, efficiency, and well-being of workers. It provided for a maximum work week of 40 hours, and a minimum wage of 40 cents an hour. This wage increase initially affected 700,000 workers; the work-week provision affected 13 million workers.[4] President Roosevelt praised the legislation. Its constitutionality was sustained by a unanimous decision of the U.S. Supreme Court.

HISTORICAL QUESTIONS & ECONOMIC ANSWERS

Why did union membership decrease during the 1920s?

After World War I, many employers took steps to try to reduce the influence of labor unions. Some employers campaigned actively for laws in support of the open-shop movement. Under open-shop rules, workers cannot be required to join or financially support a union. Other employers offered new benefits to workers—including free lunches, vacations, and pensions—to discourage unionization. Some employers became very aggressive, hiring spies to monitor and discourage unionizing activities. Some placed the names of union organizers on a "blacklist," which was distributed to other employers; blacklists warned the employers who received them not to hire particular workers because of their pro-union sympathies. Union membership declined (see Figure 1 on page 212), in part because of these actions by employers.

Why did union membership increase during the 1930s?

High unemployment and working-class poverty during the Great Depression encouraged union membership. It also generated support for the labor movement among elected officials. The Norris-La Guardia Act of 1932, the Wagner Act of 1935, and the Fair Labor Standards Act of 1938 established new rules of the game. The Norris-La Guardia Act stopped local courts from using injunctions to prevent union-organizing activities. The Wagner Act established the NLRB, which monitored elections for unions and restricted the actions that employers could take to discourage union-organizing activities. The Fair Labor Standards Act extended legal protection to basic goals of the labor movement. Union membership flourished in this political and legal environment.

Why did union membership reach a plateau in the mid-1950s and then decline?

One reason has to do with the changing composition of the economy. Employment in large manufacturing firms, like General Motors, decreased. Employment increased in new technology industries—including Microsoft, Google, Intel, eBay, and Amazon—that are nonunion. Professionals in high tech industries have a history of being uninterested in joining unions. High tech industries depend on hiring workers who can work independently and be flexible about hours, work schedules, and job responsibilities. Unions are better able to organize in workplace environments where there are uniform work rules.

Meanwhile, employment in small firms has also increased. These are firms operating primarily in the service or high-tech sector of the economy. They also depend on hiring employees who can be flexible regarding hours and duties.

Has the movement of firms to the Sunbelt been a factor in the decline of union membership?

Yes. Employment since about 1970 has grown rapidly in the Sunbelt states (Arizona, Georgia, Florida, Nevada, Texas) while declining in the states of the Northeast and Midwest. States like Georgia, Mississippi, North Carolina, Texas, and Virginia have relatively low levels of union membership. One reason is that each of these states is a right-to-work state. Right-to-work states prohibit collective bargaining agreements that require a worker to be a member of a union as a condition of employment. Right-to-work laws are similar to open-shop rules, which state that an employee cannot be required to join a union or be forced to pay union dues except under certain conditions. States like Illinois, Michigan, New Jersey, New York, and Washington are not open-shop states. They have closed-shop regulations that require employees to join a union once the union has been approved by a majority of the workers in question. These states tend to have higher levels of union membership.

Has international competition been a factor as well?

Yes. American manufacturers face stiff international competition in sectors where unions have been successful at organizing—for example, in the automobile and steel industries. This international competition has contributed to declining employment in industries where unions have traditionally been strong.

International competition within the United States has changed as well. Other nations, for example, have built automobile plants in the United States. Toyota has assembly plants in Kentucky and Texas. Honda has plants in Alabama, Indiana, and Ohio. Hyundai and Mercedes are in Alabama. Kia Motors is in Georgia, BMW is in South Carolina, and Nissan is in Tennessee. Unions have not had much success in organizing workers at these plants.

QUESTIONS for DISCUSSION

1. How did the Knights of Labor differ from the American Federation of Labor?
2. How are wage rates determined in most U.S. labor markets?
3. What were two main legal impediments to organizing labor unions?
4. How did New Deal legislation change the incentives related to unionization?
5. Why has union membership declined since its peak in 1954?

Folk Songs Helped Organize Labor Unions

If labor unions got a slow start in America, it is not because they were ignored in folk songs. Folk singers like Woody Guthrie, Pete Seeger, and Bob Dylan have written and performed hundreds of tunes protesting working conditions and extolling the virtues of membership in labor unions.

"Solidarity Forever" may be the most popular of the union folk songs. The words in the version shown here were written by Ralph Chaplin of the International Workers of the World (IWW), whose members were called Wobblies. The Wobblies often put catchy new words to the tunes of popular songs or hymns, urging workers to join the union, respect their work, and fight for their rights.

Solidarity Forever

When the union's inspiration
through the workers' blood shall run,
There can be no power greater anywhere
beneath the sun.
Yet what force on earth is weaker
than the feeble strength of one,
For the Union makes us strong.

Chorus

Solidarity forever, solidarity forever,
Solidarity forever,
For the Union makes us strong.

It is we who ploughed the prairies,
built the cities where they trade,
Dug the mines and built the workshops,
endless miles of railroad laid.
Now we stand outcast and starving

'mid the wonders we have made,
But the union makes us strong.

All the world that's owned by idle drones
is ours and ours alone.
We have laid the wide foundations,
built it skyward stone by stone.
It is ours, not to slave in,
but to master and to own,
While the union makes us strong.

In our hands is placed a power
greater than their hoarded gold,
Greater than the might of armies
magnified a thousandfold.
We can bring to birth a new world
from the ashes of the old,
For the Union makes us strong

PRIMARY SOURCE QUESTIONS for DISCUSSION

1. What main idea is emphasized in the first stanza of the song?
2. According to the song, who dug the mines? Who built the railroads and cities?
3. According to the song, who should own big business? Explain your answer.
4. The song emphasizes solidarity—that is, unity or agreement of feeling and action. From an economic perspective, why do you think solidarity was so important for the union movement?

The Rise of Public Sector Unions

The newest development in union membership can be gauged by comparing union membership in the public and private sectors of the economy. Public sector unions are unions of local, state, and federal government employees. Private sector unions organize nongovernment workers, as in the automobile and steel industries. As of 2009, union members in the public sector (7.9 million) outnumbered union members in the private sector (7.4 million), according the Bureau of Labor Statistics. Because the private sector employs five times more people than the public sector, the union-membership imbalance is especially striking.

In 1959, Wisconsin became the first state to permit municipal employees to form, join, and be represented by labor organizations. Three years later, President John F. Kennedy issued Executive Order 10988, which granted federal employees similar rights. President Kennedy's order established a framework for collective bargaining and encouraged the expansion of collective bargaining rights to other state- and local-government employees. The courts also took part in the change. Beginning in 1976, federal courts ruled that states cannot interfere with the right of government employees to join and form unions. This right is protected under the First Amendment's freedom of association provision.

The Bureau of Labor Statistics reported in 2010 that the union-membership rate for public sector workers (37.4 percent) was substantially higher than the rate for private industry workers (7.2 percent). Within the public sector, local government workers had the highest union- membership rate, at 43.3 percent. This group includes workers

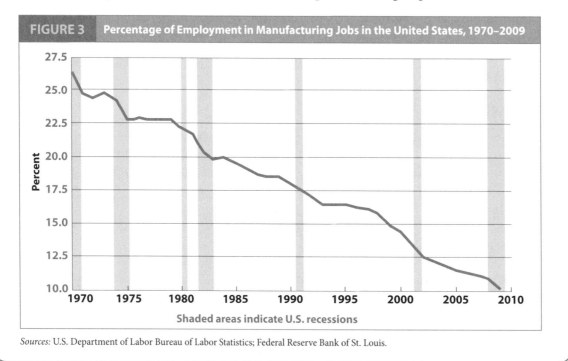

FIGURE 3 **Percentage of Employment in Manufacturing Jobs in the United States, 1970–2009**

Shaded areas indicate U.S. recessions

Sources: U.S. Department of Labor Bureau of Labor Statistics; Federal Reserve Bank of St. Louis.

TABLE 3	Total Number of Government Employees: Local, State, and Federal levels			
Year	Local	State	Federal	Total
1997	12,000,351	4,732,608	2,807,077	19,540,036
2002	13,389,169	5,074,694	2,690,149	21,154,012
2007	14,185,169	5,200,347	2,730,050	22,115,566
2009	14,479,582	6,326,022	2,823,777	23,629,381

Source: : U.S. Census Bureau, Government Employment and Payroll.

in heavily unionized occupations, such as teachers, police officers, and fire fighters.

Private sector industries with high unionization rates include transportation and utilities (22.2 percent), telecommunications (16.0 percent), and construction (14.5 percent). In 2009, low unionization rates occurred in agriculture and related industries (1.1 percent), and financial activities (1.8 percent).

What might account for these changes and differences? First, the percent of manufacturing jobs in the U.S. economy has been declining since 1970 (see Figure 3). Manufacturing has traditionally been a stronghold for union membership. Compared to manufacturing jobs, jobs in the service sector have increased. Service sector jobs include jobs in retail sales, health care, media, science, and technology—areas in which union representation has traditionally been relatively weak. Firms in the service sector tend to be smaller, often employing less than 100 employees. It is more efficient for unions to run organizing campaigns for workers in large firms, where they can reach thousands of potential dues-paying members at relatively low costs.

Second, public sector employers do not face competition in the way that private sector employers do. Competition in the private sector puts pressure on firms to improve productivity and keep costs low; that is why they try in various ways to discourage unionization. But federal, state, and local governments never go out of business. Lacking competitive pressures, they do not have a strong incentive to discourage unionization. If their costs go up, they may be able to pass those costs along to the general public, in the form of higher taxes. Table 3 shows that the number of government employees has been increasing since 1997. Government employees join unions at higher rates than do workers in the private sector. In 2009, 37.4 percent of government employees belonged to unions, up 0.6 percentage points from 2008.

THEN & NOW QUESTIONS for DISCUSSION

1. What is the latest big change in union membership?
2. Why did this change happen?
3. Who benefits from the unionization of public sector employees?
4. Who might be hurt by unionization of public sector employees?

U.S. Bureau of Labor Statistics
http://www.bls.gov

Data on labor, unemployment, unions, earnings and much more.

A History of Labor Unions from Colonial Times to 2009
http://mises.org/daily/3553

History of unions to today's times.

A curriculum of United States Labor History for teachers
http://www.kentlaw.edu/ilhs/curricul.htm#contents

Curriculum for teachers on United States Labor History.

The Origins of Labor Day
http://www.pbs.org/newshour/bb/business/september96/labor_day_9-2.html

PBS special on how Labor Day began.

Most Union Members Work for Government
http://www.nytimes.com/2010/01/23/business/23labor.html

A recent article summarizing changes in union membership.

Did Rosie the Riveter Win the Battle for Working Women?

Rose Will Monroe had known hard times, growing up during the Great Depression in a family of nine brothers and sisters in Pulaski County, Kentucky. She married young, and hard times followed her when she lost her husband in a car accident. Still in her early twenties, with children of her own to support, she moved to Michigan and took a job working in a Ford Motor Company plant. There, almost by chance, she became one of the most recognizable characters of World War II. She was the real person behind the popular image of Rosie the Riveter, the woman whose determination to win on the home front symbolized the spirit of a generation of Americans whose lives were changed by war.

Monroe's story illustrates the way in which World War II transformed the lives of many civilians as well as military personnel. During the war, the U.S. government did not, for the most part, create and operate its own plants to produce military goods. Rather, it relied on U.S. industry to retool and supply goods for the war effort. Monroe was part of that effort—working in a Ford Motor plant, riveting together parts of B-29 and B-24 bombers. Her move from Kentucky to find work in Michigan provides one example of a broader pattern of internal migration brought about by the war.[1]

By late 1945, the war was won, and many women who had gone to work in war-related jobs returned to their prewar roles. Permanent social change had been set in motion, however, and the proportion of women working outside the home would be significantly higher in succeeding generations. To what extent did Rosie the Riveter and her colleagues set this change in motion? Did their example turn the tide, creating a movement that would eventually win the battle for working women? Or were Rosie and other women who found new work during the war merely symbols of underlying economic changes that would have brought more women into the workforce even if the war had not occurred?

Rose Will Monroe

KEY ECONOMIC CONCEPTS

Employed	Opportunity cost
Labor force	Scalable output
Labor force participation	Scarcity
	Unemployed

The Historical Context
An Economy Mobilizes for War

The Great Depression did not fully end until the 1940s, when swift mobilization for World War II put millions of Americans back to work. As younger men left civilian jobs to serve in the military, U.S. employers faced a scarcity of workers. Could they find the workers they needed by hiring women? Women had long been employed in clerical and supporting jobs. The war encouraged employers to begin hiring women for assembly line production jobs, where they would use tools to make new products.

Women had previously been regarded as not well suited for production jobs, but, given the chance, they proved to be highly productive. The popular culture picked up on their new status as vital workers. A song written in 1942 introduced the character Rosie the Riveter, extolling the role of wartime production in the quest for ultimate victory. Although the song was not written specifically about Rose Will Monroe, it helped her get a part playing Rosie in a wartime movie filmed at the Ford plant where she worked. She was a real

"Rosie." She actually was a riveter, and she fit the image of "Rosie the Riveter" already established in popular consciousness. She later appeared in other films and posters encouraging the war effort.

The Economics of Labor Force Participation

An important element in any economy is its labor force. The **labor force** consists of all those who are working (the **employed**) plus those who are seeking work but unable to find it (the **unemployed**). The size of the labor force can change over time as people make ongoing decisions about work and other priorities.

In all such decisions, people deal with **scarcity**, the inability to satisfy all wants at the same time. The ultimate form of scarcity everyone faces is scarcity of time. No one, fabulously wealthy or not, gets more than 24 hours a day to do what he or she wants to do.

Because time is scarce, people are unable to have as much income *and* as much time away from work they would like. Instead, they trade off time for work against other uses of time as they make their decisions. Most workers would like to have more time away from the job for their other responsibilities, and for recreation and leisure. However, they also understand the tradeoff: with less work, they most likely would have less income.

As economic circumstances change, people respond, rethinking their decisions about time for work and time for doing other things. Here are some examples:

- When the economy gets better, emerging from a period of recession or depression, people become more optimistic about finding jobs. More of them seek jobs.

- When wages go up, many people find their tradeoffs altered. Higher wages provide a greater reward for giving up time away from the job, and people tend to work more.

- As wages increase over long periods of time, the tradeoffs can create different scenarios. Higher pay provides a greater reward for working, but with more money many people also desire more time away from the job. Over

The image most associated with Rosie the Riveter is represented in this poster by J. Howard Miller, titled "We Can Do It." The image actually had limited circulation during World War II, but later it became the most recognizable image of Rosie the Riveter. Note that the poster does not actually identify the woman as Rosie or as a riveter. The model was Geraldine Doyle, a Michigan factory worker.

long periods of time, people may choose a shorter work week—as they did between 1910 and 1980, when the average U.S. work week fell from 55 hours to below 40 hours.[2] The shorter work week came about through a combination of individual choices and new laws reflecting labor's influence on the political system.

In addition to general circumstances of this sort, other forces affected 20th-century American women more specifically as they made economic decisions:

- As work increasingly became more mechanized, the brute strength once required for work in agriculture and manufacturing became less important. This change reduced some disadvantages women previously had faced in the workforce.

- As clerical, sales, and professional jobs grew in importance, and women's educational attainment increased, there was, increasingly, a good fit between new jobs and women qualified to fill them.

- As time-saving products came into widespread use in American homes, it became less important for every home to have a homemaker present full-time. (Think about the difficulty of preparing meals without access to frozen foods or microwave ovens, as in World War II times.) As new products lessened the need for women to work full-time as homemakers, women increasingly found employment outside the home.

The social context also influenced women's participation in the labor force. Early in the 20th century many Americans believed it was improper to employ married women to work outside the home. This belief was built into various policies sometimes called "marriage bars." The marriage bars meant that employers generally would not hire married women; also, employers generally would fire single women on the payroll if they got married. Marriage bars were instituted before the 1930s and expanded during the Depression.[3] They represented a strong consensus that women should not be employed in cases in which their employment would "take work away" from unemployed married men.

World War II brought important changes to this picture of women's place in the labor force. Employment depends on supply and demand, and the war caused both to increase. The war led to increased demand for women workers to replace men who entered military service. The labor supplied by women increased in response to new opportunities and patriotic advertising campaigns such as those featuring Rosie the Riveter. Many employers dropped marriage bars.

For women who entered the labor force during the war, there were lasting effects. Women demonstrated their productivity in jobs traditionally held by men. The wartime experience ushered in a new social and economic model in which, increasingly, women would work outside the home.

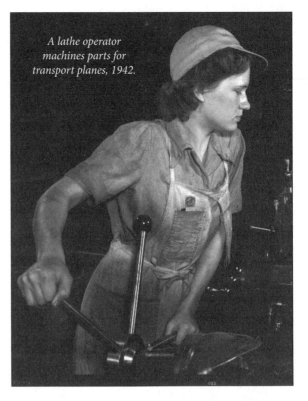

A lathe operator machines parts for transport planes, 1942.

HISTORICAL QUESTIONS & ECONOMIC ANSWERS

What was the long-term trend for working women in the 20th century?

The percent of adults employed or seeking employment is known as the **labor force participation rate**. Table 1 shows how this rate grew steadily for women in the 20th century. Comparable data for the 1930s are not shown here, but the trend is clear. At the turn of the 20th century, only 22.1 percent of women were working outside the home. By 2000, the figure had risen to 60.7 percent.

What happened to women's labor-force participation rates during World War II?

In 1940, before the United States entered World War II, 27 percent of women participated in the labor force. At the height of women's employment in 1945, women made up more than 36 percent of the labor force—more than five million additional women had begun working

TABLE 1		Labor-Force Participation by Men and Women, 1900–2000				
Year	Total Labor Force	Total Men in Labor Force	Total Women in Labor Force	Overall Labor-Force Participation Rate	Labor-Force Participation Rate for Men	Labor-Force Participation Rate for Women
1900	27,554,086	22,388,264	516,5822	57.7%	91.7%	22.1%
1910	36,236,003	28,691,821	754,4182	60.2%	92.1%	26.0%
1920	40,196,595	31,980,647	821,5948	57.8%	90.4%	24.1%
1940	52,651,801	39,720,491	12,931,310	55.6%	84.7%	27.1%
1950	59,325,379	42,847,530	16,477,849	56.0%	83.2%	30.3%
1960	67,316,826	45,159,094	22,157,732	57.6%	81.4%	36.1%
1970	79,764,936	49,180,233	30,584,703	56.7%	77.0%	42.0%
1980	104,139,944	59,623,610	44,516,334	60.9%	75.8%	50.5%
1990	122,806,586	66,350,709	56,455,877	64.2%	75.3%	57.5%
2000	140,454,000	74,517,000	65,937,000	67.2%	74.2%	60.7%

Source: : U.S. Historical Statistics, series Ba340 –Ba345 1900–1990.

in jobs outside the home.[4] Figure 1 shows how women's labor-force participation grew suddenly with the onset of the war and then declined when the war ended. (Table 1 and Figure 1 are based on slightly different measures of women's labor-force participation, yielding slightly different reported rates for 1950.)

Did World War II instantly change women's roles?

No. When the war ended, many women returned to traditional roles. As men returned from military service to civilian jobs, seniority rules displaced some women who had worked at production jobs in wartime. Other women voluntarily made way for returning male soldiers. Given the social norms of the time, two-earner families were uncommon, and many people believed that the war had caused merely a temporary departure from established patterns of work and gender roles. Women's labor-force participation dropped to 31 percent within the first year after the war ended—down five percentage points from the wartime peak, but still four percentage points above the prewar figure. It was not until the 1960s that the number increased to a point solidly above the wartime peak. By that time, however, the change would be permanent; women's labor-force participation rose steadily afterward.

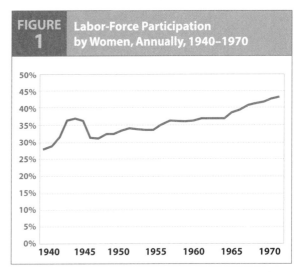

FIGURE 1 Labor-Force Participation by Women, Annually, 1940–1970

Source: Statistical Abstract of the United States, 1950, 1960, 1965, and 1971 editions. Washington: U.S. Bureau of the Census.

The image of a World War II-era woman working alongside Rosie the Riveter, and then choosing to stay on the job, is a powerful one. It seems to provide a colorful explanation of an important development in the labor force. A less colorful explanation focuses on long-term changes in the economic environment for women (the movement away from agriculture and manufacturing, for example) that made work outside the home more attractive. Which is the better explanation?

Economist Claudia Goldin used survey evidence to show that about half of all married women employed in 1950 had already been working outside the home as of 1940. These women could not have been brought into the labor force by Rosie the Riveter; they were already there. Goldin also shows that, of all women who entered the labor force in wartime, the majority left after 1944 and before 1950. "Rosie and her compatriots did not remain in the postwar labor force to the degree entrants had in normal times," Goldin reported.[5] While we cannot know for sure what would have happened if World War II had never occurred, Goldin concludes that "wartime work did not by itself greatly increase women's employment."[6]

Did economics win World War II?

During the war, many factories were converted to wartime production, and millions of women were employed in production jobs. These were two of the changes the war brought about in the U.S. economy.

Recall that **opportunity cost** is your second-best choice, or what you give up when you make a decision. When people are fully employed, the opportunity cost of mobilizing for a war can be high. High-quality workers and productive factories are diverted to wartime uses. There are large losses of consumer goods. But as the U.S. economy went to war in the early 1940s, the opportunity cost for many people and for many resources was low. The Great Depression had not fully ended, and many people were still unemployed. Unemployed people and unused resources then were put to work in the war effort—so not all the people and resources mobilized for the war effort had been diverted from high-value opportunities. As a result, losses of production in the non-military part of the economy were small.

Military historians study tactics, strategy, and the strength of opposing forces in analyzing the outcomes of specific battles. To understand the outcome of an entire war, however, it is important to study the economies of the opposing nations. The United States was successful in World War II in part because it successfully mobilized the resources of an entire economy to support troops with then-new technologies for use in building ships, tanks, and warplanes —quickly and in large numbers. The mobilization effort relied heavily on new methods economists had developed for keeping track of how resources were being allocated and used for civilian and military purposes. In fact, the Director of the U.S. Strategic Bombing Survey was later to write that economic statistics were more important than the atomic bomb in determining the war's outcome.[7]

As for the real Rosie—Rose Will Monroe—she continued to work throughout the war. She hoped to become a pilot, but she was thwarted, for a time, by rules preventing single mothers from becoming pilots. Later, she drove taxis, operated a beauty shop, and eventually founded Rose Builders, a company that built luxury homes. In her fifties, Rose did realize her dream of becoming a pilot. She died at age 77, after having achieved far more than was thought possible for a girl born in the 1920s.

QUESTIONS for DISCUSSION

1. Why is time referred to as "the ultimate scarcity"?
2. As people trade off work and nonworking uses of time, how does the wage rate make a difference?
3. Over long periods of time, do people consistently work longer hours in return for higher wages? Explain your answer.
4. If women's labor-force participation dropped immediately after World War II, why is it said that the war led to permanent changes in women's labor-force opportunities?

Rosie the Riveter Magazine Cover

This painting of Rosie the Riveter was done by noted popular artist Norman Rockwell for the cover of *The Saturday Evening Post*.

Norman Rockwell in 1921

PRIMARY SOURCE QUESTIONS for DISCUSSION

1. Rosie's feet are shown resting on a book titled, in German, *Mein Kampf* (in English, *My Struggle*). What is the significance of the book and its position beneath her feet?
2. How does this image symbolize a new view of women's capacity to work at production jobs, revealed during the war?
3. Compare this image with the "We Can Do It!" poster shown at the beginning of this chapter. Which image is more obviously associated with the character of Rosie the Riveter? Explain your answer.
4. Does the riveter depicted on this magazine cover seem likely to continue working in manufacturing after the war? Explain your answer.

Rosie and Oprah

Rosie the Riveter's story illustrates the changing role of women in the economy in the 1940s. Figure 2 shows that, in 1940, men were far more numerous than women among professionals, managers, clerical and sales employees, craftsmen, and laborers. Among the major categories of employment tracked by the government, only in services were women more numerous than men. As a manufacturing worker, Rosie would have been unusual in the prewar environment.

Today things have changed dramatically. Figure 3 summarizes similar information for 2009 (its classifications of workers differ somewhat from the 1940 definitions), showing an increase of millions of women in the labor force. By 2009, women outnumbered men in the ranks of management and professional employees, sales and office jobs, and service jobs. Men outnumbered women in natural resources and construction, which includes farming, mining and fishing. Men also outnumbered women in production and transportation work.

Statistically, opportunity for women today is a mixed bag. There have been major gains in some areas, with little change in others. As Table 2 shows, women's educational attainments have outstripped those of men; at the same time, men continue to dominate upper-management positions. In 2010, women held only 3 percent of Chief Executive Officer positions among the top 500 U.S. companies, as listed by *Fortune* magazine.

Rosie the Riveter symbolized working women in the 1940s; today there is much to learn from the example of Oprah Winfrey, a television host, actress, producer, entrepreneur, and media executive. Winfrey was born to a single mother in Mississippi; she spent much of her childhood in poverty. She ran away from home at age 13 and had a troubled adolescence before enrolling at Tennessee State University in Nashville.

Winfrey found early and sustained success working in broadcasting, beginning in Nashville and continuing with talk shows in Baltimore and Chicago. In 1986 she launched

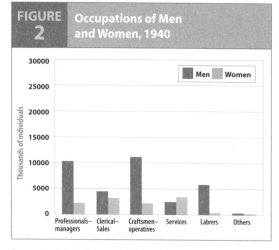

Source: Statistical Abstract of the United States 1950,
Washington: U.S. Census Bureau, Table 222, p. 184.

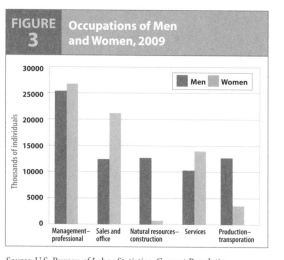

Source: U.S. Bureau of Labor Statistics, *Current Population
Survey,* Table 9: Employed Persons by Occupation, Sex, and Age.

TABLE 2	Selected Statistics about Women, Men, and Work-Life Decisions
Women earned about 57 percent of all college degrees conferred in 2007–2008.	
Today, women earn more doctoral degrees than men do.	
In 2009, 7 percent of female professionals were employed in the relatively high-paying computer and engineering fields, compared to 38 percent of male professionals.	
Among the top 500 U.S. companies listed by *Fortune* magazine, a total of 15 (3 percent) have female chief executive officers.	
On an average workday in 2009, employed married women spent 1.6 hours in household activities, compared with under 1 hour for employed married men. Surveyed women also spent more time as caregivers to other family members.	

Source: White House Council on Women and Girls. "Women in America: Indicators of Social and economic Well-Being," March 2011.

her nationally syndicated talk show, the *Oprah Winfrey Show*. Its runaway success positioned Winfrey to create a media empire complete with television, magazine, and online properties including the Oxygen Network and the new Oprah Winfrey Network (OWN). Winfrey's financial success made her the richest African American of the 20th century, according to *Forbes* magazine, and enabled her to carry out extensive charitable work. *Business Week* designated Winfrey as the greatest black philanthropist in American history.[8]

Winfrey's success illustrates a number of key features of the American economy in the 21st century. Unlike Rosie's success in manufacturing, Winfrey's success came in media industries. Instead of making physical objects, Winfrey's enterprises produce information and programming. Her success could have occurred only in a technologically advanced economy in which progress had been made against old barriers of race and gender.

Winfrey is, in a technical sense, a superstar. The word "superstar" refers generally to someone with dazzling skills in any field, but it has a specific meaning in labor economics. The key to being an economic superstar is excelling at producing an output that is **scalable**—that is, an output that can be increased in size at little or no additional cost. Oprah Winfrey's output is scalable. Once an Oprah talk show or article has been produced, it can be delivered to ever-larger audiences at little expense via broadcasting, publishing, and the Internet. Advertisers value these huge audiences and will pay top dollar to reach them. Thus, increasing revenue a hundred or a million times by "scaling up" is certainly possible for a superstar. In contrast, even the best riveter (or other manufacturing employee) could think of increasing production and pay by only a few times its original level. Given the economics of scalable enterprises, the wealthiest media star will always be richer than the wealthiest riveter. Economists Robert Frank and Philip Cook believe scalable enterprises have become important to the economy; in describing the impact of scalability, they refer to an emerging "winner-take-all society."[9]

In addition to illustrating the increasing importance of media and the economics of superstars, Oprah Winfrey's story shows how top-rank positions in the media industries today are open to women and minorities to a degree not foreseen during the time of Rosie the Riveter. Although Rosie and her colleagues did not instantly change the workforce or the social attitudes surrounding it, they symbolized ongoing changes that made the phenomenon of Oprah Winfrey possible today.

THEN & NOW

1. What does it mean to say that an output is scalable? Is a rock star's latest song scalable?
2. If the wealthiest rock star is richer than the wealthiest accountant, is the average rock musician wealthier than the average accountant? Why or why not?
3. How important is physical strength in most jobs today?
4. What happens to the inequality of wealth if scalable enterprises become a bigger part of the economy? Why?
5. Do you believe a society can have a high standard of living if it moves away from agriculture and manufacturing—that is, away from making tangible things as opposed to intangible services? Explain your answer.

Web Resources

Rose Monroe:
http://www.footnote.com/page/38366711_rose_l_monroe

This resource contains a biography and other information on Rose Monroe.

Rosie the Riveter—Real Women Workers in World War II:
http://www.youtube.com/watch?v=04VNBM1PqR8

This video from the Library of Congress explores the "Rosie the Riveter" image and the experience of actual women workers during the war.

Women's History Timeline:
http://www.biography.com/womens-history/timeline.jsp

This interactive timeline has photo resources and descriptions from 1777 to the present day.

The Oprah Winfrey Phenomenon:
http://www.oprah.com

Official Oprah Winfrey website, with links to a wide variety of related material and videos.

Why Did the U.S. Economy Grow after World War II?

"Kissing the War Goodbye," taken by U.S. Navy photojournalist Victor Jorgensen, shows a sailor kissing a nurse in New York's Times Square on "V-J Day," the day victory over Japan in World War II was announced.

It was a violation of social custom: a long kiss from a total stranger. Etiquette was cast aside, however, on August 14, 1945, as a nation exhausted from World War II celebrated the war's end. New York's Times Square was full of people overjoyed at the end of the war. A photographer was on the scene, and the kiss between a returning sailor and a wartime nurse became symbolic of the moment.

Looking back now, that day in August might seem to have been no day for worrying, but at the time many Americans were fearful for the economy. They had lived through the Great Depression, which at one point sent the unemployment rate higher than 20 percent (see Figure 1), and it was only World War II, many believed, that had ended the Depression. Wartime demands brought back high employment and prosperity. The unemployment rate dropped, reaching a record low of 1.2 percent in 1944. But now that the war was over, would the economy fall back into a depression?

| FIGURE 1 | Unemployment Rate of the Civilian Labor Force, 1929–1964 |

This figure shows the unemployment rate from the start of the Great Depression in 1929 to the end of the postwar "baby boom" in 1964.

Source: "Labor force, employment, and unemployment," *Historical Statistics of the United States*, series Ba-475.

KEY ECONOMIC CONCEPTS

Aggregate demand	**Multiplier effect**
Aggregate supply	**Ration**
Forced saving	**Rationing**
G.I. Bill	**War Bond**

In fact, the Great Depression did not resume after the war. Instead the economy entered into a long period of prosperity. Although there were a few bumps along the road, it was a time marked by high employment, steady growth of output, and new standards of material comfort in housing and transportation. As we look back now, the period of postwar prosperity seems almost to have been inevitable, but recovery was far from certain at the time. Why did the economy perform so well after World War II instead of slipping back into a depression?

The Historical Context
Difficulties of Standing Down from War

After World War I ended in 1918, the U.S. economy experienced a reduction in economic activity. Military contracts were cancelled, government spending on armaments fell, and there was no alternate source of economic activity to pick up the slack. The unemployment rate jumped from 1.4 percent to 11.7 percent, and many Americans who fought in the war could not find jobs in the civilian economy.[1] Similar downturns had followed earlier wars, but the slump after World War I was especially severe.

At the end of World War II, American policymakers feared that the World War I pattern would repeat itself. National concern over this possibility led to legislative action. In 1944, even before the war's end, returning soldiers were granted benefits under the G.I. Bill of Rights. The **G.I. Bill**, as it was known, provided

Franklin D. Roosevelt signs the G.I. Bill, June 22, 1944.

unemployment benefits to returning soldiers, loans for those wishing to start businesses, and benefits for those seeking a college education or more training. Soon afterward, President Truman signed the Employment Act of 1946, calling for the government to promote "maximum employment, production, and purchasing power."[2] The Employment Act gave the president and Congress authority to use taxing and spending to promote economic growth. It also set up a Council of Economic Advisers to consult with the president on how to achieve national economic goals.

The Economics of Aggregate Demand and Aggregate Supply

One important influence on an economy's performance is the level of **aggregate (or total) demand**, the amount of goods and services people want to buy. This factor differs from the demand for any individual good or service, such as oranges or haircuts.

Aggregate demand has four major components:

- consumer purchases of goods and services,
- business purchases, particularly purchases of factories and equipment,
- government purchases of goods and services, and
- exports of goods and services to the rest of the world.

When aggregate demand grows briskly, businesses find it easy to sell their products and workers quickly find jobs. When aggregate demand decreases, fewer products and services are needed, so fewer people are employed, and the economy slows down.

Aggregate demand tells half the story of a thriving economy—but only half. The other half has to do with **aggregate (or total) supply**, the amount of goods and services that producers want to provide. The output of all enterprises, from the smallest hot dog stand to the largest technology firm, is included in aggregate supply. Growing aggregate supply means that there will be plenty of goods and services for customers to purchase.

The balance between aggregate demand and supply is important. If aggregate demand is greater than aggregate supply, people are seeking to buy more goods than are currently available. Shortages appear everywhere. Just such a development occurred in the United States in 1973. *Newsweek* magazine ran a famous cover showing Uncle Sam holding up an empty basket, with the headline "Running Out of Everything." On the other hand, if aggregate demand is less than aggregate supply, the economy will slow down. In the Great Depression, aggregate demand was hit hard by bank failures and unemployment. Goods remained on store shelves, unsold, as the economy got worse and worse. However, if aggregate demand and aggregate supply are increasing at similar rates, the economy will grow, goods and services will remain affordable, and new jobs will be created.

HISTORICAL QUESTIONS & ECONOMIC ANSWERS

Why did production grow rapidly during the war?

In the Depression, aggregate demand had been insufficient to support robust economic activity. As the economy moved out of the Great Depression and into World War II, aggregate demand expanded greatly. Beginning in 1941, the government added its demands for armaments and supplies to the relatively small private demand then prevailing. The United States armed for war largely by converting civilian facilities over to wartime production. Auto plants, for example, were used to manufacture military vehicles and even warplanes. This aggregate-supply response was important, because aggregate demand does not by itself create goods. Rather, it is aggregate supply responding to aggregate demand that results in additional output. Figure 2 shows the components of aggregate demand from 1929 to 1963. World War II spending by the government shows up as a huge bump in the graph from 1941 through 1945.

With huge government purchases added to aggregate demand, it was hard for aggregate supply to keep up. To help resolve that difference, the government controlled the distribution of key materials such as gasoline and sugar, allowing each household a small share. This controlled distribution is called **rationing**, and each household's share was a **ration**. The war effort also included collection of used materials such as aluminum, tires, and paper. These so-called "scrap drives" were another way to meet the aggregate demand total that had been swelled by military demand.

Why did production grow so fast after the war?

The components of aggregate demand help to explain why postwar economic activity was so strong. Consumption spending was boosted by the return of soldiers and the lifting of restrictions on buying goods that had been needed for the war effort.

During the war there had been **forced saving**—that is, an involuntary reduction in people's spending. People serving in the military and people working on the home front had growing incomes, some of which they could not spend as they wished. Their spending was restricted by rationing's limits on purchases of goods such as gasoline, tires and even sugar. Some other consumer goods, such as new cars or refrigerators, were not available at all. Because people faced limits on spending, many of them were able to save money—in bank accounts or by means of savings bonds. These bonds, renamed **War Bonds** in recognition of the emergency, were issued by the government. Through the use of War Bonds, citizens lent the government money for the war effort. The bonds represented the government's obligation to repay those loans, with interest.

Forced savings and savings in the form of War Bonds added up to substantial total savings available for consumption at the war's end. With money from their savings, as well as post-war salaries and wages, many American consumers were able to spend heavily on goods and services that had been unavailable during wartime. The Depression had stirred up fears that aggregate

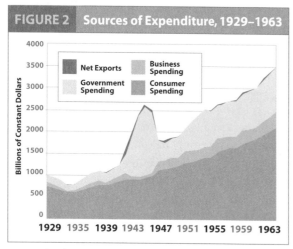

FIGURE 2 Sources of Expenditure, 1929–1963

Billions of Constant Dollars

- Net Exports
- Government Spending
- Business Spending
- Consumer Spending

1929 1935 1939 1943 1947 1951 1955 1959 1963

This figure shows sources of expenditure from the start of the Great Depression in 1929 to 1963.

Source: U.S. Department of Commerce, Bureau of Economic Analysis, "Table 1.1.6: Real Gross Domestic Product," *National Income and Product Accounts.*

supply and aggregate demand would be out of balance when the war came to an end. Those fears vanished as soldiers returned to civilian employment, the economy shifted over to production of goods and services for civilians, and strong growth in consumer spending took over.

How did the multiplier effect influence the postwar economy?

Economists describe the waves of spending that occur in an economic upturn as a **multiplier effect**. One person spends money; others receive the money as income they earn for producing and selling the goods and services the consumer buys. These new recipients pass the money on when they buy things. The money they spend becomes the salaries of the people who make and sell the things purchased—and so on.

The multiplier effect had operated in reverse during the Depression. One dollar's reduction in spending caused a multiplied reduction, as less spending flowed through the economy. After the war, the multiplier effect returned to normal, with each dollar of new spending stimulating still more spending. Think about it this way: soldiers came home from the war, got jobs, got married, and bought new houses and furniture. Money spent on houses and furniture became income for everyone involved in supplying the necessary materials and labor: wood and fabric suppliers, timber-cutters, carpenters, roofers, electricians, and others. The new income generated by such spending made it possible for all these suppliers to engage in spending as well, keeping the multiplier effect going.

Overall, what happened to aggregate demand and aggregate supply after the war?

Figure 2 (see p. 236) illustrates the overall story in aggregate demand. Starting in late 1945, consumer and business spending went up sharply. This increased spending offset reduced government spending as the war effort wound down—not totally, but enough that production and employment could grow rapidly. Besides spending by consumers, businesses, and

These Fords are ready to roll off a 1949 assembly line. Cars had been especially scarce during the war, as plants were converted to produce tanks, warplanes, and ships. Eager buyers snapped cars up when they became available after the war.

government, the one remaining element in aggregate demand was exports. But at this point in U.S. history, world trade was much smaller than it is today. Exports were relatively small, and they were partially offset by imports from the rest of the world. As a result, international trade shows up only as a tiny fringe on the overall totals in Figure 2.

Just as aggregate demand responded quickly to the end of the war, so too did aggregate supply. Producers rapidly stopped producing war materials and threw their resources into producing cars and tractors instead of tanks and submarines, stoves and refrigerators instead of helmets and rifles, highways in Iowa instead of airfields in the South Pacific, and on and on— a full range of civilian goods. The ranks of the employed, particularly women, grew quickly. Many women who had worked temporarily in the war effort left their jobs, some returned to work before long, and some were more than replaced by other women entering employment for the first time. New machines and automation sped up production, helping to drive the increases in aggregate supply.

How was employment maintained with the return of millions of soldiers?

Several factors helped the United States make the transition from a war economy to a peacetime economy. Reductions in wartime spending by the government were partially offset by other components of aggregate demand. With the demand for goods and services high, employers were looking to hire and keep workers.

The G.I. Bill provided an important means of transition for returning soldiers. Table 1 lists key facts about how veterans used benefits from the G.I. Bill. The provisions for education and training were especially important. Veterans seeking additional schooling did not immediately return to the labor force, which allowed time for available jobs to increase. Also, veterans who received training and higher education with support from the G.I. Bill built up their human capital. When they did return to work, they returned with new skills and knowledge, enhancing their qualifications and making them more productive as employees.

TABLE 1	G.I. Bill Facts
In the peak year of 1947, veterans accounted for 49 percent of college admissions.
By 1956, 7.8 million of 16 million World War II veterans had participated in an education or training program.
From 1944 to 1952, the G.I. Bill provided backing for 2.4 million home loans for World War II veterans.
Few veterans collected on unemployment pay provided for in the G.I. Bill, and less than 20 percent of the funds set aside for unemployment were used.

Source: "Born of Controversy: The G.I. Bill of Rights," *U.S. Veterans Administration.*

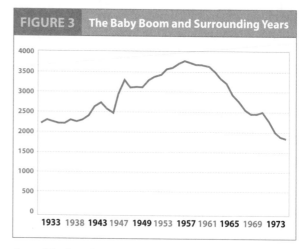

| FIGURE 3 | The Baby Boom and Surrounding Years |

Source: "Total Fertility Rate and Birth Rate," *U.S. Historical Statistics,* series Ab-52.

What was the effect of the "Baby Boom" on economic growth?

Apart from its effects on demand and production, World War II had another important economic effect, wrapped up closely with the personal plans of millions of individuals. Because millions of Americans were drawn into military service and wartime production, many marriage plans were put on hold during the war. When the war ended, people who had put off marriage began getting married, in great numbers, and babies soon began arriving in the so-called "Baby Boom." Figure 3 describes the Baby Boom, which started with an upward jump of births in 1946–1947. (The figure uses an overall measure of births called the "total fertility rate.") The upward trend peaked in the late 1950s, followed by decline through the 1960s. By the end of the boom, 73.7 million new Americans had been born.[6]

The Baby Boom had immediate and lasting effects on the U.S. economy. Young families of the late 1940s bought houses, cars, furniture, and many other goods, feeding the consumption total that goes into aggregate demand. Houses and cars were interrelated, in that cars provided mobility, which contributed to the growth of residential areas outside cities, or suburbs. As they aged, the children of the Baby Boom (they are sometimes referred to as "Boomers") had continuing effects on the economy.

World War II veteran, Orlin Munns, during the war (inset) and shortly thereafter with his young children. The sudden increase in births following the war was called the "Baby Boom."

Was postwar economic performance better than expected?

Yes. Although the transition to peacetime was not always smooth or easy, the overall performance of the economy was impressive. In 1946 President Harry S. Truman said Americans could build "a country in which the rewards we enjoy can be doubled within the life span of many of those now living."[3] In the 50 years after this message went to Congress, individuals' earnings after taxes went from $8,409 to $26,061.[4] That is, earnings more than tripled—easily exceeding President Truman's prediction.

Summing Up

This chapter about the postwar U.S. economy begins with a photograph of a sailor and a nurse kissing in Times Square. Although the photo is famous, the identity of the two people has not been conclusively established. *Life* magazine, which published the most famous photo of the kiss, says a few nurses and dozens of sailors have claimed to be the subjects of the photo. New Yorker Edith Shain came forward in the 1970s with an early and credible claim that she was the nurse. She had not identified herself before. "I didn't think [the photo] was dignified, but times have changed," she later told the magazine.[6] Perhaps the most credible of those claiming to be the sailor was Glen McDuffie, of Houston. McDuffie passed polygraph tests, was able to identify other sailors in Times Square that day, and had facial characteristics similar to those of the sailor in the photo, according to a forensic test done by a Houston expert.[7]

Whether or not Shain and McDuffie were the two people shown in the photograph, they found employment, not a return to economic depression, in the booming postwar economy. Shain became a kindergarten teacher in Los Angeles, while continuing to work occasionally as a nurse. After retiring in the early 1980s she became a producer for a public-access TV talk show.[8] McDuffie worked for the U.S. Postal Service, played semi-professional baseball, raced cars, and worked in a florist's shop.[9] Both of them belonged to the generation that won the war and saw a long run of prosperous postwar years—not a return to depression conditions.

In her later years, until her death in 2010, Edith Shain promoted veterans' events and causes.

QUESTIONS for DISCUSSION

1. Did the U.S. economy achieve zero unemployment during World War II? Is a zero unemployment rate realistically achievable for the U.S. economy? Explain your answer.
2. What fear prompted passage of the Employment Act of 1946? Was it a reasonable fear at the time? Explain your answer.
3. What was the G.I. Bill of Rights? How did it ease the transition from a wartime to a peacetime economy?
4. Given that spending by government declined after the war ended, why was there not a big drop in aggregate demand, hurting the economy?

The Way You Live at Levittown

This photograph from a promotional brochure shows a neighborhood scene in Levittown, Pennsylvania, named for real estate developer William Levitt. From the late 1940s and into the decade of the 50s, Levittown developments offered homes away from the city for the Baby Boomers and their parents. Levittown's homes were built from a limited number of standardized floor plans, commonly with two bedrooms and 750 square feet of space. Prices ranged from about $9,000 to $18,000. The required down payment was $100. War veterans could buy a "Levittowner" for no money down. It was "democracy in real estate," Mr. Levitt declared. The upbeat tone associated with Levittown housing is evident in the promotional language that came with the brochure. "Look through these pages," the brochure says to the reader, "for the modern answer to your housing problem. See how beauty, utility and craftsmanship have been combined to give you the glamorous exteriors and the unique, new floor plans from which to choose the home you have always wanted." The homes found ready buyers. In the post-war years, many Americans were eager to own new homes in the suburbs.

PRIMARY SOURCE — QUESTIONS for DISCUSSION

1. What family structure is represented in the image? Why would the developer depict this type of family structure in the late 1940s and 1950s? Explain your answer.
2. Based on the image, how many cars per household do you believe the planners of Levittown expected people to own? Was that a reasonable expectation for the times?
3. In what ways would you expect a current-year brochure for a housing development to differ from what you see in the Levittown image? Explain.

The Boomers Grow Up

The Baby Boomers, born between 1946 and 1964, were the children who grew up as their parents pioneered the suburbs and redefined modern American life after World War II. Authors Steve Gillon and Nancy Singer Olaguera attribute a large cultural influence to the Boomers, pointing out how television shows and movies shaped postwar American culture. "Since that national culture was initially directed at Boomers as young consumers and then controlled by them, it includes their unique generational imprint. Today, American culture is Boomer culture."[10]

There is some overstatement in this last claim; American culture has evolved considerably since the 1950s. Still, the imprint of the Boomers has not faded away entirely—as is evident, for example, in ongoing demand for education, mobility, single-family housing, and certain forms of popular entertainment. Do popular motion pictures today reflect story lines and character types that were also popular in movies viewed by grown-up Boomers? Examine the lists shown in Table 2 and see how many similarities and differences you can identify.

The Baby Boomers Today

After pioneering in the suburbs as children, the Baby Boomers continued to generate economic waves as they aged. As students, they created an increased demand for education (see Figure 4). As they completed their schooling, they joined the labor force and added to the economy's aggregate supply. When the Baby Boomers entered their peak earning years in the 1990s, they fueled the demand for luxury goods and

TABLE 2	Influential Movies of the Baby Boomer Generation and the Top 10 Films of 2000–2010		
Boomer Generation Movies	**Year**	**Top 2000–2010 Films**	**Year**
1. The Big Chill	1983	1. Avatar	2009
2. The Graduate	1967	2. The Dark Knight	2008
3. Woodstock	1970	3. Shrek 2	2004
4. Easy Rider	1969	4. Spider-Man	2002
5. A Hard Day's Night	1964	5. Pirates of the Caribbean: Dead Man's Chest	2006
6. Apocalypse Now	1979	6. Lord of the Rings: Return of the King	2003
7. Butch Cassidy and the Sundance Kid	1969	7. Spider-Man 2	2004
8. Dr. Zhivago	1965	8. The Passion of the Christ	2004
9. Star Wars	1977	9. Star Wars Episode III: Revenge of the Sith	2005
10. Saturday Night Fever	1977	10. Lord of the Rings: The Two Towers	2002

Sources: Paul Briand, "The Top Best Baby Boomer Movies," September 30, 2008, available online: http://www.examiner.co/baby-boomer-in-national/the-10-best-baby-boomer-movies; Box Office Mojo, All Time Box Office," available online: http://boxofficemojo.com/alltime/adjusted.htm

services and for continuing education for their children.

The Boomers today are a large generation, generating demand for medical care and retirement needs. Many Boomers could use saved-up resources to meet a portion of their medical care and retirement needs. Among other motives people have for saving, one is to set aside money to smooth out fluctuations in the standard of living as it changes over time, from young adulthood through retirement. Most people would like to have a steady standard of living rather than a feast

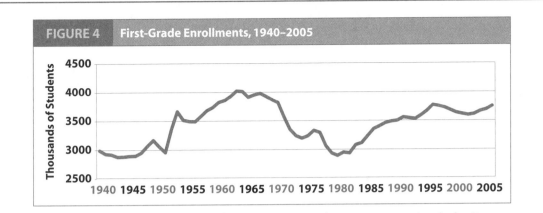

FIGURE 4 First-Grade Enrollments, 1940–2005

First-grade enrollments show the influence of the Baby Boomers, beginning in 1952, when the first Boomers turned six years old, and continuing through the mid-1980s, when the many Boomers' children began first grade.

Source: U.S. Historical Statistics, "Enrollment in Public Elementary and Secondary Schools, by Grade," series Bc22.

during the working years and a famine after retirement. Social Security and other programs help with retirement needs, but these programs are designed only to supplement, and not replace, individuals' saved resources.

As a large generation, the Boomers created a high demand for loans to buy houses and cars when they were young adults. It was hard for them to save money during those years. Next, as they built up seniority and experience in their jobs, they entered their peak earning years. During that time many of them were able to pay down debt and save. Today the life-cycle priority for many Boomers will involve withdrawals from savings to fund medical care and retirement needs.

Did the Boomers do a good job of saving?

Some observers think not. "The Baby Boom generation is pitifully unprepared for the future," wrote columnist Ben Stein. "The average savings for Baby Boom households is less than $50,000, not including their homes. Even including the equity [that is, the value minus the debt owed] in their homes, it's not much over $100,000. And roughly half of all boomer households have either little retirement savings or none."[11] Social Security will be the primary source of retirement income for such boomer households.

However successful or unsuccessful they are financially, the Boomers' influence will be long-lasting. The youngest boomers will not hit age 65 until the year 2029.

THEN & NOW   QUESTIONS for DISCUSSION

1. When a wave of people (such as the Baby Boomers) ages through a span of years in an economy, do they increase aggregate demand or aggregate supply or both? Explain your answer.
2. Over a lifetime, in which years are people able to save the largest amounts of money? Why? In which years are people typically borrowing the most money? For what purposes?
3. Authors Steve Gillon and Nancy Singer Olaguera say, "American culture is Boomer culture." Look at Table 2, showing the 10 most influential Boomer movies and more recent movies. How many of those Boomer movies are you familiar with? Based on that list, is it true that "American culture is Boomer culture"? Explain your answer.

Levittown Historical Society
http://www.levittownhistoricalsociety.org/

Website maintained by the Levittown Historical society, with history and photographs.

Levittown, Pennsylvania: Some History On It
http://www.youtube.com/watch?v=pHnIjpndAnM

Black-and-white video on Levittown history, open-captioned.

Boomers' Life
http://www.boomerslife.org/

A website with information on the Baby Boom generation, including music, people and issues.

Boomers Rocked the Culture
http://www.usatoday.com/life/lifestyle/2010-12-30-boomerarts30_CV_N.htm

Useful report on boomer culture from USA Today.

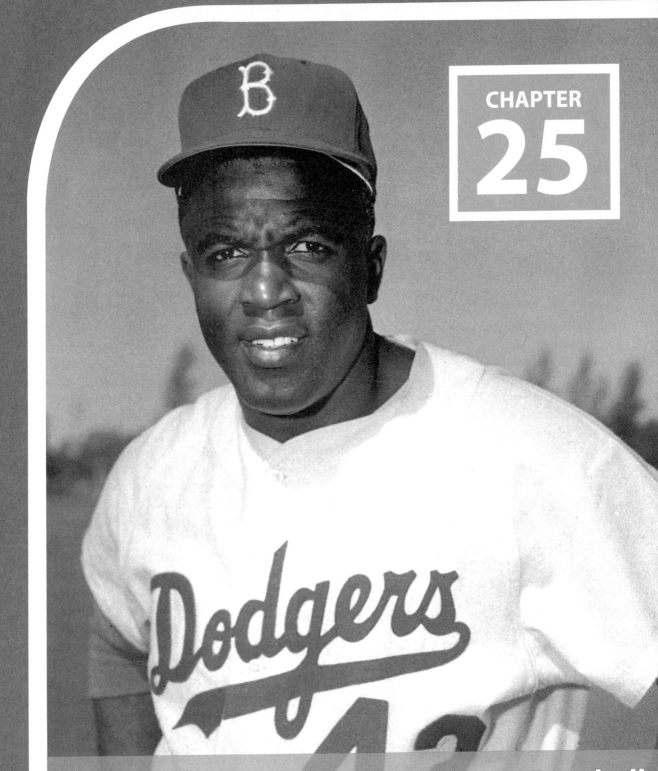

Who Desegregated Major League Baseball: Adam Smith or Jackie Robinson?

*Jack Roosevelt (Jackie) Robinson, major league
baseball player and civil rights activist.*

Racial Segregation in Major League Baseball

The story is well known to avid baseball fans. In 1947, Branch Rickey, president of the Brooklyn Dodgers, signed Jackie Robinson (1919–1972) to be the first African American baseball player in the major leagues. It took courage and determination on Rickey's part and Robinson's to make the move. After all, racial segregation in 1947 was widespread in the United States. How would fans react? How would players react? These concerns may seem odd today, but in 1947 no one knew the answers.

Adam Smith (1723–1790) certainly did not play baseball, and he probably was not a fan of cricket, an early version of the game. Smith is regarded as the founder of modern economics. He wrote his classic book, *The Wealth of Nations*, 143 years before Jackie Robinson was born. Could Smith's ideas have helped to desegregate major league baseball?

To begin thinking about that question, consider Smith's contention that individuals

KEY ECONOMIC CONCEPTS

Cartel	Monopoly
Competition	Monopsony
Invisible hand	Profit
Labor market	Profit motive

acting in their own self interest, pursuing profits in competitive markets, can produce good outcomes for others. By pursuing his own interest, Smith wrote, an individual "frequently promotes [the interest] of the society more effectually than when he intends to promote it." The explanation for this contention has to do with competition. In free markets, **competition** refers to producers seeking to outdo one another by keeping prices low, providing high-quality goods and services, or both. Society as a whole benefits from these competitive efforts. Individuals seeking their own profit thus promote the economic interest of others, as if they were guided by what Smith called the **invisible hand** of the market.

In this chapter we explore competition as a force that helps to explain Jackie Robinson's success and the success of other African American ball players who subsequently signed with major league baseball teams. What role did competitive labor markets and profits play in desegregating major league baseball?

The Historical Context
Racial Segregation after the Civil War

Even after the Civil War ended in 1865, racial discrimination persisted in the United States. Several states and local governments enacted Jim Crow laws to keep African Americans segregated from white Americans. In southern states, nearly every public setting—including schools, buses,

Branch Rickey

railroad passenger cars, restrooms, swimming pools, pool halls, and restaurants—was marked by racial segregation. Racial segregation was also widespread in northern states, enforced more by custom and social arrangements than by Jim Crow laws. Segregation was not limited to remote, isolated areas. The U.S. armed forces were segregated. In the 1920s, an African American man could not enlist in the U.S. Navy. President Woodrow Wilson segregated federal offices in Washington, D.C. Opportunities for African Americans to push back against segregation through political action were limited by the fact that poll taxes and literacy tests kept many African Americans from voting.

It would take many years, several momentous Supreme Court decisions, and some far-reaching federal legislation before schools and other institutions took effective action to desegregate. In some economic sectors, however, people abandoned racial segregation more quickly—years ahead of the civil rights legislation enacted in the 1960s. Major league baseball provides a perfect example. Jackie Robinson became the first African American baseball player to play in the National League in 1947, and others soon followed.

Why might some labor markets—including major league baseball—act more quickly than others to move away from racial segregation?

The Economics of Labor Markets
The ABCs of Hiring the Best Worker

A **labor market** is any place or situation in which employers are trying to hire workers and workers are trying to find jobs. Let's explore how labor markets work before returning to the story of Jackie Robinson and Branch Rickey.

It's obvious that racial discrimination causes economic harm to its victims. What is less obvious is that discrimination is also bad for businesses. Business owners are guided by the **profit motive**; they try to earn as much revenue as they can in hopes of making a **profit**. Profit is the money a business has left after it pays for all its operating expenses—rent, wages, utilities, and so on. Making a profit requires hard work and

close attention to the actions of competitors. In these efforts, it is important for business owners to hire the most talented, productive workers they can find. If they do not hire the best workers available, they might wind up losing money; eventually, they might fail altogether and have to close down. It would be a disadvantage, therefore, for a business owner to be influenced by racial prejudice or other sorts of bigotry in decisions about hiring. The talented African American not hired by a bigoted employer might get hired instead by a competitor—one looking only for the best available employee, regardless of race. In this way, discrimination on the basis of race (or other considerations unrelated to competence) can impose high costs on bigoted business owners.

Consider an example unrelated to baseball. Imagine that Cutty Coleman is the owner of Cutty's Pretty Good Lawn Cutting Service, a small lawn-care business. Cutty has decided to expand the business; he plans to hire one new employee. The following three people apply for the new job:

Applicant A can cut and trim two average-size lawns between 8:00 a.m. and 12:00 noon, using the company's standard riding mower, the standard walking power mower, and the gas-powered trimmer. This applicant wishes to be paid $10 per hour.

Applicant B can cut and trim three average-size lawns between 8:00 a.m. and 12:00 noon, using the company's standard riding mower, the standard walking power mower, and the gas-powered trimmer. This applicant wishes to be paid $10 per hour.

Applicant C can cut and trim four average-size lawns between 8:00 a.m. and 12:00 noon, using the company's standard riding mower, the standard walking power mower, and the gas-powered trimmer. This applicant wishes to be paid $10 per hour.

Which person should Cutty hire? He should hire Applicant C. Applicant C can do more than the other applicants to increase the number of lawn jobs Cutty's business can complete per day. With Applicant C on board, Cutty's business will be able to earn more income and a larger profit.

But now imagine that Applicant C is a member of a group (age-related, or racial, or religious, for example) about which Cutty holds prejudicial, bigoted views. Should Cutty hire Applicant C anyway? He should. Cutty might be prejudiced against Applicant C, but he would undercut his capacity to earn a profit if he failed to hire Applicant C.

The example shows how competitive labor markets make it costly for business owners who allow prejudices to stand in the way of hiring the best available workers. It also helps us to see that maintaining racial discrimination on a broad scale would require a great deal of effort—and the support of local or state laws—because the profit motive would work continually against racial discrimination. In fact, during the Jim Crow era, many business owners in the South wanted to hire African American employees and serve African American customers. But the Jim Crow laws made it difficult or impossible to conduct business in this way.

HISTORICAL QUESTIONS & ECONOMIC ANSWERS

Is major league baseball a business like other competitive businesses?

Not exactly. In fact, economically speaking, major league baseball is one of a kind. Baseball club owners are exempted from federal antitrust laws, although no other business is. The exemption is a result of a 1922 Supreme Court ruling in the case of the *Federal Baseball Club of Baltimore, Inc. v. National League of Professional Baseball Clubs*. This case was an unusual one, filled with odd twists. For example, the Court was not concerned with the fact that the defendants were involved in a sport. What mattered, instead, was that major league baseball clubs were profit-seeking businesses and they were clearly engaging in commerce across state lines.

Nonetheless, the Supreme Court decided that organized baseball was not engaged in interstate commerce, according to their legal definition of that term. Moreover, the Court held that major league baseball was not a monopoly as defined by the Sherman Antitrust Act. A **monopoly** is traditionally understood to be a market with only one seller of a unique good or service. The Justices reasoned that attempts by club owners to sign baseball players were not attempts to establish a monopoly.

If it is not a business engaged in interstate commerce, or a monopoly, is major league baseball a cartel?

Yes, major league baseball is a government-sanctioned cartel. A **cartel** is an organization of producers or suppliers who make agreements with one another about how to run their businesses. The Organization of Petroleum Exporting Countries (OPEC) is perhaps the most well-known cartel in existence today. The 12 members of OPEC try to control the price of petroleum by enforcing agreements among themselves to limit oil production. Similarly, major league baseball clubs are permitted to enter into agreements about how they will operate—instead of simply competing against one another in the marketplace. For example, they can decide where baseball teams will be located, how baseball farm clubs will operate, and how baseball players will be drafted and signed. Their real power lies in the fact that baseball club owners are the sole purchasers of professional baseball talent. Economists have a name for this: if you are the sole buyer of a good or service, you operate a **monopsony**. That is something close to monopoly power. No other American business has this sort of monopsony clout.

Prior to the breakthrough made by Branch Rickey and Jackie Robinson, major league baseball club owners had agreed that they would not employ African American players. This decision almost certainly was influenced by racist views among club owners; nonetheless, it probably was based on two economic considerations as well. First, club owners would have been unsure how baseball fans would react to racially integrated teams. Would white fans pay to see black players play baseball with white players? Second, some white players had made it clear that they did not want to compete with African American players. Some feared losing their jobs. Some threatened strikes or violence.

The Profit Motive and the Rickey-Robinson Story

Despite the fact that major league baseball operated a legal cartel, club owners did compete with one another. The profit motive came into play: they all wanted to win ball games and make money. Competition of this sort erodes the power of cartels to enforce the agreements cartel members have made. Members always have an incentive to break their agreements and "cheat." Major league baseball club owners were no exception. In competing to win and earn a profit, they could not easily ignore the advantage they might gain by cheating on the cartel—by hiring the best available ball players, regardless of race.

There was an ample supply of talent outside the cartel. African American baseball leagues fielded dozens of African American professional and semi-professional baseball teams from 1887 to 1950. The Negro National League, founded in 1920, was especially successful.

There were also barnstorming African American teams—the Omaha Tigers and the Miami Giants, for example. Barnstorming teams traveled in circuits, often in the South and Midwest, playing baseball wherever an entrepreneur could rent a ball park and find fans willing to buy tickets. The most famous barnstormers were the Satchel Paige All Stars (all African American players) and the Dizzy Dean All Stars (all white players). They toured the nation every October from 1934 to 1945; they were watched by thousands of fans.

Life for ball players in the African American leagues and the barnstorming circuits was not easy. The work was hard and the pay was low, except for stars like Satchel Paige. Continual travel, mostly by bus, was exhausting. Players often had trouble finding hotels, restrooms, and restaurants that would accommodate them. For those who thought they had what it takes to play in the major leagues, the prospect of moving up to the majors, for better pay and improved working conditions, was highly attractive.

Given the competitive pressure they faced, and this rich source of talented players not yet hired for the major leagues, did some club owners try to hire African American players? You bet. Because pay in the African American leagues was much lower than major league pay, club owners knew they could hire excellent African American ball players for lower salaries than they were paying white players. As early as 1944, Bill Veeck tried to buy the slumping Philadelphia Phillies. His plan was to sign several African American players—Satchel Paige, Roy Campanella, Luke Easter, Monte Irvin, and many others were available—to turn the club around. Veeck failed in his effort to buy the Phillies, but he later became the owner of the Cleveland Indians. Almost immediately, he signed Larry Doby as the first African American player in the American League, in 1947.

Table 1 lists major league ball players who started out playing in the African American leagues. It is a selective list, but it suggests the wealth of talent the major league teams would eventually draw upon.

TABLE 1	Major League Ball Players Who Had Played in the African American Leagues
Players	**African American League Teams**
Hank Aaron	Indianapolis Clowns
Willie Mays	Birmingham Black Barons
Jackie Robinson	Kansas City Monarchs
Monte Irvin	Newark Eagles
Larry Doby	Newark Eagles
Roy Campanella	Baltimore Elite Giants
Sam Jethroe	Cleveland Buckeyes
Orestes "Minnie" Minoso	New York Cubans
Leroy "Satchel" Paige	Kansas City Monarchs
Joe Black	Baltimore Elite Giants

Source: http://www.negroleaguebaseball.com

Major league club owners wanted to build winning teams, and tapping into a new source of talent could help them do that. Winning teams attract fans to the ballparks. More fans generate more revenue and larger profits.

Competition for talented players and loyal fans was especially intense in big baseball markets like New York City. After World War II, New York City had three professional baseball teams—the Brooklyn Dodgers, the New York Yankees, and the New York Giants. Mass transit in New York would enable fans to shift loyalties easily from a losing club to a winning club. In that competitive market, owners were obliged to do everything they could to attract fans. Having a winning team was one way to do it. Having spectacular players was another. What if you could offer both?

Enter Branch Rickey and Jackie Robinson. Like Jackie Robinson, Rickey was a competitor. He started out playing catcher with two major league baseball clubs. Although he turned out to be a mediocre ball player, he became a highly successful major league manager and executive. Known as a great innovator, he invented baseball's farm system and spring training. He made use of batting cages, batting helmets, and pitching machines. He is best known, however, as the man who signed Jackie Robinson to play for the Brooklyn Dodgers.

Going into 1946, it seemed likely that the '46 World Series would be played by the two dominant teams in baseball at the time—the Boston Red Sox and the St. Louis Cardinals. The Red Sox were led by Ted Williams, the greatest hitter since Babe Ruth, with 521 home runs and a

Jackie Robinson and Branch Rickey in February 1948.

career batting average of .344. The Cardinals were led by "Stan the Man" Musial, also an excellent hitter. Musial collected 3,630 hits and 475 home runs during his career.

But the pattern of team dominance was soon to change. In 1946, Rickey signed Robinson, who played that year for the Montreal Royals. The Brooklyn Dodgers finished the 1946 season two games behind the Cardinals. Robinson played his rookie season with the Dodgers in 1947, and he soon became the biggest attraction in baseball. Huge crowds turned out to watch him play. The Dodgers won the National League pennant in 1947, and they won it again in 1949, 1952, 1953, 1955, and 1956. Robinson was selected as Rookie of the Year in 1947. In 1949 he led the National league with a .342 batting average and was named the National League's Most Valuable Player. He helped the Dodgers win a World Series in 1955.

Rickey, keenly aware of his overnight success in signing Robinson, quickly signed other African American players including Roy Campanella and Don Newcombe. Between 1947 and 1957, African Americans playing for the Dodgers won five Most Valuable Player awards and four Rookie of the Year awards. Racial integration in the National League electrified the country, and the National League pulled ahead of the American League in fielding higher-quality teams.

Teams that signed African American players were rewarded on the field and in their pocketbooks. By comparison, teams that were slower to react, failing to sign African American players, were disadvantaged. James Gwartney and Charles Haworth studied the impact of African American players in the early years of baseball desegregation. They found that the number of African American players was a significant factor related to the number of games a team won. From 1950 to 1955, the inclusion of an African American player on a major league team resulted, on average, in an additional 3.75 wins per year. What about revenues? Were club owners correct, early on, to worry that baseball fans might stay away if the clubs signed African American players? Not at all. Gwartney and Haworth also found a strong, positive relationship between fan attendance and the number of African American players on a team. On average, each additional African American player on a team was associated with between 55,000 and 60,000 additional home-team admissions annually during the 1950s.

QUESTIONS for DISCUSSION

1. What was Adam's Smith "invisible hand" of the market place?
2. How is major baseball one of a kind, economically?
3. Why is major league baseball considered a cartel?
4. What does it mean to say that major league baseball clubs hold a form of monopsony power?
5. Why is it in the self-interest of business owners to hire the most productive workers they can find?
6. How did the desire to win ball games influence Branch Rickey's decision to sign Jackie Robinson?
7. What happened to the revenues and records of baseball teams that signed African American players?
8. Who desegregated major league baseball: Jackie Robinson and Branch Rickey, or Adam Smith?

Branch Rickey Speaks Out

PRIMARY SOURCE

On January 20, 1956, Branch Rickey gave a speech at a banquet held by the One Hundred Percent Wrong Club, in Atlanta, Georgia. In his speech, Rickey described the problems he faced in the 1940s when he decided to desegregate major league baseball by signing Jackie Robinson to play for the Brooklyn Dodgers. Here is a short excerpt from the speech:

"I know that America … is more interested in the grace of a man's swing, in the dexterity of his cutting a base, and his speed afoot, in his scientific body control, in his excellence as a competitor on the field. America, wide and broad, and in Atlanta, and in Georgia, will become instantly more interested in those marvelous, beautiful qualities than they are in the pigmentation of a man's skin, or indeed in the last syllable of his name. Men are coming to be regarded of value based upon their merits, and God hasten the day when Governors of our States will become sufficiently educated that they will respond to those views."

Source: Library of Congress, Manuscript Division, Branch Rickey Papers.

PRIMARY SOURCE **QUESTIONS for DISCUSSION**

1. What is Branch Rickey's main point in this speech?
2. How does Rickey's point compare to Adam Smith's point about profits and the invisible hand, as quoted early in this chapter?

This chapter has focused on racial discrimination against African Americans in major league baseball. There are, of course, other forms of discrimination.

The "gender gap" is a topic of hot debate, often in the news. What is the gender gap? Actually, there are two types. The first gender gap is the difference between men's and women's participation in the labor force. The Bureau of Labor Statistics reports that women's labor-force participation, which was about 34 percent in 1950, increased significantly during the 1970s and 1980s, climbing to almost 58 percent in 1990. In 1999, women's participation rate reached a peak of 60 percent. By 2000, however, this rate had declined slightly, to 59.9 percent; since then it has displayed a pattern of slow decline in each successive period, falling to 59.3 percent in 2005. The participation rate of women is projected to be 59.4 percent in 2020 and 55.1 percent in 2050.

The second gender gap—the one that gets the most attention—is the gap between men's earnings and women's earnings. Men generally earn more money than women do. The earnings gap has narrowed over the past several years. It was 40 percent in 1970. It declined to about 20 percent in 2010.

Why is there still any gap in wages? One possibility is that the gap is caused by ongoing discrimination against women. Certainly women have been victims of discrimination in the workplace. Another possibility is that, compared to men, women are more likely to work part-time, choose careers in lower-paying fields, work for government or non-profit organizations, and have fewer years of work experience than men of the same age. Many of these work-related differences reflect the fact that women generally have more family responsibilities than men do. When information about wages is adjusted for differences in education, experience, and type of job, there is no significant difference between the earnings of men and women who have never married and never had a child.[1]

As a society, we have become increasingly attentive to issues of gender discrimination. Title VII of the Civil Rights Act of 1964 forbids discrimination on the basis of sex in hiring, promotion, and other conditions of employment. People who believe that they have experienced discrimination may file charges against their employer with the U.S. Equal Employment Opportunity Commission (EEOC), which enforces the law. If a person wins the case, he or she may be reinstated, receive back pay, be promoted, or be provided with some other form of compensation.

Recall the incentives that influenced owners of major league baseball clubs, encouraging them to hire the best possible workers. The same logic applies to the hiring of women. Employers have a strong incentive to hire the most productive workers they can find, regardless of gender. The incentive is the advantage that follows when a business develops a strong, productive workforce. This incentive has, to date, played an important role in reducing the two gender gaps, though it has not eliminated either one.

THEN & NOW QUESTIONS for DISCUSSION

1. Which remedy do you think is more likely to reduce discrimination against women in the workplace: legislation like Title VII or the incentives that encourage business people to hire the best possible workers? Explain your answer.

Web Resources

Racial Segregation in Major League Baseball
http://mlb.mlb.com/la/history/jackie_robinson_timeline/timeline_index.jsp

An overview from the Major League Baseball association.

Racial Segregation after the Civil War
http://www.pbs.org/wnet/jimcrow

Jim Crow, history and laws.

The Profit Motive and the Rickey/Robinson Story
http://memory.loc.gov/ammem/collections/robinson/jr1940.html

African American baseball league timeline.

The Jobless Gender Gap
http://finance.fortune.cnn.com/2010/10/08/why-the-jobless-gender-gap-persists

Fortune Magazine provides yet another perspective on the gender gap.

How Did the Marshall Plan Become a Model for Foreign Aid Programs?

Two German workers take a lesson in mechanics on a tractor provided by the Marshall Plan after World War II.

A German coal miner introduces himself as "Hans Fisher. Age 26. Profession: Optimist." It is 1949, and although Hans's Ruhr region in Germany was bombed out in the war, Hans clearly sees what went wrong and how to correct it. He tells us that "when people get hungry enough or cold enough or hopeless enough, they start to look for the easy answers—uniforms and slogans and violence and barbed wire." That outlook led the Nazis to power in Germany and on to a destructive war. The better alternative lies in freedom and economic development.

But how to get started? Hans says American aid to Europe is the answer. The aid program known as the **Marshall Plan** will bring billions of dollars to Germany. That money will enable Germans to buy production equipment and help the German economy to get back on its feet. With what they produce, Germans will export to the world and use their earnings to recover from the war. By the time he has finished telling his story, Hans identifies himself differently: "Name: Hans Fisher. Profession? Just call me a Marshall Planner."

George C. Marshall at a Harvard University graduation in 1947, where he delivered a speech proposing the Marshall Plan.

KEY ECONOMIC CONCEPTS

Command economy	**Infrastructure**
Comparative advantage	**Marshall Plan**
Foreign aid	**Mixed economy**
Gross Domestic	**Primary effects**
Product (GDP)	**Secondary effects**

As you watch Hans in the 1949 film *Me and Mr. Marshall*,[1] you get the idea that his praise for the Marshall Plan is just a little too perfect. In fact, Hans is a made-up character, and *Me and Mr. Marshall* is a promotional film. But is the underlying idea of the film historically and economically correct? How did the Marshall Plan become known as the model for foreign aid programs?

The Historical Context
Europe's Recovery from War

Shortly after World War II ended, it seemed that Europe would recover quickly from wartime death and destruction. By the end of 1945, European nations were reporting that industrial production had returned to 60 percent of its prewar level. The situation was even more favorable in France, Belgium, and the Netherlands, where spring 1946 saw production levels reach 90 percent of their prewar levels. But then the harsh winter of 1946–47, followed by crop failures and other problems, brought extreme scarcity of food and fuel. Conditions were even worse in Germany, where national output fell 70 percent from 1945 to 1947.[2]

The United States economy, on the other hand, made a highly successful transition from wartime to peacetime, with employment and output expanding rapidly. Alone among the major powers, it had suffered only minor damage to its industries and infrastructure during the war.

After the war, U.S. foreign policy in Europe was directed toward countering the Soviet Union (Communist Russia and associated states). Although the United States and Russia had been allies in the war, their relationship soured quickly after the war's end. Eastern Europe fell under Soviet influence, and the United States worried about the military strength of the enlarged Soviet empire.

The vision of a resurgent Western Europe with democratic governments and strong economies was attractive to U.S. policymakers. Europe had experienced two devastating wars in less than 50 years. If Western Europe could rebound, and make itself prosperous and free, perhaps its nations would be uninterested in war. Furthermore, a prosperous, strengthened Western Europe would block continued expansion of Soviet influence.

The postwar U.S. economy clearly had the capacity to aid the struggling economies of Europe and to promote its foreign policy interests with an aid program—but would it? U.S. Secretary of State, George C. Marshall, saw the possibilities; by developing the right sort of economic policy and foreign policy, the United States could promote its own interests while also easing hardships in Europe. Toward that end, in 1947, he formulated the European Recovery Program that would be known thereafter as "the Marshall Plan."

Harry S. Truman signs legislation authorizing the Marshall Plan in 1948.

(Above) The first consignment of sugar under the Marshall Aid Plan arrives in London. (Left) Aid packages were shipped with this label.

The Economics of Foreign Aid

Foreign aid, a granting of money or resources from a donor nation to a recipient nation, might seem to be a simple transfer. It would seem to make the donor country worse off—after all, that country gives up resources it could otherwise spend domestically. It would seem to make the recipient country better off by expanding its opportunities. Both of those assumed effects, however, could be wrong.

1. The donor country may be better off.

Even in terms of its own self-interest, the donor country may be better off. Foreign aid provided by the United States may strengthen U.S. trading partners, improving the quality of imports from them and the United States' ability to export to them. Frequently there are particular groups within a nation who benefit from foreign aid to others, including farmers who grow crops intended for shipment abroad. Foreign aid may also accomplish foreign policy objectives, strengthen alliances, and allow for reduced use of U.S. forces abroad.

2. *The recipient county may be worse off.*

The **primary effect** of an economic policy, its intended and most visible result, is easy to recognize. The primary effect of foreign aid is to increase resources available to the recipient. Foreign aid also has secondary effects, results that are not intended and may work against the primary effects. The **secondary effects** of foreign aid may reduce the effectiveness of aid or even make the recipient nation worse off. Here are some of the reasons:

- As foreign aid goods flood in, they lower the prices people pay to native sellers of the same goods, hurting local producers and possibly putting them out of business. As an example, The *Wall Street Journal* reported that foreign aid money was abundant after the 2010 earthquake in Haiti. "But only a tiny fraction of that money [was] spent in Haiti, buying

goods from local businesses. Worse, the aid [had] the unintended consequence of making life harder for many businesses [there], because of competition from free goods brought in by relief agencies."[3]

- Foreign aid may be poorly designed. What works well in one social and cultural setting may fail badly elsewhere. For example: the "Reindeer People" (the Eveny of northern Asia) abandoned their nomadic herding culture after receiving outside aid that concentrated them in settlements, only to experience social pathology, alcoholism, and tooth decay from a non-native diet. Urbanization that worked in Europe proved to be a failure among the Eveny people.[4] The greater the cultural differences between donor and recipient, the harder it is to make foreign aid work.

- Although foreign aid may help a recipient nation in the short run, over the long run the nation may become dependent on the aid. This long-term dependence may leave a nation worse off than if it had not received aid.

Children in Greece wait in line for bread made from Marshall Plan flour just days before Christmas.

Many governments are aware of these secondary effects and have concluded that, in view of the primary effects, foreign aid can nonetheless be useful as one element of an overall foreign policy. The best foreign aid programs are designed to minimize unwanted effects. Because of those effects, however, foreign aid can have very different consequences in different times and places. In Europe after World War II, the setting was favorable. The United States transferred billions of dollars in aid, with good effect, to Europe's struggling economies under the Marshall Plan.

The Marshall Plan had four major provisions:

1. The plan provided resources that enabled European governments to make loans to their businesses to promote increased growth.

2. When businesses that received aid repaid their loans, the repayments went to local governments; the local governments used the revenue to build or repair basic facilities such as ports, roads and railways. (These basic facilities are known as **infrastructure**; infrastructure was a critical need after the damage and destruction caused by World War II.)

3. Participating governments were required to make reforms that favored market rather than government-controlled solutions to economic problems. Some nations in Eastern Europe, with economies under strong government control, were offered Marshall Plan aid but rejected it because of this condition.

4. A single European coordinating body for the Marshall Plan reported back to the United States.[5]

As the Marshall Plan kicked in, European economies began to grow. Unintended secondary effects were minimal, as European businesses thrived and their governments improved the infrastructure. It was clearly a temporary program, and no long-term dependence resulted.

Was the Marshall Plan "large"?

Yes. It involved transferring about $13 billion from the United States to Europe. (Table 1 shows the total aid transferred by country and year.) That was a large sum overall, amounting to 1.2 percent of the U.S. economy's total production. Today all U.S. foreign aid, to Europe and the rest of the world, is well below half a percent of the U.S. economy.[6] Although the Marshall Plan was large, it was relatively affordable. The agricultural and industrial base of the U.S. had come through the war unscathed, and its economy recovered much more quickly than Europe's.

TABLE 1	Marshall Plan Expenditures by Nation, in Millions of Dollars		
NATION	1948–1949	1949–1950	1950–1951	Cumulative
Austria	232	166	70	468
Belgium and Luxembourg	195	222	360	777
Denmark	103	87	195	385
France	1,085	691	520	2,296
Germany	510	438	500	1,448
Greece	175	156	45	376
Iceland	6	22	15	43
Ireland	88	45	0	133
Italy and Trieste	594	405	205	1,204
Netherlands	471	302	355	1,128
Norway	82	90	200	372
Portugal	0	0	70	70
Sweden	39	48	260	347
Switzerland	0	0	250	250
Turkey	28	59	50	137
United Kingdom	1,316	921	1,060	3,297
Totals	4,924	3,652	4,155	12,731

Source: Roy Gardner, "The Marshall Plan Fifty Years Later: Three What-Ifs and a When," in Martin Schain and Tony Judt, *The Marshall Plan Fifty Years Later* (New York: Palgrave MacMillan, 2001), p. 120.

How well did Europe's economies recover?

At the end of the Marshall Plan's funding in 1952, all the participating nations had expanded their economies to beyond their prewar size. For all the participating nations taken together, total production in 1951 was 35 percent higher than it had been in 1938. The foundations for long-term prosperity had also been laid, and the economies of Western Europe experienced healthy growth for the next two decades.[7]

How did the Marshall Plan promote recovery?

The Marshall Plan's supporters have called it "history's most successful structural adjustment program."[8] It promoted the growth of local business and infrastructure. It operated with clear lines of reporting to the United States. In addition, supporters believe the Marshall Plan successfully promoted a "social contract"—that is, an informal agreement among many Europeans about goals to be sought in society generally. After the war, European economies might have fractured into squabbling interest groups making unreasonable demands—labor and management going for bigger pieces of the economy rather than working to make the economy itself bigger. The Marshall Plan has been cited as one force among many that led to a social contract in which labor implicitly agreed not to bargain aggressively and management agreed to make long-term investments for improved productivity.

Whatever the combination of forces, European governments moved toward **mixed economies**, characterized by shared control by business and government. They turned away from the model favored by the Soviets—**command economies** controlled by the government. After several difficult years following the war, Europe grew rapidly.

How did recipient nations contribute to the Marshall Plan's success?

When the war ended, the European nations, and Germany in particular, continued at first

Workers unload Marshall Plan–funded coal in the Netherlands.

to maintain centralized control of businesses. Gradually they lifted their controls. In West Germany the Director of Economics, Ludwig Erhard, engineered the removal of controls on trade, distribution, production, and prices. Erhard also led currency reforms that stabilized West German money. Right after the war, Germans still used Nazi money, the Reichsmark, and it was uncertain how much that money might be worth in the future. Under Erhard, the new Deutschemark replaced the old money, with government guarantees about the value of the new currency. All this happened shortly before Marshall Plan aid began arriving. The stage was then set for solid economic growth in West Germany.

In France, Italy, and Belgium a similar pattern developed as these European economies phased out wartime economic measures and Marshall Plan aid arrived. Although circumstances varied from one recipient nation to another, internal reforms accompanied by Marshall Plan expenditures led to strong economic growth. Statistically it is difficult to separate out the contributions of the various factors working together. Some economists believe internal reforms were more important than Marshall Plan aid,[9] while others see the aid as vital to solidifying those reforms.[10] However the credit is allocated, it is clear that the European economies were working hard to recover when the Marshall Plan took effect.

Was it important for the U.S. economy to be number 1?

No. The best broad measure of economic well-being is total production (**Gross Domestic Product** or **GDP**) per person. World ranking, especially by overall GDP, has little or no meaning. For the United States, being number 1 in GDP, by a large margin, was possible only because Europe (especially Germany) and Japan had been devastated by war. Their economic weakness did not strengthen the United States. Had they been stronger, they would have been capable of supplying more imports to improve the quality of life in the United States. They would also have been capable of demanding more exports from the United States, improving overall American economic activity.

People do well economically when they can trade freely with others who can produce wanted items at a low opportunity cost. Recall that a producer with a lower opportunity cost than a trading partner is said to have a **comparative advantage**. As recovering European industries developed exports for which they had a comparative advantage, they and their trading partners in Europe and the United States benefited from mutual trade.

QUESTIONS for DISCUSSION

1. How could a foreign aid program benefit people in the United States, such as farmers?
2. How could a foreign nation's businesses be hurt by aid from the United States?
3. Why could the United States better afford to provide foreign aid than its wartime allies after World War II?
4. Which is a more important measure of well-being: an economy's overall GDP or its average GDP per person? Explain your answer.
5. Would the United States have been better off after the war if its trading partners had remained weak? Why or why not?

The Marshall Plan as a Bike Lesson

This cartoon by Dorman Smith in the *Phoenix Gazette* shows an American taxpayer in the form of a father encouraging his son, Europe, to "keep pumpin." This cartoon appeared in 1949, after Marshall Plan expenditures had begun.

Dorman Smith in The Phoenix Gazette, NEA

"He's finally getting the hang of it."

PRIMARY SOURCE QUESTIONS for DISCUSSION

1. What is the goal of the Marshall Plan, according to the cartoon? If this goal is not achieved, what would the alternative be?
2. As depicted, is the Marshall Plan a failure, an immediate success, or a work in progress? Explain your choice.
3. Do you believe a European in the late 1940s would have found the cartoon insulting? Explain your answer.

The photographs in magazines and televised news reports are heart-wrenching, reflecting the underlying tragedy: young African children on the verge of starvation. No wonder governments and private aid organizations have responded with massive foreign aid to Africa. Unfortunately, foreign aid sent to Africa has been successful only in part, barely holding the line, in some areas, against poverty and hunger.

More substantial long-term success has been hard to achieve. In response, economist Glenn Hubbard and others have proposed a "Marshall Plan for Africa." The Marshall Plan's effects in Europe promoted growth of local businesses, Hubbard explains, but African aid has concentrated on funding government and nonprofit projects rather than strengthening local business. "The Marshall Plan worked. Aid to Africa has not. An African Marshall Plan is long, long overdue," Hubbard says.[11]

Figure 1 shows how Africa has missed out on worldwide economic growth. When the rest of the world was industrializing (1870–1913), Africa was lagging. The differences have become more profound over time.

Although the story of foreign aid to Africa is too big to capture with any one example, a Norwegian plan to help the Turkana tribe in Kenya illustrates some of the issues. The plan involved training 20,000 members of the tribe to catch fish from an inland lake; tribe members would build a plant to freeze the catch for export. Donors paid for the training and the plant. Unfortunately, in Kenya's hot climate, the freezer plant took too much energy to operate. The plant was an economic failure; it closed after operating for less than a week in 1981. Worse, some of the Turkana who turned from livestock herding to fishing

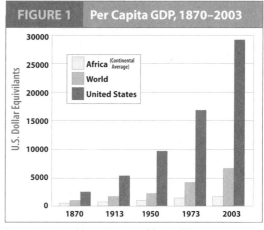

FIGURE 1 Per Capita GDP, 1870–2003

Source: Angus Maddison, *Contours of the World Economy 1–2030 AD: Essays in Macro-Economic History* (Oxford: Oxford University Press, 2007), p. 382.

in anticipation of the project were then dependent on aid from outside. Culturally, the development project had not fit the Turkana well because the tribe considered cattle as wealth and fishing as taboo.[12]

In its strategy, the Norwegian plan to aid the Turkana was strikingly different from the Marshall Plan. Rather than strengthening a local enterprise, it sought to create an entirely new business. It attempted to transplant a successful business idea from Norway to Kenya, where conditions were different, without adequate allowances for the differences. It did not take account of cultural differences.

In calling a Marshall Plan for Africa long overdue, Hubbard is both paying tribute to the effectiveness of the original Marshall Plan and delivering an unfortunate verdict on African aid to date. Still, Hubbard concludes optimistically: "More than half a century after the United States helped rebuild a war-torn Europe, it's time Africa got the same chance."[13]

QUESTIONS for DISCUSSION

1. According to Hubbard, how has modern aid to Africa differed from Marshall Plan aid?
2. Why did the Norwegian plan to aid the Turkana in Kenya fail? What might have been done differently to promote a better outcome?
3. If the example of the Marshall Plan were followed closely in African aid, would the results be successful? Explain your answer.

Web Resources

The Marshall Plan speech
http://www.usaid.gov/multimedia/video/marshall/marshallspeech.html

The text of the Marshall Plan speech delivered at a Harvard University commencement.

Me and Mr. Marshall
http://www.marshallplanimages.com/me-and-marshall

A black-and-white film promoting the Marshall Plan in aiding European reconstruction after World War II

For European Recovery: The Fiftieth Anniversary of the Marshall Plan
http://www.loc.gov/exhibits/marshall

This Library of Congress online exhibition includes a wealth of resources about the Marshall Plan, reactions to it, and evaluation of wartime recovery in Europe.

A Marshall Plan for Africa
http://www.foreignpolicy.com/articles/2009/08/13/think_again_aid_to_africa

From Foreign Policy magazine's website, Glenn Hubbard's brief for a Marshall Plan-like model for foreign aid to Africa.

What Were the Origins of the African American Middle Class?

This 1942 photo shows a reading lesson in an African American school in Washington, D.C.

A Business Startup in a Time of Change

Judging from his background, George Johnson faced slim chances of financial success. He was born in Mississippi in a three-room sharecropper's shack in 1927. As an African American in the Deep South of the 1920s, he faced a future of segregation and discrimination.

Johnson's childhood was difficult. He was only two years old when his parents separated. His mother, Priscilla, moved the family to Chicago, where they endured the Great Depression together. Young George showed a spirit of enterprise at an early age, shining shoes to make money as an eight-year-old. He worked other jobs, too, at a restaurant and a bowling alley, while continuing his education. Although he never finished high school, he did get a job at a cosmetics firm, and he continued to put his enterprising spirit to good use.

You may have heard the expression "on a shoestring"—as in "They managed to buy that house on a shoestring." The expression refers to financing that is very small and casual. George

George and Joan Johnson, founders of the noted minority enterprise Johnson Products, in 2010.

KEY ECONOMIC CONCEPTS

The Great Migration   **Invest**
Human capital   **Middle class**

Johnson and his wife, Joan, started a company on a shoestring. With a $250 "vacation loan" and another $250 borrowed from a friend, they launched Johnson Products in 1954. Their niche was hair-care products for African American consumers. The company grew slowly at first; however, after years of continued growth, it became, in 1971, the first African American-owned company traded on the American Stock Exchange.[1] As the company continued to do well, George Johnson became a multi-millionaire.

George Johnson has been remarkably successful. Still, his story is not altogether surprising. African Americans made substantial economic progress throughout the 20th century. Even before the civil rights movement of the 1960s, many African Americans attained middle-class status. What were the origins of the 20th century African American middle class?

The Historical Context
The Great Migration

George Johnson participated in a large demographic shift known as **The Great Migration**—the widespread movement of African Americans out of the South between 1910 and 1930. In all, about 1.75 million individuals relocated in that time.[2] This movement was followed by a second Great Migration, not as widely noted as the first, in which an even larger number of African Americans, possibly five million or more, moved out of the South from 1940 to 1970.

A group of African American migrants from Florida make their way to New Jersey, 1944.

The first Great Migration came in response to a combination of factors that made the South increasingly unattractive to African Americans. One factor had to do with farming. African American farmers in the South were more likely to work on land they did not own; their income was a portion of the crop they harvested for the land owner. This arrangement was referred to as sharecropping; it was more common in the South than elsewhere. The small income sharecroppers earned made it difficult for them to save enough money to buy land and become independent farmers.

A second factor was heightened racial discrimination. As southern states regained their autonomy in the aftermath of the Civil War, racial discrimination and segregation worsened with the passage in many states of Jim Crow laws. Violence against African Americans became an ever-present threat in some areas.

Meanwhile, outside the South, industrial expansion and reduced immigration from Europe created job opportunities in well-paying manufacturing jobs. As African Americans began to discover these opportunities and relocate in the North, Midwest, and West, they sent information back to friends and relatives in the South, and they provided assistance to new arrivals. Thus, as the South was becoming less attractive to African Americans, other regions were becoming more attractive.

The Great Migration contributed to an increase in African Americans' educational achievement. Figure 1 shows a striking increase in school enrollments among nonwhite Americans from 1850 to 1950. During the era of slavery,

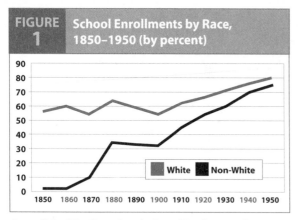

FIGURE 1

School Enrollments by Race, 1850–1950 (by percent)

White   Non-White

Source: "School Enrollment Rates by Sex and Race," *Historical Statistics of the United States,* Series Bc439 and Bc440.

nonwhite school enrollment nationally stood at 1.8 percent, compared with 56.2 percent for white enrollment. Nonwhite enrollment jumped sharply after the Civil War, to 33.8 percent, and then leveled off and declined slightly until resuming a sustained increase after 1900. By 1950, during the second Great Migration, the enrollment gap between whites and blacks had closed to 4.5 points. This figure does not mean that African Americans had gained equalization of educational opportunity, especially not in areas with racially segregated schools, but it does reflect a remarkable increase in school attendance.

School attendance provides one measure of educational progress; literacy provides another. Economists R.A. Margo and William J. Collins found a similar gap in literacy between white Americans and African Americans from 1870 to 1930. However, they also found that the literacy gap declined steadily over that period. One important mechanism was the establishment of schools for African American children in the South, where slavery had earlier suppressed schooling for African Americans. Gains in literacy brought substantial economic gains to African Americans, even in the presence of segregation and discrimination. Increased education also was associated with the Great Migration, as those moving out of the South tended to have higher educational levels than those who remained.[3]

For George Johnson, these demographic changes meant that he would find a thriving and growing African American community in Chicago when he arrived there in 1929. When African Americans left the South, they moved disproportionately to cities, where incomes were higher. There would be urban consumers for products such as Johnson's, in the North and the South.

The Economics of Human Capital and Internal Migration

Human capital consists of a person's skills, knowledge, and abilities. People are said to **invest** in human capital—for example, by completing high school and mastering work-related skills. Investments in human capital are similar to other investments in an important way. When you invest money, you give up the use of the money now, expecting to get back even more money in the future. When you give up time and money to go to school now, you are investing in your human capital, hoping to gain from your education in the future. Getting additional education is a well-tested strategy for earning more income.

Formal schooling is not the only way to increase human capital. On-the-job training and apprenticeships also help people to be more productive. Beyond these examples, anything you do to improve your skills, knowledge, and abilities will add to your human capital.

Deciding to move from the South to the North might seem to differ greatly from deciding to get additional schooling. Economically, however, the choices are similar. Both involve giving up something now in order to gain something valuable in the future. The expected gain typically involves higher earnings, often with greater possibilities of advancement. Some people also find it rewarding to leave the past behind and make a new start in a new place.

All of these forces were in evidence between 1910 and 1930 during the first Great Migration. Similar forces applied between 1940 and 1970 during the second Great Migration. African Americans increasingly were developing more human capital.

HISTORICAL QUESTIONS & ECONOMIC ANSWERS

What does it mean to be "middle class"?

There is no single, agreed-upon definition of what it takes to be **middle class**. Most people would say, however, that the middle class is made up of those whose incomes fall in a middle-income range: above the poverty level, but not high enough for them to be considered wealthy. Here are some elaborations of that general idea that have been commonly accepted at various times in U.S. history:

- Having an income sufficient to enjoy a "comfortable" standard of living. In the first half of the 20th century, many Americans earned enough income from employment in blue-collar jobs to attain a comfortable standard of living.

- Having a "white-collar" job, not necessarily in one of the high-status professions. Office clerks and sales people were said to hold white-collar jobs throughout much of the 20th century.

- Having an income at least twice the federal poverty level. The federal poverty level is an estimate of the minimum income required to provide a family with basic necessities such as food, shelter, and clothing.

- Having a college degree.[4]

Notice that these criteria can be overlapping or contradictory. Someone holding a college degree today might receive less income than twice the federal poverty level; someone with a well-paying industrial job can be "blue-collar" but still, today as in the past, earn a middle-class income. Of all Americans today, 53 percent view themselves as middle class. Among African Americans today, 50 percent view themselves as middle class.[5]

What is the statistical evidence that African Americans entered the middle class in large numbers after 1910?

The longest-running evidence comes from government data on occupations. Table 1 shows information about the occupations of African Americans beginning in 1890, 20 years before the first Great Migration. This overview extends through 1970, the year in which the second Great Migration ended. The overview shows steady growth in white-collar employment, with large gains in the "professional, technical and administrative" and "clerical and sales" categories.

Another measure of middle class membership is holding a college degree. The U.S. Census

TABLE 1	Occupational Distribution of African Americans, 1890–1970, by Percentage								
Occupation	1890	1900	1910	1920	1930	1940	1950	1960	1970
Professional, technical and administrative	1.1	1.2	1.3	1.7	2.5	3.8	5.1	6.1	10.6
Clerical and sales	0.9	0.6	0.4	0.8	0.7	1.8	4.6	7.3	16.0
Manufacturing and mechanical	5.8	6.9	10.6	18.7	18.6	13.1	24.1	25.7	27.0
Trade, transportation, and communication	3.8	4.6	6.0	9.4	10.5	--	--	6.3	5.7
Personal service	16.0	21.2	14.2	23.0	19.3	11.7	15.2	16.9	20.0
Domestic service	13.1	11.8	11.9		9.3	22.4	15.1	15.0	8.3
Nonfarm labor	--	--	--	2.2	2.0	14.2	15.5	12.6	9.4
Agricultural	56.2	53.7	54.6	44.2	36.1	32.3	16.5	8.1	3.0

Source: : Stephan Thernstrom, Ann Orlov and Oscar Handlin, *Harvard Encyclopedia of American Ethnic Groups* (Cambridge, MA: Belknap Press of Harvard University Press, 1980), p. 21.

began asking a question about this in 1940, at the beginning of the second Great Migration. Table 2 shows a steady increase in African American college participation during the time.

Yet another measure of middle-class membership is income at least twice the poverty level. For the years before 1959 (before the government collected detailed information on race and poverty), guesswork is necessary, but Figure 2 provides a reasonable approximation. It shows the estimated percentage of African American families with incomes more than twice the federal poverty level. The information summarized in Figure 2 indicates an overall upward trend, but with some setbacks from 1947 through 1971.

Why do most people consider middle-class status important?

People consider middle-class status important because it marks their full integration into American culture. Middle-class status is also thought to protect against adversity across generations. That is, children from middle-class families are less likely than others to fall into poverty. This generalization, however, may not apply across the board. One recent, widely cited report has found sharp differences across races in this effect of middle-class membership: 45 percent of black children from middle-income families ended up "near poor," while the corresponding number of "near poor" for white children from middle-income families was 16 percent.[6]

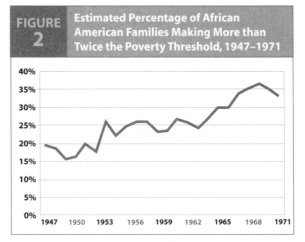

What methods did African Americans use to enter the middle class?

Well-paid industrial jobs outside the South were a major entry ticket for African Americans in the early 20th century. College education also became important—obtained from traditionally black institutions and from colleges and universities in general. Small-business ownership continues to be an important route to the middle class. A recent study estimates that African Americans are 50 percent more likely to engage in business start-ups than their white counterparts.[7]

Were African American leaders in agreement about the best approach to economic progress?

No. Some leaders favored self-help in the African-American community and a nonconfrontational approach in relationships with others. The leading supporter of this view was Booker T. Washington, founder and president of Tuskegee Institute, in Alabama. Washington believed that markets would reward hard work and bring about racial reconciliation. "No race that has anything to contribute to the markets of the world is long in any degree ostracized," he said.[8]

Critics believed Washington was conceding too much. Led by W.E.B. Du Bois, they called for a movement to ensure full political and economic equality for African Americans. Du Bois was a

TABLE 2	African American College Participation	
YEAR	Percentage of African American Males Completing 4 or More Years of College	Percentage of African American Females Completing 4 Years or More Years of College
1940	1.4	1.2
1950	2.1	2.4
1960	3.5	3.6
1970	4.5	4.4
1980	7.1	8.1
1990	11.9	10.8

Source: U.S. Historical Statistics, "Years of school completed, by sex, race, and ethnicity."

college professor and researcher who became a co-founder of the National Association for the Advancement of Colored People. To those who asked for patience in improving race relations, he responded: "Now is the accepted time, not tomorrow, not some more convenient season."[9] To those who shrank back from the cost, he responded, "the cost of liberty is less than the price of repression."[10]

Washington's and Du Bois's approaches, although different in their political implications, illustrate fundamental principles of economic reasoning. Greater human capital leads to higher earnings. Markets promote opportunity, yet markets operate within the rules of the game set by political institutions. Fundamental changes in those institutions, spurred by the civil rights movement, would also be necessary.

How did the beginnings of economic success for African Americans interact with the civil rights movement?

Between 1940 and 1950, African American men saw their annual earnings increase on average from $4,956 to $8,655 (in inflation-adjusted dollars). The increases resulted from migration, improved job opportunities, and overall growth in the U.S. economy. These increases meant that African Americans were becoming a powerful commercial force when the civil rights movement arrived in the mid-1960s. Although earnings were increasing rapidly for African Americans, they were substantially below those of white Americans, which increased from $11,441 to $15,677 in the same ten 10-year period.[11]

Did northward movements of African Americans continue throughout the 20th century?

No. There was a reversal later in the century. By the century's end the South was attracting African American migrants from the Northeast, Midwest and West. Southern metropolitan areas, especially Atlanta, drew large numbers.

The term "brain drain" is sometimes used to describe a negative effect that occurs when talented people leave an area. There was an opposite effect, a "brain gain," in the migration of African Americans to the South late in the 20th century, since many of the migrants held college degrees. "The 'brain gain' states of Georgia, Texas, and Maryland attracted the most black college graduates from 1995 to 2000, while New York suffered the largest net loss," according to William Frey. Reasons for the reverse migration, Frey reported, include economic growth, improved race relations, and "long-standing cultural and kinship ties" among black families. The migratory trend promoted growth of the African American middle class in southern cities.[12]

QUESTIONS for DISCUSSION

1. When did significant increases in nonwhite school enrollment begin occurring? Did they predate the Civil Rights movement of the 1960s?
2. How can people increase their human capital apart from gaining more formal schooling?
3. How is investing in human capital similar to investing money?
4. In what sense is deciding to move to a new job like investing in human capital?
5. Which is harder: moving within a nation or moving to another nation? Why?
6. Is a college graduate automatically considered "middle class"? Why or why not?
7. How hard is it for people to achieve middle-class status in the United States today if they are not born into that class? Explain your answer.

A President Takes Notice of the Great Migration and Its Importance

The passage that follows is from a speech delivered by President Warren G. Harding on October 26, 1921, in Birmingham, Alabama. It was the first presidential speech in the South calling for racial equality. (Note that the language of the time employed the archaic terms "Negro" and "colored" for African Americans.)

The World War brought us to full recognition that the race problem is national rather than merely sectional. There are no authentic statistics, but it is common knowledge that the World War [World War I] was marked by a great migration of colored people to the North and West. They were attracted by the demand for labor and the higher wage offered. It has brought the question of race closer to the North and West, and I believe, it has served to modify somewhat the views of those sections on the question. It has made the South realize its industrial dependence on the labor of the black man and made the North realize the difficulties of the community in which two greatly differing races are brought to live side by side. I should say that it has been responsible for a larger charity on both sides, a beginning of better understanding and in the light of that better understanding perhaps we shall be able to consider this problem together as a problem of all sections and of both races, in whose solution the best intelligence of both must be enlisted.

Source: "Harding Says Negro Must Have Equality in Political Life," *New York Times*, October 27, 1921, p. 1.

President Warren G. Harding arrives in Birmingham, Alabama, for a key speech on race relations.

QUESTIONS for DISCUSSION

1. Does President Harding express certainty about the size of population movements during World War I? Why or why not?
2. In President Harding's view, are race relations a regional or a national problem? What economic and demographic event caused the nation to come to this realization, according to President Harding?
3. To what does President Harding attribute the large-scale migration?
4. According to President Harding, what key economic element does the South have to acknowledge because of the Great Migration? How have Southerners come to realize this?

Continuing Musical Influences from a Migration Long Past

Today's most noted pop artists owe a debt to the Great Migration, according to music critics Mike Householder and Jeff Karoub. Their reasoning is that pop artists today are highly influenced by a sound that originated in Detroit in 1959, the "Motown" sound. Motown featured African American artists and was run by African American executives. Householder and Karoub ask:

> Would there be a Beyoncé or Mariah Carey had Diana Ross, Martha Reeves and Gladys Knight not come first? . . . How about Kanye West and Justin Timberlake? What would have become of their musical careers had Motown not blazed a trail with the likes of Michael Jackson, Smokey Robinson, Marvin Gaye, Stevie Wonder, The Temptations and The Four Tops?[13]

Before Motown, American rock and roll was tame and showmanship was lacking. After Motown, a wide variety of artists adopted its strong bass lines, rhythm and blues-inspired accompaniment, and brilliant vocals. Before Motown, African American artists played mostly to black audiences. After Motown, African American artists crossed over to play for multiracial, nationwide audiences. Householder and Karoub see the Motown influence as stretching across the entire contemporary musical landscape.

The founding father of Motown Records was Berry Gordy, whose parents moved from Georgia to Detroit during the Great Migration. Gordy combined Deep South influences with the urban energy of Detroit in formulating the distinctive Motown sound. The artists that came to prominence through Motown and other record labels also were children of the Great Migration, according to the Pulitzer Prize-winning author Isabel Wilkerson, who lists these examples:

- The Jackson 5 (including, most notably, Michael Jackson), who were from Gary, Indiana, after their father had migrated from Arkansas;

- Diana Ross, whose parents had migrated to Detroit from West Virginia and Alabama;

- Miles Davis (a jazz musician, not known as a pop performer), whose parents had migrated from Arkansas to Illinois; and

- John Coltrane (also a jazz musician), who moved from North Carolina to Philadelphia at age 17.

Wilkerson spent 15 years studying the Great Migration in preparation for her book *The Warmth of Other Suns*.[14] She told an interviewer, "It is hard to separate out the legacy of this great migration because it's so embedded in our culture." On the overall effect of the migration, Wilkerson says, "There are certain things that we take for granted that simply would not have existed without the Great Migration."[15]

The Great Migration provides an example of how individual decisions drive social and economic change. "It was a leaderless migration. People made decisions on the basis of what was in their heart, and I think this is a story of inspiration that says that so much power is within us," Wilkerson told an interviewer. "These individual people, one by one, multiplied by six million, ended up helping to change this country."[16]

QUESTIONS for DISCUSSION

1. How could African-American musicians who grew up outside the South be influenced by its music?
2. The Great Migration is referred to by Wilkerson as "leaderless." How could a movement without a leader come to involve so many people?
3. Some people think of music as pure artistry, based on such elements as talent, composition, and technique. Given the example discussed here, is music also based on economic decisions?

Web Resources

Johnson Products Company
http://www.encyclopedia.chicagohistory.org/pages/2729.html

An expanded history of Johnson Products Company.

The Great Migration
http://www.encyclopedia.chicagohistory.org/pages/545.html

An expanded history of the Great Migration.

A Brief History of Motown
http://www.time.com/time/arts/article/0,8599,1870975,00.html

This TIME magazine collection includes an audio slideshow of five of Motown's best tunes.

Why Did Communism Collapse?

Germans gather on the Berlin Wall and begin to tear it down, November 9, 1989.

Ulrike and Conny's Separate Lives

Ulrike and Conny were identical twins born in 1969 in East Germany. They were separated from each other as babies and adopted by different families. At age 12, Ulrike moved with her adoptive family to West Germany, which had a political and economic system much like that of Western Europe and the United States. Conny remained in East Germany, where the governmental system was communism. Under **communism**, property is publicly owned and a ruling Communist Party imposes a system of strong central control over all social institutions. Because they lived in countries that differed greatly in their governmental and economic systems, Ulrike and Conny lived very different lives.

In the East, Conny said, "The secret police were everywhere. There was little to buy or to eat in the shops, no freedom, and things like fashion and music were very limited." On the other side of the border, Ulrike said, "As a teenager in the West, I wanted for nothing. We had lovely summer holidays on the Mediterranean, went skiing in the winter and every Christmas and birthday I was showered with presents."[1]

KEY ECONOMIC CONCEPTS

Communism	**Scarcity**
Rules of the game	**Market economy**
Socialism	

Although Conny and Ulrike tell unique stories, the differences in their standards of living were far from unique. Most West Germans had far higher incomes than their counterparts in the East. It is natural to wonder how two countries with the same culture and language could have differed to the extent they did in material standards of living. The answer lies in differences between the East German variety of communism and the West German market economy.

For 44 years, from 1947 to 1991, the United States fought a Cold War—never declared, but always tense—against the Soviet Union and its allies. The Cold War dominated foreign policy and had wide-ranging domestic effects, from large investments in the production of weapons to schoolchildren's drills to prepare for missile attacks. It was a war of competing nations, but also of competing economic systems. Markets and self-government in the West stood in opposition to communism in the Soviet bloc. Suddenly in 1989 Soviet communism collapsed. Then, with the further dissolution of the Soviet Union in

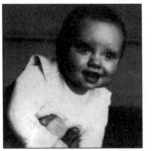

Twins Ulrike Reichenbach (left) and Conny Holzbrecher grew up under very different conditions—Ulrike in what was West Germany and Conny in what was East Germany.

1991, the Cold War was over. At the time, it was a big surprise. Why did communism collapse in East Germany and throughout the Soviet bloc? And what can we learn about communism by studying the German example?

The Historical Context
Germany Is Divided

At the time of the Yalta Conference in 1945, the United States, Britain, and the Soviet Union were close to victory over Germany in World War II. They had already begun planning for what postwar Europe would look like. At Yalta they agreed that Germany and its capital, Berlin, would be divided, that Germany would be occupied temporarily by the victorious nations' armies, and that after Germany had gotten back on its feet, the occupying forces would leave.

The occupation in the western parts of Germany was ending in 1949 when Soviet leader Josef Stalin established East Germany, formally known as the German Democratic Republic, as a separate nation. Stalin's move made the temporary division of Germany more permanent. For years there would be an East Germany and a West Germany. East Germany would be closely allied with the Soviet Union and would have communist institutions. West Germany would be allied with Britain and the United States and would have a democratic form of government.

The Economics of Market Systems and Socialist Systems

Born in the East where the state had great authority, Conny and Ulrike were put up for adoption against their parents' wishes. "Our mother was forced by the communist state to put us up for adoption because she was a young mother with three older children by our father," Conny explained. She added, "She was struggling, especially as all women were expected to work as well."[2] Conny was adopted by East German parents.

Ulrike's adoptive adoptive parents also lived in East Germany, initially. They were politically active, however, and were expelled from East

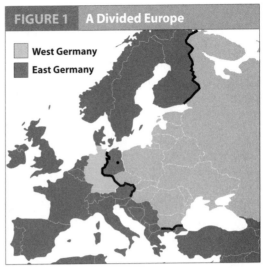

FIGURE 1   A Divided Europe

West Germany

East Germany

The map shows how Europe was divided between communist and non-communist nations after World War II. Communist nations are shown to the east and north—most of them behind the black line that represents the Iron Curtain. Not all communist nations were part of the Soviet (Iron Curtain) bloc. The black dot represents the divided city of Berlin.

Germany when Ulrike was 12. For the next eight years, Ulrike lived in the prosperous West of a divided Germany. Then, after the fall of the Berlin Wall in 1989, the two Germanys were reunited. Still later, Conny and Ulrike were reunited.

The lives Conny and Ulrike lived before they were reunited illustrate some of the consequences that followed as European governments made decisions about how to deal with **scarcity**, the mismatch between the many things people want and the limited resources available to satisfy those wants. The economic growth of the late 19th and early 20th centuries, far from putting an end to scarcity, brought new challenges. New industrial methods generated larger amounts of goods and services, and people wondered who would gain and who would lose from this development. Would the economic growth merely make the rich richer as the working classes worked harder? Or would the benefits of industrialization and growth be widely distributed?

To Karl Marx, the answer was clear. Marx (1818–1883) was a German philosopher and economist; he and Friedrich Engels were the founders of modern communism. Economic growth, Marx believed, would provide benefits for the upper class, which would take advantage of workers. However, workers would not stand for this treatment, he said. Instead they would demand that the market economy be replaced by **socialism**: government ownership of industry, with policies aimed at promoting equality. The shift to socialism would lead in turn, according to Marx, to communism, under which private property would be abolished and complete economic and social equality would be achieved. Followers of Marx participated in the Russian Revolution of 1917 and eventually took control of the Russian government. Under the leadership of Vladimir Lenin, they established a communist state, later known as the Soviet Union.

The leaders of Western Europe and the United States took a different approach to distributing the benefits of economic growth. They believed that democratic governments could guarantee individual rights while leaving most economic decisions to individuals participating in the market economy. The **market economy** would rely mainly on individual choices and market transactions between producers and consumers to deal with the problem of scarcity. Government would step in if the market economy led to abuses that could not otherwise be corrected.

Although theorists have argued about the merits of pure socialism, pure communism, and pure market economies, there have been no pure examples of these systems in the real world. In practice, the question has been: how much central control should governments exercise over the economy and individuals? The answer given would have important effects on consumers and workers. Socialist systems promised to reduce the inequality that might occur because of industrialization. Under socialism, if the owner of an industry got rich, that owner was the government. Profits could be widely distributed. Market economies promised more freedom and more opportunity. There would be incentives for producers to produce what people wanted. Along with the freedom and opportunity, however, there would be more risk. Those who did badly in a market economy would find themselves poor.

Because of the way World War II ended, Germany provided a testing ground for the two systems. In West Germany, participants in the market economy made production decisions and determined incomes. Steel provides an example of how the system worked. If consumers bought more products containing steel, their decisions would send a signal to steel producers to make more. The higher demand for steel would create more work and income for steelworkers. The increased emphasis on steel would be more a result of consumer choice than of government decree.

In East Germany's socialist economy, the government owned key industries and had power to allocate incomes and goods and services. If the East German government wanted more steel produced, it could simply issue the order. If it wanted steel workers to receive higher incomes, that could also be accomplished by decree. Because the East German government had strong central control of all social institutions from factories to schools, the system was also accurately described as communist.

Because of scarcity, market economies and socialist economies must answer three basic economic questions: what to produce, how to produce, and for whom to produce. The answers they provide serve to distinguish one system from another.

1. What to produce?

In a market economy, what to produce is determined by "dollar voting." Someone buys a bag of apples and gets to eat them. Not only that, but buying apples is like casting a vote for their continued production. Buying Golden Delicious apples is a specific vote for that product. If enough

The Trabant automobile became a symbol of East German manufacturing.

people vote for it with their dollars, Golden Delicious apples will continue to be produced. The producers will make money, giving them good reasons to keep the supply coming.

In a socialist economy, central authorities determine what to produce. If they want to move an economy away from consumer goods toward more military armament, they can. If they want to produce fewer apples and more guns, they can.

The differences became striking across East and West Germany. In the West, consumers chose from a wide array of products from all over the world. In the East, consumers had restricted choices determined by the central authorities. The banana became a symbol of the difference. Bananas, commonly available around the world, were rare in East Germany because the central authorities considered them an unnecessary luxury. (Bananas grow in the tropics and must be imported for German consumers.) Bananas even became a highly prized gift, often given to East Germans by relatives visiting from the West.[3] In the West, bananas were commonplace because people voted for them with their money—easily covering the cost of importing them and returning a profit to grocery stores that stocked them.

Notice how scarcity forces the issue. No society can have all the foods it wants in unlimited quantities. In Germany, however, the West's market system was more effective than the East's socialist system in dealing with scarcity. Consumers' dollar votes for particular products caused those products to be supplied. In the East, central authorities made the decisions but struggled with providing the mix of goods that would satisfy consumers and producers.

2. How to produce?

In a market economy, how to produce is determined by the cost of resources. If fuel is expensive and insulation is cheap, merchants will conserve on fuel by building highly insulated stores. If labor is very expensive, builders will get a ditch dug by hiring a backhoe and operator, not by hiring 12 people with 12 shovels. Notice that in a market economy there is no central authority telling people where to work; instead, they find the best jobs they can.

East German border guards man a guard tower at the border between East and West Germany.

In a socialist economy, central authorities decide how output is to be produced. They decide on the technology and they assign people to jobs. The central authorities, unlike the producers in a market system, are not guided by profit but instead by whatever goals they choose to adopt. In East Germany, the primary goals were heavy manufacturing and military armament.

In East Germany, central control took the form of production quotas (linked to the state's primary goals) assigned by the government to individual industries and the whole economy. There were two Five-Year Plans and a Seven-Year Plan; each specified ambitious production targets and empowered the state to allocate key resources to achieve the targets. Production often fell short of the plans.

3. For whom to produce?

In a market economy, output ordinarily goes to those who are willing and able to pay. When the output is a concert ticket, there are no great moral issues arising from this system. If you like the music, you pay for a ticket and attend the concert. If you do not like the music, no one forces you to attend. And if some people cannot afford tickets, there is no great social concern; a concert is not a life-or-death matter. A similar attitude would apply to the distribution of many goods and services in a market economy.

When a vital good is allocated by markets—say, the oil used to heat a home in wintertime—many people do have qualms about the outcomes of market distribution. We are unwilling to let people freeze simply because they are unable to afford fuel, and so we do not allocate heating oil (or medical care, or housing) purely through markets. For those unable to pay, market economies have adopted a variety of programs to assist people who would otherwise be left out. Still, most goods and services in a market economy go to those willing and able to pay.

As we saw, a socialist government can directly answer the question of "for whom?" to produce. Such a government owns key industries and has power to allocate incomes and goods and services. The central authorities can set pay scales across the economy and, if they wish to do so, they can control the prices of vital goods and services to make them more affordable. In East Germany, low-cost housing and basic foodstuffs led to low poverty rates. Government policy also made most luxury items expensive and scarce.

East Germany was widely considered the most prosperous of the Soviet bloc nations in Eastern Europe. Even so, it was considerably less prosperous than West Germany. The economic system in West Germany was market-oriented (the government did not own all the means of production and distribution), but with a stronger role played by the central government, and with more generous welfare assistance, than the economy in the United States.

HISTORICAL QUESTIONS & ECONOMIC ANSWERS

Why did West Germany's economy grow faster than East Germany's?

West Germany protected the right to own private property; it also preserved personal incentives for its citizens. One incentive was profits. Business owners knew that if they developed new products or cut costs, they would be able to keep their after-tax profits. In the East, profits generated in any enterprise belonged to the state. This arrangement blunted the incentive to earn profits in the first place, and also discouraged innovation and efficiency.

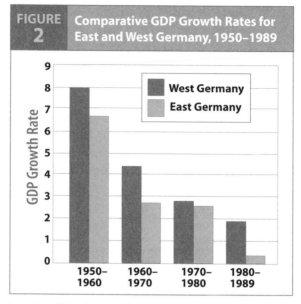

FIGURE 2 Comparative GDP Growth Rates for East and West Germany, 1950–1989

Source: Jaap Sleifer, *Planning Ahead and Falling Behind: The East German Economy in Comparison with West Germany 1936–2002* (Berlin: Akademie Verlag GmbH, 2006), p. 50.

Also, East Germany's economy was closely associated with the slow-growing Soviet bloc of nations. East Germany had been founded at the direction of Soviet leader Josef Stalin, and it was integrated into the Soviet economic sphere. By the early 1980s, it had become apparent that Soviet-style central planning would not compete well in a world increasingly characterized by global trade and competition.[4] The Soviet system's strength was in heavy industry and production of military armaments. It was not well suited for dealing in consumer goods, services, or intellectual property—all industries that require creativity and initiative that is difficult to administer centrally.

Figure 2 shows comparative growth rates for the East and West German economies from 1950 to 1989. West Germany outstripped the East in each 10-year period. Postwar recovery pushed both nations' growth rates upward in the 1950s, followed by more normal growth rates in the 1960s and 1970s. The slowing world economy pushed West Germany's growth rate to around two percent in the 1980s, but that rate was still stronger than the rate of East German growth. By reunification in 1989, East Germany's growth rate had fallen to 0.3 percent.

What made the Wall come down in 1989?

The Berlin Wall was the most prominent symbol of the East-West division. It was a militarized barrier that kept East Germans from migrating to West Berlin. East German border guards were ordered to use armed force if necessary to prevent migration. Tension grew throughout the time of the Wall. There were some daring escapes from East Germany over the wall, and there were sad stories of refugees being shot and killed by border guards.

All this changed in 1989. East Germans had long been free to travel back and forth to Hungary, a member of the Soviet bloc. In August 1989, Hungary opened its border with non-communist Austria. East Germans then could travel to Hungary, and then to Austria and then—anywhere. Thousands of East Germans left through Hungary, not intending to return. After several months of jockeying about who could leave East Germany and when, thousands of East Germans massed at the Berlin Wall, eager to leave. By then the border guards were unwilling to use force and unwilling to stop the exodus. The Wall began to come down on November 9, 1989.

Since November 1989, historians and journalists have struggled to make sense of the night the wall began to come down, attempting to put together a timeline of decisions that might have caused it to happen. They have not succeeded. Seemingly random factors, such as the need to make key decisions when officials were asleep and not to be disturbed, were important. A study by the *Washington Post* published in 2009 concluded: "[M]omentous events are also a sort of ambush of history, when all those long-term pressures come together in an unexpected way. The opening of the Berlin Wall, largely unintentional, was such an event, an unsettling thought for those who see history as the result of strategy and planning by pivotal leaders."[5]

Did other communist nations have experiences similar to Germany's?

The German experience was not unusual. All over the world, communist nations have found their economic systems to be ill-suited to the global economics of 1989 and beyond.[6] Communist nations could fix prices and incomes within their borders, but those prices often turned out to make no sense. In Poland, for example, the central government once set the price of bread very low so that everyone could afford bread. The price was so low, however, that farmers would buy packaged bread and feed it to their pigs. It was cheaper than hog feed. Store shelves were bare as bread intended for people went to pigs.

In China, pure socialism worked poorly. After the Chinese authorities abandoned early socialist efforts, a home-grown blend of markets and central government put China on a path toward strong economic growth. Even Cuba and North Korea, the nations most devoted to communism recently, have found that pure communism is difficult to manage. The lack of incentives for innovation and efficiency has left both nations lagging in their efforts to deal with scarcity.

Although the German experience with communism was not unusual, it was striking because it showed how people with a common language and culture might achieve very different economic results, given different political and economic systems. As we saw in Chapter 1, the **rules of the game** matter.

QUESTIONS for DISCUSSION

1. How did Germany become a divided nation after World War II?
2. How do market and socialist economies differ in deciding what goods to produce?
3. How did the banana become a symbol of East-West differences in Germany?
4. Based on the German experience, how can an economic system be responsive to consumers if the government does not require a consumer focus?
5. Why would communist countries have difficulty succeeding in a global economy where computers and innovation are more important than strength in heavy manufacturing?

Why Did Communism Collapse?

The Trabant, and the Fall of the Wall

PRIMARY SOURCE

Below is an account of the fall of the Berlin Wall, written by someone who was there. Andreas Ramos was born in Colombia and grew up in the United States, but he had studied in Germany and was living in Denmark when rumors grew that something big was about to happen in Berlin. Ramos and some friends got a car and started driving toward the divided capital city. Here is what Ramos said happened next:

At the border city of Braunschweig (Brunswick), on the German side, we began to see the first Trabants. These are small East German cars. They don't just look like toy cars, they look like Donald Duck's car. [The Trabant] was designed by a famous East German industrial designer during the 50s and it never changed. It's the only car in the world with tail fins. It has cheap, thin metal that rusts easily. The two-stroke engine buzzes like a lawn mower and pumps out clouds of smoke. God help you if you're standing near one. Trabants, which Germans call Trabis, have a top speed of about 50 miles an hour. . . .

We finally reached the border just after midnight. The East German border was always a serious place. Armed guards kept you in your car, watching for attempts at escapes. Tonight was a different country. Over 20,000 East and West Germans were gathered there in a huge party: as each Trabi came through, people cheered and clapped. East Germans drove through the applause, grinning, dazed, as thousands of flashbulbs went off. The traffic jam was spectacular. The cloud of light turned out to be the headlights of tens of thousands of cars in a huge cloud of Trabi exhaust fumes. We got out of [our] car and began walking. Between lanes of cars, streams of people were walking, talking together. Under one light, a group of musicians were playing violins and accordions and men and women were dancing in circles. Despite the brilliantly cold night, car windows were open and everyone talked to each other.[7]

This painting on the Berlin Wall shows an East German Trabant smashing through the wall, symbolizing East Germans' new freedom to travel beginning in 1989.

PRIMARY SOURCE — QUESTIONS for DISCUSSION

1. How was the Trabant car symbolic of what went wrong with economies in communist countries?
2. According to Ramos, why was the East German border ordinarily a secure and serious place?
3. Why did East German border guards not stop the exodus in 1989?

THEN & NOW

East and West Germany Today

There is only one Germany today, more than 20 years after the fall of the Wall. No one made Germany an experiment deliberately, but the result has been a "natural experiment" in the effects of different institutions. Economists have had an opportunity to see how the change after 1989 continues to affect the former East German economy. If the problem with East Germany was a communist economic and political system, then removing that system should make incomes and opportunities converge in the former East and West German nations.

When the Wall fell, there were predictions that it would take decades for East Germany to recover. Fortunately, those predictions were wrong. Money from the west flowed eastward quickly, permitting rapid upgrades in production of goods and services. Germans once again could move freely around the country to homes and jobs best suited to their tastes and abilities. As a result, the former East Germany has caught up in important ways:

- The goods and services available per person in the East have reached levels 80 to 85 percent as high as the Western levels—differences that are comparable to the differences between poorer and richer areas within West Germany. Although the figures are not directly comparable, in the United States people in the poorest states have incomes about 80 percent as high as the national average of income per person.[8]

- Ownership of durable goods such as cars and appliances has become more nearly equal across the former East and

TABLE 1	Durable Goods Ownership in East and West Germany, 1993–2007		
	1993	1998	2007
DURABLE GOODS	East/West	East/West	East/West
Automobile	66/74	71/76	72/78
Landline telephone	49/97	94/97	95/96
Cell phone	-	11/11	82/82
Personal computer	16/22	36/43	70/73
Internet access	-	5/9	56/61
Television	96/95	98/95	97/96
Cable access	-	64/51	61/48
Satellite dish	-	30/29	33/41
Video recorder	36/48	61/63	71/69
Refrigerator	95/95	99/99	99/99
Microwave oven	15/41	41/53	68/69
Dishwasher	3/38	26/49	54/64
Washing machine	91/88	94/91	99/95
Dryer	2/24	14/33	22/44

Source: Michael C. Burda, "The East German Economy in the Twenty-First Century," prepared for a conference of the German Historical Institute, Washington D.C., September 2009.

West Germany. Table 1 shows ownership rates in 1993, 1998, and 2007. In the case of cars, ownership rates converged to within six percentage points. In computer ownership the gap fell to three percentage points. There was no gap in ownership of cellphones.

- Life expectancy, in some ways the most comprehensive indicator of well-being, has nearly converged. For women, expected years of life are now equal across the East and West. For men, life expectancy has converged to within one year, with the West still ahead.[9]

As for Conny and Ulrike, it is obvious they lived differently under different economic and political systems. But there were apparently powerful unseen influences making their lives convergent despite all that. Both of them loved art and painting as children. They studied the same subjects at school and chose the same career, event management. Living their separate lives, both of them married young and had their first children, daughters in both cases, when they were 19. Each went on to have three children. Before meeting each other, they even liked the same clothing styles, makeup, and hairstyles. After the Wall fell in 1989, they were amazed to learn how similar their personal lives had been despite the large difference in their surroundings for two-thirds of their lives.[10]

THEN & NOW — QUESTIONS for DISCUSSION

1. Does the example of post-World War II Germany provide a good comparison of market vs. socialist economies? Or is the comparison flawed? Explain your answer.
2. What evidence is there that conditions in the former East Germany have improved after reunification with West Germany?
3. The goods and services available per person in the former East Germany now have reached 80 to 85 percent of the West German levels. Do you believe the remaining differences are acceptable? Explain your answer.

Web Resources

The Twins Brought Up on Either Side of the Iron Curtain
http://www.dailymail.co.uk/femail/article-503775/The-twins-brought-Iron-Curtain--lived-identical-lives.html

A British newspaper's in-depth story of Ulrike and Conny.

The Fall of the Berlin Wall: A Personal Account
http://andreas.com/berlin.html

Andreas Ramos's first-person account of the fall of the Berlin Wall.

The Organization for Economic Cooperation and Development
http://oecd.org

This Paris-based organization has excellent web resources on European countries, which are prominent among its 33-nation membership.

VoxEU: The Voice of the European Union
http://www.voxeu.org

Policy analysis and commentary by leading scholars of the European Union.

How Did the Economy Influence Presidential Elections in the Stagnant Seventies?

Cars line up for fuel at a gas station during the energy crisis of the 1970s.

Archie Goes on Strike

KEY ECONOMIC CONCEPTS

Consumer Price Index	Inflation
	Interest rate
Deficit	Misery Index
Federal funds rate	Money supply
Gross Domestic Product (GDP)	Recession
	Unemployment rate

All in the Family was a popular situation comedy broadcast on the CBS television network from 1971 to 1979. The series starred Carroll O'Connor as Archie Bunker, Jean Stapleton as Archie's wife, Edith, and Sally Struthers as their daughter, Gloria, who was married to Michael Stivic, played by Rob Reiner. In 1974, the program began a four-part series called "The Bunkers and Inflation." The first episode began with the news that Archie's union was going on strike for higher wages. The union demanded higher pay because inflation that year was running at 11 percent. High inflation means high prices, making it difficult for workers to get by on their salaries. The unemployment rate was 5.6 percent in 1974; it went up to 8.5 percent in the following year. When the strike ended, Archie did get a raise, but the Bunkers were in no better financial shape than they were when strike began. The Bunkers and Stivics had good reason to worry about the souring economy that was affecting middle-class families.

The Bunkers and Stivics may or may not have understood exactly how the economy was changing. Not many people really did. A new word was coined to describe the change: *stagflation*. Stagflation combines two ideas. The

Rob Reiner, Sally Struthers, Carol O'Connor, and Jean Stapleton in a scene from the T.V. series "All In The Family."

first is stagnant (zero or slow) economic growth, with high levels of joblessness. The second is high levels of inflation.

The stagflation of the 1970s replaced a long period of prosperity, for the Bunker family and millions of real American households. Usually, bad news about the economy is also bad news for the American president. Did the sour economy of the 1970s cost President Jimmy Carter reelection in 1980?

The Historical Context
The Stagnant Seventies

The period after World War II stood in stark contrast to the period in which American families made economic sacrifices to support the war. The decades of the 1950s and 1960s were marked by a growing economy and increasing prosperity. In the 1960s, Gross Domestic Product (GDP) grew on average at nearly 4.5 percent when adjusted for inflation. (**Gross Domestic Product** is the final value of all the goods and services produced in the nation.) In no single year during the 1960s did GDP fall. In three years during the decade (1962, 1965 and 1966), growth in real GDP exceeded 6 percent.

But in the decade of the 1970s, the economy performed at a lower rate. The growth of GDP adjusted for inflation averaged close to 3 percent. The year of highest real growth was 1973, with GDP growth of 5.8 percent. In two years (1974 and 1975), GDP actually declined. By 1979, there was double-digit inflation and persistently high unemployment. The economy was stuck in a ditch.

The Economics of Stagflation

To understand the events of the 1970s, it helps to have a good grasp of three important economic concepts: inflation, the Consumer Price Index (CPI), and unemployment.

Inflation. Most people think inflation means rising prices. That is basically correct. Inflation is a sustained rise in prices. But not every price increase represents inflation. You may notice that the price of a cup of gourmet coffee or a favorite pasta dish goes up. But at the same time the prices of other things like eggs and bananas may go down. Inflation is different. **Inflation** is a sustained increase in average prices *across the economy*.

In the 1970s, economists often emphasized two causes of inflation. One of these was widespread increases in the cost of production. Rising labor costs throughout an economy, according to this view, might set off inflation. The strike of Archie Bunker's union was intended to increase wages for its workers. It did, but that increase might merely add to inflation. No matter how hard Archie worked, he might never make headway because all the other Archie Bunkers would also be getting higher wages. As those wages went up, they would increase costs of production throughout the economy, making it harder and harder for anyone to get ahead. And as production costs went up, prices would go up to cover those costs. The same analysis holds for rising costs of gasoline and oil. An unexpected increase in the price of gasoline makes it more costly to produce many goods and services. Gasoline and related fuels are used in almost every industry, so virtually everything becomes more expensive to produce when gasoline and other fuel prices rise.

A second cause of inflation emphasized in the 1970s has to do with spending. Inflation can get started, according to this view, when total spending by businesses and government is too high. "Too high" is difficult to define in this context, since spending that at first seems to be very high may turn out later to have been a good idea. But spending might be too high when consumers or businesses are taking out more and more loans or reaching into savings to buy more and more stuff. And government spending might be too high when it requires more and more borrowing to pay for more and more programs over many years. If total spending exceeds the maximum amount of goods and services the economy can produce, prices go up.

Once inflation starts, it can be hard to stop. In an inflationary period, consumers may begin to think that high prices will only keep rising.

According to that assumption, it makes sense to buy that new car or boat or house *now*, because in no time it will cost even more!

The Consumer Price Index (CPI). The **Consumer Price Index (CPI)** is a measure of changes in the prices of goods and services commonly bought by consumers. Economists at the Bureau of Labor Statistics (BLS) developed the CPI for use in estimating inflation. Here is how it works. Economists collect price information for a "market basket" of goods and services. The information is provided by thousands of families and individuals. These people report what they actually buy in a given time period (food, housing, clothing, transportation, and so on) and the prices they pay for what they buy. Economists then weight the prices of these goods and services according to how much the average consumer spent on these items in a selected year. Items on which consumers spend a great deal of income—food and housing, for example—are given more weight than toys and haircuts.

Then economists calculate how much the cost of the market basket has changed. One time period (say, 1982–1984) serves as a base period. CPI calculations show how current prices compare with prices from that base period. The difference—"The CPI was up 3.8 percent," say—provides an estimate of the rate of inflation for the time in question. Inflation rates in the United States vary from year to year. The annual percentage change over the past 30 years has been as low as -0.4 percent in 2009 and as high as 13.5 percent in 1980.

The Unemployment Rate. The **unemployment rate** is the number of people who have no job and are actively looking for work, divided by the labor force (all civilians aged 16 and above who are either employed or actively looking and available for work). Unemployment rates in the United States also vary from year to year. The annual unemployment rate over the past 30 years has been as low as 4 percent in 2001and as high as 9.7 percent in 1982.

Gas ration stamps being inspected at the Bureau of Engraving and Printing, Washington, D.C.

World Affairs and High Inflation in the 1970s

Two developments in world affairs explain why U.S. inflation rates were high in the 1970s. The first had to do with war. The United States fought a war in Vietnam from 1964 to 1973. Early in the war, President Lyndon Johnson's economic advisor, Walter Heller, recommended tax increases to help pay for it. Heller's advice was ignored. Government spending, driven by wartime needs, subsequently increased faster than tax revenues. The wave of spending set off inflation.

The second cause was an unexpected increase in production costs, brought about by rising oil prices. The rise in oil prices was also war-related. The Organization of Oil and Petroleum Exporting Countries (OPEC) emerged as a powerful force late in the 1960s. In October 1973, Mid-Eastern OPEC nations halted oil exports to the United States. This stoppage was intended to punish the United States for its support of Israel in the Yom Kippur War, fought in October 1973, between Israel and a coalition of Arab states. OPEC's action reduced the supply of oil in the United States and caused oil prices to increase. The increase in oil prices had ripple effects, since

President Richard Nixon with some of his economic advisors, 1971.

oil is used in the manufacture of thousands of products and in the fuel that is needed to move products from place to place. OPEC had induced an "energy crisis" in the United States.

It took time for Americans to adjust to the energy crisis. Some consumers changed their behavior, turning down their thermostats in winter and wearing heavy sweaters. Some stopped decorating their houses with lights at Christmas time. Some demanded and got more fuel-efficient cars. Businesses found ways to be more efficient in their use of fossil fuels. New competition emerged in the oil industry as new sources of petroleum were discovered in the North Sea, off the coast of the United Kingdom. But the inflationary damage had been done.

Inflation Defeats Presidents Nixon, Ford, and Carter

President Richard Nixon was elected to the White House in a close race in 1968. He did not want a sour economy to cost him his chance for reelection in 1972. Economic conditions had begun to deteriorate as he took office. The inflation rate, which had averaged 1.6 percent from 1960 to 1964, rose to an average of 5 percent under President Nixon. Unemployment was also up from the 3.5 percent level of the late 1960s to 5 percent.

President Nixon searched for a way to reduce inflation without slowing the economy and increasing unemployment. He settled on the idea of imposing a system of wage and price controls, beginning in 1971. It was called the New Economic Policy. For an initial 90-day period, this policy froze wages and prices. A Cost of Living Council was appointed to manage the nation's wages and prices. After the initial 90 days, the controls were gradually relaxed and the system seemed to be working. Inflation dropped to 3.2 percent in 1972. President Nixon gained enough economic success to help him to win re-election in 1972.

In the months that followed Nixon's reelection, inflation began to pick up again, largely in response to wage increases. President Nixon re-imposed a freeze in June of 1973. Once again, government officials took charge of setting prices and wages. This time, however, it was apparent that the control system was a failure. Shortages of consumer goods began to show up. Some ranchers stopped shipping their cattle to the market. Some farmers drowned their chickens rather than sell them at a loss. Responding to the shortages, shoppers emptied out grocery store shelves. The wage and price controls system was abolished in April 1974. But when the controls were lifted, inflation once again skyrocketed, reaching a rate of 11 percent for 1974. Price controls had suppressed inflation, but they did not address its causes.

President Gerald Ford made the next attempt to fight inflation. He was not about to go back to wage and price controls. His program, beginning in 1974, was called "Whip Inflation Now" (WIN). President Ford described inflation as "enemy number one" and encouraged people to take voluntary actions—as people had done during World War II—to restrict their spending and save more money for the general good of the nation. If total spending could be decreased, Ford believed, the upward pressure on prices would be reduced. Campaign buttons were printed with the WIN slogan, and there was much talk about what people should do. But the WIN program also failed.[1]

Jimmy Carter defeated Gerald Ford in the presidential election of 1976. Newly-elected President Carter wanted to reduce the unemployment rate and provide increased social benefits. He increased Social Security benefits, farm subsidies, and welfare programs. The federal deficit exploded. A **deficit** exists when

TABLE 1	Rates of Inflation, 1974–1984
Year	Annual Percentage Change in the Consumer Price Index
1974	11.0
1975	9.1
1976	5.8
1977	6.5
1978	7.6
1979	11.3
1980	13.5
1981	10.3
1982	6.2
1983	3.2
1984	4.3

Source: U.S. Bureau of Labor Statistics.

federal spending exceeds revenues collected from taxes. The federal government had been running up deficits since 1969, borrowing funds to pay for increased spending. The deficits continued each year under President Carter: $53 billion in 1977, $59 billion in 1978, $40.7 billion in 1979, and $73.8 billion in 1980. The high levels of federal spending contributed to increased inflation.[2] Table 1 shows the rates of inflation from 1974–1984. The rise begins in 1976; it topped out at 13.5 percent in 1980.

President Gerald Ford debates Jimmy Carter in Philadelphia, 1976.

HISTORICAL QUESTIONS & ECONOMIC ANSWERS

How did the inflationary spiral finally end?

In August 1979, President Carter appointed Paul Volcker as Chairman of the Federal Reserve Board. Volcker changed Fed policy in the fight against inflation, influenced by the thinking of economist Milton Friedman. Friedman had long argued that the underlying cause of inflation is neither increased costs of production nor excessive total spending. Instead, he argued, sustained inflation is caused by sustained growth in the **money supply**—the total amount of money available in the economy at a given time. The money supply might not be exactly what you think it is. It includes currency—those dollars in your purse or wallet—but it also includes deposits in checking accounts. In fact, most of our money supply is the money held in checking accounts. The money supply is controlled by the Federal Reserve.

In other words, Friedman argued inflation is caused when there is "too much money chasing too few goods." Inflation sets in when the money supply increases faster than the amount of goods and services being produced by the economy. Think about an imaginary economy that produces only one consumer good, apples. If it produces five pounds of apples and has a money supply of $5, then as the money supply is spent, the price of apples is $1 per pound. If that economy's money supply goes up to $10 with no increase in the amount of apples being produced, people have more money to spend on the same amount of apples. In other words, $10 will go chasing after five pounds of apples. The price will be $2 per pound. This simple economy could solve its inflation problem by allowing the money supply to grow only as fast as apple production grows.

The U.S. economy is much more complex than an apples-only economy, but the cure for inflation is similar, according to Friedman. To control inflation, we need to reduce the amount of money in circulation to match the production of goods and services.

How would Friedman's cure operate to bring down the inflation rate? The answer lies in changing **interest rates**, the percentage paid by borrowers on loans. Higher interest rates discourage people from taking out loans to pay for business expansion and consumer spending. Who wants to build a new plant or buy a new car or home by taking out a loan at double-digit interest rates? Raising interest rates thus decreases the amount of money that banks lend out; that decrease, in turn, slows down the flow of money into the money supply.

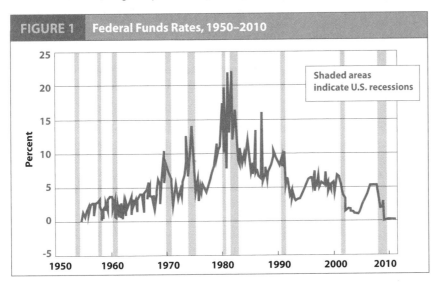

FIGURE 1   Federal Funds Rates, 1950–2010

Shaded areas indicate U.S. recessions

Source: http://research.stlouisfed.org/fred2/series/DFF

Figure 1 shows changes in the federal funds rate from 1950 to 2010. The **federal funds rate** is a key interest rate controlled by the Federal Reserve. It is the interest rate banks charge one another for loans. It influences other interest rates charged by banks on business loans and loans for consumer purchases. Acting in his capacity as chairman of the Federal Reserve, Paul Volcker began to raise the federal funds rate in 1979. Notice the spike of the federal funds rate in 1981. Other interest rates then increased, and loans became more expensive. People cut back on buying cars and homes, and businesses slowed down on borrowing.

Wouldn't reducing the money supply by raising interest rates hurt the economy?

Yes. The increase in interest rates after 1979 caused a recession. A **recession** is a significant decline in economic activity lasting several months, accompanied by high unemployment. After the Fed raised interest rates, business activity stalled. Families could not buy homes or cars unless they were willing to pay very high interest rates on loans. With a reduction in purchases of homes and cars, some people who worked in industries related to automobiles and housing lost their jobs. In 1982, the unemployment rate reached 9.7 percent. Ronald Reagan was elected president in 1980. He and Volcker presided over a long and painful recession.

When did the economy begin to recover?

By 1982, inflation had been reduced to 6.2 percent, as measured by the CPI. The unemployment rate also began to decline then, but more slowly. It remained at 7 percent or above until 1987, when it dropped to 6.2 percent; it dropped again, to 5.5 percent, in the following year. GDP grew at 4.5 percent in 1983 and 7.2 percent in 1984. The economy began what was at that time the longest peacetime recovery on record.

Does the economy influence the outcome of presidential elections?

Maybe. Rightly or wrongly, American voters typically hold presidents accountable for the nation's overall economic performance. Is there a way to know in advance who might win a presidential election based on economic performance? Maybe. Arthur Okun, an economist, developed a statistic called the Misery Index in the 1960s. The **Misery Index** is calculated by adding the unemployment rate to the rate of inflation to get a measure of "misery." It is an easily-understood way to tell how the economy is performing.

When Jimmy Carter, a Democrat, ran for president in 1976 against incumbent President Gerald Ford, a Republican, Carter often referred to the Misery Index as evidence of President Ford's mismanagement. In 1975, the Misery Index was very high, at 17.5. Jimmy Carter alleged that President Ford was not competent to manage the economy even though the Misery Index declined to (a still very high) 13.8 in the election year of 1976.

In the 1980 election, the tables were turned. Ronald Reagan, the Republican candidate, enjoyed asking voters if they were better off than they had been four years earlier. The economy had worsened under President Carter, as measured by the Misery Index. In 1979 the Misery Index was 17.1, and it climbed to 20.6 in the election year of 1980. President Carter lost his bid for reelection to Ronald Reagan.

Can you predict the outcome of a presidential election by reference to the Misery Index?

More or less. Examine Table 2. The fourth column from the left shows the Misery Index from 1973 to 2008. If the Misery Index declines as an election year approaches, the index predicts that the candidate of the incumbent party will keep control of the White House. For example, the 1983 Misery Index of 12.8 fell to 11.8 by the forthcoming election year—predicting a win for the incumbent. Incumbent Ronald Reagan defeated Walter Mondale for reelection, just as the Index predicted.

If the Misery Index increases as an election year approaches, it predicts that the candidate of the incumbent party will lose control of the White House. In 1979, the Misery Index stood at 17.1 percent; it jumped to 20.6 in the 1980 election year—predicting defeat for incumbent President Carter. The Misery Index was correct again.

Overall, the Misery Index does pretty well. It has correctly predicted the outcomes in seven out of nine recent elections. The Misery Index failed to predict the correct outcome in 1976, the year Democrat Jimmy Carter defeated Republican incumbent Gerald Ford. President Ford had issued an unpopular pardon of President Richard Nixon, who had resigned from office as a result of the Watergate scandal. This unique non-economic factor may have influenced the outcome of the election.

QUESTIONS for DISCUSSION

1. What major international event contributed to the growth of inflation in the 1970s?
2. What was stagflation? How could it be measured?
3. Who finally ended the inflation spiral of the 1970s? How did he do it? What was the result?
4. In your own words, describe the Misery Index.
5. How well does the Misery Index predict the outcome of presidential elections? Explain your answer.

TABLE 2	The Misery Index 1973–2008				
YEAR	Unemployment Rate (A)	Inflation Rate (B)	Misery Index (A+B)	Presidential Candidates	Winner Consistent with the Misery Index Prediction?
1973	4.9	6.2	11.1		
1974	5.6	11.0	16.6		
1975	8.5	9.0	17.5		
1976	7.7	6.1	13.8	Carter(D)/ Ford(R)	No
1977	7.1	6.5	13.6		
1978	6.1	7.6	13.7		
1979	5.8	11.3	17.1		
1980	7.1	13.5	20.6	Carter(D)/ Reagan (R)	Yes
1981	7.6	10.3	17.9		
1982	9.7	6.2	15.9		
1983	9.6	3.2	12.8		
1984	7.5	4.3	11.8	Mondale(D)/ Reagan(R)	Yes
1985	7.2	3.6	10.8		
1986	7.0	1.9	8.9		
1987	6.2	3.6	9.8		
1988	5.5	4.1	9.6	Dukakis(D)/ Bush(R)	Yes
1989	5.3	4.5	9.8		
1990	5.6	6.3	11.9		
1991	6.8	3.3	10.1		
1992	7.5	3.0	10.5	Clinton(D)/ Bush(R)	Yes
1993	6.9	3.0	9.9		
1994	6.1	2.6	8.7		
1995	5.6	2.8	8.4		
1996	5.4	3.0	8.4	Clinton(D)/ Dole(R)	No prediction
1997	4.9	2.3	7.2		
1998	4.5	1.6	6.1		
1999	4.2	2.2	6.4		
2000	4.0	3.4	7.4	Gore(D)/ Bush(R)	Yes
2001	4.7	2.8	7.4		
2002	5.8	1.6	7.4		
2003	6.0	2.3	8.3		
2004	5.5	2.7	8.2	Kerry(D)/ Bush(R)	Yes
2005	5.1	3.4	8.5		
2006	4.6	3.2	7.8		
2007	4.6	2.8	7.4		
2008	5.9	3.8	9.7	Obama(D)/ McCain(R)	Yes

Presidential winners are in blue.
Source: U.S. Bureau of Labor Statistics.

President Carter Addresses the Energy Crisis of 1979

PRIMARY SOURCE

In 1979, OPEC announced another round in a series of oil price increases. Gas prices again took off. In some places, like California, there were long lines of people waiting at gas pumps. Americans, weary of stagflation, did not sense any way out. Much of that anger was directed toward President Carter, whose approval ratings dropped as the crisis deepened.

On July 15, 1979, millions of Americans tuned in to hear President Carter speak about the economic crisis. His speech was later called the "Malaise Speech," based on the meaning of "malaise" as "a general feeling of being unwell." Here is an excerpt from his speech.

… I want to speak to you first tonight about a subject even more serious than energy or inflation. I want to talk to you right now about a fundamental threat to American democracy….

The threat is nearly invisible in ordinary ways. It is a crisis of confidence. It is a crisis that strikes at the very heart and soul and spirit of our national will. We can see this crisis in the growing doubt about the meaning of our own lives and in the loss of a unity of purpose for our Nation.

The erosion of our confidence in the future is threatening to destroy the social and political fabric of America.

[T]oo many of us now tend to worship self-indulgence and consumption. Human identity is no longer defined by what one does, but by what one owns. But we've discovered that owning things and consuming things does not satisfy our longing for meaning. We've learned that piling up material goods cannot fill the emptiness of lives which have no confidence or purpose.

The symptoms of this crisis of the American spirit are all around us. For the first time in the history of our country a majority of our people believe that the next five years will be worse than the past five years. Two-thirds of our people do not even vote. The productivity of American workers is actually dropping, and the willingness of Americans to save for the future has fallen below that of all other people in the Western world.

Available at http://www.pbs.org/wgbh/americanexperience/features/primary-resources/carter-crisis

Toward the end of the speech, President Carter called for several new actions to address the energy crisis. He called for setting limits on imports of petroleum, increased spending to develop alternative sources of energy, and mandates for reducing energy consumption.

PRIMARY SOURCE QUESTIONS for DISCUSSION

1. According to President Carter, what were the problems facing Americans in 1979?
2. What actions did President Carter propose?
3. Do you think these proposed actions would have been effective? Explain your answer.

The Economy and the Mid-Term Elections of 2010

When President Carter lost his reelection bid in 1980, the Misery Index stood at a painful 20.1 percent. It represented a combination of high inflation and unemployment. Things were different by 2008, when Barack Obama defeated John McCain to become president. The Misery Index then was nowhere near its 1980 level. Nonetheless, the Misery Index correctly predicted the 2008 outcome. The Misery Index for 2007 stood at 7.4, and it increased to 9.7 in 2008, predicting a victory for Obama over McCain.

President Obama faced a different situation in 2010. His party, the Democrats, took a pounding in the mid-term elections held on November 2, 2010. Republicans gained a net 63 Congressional seats from Democrats and took control of the House of Representatives. Republicans also gained six seats in the Senate, but fell short of gaining a majority in that body. While the party controlling the White House usually loses seats in a mid-term election, losses for the Democratic Party in 2010 were greater than usual. Could the economy have been the key variable in the election?

Table 3 shows the Misery Index for the months leading up to the November 2, 2010 elections. The Misery Index increased between September and October of 2010, but just barely. Does this small change

TABLE 3	Misery Index, 2010		
Month	Unemployment Rate	Consumer Price Index	Misery Index
Aug.	9.6	0.3	9.9
Sept.	9.6	0.1	9.7
Oct.	9.7	0.2	9.9

Source: U.S. Bureau of Labor Statistics.

explain the Republican victory? Perhaps, but it seems unlikely. Three other factors probably contributed.

First, the growth of GDP had been sluggish. In 2010, the economy was recovering very slowly from the recession of 2007–2009. In the first quarter of 2010, GDP increased by 3.7 percent. It increased by 1.7 percent in the second quarter, and by 2.7 percent in the third quarter. This level of economic growth, however, is not enough to reduce the unemployment rate.

Second, because of slow growth in GDP, unemployment in 2010 remained at a historically high level. In 2006 and 2007, before the recession, the annual unemployment rate was 4.6 percent in both years. In 2009, it had climbed to 9.3 percent. Finally, some voters may have been concerned about continuing levels of high federal deficits. The 2010 deficit was $1.29 trillion; it followed an all-time high of $1.41 trillion in 2009.

THEN & NOW QUESTIONS for DISCUSSION

1. What were the results of the 2010 mid-term elections?
2. How does the party in power usually do in the mid-term elections?
3. Did the performance of the economy contribute to the outcome of the 2010 mid-terms? Explain your answer.

The Economics of Stagflation
http://www.bls.gov/cpi

CPI tables from the Bureau of Labor Statistics.

Inflation Defeats Presidents Nixon, Ford, and Carter
http://millercenter.org/scripps/archive/speeches/detail/3283

Gerald Ford's WIN speech in 1974.

The Economy and Presidential Elections
http://www.miseryindex.us

The Misery Index website.

President Jimmy Carter
http://www.pbs.org/wgbh/amex/carter/filmmore/ps_crisis.html

Full text of President Carter's "Crisis of Confidence" or the Malaise Speech.

Bureau of Labor Statistics
http://www.bls.gov

Use the BLS website to get the very lastest data on inflation and unemployment.

Is the Information Revolution as Big as the Industrial Revolution?

A network server room.

They were always proud parents, but Mary and William would later admit feeling some disappointment when their son told them he was dropping out of college. Who wouldn't? William was a successful lawyer and he had hoped his son would follow in his footsteps. Mary and William had worked with their son throughout his high school years to make sure he would have the kind of academic record needed to get into a top college. When Harvard admitted him, their son was on the fast track to success.

But now he said he was dropping out to build a small business that he and a longtime buddy had started. A career in law had become a long shot at best. Mary and William were supportive; they told their son they understood his decision. Young William, named after his father, was intellectually brilliant and a hard worker. Surely he would succeed. Still, their doubts would not go away.

If Mary and William could have seen into the future, those doubts would have vanished. Their son was William H. Gates III—Bill Gates. He became a multi-billionaire by transforming his dorm-room startup, Microsoft, into an

Bill Gates, at age 27, poses in his executive office at the startup software firm Microsoft in 1982.

KEY ECONOMIC CONCEPTS

Creative destruction
Networks
External benefit
Externality

Metcalfe's Law
Scalable output
Speculative bubble

international technology giant. Then, after the company matured, he stepped back and turned to work in charity, giving away billions of dollars to help others, through the Bill and Melinda Gates Foundation.[1]

What made it possible for a college dropout's startup business to become a multi-billion dollar international corporation? Why did computers, behind the scenes in business for three decades, suddenly become important to ordinary individuals and to the economy as a whole? Is the Information Revolution as big as the Industrial Revolution?

The Historical Context
A Missing Revolution

The Industrial Revolution (in the United States, 1820–1870) changed societies. Economies went from being mostly agricultural to mostly industrial. People left rural areas and moved to cities, which grew rapidly. The amount of goods and services available grew sharply because of the efficiency of manufacturing. Individuals and societies sometimes struggled with the changes.

Would the computer industry also usher in revolutionary changes? Early on, that did not seem likely. Practical electronic computers were first developed in the 1940s, spurred on by war-related research and development. Businesses began to use computers extensively in the 1950s. Those computers did not look or work much like today's computers. The hardware was so big

This multi-room computer of the 1960s had less processing power than a cellphone has today.

that a single computer might fill several rooms. Computers were kept at a distance from their users by their operators, who would accept programs and give back the printed results.

Before the 1970s, people did not want a computer at home—what could you do with it? Apple Computer's founders, Steve Jobs and Steve Wozniak, answered that question by building a small and versatile computer in the Jobs family garage. Their first widely distributed computer, the Apple II, could turn itself from a word processor to an accounting ledger to a game player. Users could touch and play with the computer without the intervention of operators. This is all commonplace now, but it was revolutionary at the time. It helped take Apple from a garage workplace to a position among global technology giants.

Even so, with people buying Apple II computers to play games and businesses installing room-size computers, nothing about early computers seemed likely to cause big changes in peoples' lives. Businesses invested heavily in computers, but business people still interacted with customers much as they had before. In fact, business spending on computers looked rather unproductive. Economist Robert Solow joked in 1987, "you can see the computer age everywhere [except] in the productivity statistics."[2] Computers were supposed to revolutionize the economy, but the revolution was missing.

Then, in the 1990s, the Internet took off. Investments in information technology began to pay off handsomely. Previously unknown startups became household names: Amazon.com, Google, and Facebook, to name just three. New millionaires appeared overnight. Bill Gates, whose success would have been remarkable even if his company had stayed focused on its original operating software, became a multi-billionaire. Even the economy-wide productivity statistics started to show major effects from information technology. As people looked into the future, it seemed a reasonable possibility that society was on the verge of a change as big as the Industrial Revolution.

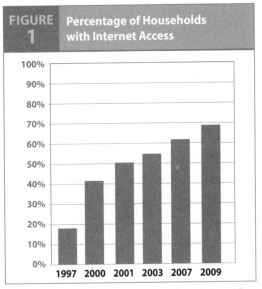

| FIGURE 1 | Percentage of Households with Internet Access |

Source: Current Population Survey, Washington: U.S. Census Bureau.

The Economics of the Information Revolution

When analysts use the term "Information Revolution" today, they refer to two interrelated developments:

1. Widespread low-cost computing, and
2. Widespread low-cost telecommunications (voice, text and data).

Both developments are important. Their significance is emphasized in the term sometimes used to describe them in tandem: the "Information and Communications Technology (ICT) Revolution."[3]

These two developments permitted **networks** (interconnected systems of devices or people) to grow and thrive. In the process, computers went from being massive pieces of business equipment to showing up in small devices everywhere—in classrooms, under the hoods of cars, and even in your cellphone.

To understand the Information Revolution, you have to understand the idea of an externality. An **externality** is an effect that a transaction has on a bystander who is not directly involved. For example, if your neighbor is a gifted musician who plays on the back porch, you get free access to the music. That would be a positive externality or **external benefit**.

The most well-known externalities are bad for bystanders, as with pollution. However, external benefits are especially important in the case of computers and information technology. People throughout society get benefits from other people's transactions. One prominent example is the large set of free software that programmers have written and given away. Other external benefits come from millions of computer users being able to interact on hardware that gets better and faster all the time. From the time they were first developed, computers have rapidly improved. You may have heard that today's cars have more computing power than the Apollo moon spacecraft. That is no urban legend; they do.[4]

We can get a good grasp of how the Internet has taken off if we combine the concept of external benefits with **Metcalfe's Law**. Attributed to electrical engineer Robert Metcalfe,[5] this law says that when the number of users of a network doubles, the value of the network quadruples. (Twice as many users will make the network four times more valuable.) Although it sounds precise and mathematical, in application the law simply states the fact that networks get much better as more people can connect.

Think back to a time when only one person had a phone capable of text-messaging. That phone would not be very valuable, would it? There

```
————————————————  INTERNET  ————————————————

                Your Internet ID: monopoly@host.yab.com
—————————————————————————————————————————————————————————————————
              Getting Files                  Finding Information
    [A]  Find Files on the Net (Archie)  [G]  Search for Information (Gopher)
    [F]  Get Files from the Net (FTP)    [W]  Hypertext Search (WWW)
    [Y]  File Transfers for Net Account  [Q]  Query About Someone (Finger)
              Entertainment                       Messages
    [M]  MUDs (Games)                    [E]  Internet E-Mail
    [I]  Internet Teleconference (IRC)   [U]  Internet Message Areas (Usenet)
    [J]  Tintin Interface for MUDs                  Help
              Miscellaneous              [D]  Detailed Reference Text
    [B]  Unix Shell Access (BASH)        [H]  Help Using Internet Functions
    [T]  Connect to Other Sites (Telnet) [K]  If You're Stuck at "Password"
              SLIP Access (Mosaic, NetScape, etc)
    [S]  SLIP - Graphical Interface      [C]  How To Configure SLIP Access
    [P]  PPP - Point-to-Point Protocol

  Your Choice (A,B,C,D,E,F,G,H,I,J,K,M,P,Q,S,T,U,W
  (N)onstop, (Q)uit, or (C)ontinue?
  Menu: <Ctrl R-Shift>               2400 8N1          VT100     Online
```

The early Internet was mostly text-based, without any graphics, as shown on this Bulletin Board System (BBS) screen from 1994.

would be nobody else to receive or send texts. But as more phones for texting came into use, texting became far more valuable. The text-message network's value shot up rapidly.

When the Internet began to take off in 1992, users' experience with it was far different from users' experience today. Home users dialed in, tying up the phone line for the time they were online. The home computer was a large desktop box with a TV-style monitor. Most of the content available on the Internet was text rather than graphics. Complex programs had to be used to bring up Internet content because the browser (like Internet Explorer or Firefox) had not yet been developed. But that did not matter much because there were only 26 websites, by one count.[6]

As the Internet began to grow, external benefits and Metcalfe's Law kicked in. Programmers who previously had to swap disks soon could exchange code by e-mail. The trickle of free software became a flood. With computers quickly becoming better and faster, better-quality graphics and then full-motion video appeared on the exploding number of websites. With more users getting Internet access all the time, content and connections grew. Users could assume that most people and almost all businesses would have Internet access.

Small numbers of Facebook users rapidly became millions. Facebook had little usefulness if your friends were not on it, and a lot of usefulness if they were. Your benefit from Facebook went up greatly as more of your friends joined (Metcalfe's Law again), until you reached the point at which you could invite all your friends to a party with one post. The combined effect was stunning.

Both aspects of the Information Revolution—improved computer power and improved telecommunications—were important. The big change with the Internet in place was that computers could talk to one another. For an individual computer user, even a great deal of computing power meant little without access to outside information. With information from other computers, people could produce and consume in ways they had not even thought of before. Ventures such as YouTube, eBay and Facebook became possible. The network of people and devices was the key.

In the 1990s and beyond, computers—long regarded as a disappointment for the economy—became a major driver of growth. Economists found that, as labor productivity zoomed upward in the late 1990s, information technology was responsible for about two-thirds of the boost.[7] But how about that "revolution"? Was it real? Economist Robert Gordon thought not, pointing out that the major effects of information technology were in the making of computers themselves, and of durable goods. He concluded that the effects of information technology were less than the effects of other famous historical inventions such as the electric light, automobiles, or airplanes.[8]

HISTORICAL QUESTIONS & ECONOMIC ANSWERS

Who invented the Internet?

There was no one inventor of the Internet. It originated within a small band of government researchers, the Advanced Research Projects Agency (ARPA). Although researchers had written theoretical papers about computer networks in the 1960s, it was ARPA in 1969 that implemented the ideas with a link between a computer at the University of California Los Angeles and another computer at the Stanford Research Institute. Before year's end there were four computers on the tiny network, called ARPANET.[9]

ARPA researchers found that their network provided a convenient way to exchange comments, data, and messages. E-mail was a natural application of the network. But keep in mind, before sending mail in those days, researchers would first have to ask whether the recipient used e-mail. A "yes" answer was not assured. Once the basic network was established, however, people rapidly saw the benefits of being connected. First researchers and scientists, and then people in universities, began using the networks. As more businesses and personal users got connected, there were large leaps in the capability and interconnection of the networks that grew into the Internet. Metcalfe's Law applied with full force; the value of the network went up dramatically as more people joined.

Is the Internet an example of government success? Of private market success?

The answer is "yes" to both questions. The basic research required for the first computer networks was speculative and risky. The early results were not ready to be commercialized. The positive externalities, though, were potentially huge. In such instances there is a strong case for government-subsidized basic research. In a similar way, basic medical research with little immediate commercial value may be supported by government programs.

In the growth years of the Internet, however, entrepreneurs developed the new ideas. Amazon.com, the pioneering online bookstore, combined its book-selling expertise with the Internet's capabilities to become a household name and a business success. YouTube.com, the video site, became famous for its user-contributed video content and became profitable through advertising. The Internet provides a model for business-government interaction in which government supports basic research on infrastructure and the market discovers and implements new applications.

What is "creative destruction" and how does it apply to the Internet?

The economic historian Joseph Schumpeter was impressed with how private enterprise excelled in delivering new products at low cost. But he thought major economic progress and growth did not come merely by making small improvements in existing goods and services. Rather, Schumpeter theorized, the big results came when totally new ideas blew away established firms. He called these winds of change "gales of creative destruction."[10]

As it is applied today, the term **creative destruction** refers to innovation by entrepreneurs that spurs economic growth, even while sharply reducing the value of companies based on older technology. The innovation of word processing, for example, would sharply reduce the value of any company that tried to rely on selling typewriters.

Schumpeter recognized that when trains displaced slower means of transportation in history, some people were hurt. The process was repeated when trucks and cars displaced trains, and again when airliners became the fastest way to travel for long distances. Schumpeter thought that gains made through creative destruction were more important than protecting existing firms. The process of creative destruction would be beneficial to the overall economy, even as it was destructive in some ways.

The Internet has dramatically changed the way certain businesses operate. Selling local classified advertisements has long been a profitable enterprise for newspapers, but Craigslist and eBay have done away with major chunks of classified print advertising. Now some print newspapers are on the endangered list, and some have already folded. Local bookstores were long insulated from national competition, since ordering books from more distant sources required spending considerable time and effort. With the advent of Amazon.com, ordering a book from a distant source became as simple as clicking a mouse. Even video rental stores—themselves a technological innovation—found their market threatened by online streaming of movies over the Internet. In creating new businesses and subjecting old ones to severe stress, the Internet is an excellent example of creative destruction.

Internet retailers like Amazon.com have changed the way many consumers and businesses buy and sell goods.

What does "scalable" mean, and how does that apply to the Internet?

Scalable means capable of being increased in size at little or no additional cost. Some economic activities, such as medical care, are not scalable. To get more patients treated, hospitals and clinics need to employ more doctors and nurses and staff. The cost is high. Many Internet activities, however, are scalable. Once enterprises such as iTunes and Facebook took off, they were able to expand greatly in size with impressively low costs. In scalable enterprises, being first in a market is a big advantage because the leader can grow quickly and inexpensively.

National borders mean little to a scalable business on the Internet. Output can be expanded easily to other countries, as compared with expanded output for the manufactured products that were so important in the 20th century. In the case of a business such as iTunes, for which the product is a digital music file, delivery to any destination occurs over the Internet without any product being physically shipped.

So, is the Information Revolution as big as the Industrial Revolution?

This chapter began with the question: Is the Information Revolution as big as the Industrial Revolution? Before the Internet, the answer was "no." Computers showed much promise, but before the Internet came into play they had a limited effect on economic activity. After the Internet, the answer is "we are not sure." Table 1 shows some comparisons.

TABLE 1	Selected Facts about the Industrial Revolution and the Information Revolution	
	Industrial Revolution in the United States (1820–1870)	Information Revolution (1955–current)
Economic growth across the period	646%	429%
Population growth across the period	315%	85%
Urban percentage of population	Went from approx. 8% to 25%	Went from approx. 64% to 81%

Sources: U.S. Historical Statistics, "Gross domestic product: 1790–2002," Series Ca9; Federal Reserve Bank of St. Louis, "Real Gross Domestic Product," U.S. Census Bureau Quick Facts.

Information technology and telecommunications have already changed the way people work and interact, but the changes we have seen so far may be just the beginning. The Internet reached widespread adoption in 1992. Given that take-off point, the information revolution has only recently begun.

Possibilities for future developments seem almost unlimited, or unnerving. Some analysts look to a future time when all of us will have tiny computers implanted in our heads, hooked up to our brains and nervous systems.[11] If this came to pass, all of us would have access to boundless information and computational power just by thinking about what we wanted to know or calculate. An economy and society composed of such computer-people would be vastly different from today's economy—perhaps making the Industrial Revolution look small by comparison.

QUESTIONS for DISCUSSION

1. Why was computing power alone insufficient to bring about the Information Revolution? What second element was necessary, and why?
2. Suppose someone developed a new social networking site, far better than the one you use most often now. Would you want to join that new site? What would determine your answer?
3. Do you think the government should have a policy of paying money to compensate for creative destruction—for example, making payments to newspaper publishers hurt by online advertising? Explain your answer.
4. Do you believe the Information Revolution will be as big as the Industrial Revolution? Explain your answer.

A Prediction that Was Not So Stupid

Computing pioneer Ken Olsen, co-founder of Digital Equipment Corporation, was endlessly teased about supposedly predicting in 1977, "There is no reason anyone would want a computer in their home." The prediction has since been included on lists such as "Famously Wrong Computer Predictions" and "Stupid People, Bad Predictions."[12] As it turns out, he did not get it so wrong.

Olson was reacting to the then-common idea that a single computer would be extensively used for home control applications. "Images of the fully computerized home that automatically turned lights on and off and that prepared meals and controlled daily diets were popular," wrote technology historian Edgar H. Schein. This idea of the computer had been popularized by an animated cartoon series "The Jetsons," in which a computer did everything from cooking in the kitchen to walking the dog. Since Olson's quotation referred to the idea of a central home control computer, the growth of home computers for entertainment and productivity does not invalidate his statement.

Below is what Olson later told an interviewer:[13]

> This is, of course, ridiculous because the business we were in was making PCs, and almost from the start I had them at home and my wife played Scrabble with time-sharing machines, and my sixth-grade son was networking the MIT computers and the DEC computers together, hopefully without doing mischief, using the computers I had at home. Home computers were a natural continuum of the "personal computers" that people had at work, in the laboratory, in the military.
>
> I did make a number of statements and still make statements that people don't understand about computers, or delight in misquoting. A long time ago when the common knowledge was that PCs would run our lives in every detail, I said that if you stole something from the refrigerator at night you didn't want to enter this into the computer so that it would . . . mess up the computer plans for coming meals."

PRIMARY SOURCE QUESTIONS for DISCUSSION

1. When Olson said, "There is no reason anyone would want a computer in their home," did he have computers in his own home? Explain your answer.
2. Predictions of a single computer controlling the home were made at a time when computers were large and expensive. How did changes in cost and technology make that prediction unlikely to be realized?
3. Given that it is now easy and inexpensive to have computer-controlled lights, why do you think so many people still use ordinary light switches on the walls of their homes?

Speculative Bubbles, "This Time Is Different," and a 2009 Breakup

In a time of rapid change, financial markets can get ahead of the real economy—the ordinary arena in which people work, buy food and clothing, and so on. This is a continuing theme in American economic history. When financial markets outrun the real economy, stock prices become unsustainably high and a crash becomes inevitable.

Just such an episode occurred in the history of the Internet. This episode is known as the "dot-com bubble." The term refers to the rapid rise in technology-related stock prices from 1995 to 2000. Recall that a **speculative bubble** is an unsustainable increase in prices. The dot-com bubble occurred when technology-related stock prices rose far above their long-term values. The phenomenon was named after new firms, such as Amazon, that had ".com" in their company names to refer to their websites.

If investors think they are involved in a bubble, they will want to get out before the bubble pops. Therefore few investors knowingly buy into a bubble. Investors who forge ahead in risky areas prefer to believe that something big is going on—perhaps something as big as the Industrial Revolution of the 1800s. They may persuade themselves that "This Time Is Different" (a phrase later adopted as the title of a book subtitled "Eight Centuries of Financial Folly"[14]): this time stock prices will continue to go up, indefinitely. In the dot-com world, some people believed companies would create wealth without having to build plants and stores. Therefore conventional limits to their value would not apply.

A famous merger illustrates the problems with assuming that "This Time Is Different." Time Warner has long been an established media giant, its properties including Time Inc., Warner Brothers Entertainment, Turner Broadcasting, and HBO. In January 2001, Time Warner merged with America Online (AOL) to form a new company, AOL Time Warner. Putting "AOL" first in the title was deliberate because Time Warner wanted to take advantage of the dot-com frenzy. It was remaking itself as a new media company. The pitch was that with the power of America's leading online company, the old media giant would rise to new heights.

The merger went badly, however. AOL's strength was in Internet service delivered over telephone lines ("dialup" service). As important as that was in the 1990s, faster and better ways of connecting to the Internet had already begun to appear. The newly merged company turned out to be a media giant plus an unspectacular Internet firm. The merger was a disaster that lost billions of dollars. Only three years after the merger, the company dropped the "AOL" in its name and went back to being "Time Warner." The merger was finally undone with a breakup in 2009.[15]

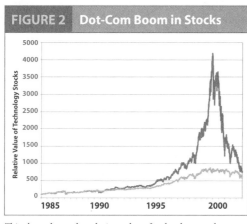

FIGURE 2 Dot-Com Boom in Stocks

This chart shows the relative value of technology stocks compared with a widely followed stock market average, the Dow Jones Industrial Average. Technology stocks, represented by the upper line, reached unsustainably high prices, peaking in 2000 before falling back to more reasonable valuations.

Source: Yahoo Finance, Dow Jones Industrial Average.

In retrospect, there clearly was excessive optimism about the merged future of AOL Time Warner. "We're kicking off the new century with a unique new company that has unparalleled assets and the ability to have a profoundly positive impact on society," said AOL head Steve Case at the time.[16] Some investors apparently assumed that anything with dot-com in the name would become a success. That turned out to be wrong.

Investors seem slow to learn about bubbles. After the dot-com bubble burst in 2000, a bubble in housing prices developed.

Though housing prices had gone through their ups and downs before, some investors felt "this time is different"—and made bets that housing prices would only continue to rise. Those bets came crashing down in the recession of 2007–2010, followed by large losses on the part of homeowners, real estate investors, and others throughout the financial system. Both the experience of AOL Time Warner and the housing crash suggest that an investor should be cautious when told, "this time is different."

THEN & Now QUESTIONS for DISCUSSION

1. What is a "bubble" in stock market prices, and how did the 1995–2000 bubble get its name?
2. Previous bubbles made prices go up before they burst. How did adherents of the idea that "This Time Is Different" persuade themselves that the dot-com bubble would not burst?
3. Why would 1990s strength in dial-up Internet service, a key feature of American Online, be less valuable after 2000?
4. At the time of the America Online-Time Warner merger, well informed people thought the merger would be a success. Why were they wrong?
5. Are all industries susceptible to bubbles? That is, should investors ever accept an argument that says "This Time Is Different," implying that the value of an investment would always go up and never come down?

Web Resources

A Brief History of the Internet
http://www.isoc.org/internet/history/brief.shtml

This site, maintained by the Internet Society, includes resources on every stage of the Internet's development.

How the AOL-Time Warner Merger Went So Wrong
http://www.nytimes.com/2010/01/11/business/media/11merger.html

An in-depth look at one of the biggest disappointments in the history of mergers, assembled by the New York Times.

Bill Gates Biography
http://www.biography.com/articles/Bill-Gates-9307520

A biography including an extensive text and multiple videos.

Net Neutrality from the *New York Times*
http://topics.nytimes.com/topics/reference/timestopics/subjects/n/net_neutrality/index.html

This "Times Topic" includes a description of a central issue in Internet regulation, with links to news coverage and commentary.

Is Free Trade Out of Date?

*A World Trade Organization conference
in Geneva Switzerland, 2009.*

Governments can encourage trade between nations or they can discourage trade. To discourage trade, governments adopt protectionist policies. **Protectionist** policies discourage trade by imposing tariffs, quotas, and other restrictive measures. **Tariffs** are taxes on imports; they increase the cost of imported goods and thus discourage consumers from buying them. **Quotas** are limits on imports; a quota on imported automobiles means that only so many (the number set by the quota) of those automobiles may be imported. The intended effect of tariffs and quotas is to protect domestic industries from international competition. The opposite of protectionism is free trade. **Free trade** is a system in which goods and services may be bought and sold internationally with minimal interference from governments.

In the aftermath of World War II, U.S. policy has generally favored free trade over protectionism. The protectionist policies of the 1930s taught a lesson that influenced U.S. policy leaders after the war. The Smoot-Hawley Tariff Act of 1930 raised tariffs on 20,000 imported goods. European and Canadian trade partners of the United States swiftly retaliated by imposing tariffs on goods imported from the United States. Trade was stifled. Businesses lost international customers. Consumers lost access to less expensive goods and services. Standards of living were reduced among trade partners in the midst of the Great Depression, the largest economic downturn in history. Nobody wanted to repeat that history of losses caused by protectionism..

Fast forward to 2007, when the U.S. economy took another historic nose dive—the worst downturn since the Great Depression. Evidence of the downturn was seen in towns and cities across the nation. Niagara, for example, is a town of 1,800 residents in

KEY ECONOMIC CONCEPTS

Absolute advantage	Outsourcing
Comparative advantage	Scarcity
Exports	Specialization
Free Trade	Tariff
Imports	Quota
Opportunity cost	Voluntary trade
Protectionist policies	

Marinette County, Wisconsin. In 2008, the New Page paper mill in Niagara closed its doors and laid off nearly 300 workers. Tom Sielaff, 49, lost his job. He had worked at the mill for 30 years. His brother Ron, 57, also lost his job. These losses were a shock to the community, but the cause of the problem was not new. Demand for the coated paper produced at New Page had been falling for years. From 1990 to 2008, Niagara had lost nearly 67 percent of its paper mill jobs. Unemployment in the Marinette County reached 11.7 percent. Although this is a far cry from the unemployment rate of 1933, people like Tom and Ron had never experienced anything like it. Some politicians, from the region argued that the job losses were caused by international competition from paper mills in Finland and China.

When unemployment is at high levels and plants are being closed, perhaps because of international competition, is it in America's best interest to engage in protectionism—that is, to establish barriers against free trade? Or is free trade still good for America?

The Historical Context
World Trade after World War II

After World War II, the industrial nations of world engaged in a series of negotiations aimed at reducing trade barriers. They established the

Bill Clinton makes a speech in support of NAFTA to the Washington Chamber of Commerce.

General Agreement on Tariffs and Trade (GATT). GATT is a United Nations Agency created by treaty to promote trade by reducing tariffs and quotas. From 1948 to 1994, GATT wrote rules for trade that substantially reduced tariff barriers for manufactured goods in the industrial countries. These tariff reductions helped promote the tremendous expansion of world trade that followed World War II and the subsequent rise in per capita incomes among developed and developing nations.[1] The successor to GATT is the World Trade Organization (WTO), established in 1995. The WTO is now the forum in which member countries negotiate reductions in trade barriers. It has 153 members and is headquartered in Geneva, Switzerland.

Regional Trade Agreements (RTAs) provide another means of reducing trade barriers. There are nearly 500 RTAs worldwide. The United States has RTAs with 17 countries including Australia, Bahrain, Israel, Jordon, Peru, and Singapore. The RTA of greatest interest to Americans is the North American Free Trade Agreement (NAFTA). NAFTA was established in 1994 under President William Clinton. The members are Canada, Mexico, and the United States. Under the terms of NAFTA, the United States, Canada, and Mexico agreed to phase out all tariffs on merchandise trade and to reduce restrictions on trade in services over a decade.[2] Canada is the United States' top trade partner, followed by China and Mexico.

Although America has generally promoted free trade since World War II, there have been periods in which American policy favored protectionism. In the 1970s, the economies of Germany and Japan had recovered from the devastation of World War II. The United States no longer dominated the global economy to the extent it once had. American industry faced increased international competition in the manufacturing of steel, automobiles, electronics, textiles, and shoes. In this context, American automobile manufacturers and the automobile workers' union worked together to fight for government protection from international competition. In 1981, they were able to obtain "voluntary export restraints" on cars imported from Japan. These were quotas; they reduced the number of cars imported from Japan and they helped to protect the jobs of some American auto workers. They also increased the prices American consumers paid for automobiles. Economist Alan Blinder determined that, by increasing prices, the quotas cost American consumers about $160,000 for each auto-worker job saved.[3]

Is Free Trade Out of Date?

These "voluntary export restraints" have now been dropped. American auto makers have made progress in competing against Japanese imports. And the United States has for the most part continued to support the expansion of free trade. It has continued to negotiate RTAs to strengthen trade relationships with other nations. After 2000, the United States negotiated free trade agreements with Columbia, South Korea, and Panama.

The Economics of Free Trade

Economists since the time of Adam Smith have argued in favor of free trade among nations as the path toward prosperity. Some Americans, such as Tom and Ron Sielaff, would most likely disagree. They experienced serious personal losses, perhaps as a result of international competition.

But it would be a mistake to view trade policy as an issue that pits a handful of economists against the rest of the American public. In their everyday lives, ordinary Americans benefit regularly from free trade, even though they probably don't pause to think about it.

Thinking about the everyday benefits of free trade requires attention to two concepts: specialization and voluntary trade. **Specialization** is doing what you can do best, at a low cost; **voluntary trade** is engaging in transactions freely, without barriers or coercion. For example, suppose you decide to get a haircut. You probably won't try to cut your hair yourself. Instead, you might head for a discount hair-styling shop, where the stylist or barber specializes in cutting hair at discount rates. If you do that, your decision will mean one less customer for a high-end hair salon somewhere in your vicinity, where you could have gone instead. But no one suggests that high-end salons should be protected against competition from discount hair stylists. Common sense suggests that, if you choose to do so, you should be able to engage in voluntary trade with the discount stylist. In the exchange, you'll receive a haircut at a discount price; the stylist will receive income from you. You and the stylist will be better off, thanks to the

Adam Smith, author of The Wealth of Nations.

exchange—the free trade—you've made.

What is true of domestic trade is also true for international trade. Economist Alan S. Blinder emphasizes the point by reference to shoe manufacturing:

> Spain, South Korea, and … other countries manufacture shoes more cheaply than America can. They offer them for sale to us. Shall we buy them … with money we earn doing things we do well—like writing computer software and growing wheat? Or shall we keep "cheap foreign shoes" out and purchase more expensive American shoes instead? It is pretty clear that the nation as a whole must be worse off if foreign shoes are kept out—even though the American shoe industry [would then] be better off. [4]

Adam Smith had precisely the same insight more than 200 years ago. Here is how he put it in 1776:

> By means of glasses, hotbeds, and hotwalls [that is, greenhouses], very good grapes can be raised in Scotland, and very good wine too can be made of them at about thirty times the expense for which at least equally good [wine] can be brought from foreign countries. Would it be a reasonable law to prohibit the

importation of all foreign wines, merely to encourage the making of claret and burgundy [wines] in Scotland?"[5]

Scarcity, Opportunity Cost, and Voluntary Trade

Blinder and Smith are writing about voluntary trade. At its core, this topic is related to scarcity and opportunity cost. **Scarcity** means that we can't have everything we want. We want too much, and our resources are too limited—too scarce—to meet our wants. One way to cope with the problem of scarcity is to increase international trade. Doing more of one thing (growing grapes in a greenhouse in Scotland, say) always requires doing less of something else (raising sheep, perhaps, without the need of a greenhouse). In other words, in a choice to make wine, or raise sheep, or do anything else, there is an **opportunity cost**. Is there a way to reduce opportunity costs? Probably so. People who trade in competitive markets strive to reduce opportunity costs by finding ways to be more productive. International trade expands competitive markets, helping producers and consumers to reduce the opportunity costs related to production.

Here is an example of how that works. Imagine that Jenny King is a world-class tennis player. She plays in all the big tournaments and has many product endorsements. Jenny is also great at mowing lawns. She can mow her lawn, a big one, in only two hours. But in the two hours it takes her to mow her lawn, she could earn $10,000 making a television commercial for Whizbang tennis shoes. What is Jenny's opportunity cost (her second-best choice) if she chooses to mow her lawn? It is $10,000.

Now suppose that Jenny has a neighbor named Scotty, who sometimes works at McDonald's. Jenny is thinking about hiring Scotty to mow her lawn; she would pay him $40 per lawn job. Scotty is not as good at mowing lawns as Jenny. It takes him four hours to mow Jenny's lawn. In that time, Jenny could mow her lawn twice. Scotty's opportunity cost (his second-best choice) for mowing Jenny's lawn is to work four hours at McDonalds, where he could earn $32. The loss of four hours' work at McDonald's translates into a $32 opportunity cost if Scotty chooses to mow Jenny's lawn. Economists would say that Jenny has an **absolute advantage** over Scotty in lawn mowing. This means that she can do more lawn mowing than Scotty can, with the same amount of resources (time and effort).

Should Jenny do both jobs—be a star tennis player and a lawn mower—or should she just play tennis and hire Scotty to mow her lawn? She should hire Scotty, unless she is uninterested in endorsement fees and other tennis-related benefits. Why? Jenny has a comparative advantage in being a tennis star. **Comparative advantage** is the ability to produce something more efficiently and at a lower cost than a competitor could produce it. Jenny can earn more income, and give up less in doing so, if she spends her time playing tennis and doing endorsements rather than dividing her time to do other things.

Scotty, on the other hand, has a comparative advantage over Jenny in mowing lawns. He is better off specializing in mowing Jenny's lawn. As long as Jenny pays Scotty more than $32 and less than $10,000, they are both better off than they would have been if the lawn-mowing exchange never occurred.

What do Jenny and Scotty have to do with international trade? Jenny's skills are like the skills of American workers. American workers are relatively well educated and highly skilled. They have an **absolute advantage** in producing many goods and services, including computers. The skills of workers in some other countries resemble Scotty's skills. Chinese workers, for example, are less costly in some manufacturing jobs than American workers are; we know this because we see clothing, television sets, and many other products from China on sale in our stores.

Economists argue that American workers should specialize in producing what they do best and then trade some of what they produce for goods produced elsewhere. For example, suppose that American workers have a comparative advantage over Chinese workers in producing new antibiotics. They can produce antibiotics more efficiently and at a lower cost than Chinese workers could. If that is so, Chinese workers

Workers wear protective suits at an electronics factory in Shenzhen, China.

should specialize in manufacturing other things. Perhaps they can produce computers at a lower opportunity cost than American workers can. If that is so, businesses in both nations should specialize and trade; in the exchanges that follow, American consumers will get computers and Chinese consumers will get antibiotics. People on both sides will be better off.

Barriers to Trade

As noted earlier, a tariff is a tax on imports. It represents an added cost to the producer, since the producer pays the tax. The United States first imposed a tariff when it enacted the Tariff Act of 1789. Tax revenue generated by the Act was a key source of income for the new federal government in a time when there was no income tax. It helped to pay for the costs of running the government and to reduce the national debt resulting from fighting the American Revolution.

A quota is a restriction on the amount of a product that may be imported into the United States. The United States has at times restricted the amount of sugar that can be imported, in order to protect producers in the U.S. sugar industry from international competition. Sugar quotas in place today have remained unchanged since 1990. As a result, the price of sugar in the

United States is significantly higher than the world price.

Most nations make some use of tariffs and quotas to protect domestic industries. Almost no producers welcome competition. American farmers, for example, would prefer not to compete with farmers in other nations. Why is that? Think about green peppers. Green peppers grown in Mexico and brought into the United States increase the supply of green peppers and lower the price of peppers at the supermarket. Domestic growers of green peppers would prefer higher prices. They might therefore lobby members of Congress to impose barriers on imports of green peppers.

People who seek trade protection are likely to emphasize one or more of three reasons to justify their position. The first has to do with national defense. Many Americans believe the United States should protect industries that are necessary to equip the U.S. military forces for war. They argue, for example, that it might be difficult to buy missiles and their spare parts from another country in time of war.

The second has to do with protecting "infant" industries. This argument states that some new industries are not strong enough to compete in the global economy with other, more established firms. They should therefore be protected for a time by tariffs or quotas, until they can recover their startup costs and begin to compete on their own. Alexander Hamilton, the first U.S. Secretary of Treasury, strongly endorsed the infant-industry argument in his Report on Manufactures in 1790.

The third is the anti-dumping argument. The term "dumping" has a special meaning in trade policy. It refers to the sale of a product in another nation at a price lower than the price charged in the producer's home markets. For example, if producers in another nation sell television sets in the United States for less than they charge for television sets at home, they are said to be engaged in dumping. That is unfair competition, according to the anti-dumping argument, and producers engaged in it should be restricted by protectionist measures.

These arguments illustrate two important characteristics of controversy over trade policy. One is that people seeking protectionist measures are not likely to come out and state that they want protection so that they can earn profits without having to outdo their competitors. Instead, they are likely to claim that they are defending an abstract value of some sort—perhaps the national interest (argument 1), or fairness (arguments 2 and 3). Claims of that sort might sound attractive in the court of popular opinion, trumping consideration of concrete details such as the higher prices caused by trade protection. The other characteristic is that emphasizing abstract values said to be at stake might prevent observers from posing follow-up questions. Exactly what is an infant industry, for example, and when does such an infant become simply a noncompetitive adult? Or again, can it be known for sure when a foreign company is selling products below cost? Does a manufacturer of tube socks in a remote province of China provide detailed cost accounting records for American competitors to examine?

Given these characteristics of how trade policy gets discussed in public, legislators acting on specific claims for protection may take their guidance more from interest-group advocacy than from economic or logical analysis. Interest-group advocacy creates incentives, and legislators, like other people, respond predictably to incentives.

What are American's top imports and exports?

Although the size of planet Earth has not changed over time, the amount of time and money it takes to move resources from one place to another has decreased enormously in recent years, setting the stage for equally enormous increases in world trade. International trade today has received a big boost from reduced costs involved in the delivery of goods.

America is the world's largest importer. In 2008, the United States bought more than $2 trillion worth of imported products. Table 1 shows a list of the top 10 American exports and imports. Goods and services produced by businesses in one country and sold to individuals or companies in another are called **exports**. **Imports** are goods and services purchased from businesses in another country. As you can see,

TABLE 1	Top U.S. Exports and Imports for 2008		
Top U.S. Exports	Amount (in billions of U.S. dollars)	Top U.S. Imports	Amount (in billions of U.S. dollars)
Civilian aircraft	74.0	Crude oil	341.9
Semiconductors	50.6	Passenger cars	125.6
Passenger cars	49.6	Pharma-ceuticals	78.9
Pharmaceuticals	40.4	Automotive accessories	64.9
Automotive accessories	39.9	household goods	61.6
Other industrial machines	38.1	Computer accessories	60.2
Fuel oil	34.9	Petroleum products	52.3
Organic chemicals	33.4	Cotton apparel	49.5
Telecom-munications	32.9	Telecom-munications equipment	44.8
Plastic materials	31.6	Video equip-ment (DVDs)	41.0

Source: http://www.worldsrichestcountries.com

the top U.S. exports are aircraft, semiconductors, and cars. Top U.S. imports are crude oil, passenger cars, and medicines.

Aren't more exports good for our economy, and aren't more imports bad?

A lot of people think so. But this is a case where economic thinking can make a real difference in understanding how trade works. At first glance, the argument for exports seems powerful. Surely it seems to make sense that if 1,000 additional U.S. passenger planes were sold in Asia, Americans would be better off. In fact, some Americans would be better off, but others would not be.

Remember that exports are made from scarce resources. To make more airplanes for export, airline manufacturers would have to use resources that other manufacturers could use to produce other goods and services in the United States. Scarcity of resources for use in those other areas of manufacturing would push prices in those areas up. The opportunity cost of increased aircraft sales would therefore be higher prices for other goods and services. Because prices for other goods and services would go up, increased export sales of aircraft would make economic sense only if U.S. consumers could purchase imported goods and services from other countries at costs low enough to offset higher prices caused by an increase export sales of aircraft.

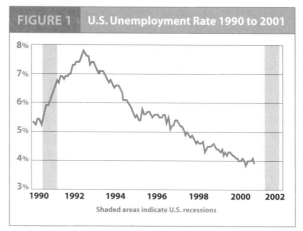

FIGURE 1 — U.S. Unemployment Rate 1990 to 2001

Shaded areas indicate U.S. recessions

Source: Federal Reserve Bank of St. Louis.

Who are the most important trade partners of the United States?

Table 2 shows the top 10 trade partners for the United States. The top three trade partners are Canada, China, and Mexico. The 10 countries listed in the table account for 65.99 percent of U.S. imports, and 61.20 percent of U.S. exports in goods.

Has the North American Free Trade Agreement (NAFTA) been an economic success?

Most observers believe it has. The concept behind NAFTA is to promote economic growth by reducing the cost of trade across all three nations—the United States, Mexico, and Canada. Since 1994, trade has increased dramatically across all three borders. For example, agricultural trade between Mexico and the United States (in both directions) increased from $7.3 billion in 1994 to $20.1 billion in 2006. Trade among businesses in Canada, Mexico, and the United States is counted in hundreds of billions of dollars. The United States imports oil worth billions of dollars from Canada and Mexico, reducing our dependence on oil from the Middle East. Supporters of NAFTA also point to the U.S. unemployment rate, after NAFTA, as an indicator of success. Figure 1 shows the decline in U.S. unemployment rate from about 1992 to about 2001. Unemployment rates also declined in Canada and Mexico during the same period.

Not everybody believes that these favorable results can be directly linked to NAFTA.

TABLE 2 — Top 10 Trade Partners for the United States, as of 2009	
Country	**Total Value of Exports and Imports in Goods (in billions of U.S. Dollars)**
Canada	429.64
China	365.98
Mexico	305.53
Japan	147.14
Germany	114.55
United Kingdom	93.20
South Korea	67.88
France	60.56
Taiwan	46.81
Brazil	46.25

Source: U.S. Census Bureau.

Developments unrelated to NAFTA—the boom in "dot-com" businesses in the 1990s, for example—also played a role. Critics of NAFTA also point to U.S. businesses that have moved production plants to Mexico; they claim that moves of this sort have cost some Americans their jobs. Here again, these claims are difficult to assess. Factors unrelated to NAFTA have contributed to changes in unemployment rates in all three NAFTA nations. While American farmers have benefited from increased exports to Mexico, it is hard to know how increased competition from American farmers may have hurt Mexican farmers.

Is outsourcing bad or good for the American Economy?

Outsourcing occurs when one firm enters into an agreement with another firm (frequently in another country) to provide services (usually at a lower rate of pay) that might otherwise be performed by the first firm's own workers. Many companies now outsource services such as managing payroll or running calling centers. Others outsource specific aspects of a manufacturing process. Have you ever called a bank or a computer tech-support number? There is a good chance that your call was picked up by someone in another English-speaking country such as India.

The economic reason for outsourcing is not very mysterious. It is another story about opportunity costs. Imagine the case of Rock Solid Community Banks. The workers at Rock Solid have an absolute advantage over workers in India in handling the bank's loan processing services. But suppose that a firm called We've Got Your Number—a calling center company in New Delhi, India—can provide the same calling center service at a lower cost than the calling center workers at the Rock Solid Community Banks. If we use the economic way of thinking, what should Rock Solid do? It should specialize in what it does best—loan processing—and outsource the calling center to We've Got Your Number.

But that is not the end of the story. Some workers at Rock Solid will be better off than others if Rock Solid sticks to loan processing and outsources its call center service. Perhaps more loan officers will be hired, but the people working in the calling center may be laid off. The pain is real for the laid-off workers and their families. Taken together, however, the opportunity-cost argument suggests that outsourcing is good for the economy as a whole. It is little different from other forms of trade.

QUESTIONS for DISCUSSION

1. What is the main argument in support of specialization and free trade?
2. What are the main arguments in opposition to free trade?
3. Which argument—for or against free trade—do you find to be most convincing? Why?

Tariffs between the
United States and Europe

The cartoon below appeared in the November 22, 1952, issue of *Collier's*, a popular American magazine at the time. The figure in the upper-left corner of the cartoon represents the United States. He seems to be shoveling money out to a European man sitting on crates of European goods. The figure looking on from the background, smoking a pipe, seems to be Josef Stalin, the head of the Communist Party of the Soviet Union. Examine the cartoon and respond to the questions that follow.

PRIMARY SOURCE **QUESTIONS for DISCUSSION**

1. Why might the cartoon suggest that the United States is shoveling money to Europe in 1952?
2. What is the European man doing?
3. Why doesn't the figure who represents Europe "shovel" his goods to the United States?
4. What does the cartoon suggest about the situation it depicts?
5. Josef Stalin, the figure standing in the background, seems to be smiling. Why might he be smiling?

A Trade War with Mexico?

NAFTA has reduced trade barriers among the United States, Canada, and Mexico. But there have been occasional flare-ups in trade relationships among these trade partners. For example, the *Wall Street Journal* reported the following account of a trade dispute between the United States and Mexico.

In the summer of 2010, Mexico announced that it had placed new tariffs on 26 previously tariff-free items it imports from the United States. It placed new tariffs, for example, on Washington apples, California oranges, and pistachios and cheeses from California and Wisconsin.

What is behind Mexico's actions? Why would it wish to make imported goods more expensive for Mexican citizens?

Mexico has argued for 15 years that the United States has failed to keep its commitments under the NAFTA agreement by refusing to allow Mexican trucking companies to operate in the United States. United States authorities have cited highway safety concerns as a reason for excluding Mexican trucks. On the other hand, U.S. trucking firms do operate in Mexico. In 2001, Mexico appealed the exclusion of its trucking companies, asking a NAFTA resolution panel to rule that the Mexican companies should be permitted to operate in the United States. Mexico won the appeal. In response to the unfavorable decision, the United States promised to conduct a pilot program that would allow Mexican drivers to operate in the United States from 2007 to 2009. The program was reported to be a success; Mexican trucks were as safe as American trucks. The pilot program ended, however, and it has not been restarted.

What is the problem? The *Wall Street Journal* suggests that pressure from the International Brotherhood of Teamsters is blocking Mexican trucks.[6] The union, many of whose members drive trucks, does not welcome competition from Mexican trucking companies.

Critics of the *Wall Street Journal* report say that the issue is not about protecting union trucking jobs. Instead, it is about public safety. The U.S. Department of Transportation, for example, reports that Mexico has inadequate safety standards for its trucking companies that it fails to enforce its standards properly. It cites questions about how many hours per day or week Mexican truckers may drive, about access to drivers' highway safety records, and about access to drug-test records.

Who is at fault here? Is a trade war looming with Mexico?

THEN & NOW QUESTIONS for DISCUSSION

1. Why might the United States not honor its commitments under NAFTA to allow Mexican trucking companies to operate in the United States?
2. Which explanation seems more likely? Explain your answer.

Web Resources

Is It Time for Protection?
http://www.bea.gov/national

GDP website

World Trade after World War II
http://www.wto.org

World Trade Organization homepage, featuring current news

Do economists regard NAFTA as a success?
http://www.export.gov/fta/NAFTA

Video highlighting some aspects of NAFTA

Is the Growth of the Federal Government Good for the Economy?

Federal employee Ralph Baughman removes a few hundred Social Security checks from a check writing machine, 1939.

In a 1994 episode of the television sitcom *Friends*, Rachel receives her first paycheck from a waitressing job. She rushes to her friends, saying "Look . . . my first paycheck!"

She tells them that she worked hard to earn her first pay check. She wiped a lot of tables and steamed a lot of milk. It was totally worth it! But when she opens her check and examines it, she says it was totally not worth it. Her paycheck is much smaller than she anticipated: "Who's FICA? Why is he getting all my money?" she asks.[1]

What Rachel didn't know is that FICA is the Federal Insurance Contributions Act (FICA) tax. It is the tax withheld from paychecks to cover Social Security and Medicare, the federal programs that provide pensions and medical care for older Americans. Perhaps you had a "Rachel" moment when you earned your first paycheck.

Like Rachel, FICA would have mystified the Founders. They had in mind a limited role for the federal government in the economy. That role, according to the Constitution, included providing for national defense, protecting private property rights, collecting taxes, regulating the value of money, and issuing patents and copyrights.

But life for Americans today differs greatly from life in 1789. The country has grown from 13 states to 50; it has taken on far-reaching international responsibilities; its social norms and its economy have evolved. In this context, how should Americans view the expansion of the federal role in the economy?

The Historical Context
The Growth of Government Spending

The federal government maintained a limited role in the economy throughout the 18th and 19th centuries. Federal spending went mainly for national defense and transportation infrastructure, such as road and canals. Most government spending took place at the local and state levels.

KEY ECONOMIC CONCEPTS

Bond	Incentives
Entitlements	Interest groups
Deficit	National debt
Government failure	Surplus
Gross Domestic product (GDP)	

Wartimes were different. Through most of its history, the federal government added substantially to its debt in times of war. In the aftermath of war, it worked to reduce its debt. The federal debt was relatively high back in 1792, owing to debts acquired in fighting the American Revolution. The debt was all but erased by 1860, but it increased again with the Civil War. In the 20th century, the debt spiked again during World War I and World War II.

During World War II, the economic role of the federal government expanded greatly. The government controlled prices for many products; it also set wages for people in many occupations. It rationed the distribution of many goods, providing Americans with coupons that allowed them to purchase only limited amounts of sugar, butter, meat, or gasoline, for example, even if they had enough money to buy more. Government officials decided how raw materials were to be used in the war effort. They drafted soldiers into the armed forces and took over whole industries. Every community and every family had some connection to the economic changes involved in the war effort.

Following World War II, the federal role in the economy changed. Price controls were lifted. Military spending declined, and factories returned to producing civilian goods. However, federal spending did not drop back to pre-war levels. By 1947, it began to increase. What might explain that renewed upward trend?

The Economics of Government Spending

The federal government spends money in three major areas:

- **Transfer payments:** These are payments of income to recipients who do not provide any goods or services in return for the payments. Examples include Social Security payments, unemployment compensation, and payments to people with disabilities. Transfer payments constitute the largest portion of federal spending today.

- **Purchases of goods and services:** This category includes, for example, payments for national defense (soldiers' salaries, military bases, aircraft, missiles, and so on), roads, national parks, federal courts, and some support for public education.

- **Interest on the national debt:** The federal government in recent years has often spent more than the tax revenue it has taken in. To close the gap between spending and income, the federal government borrows money. It sells bonds. A **bond** is a certificate. It states that the person who bought the bond has made a loan to the government; it also states a promise to pay the bond's owner the amount borrowed, plus interest. The money raised by selling bonds is used to meet the government's spending obligations.

Figure 1 shows government spending from 1929 to 2010. Note the increased level of government spending during World War II. Also note how spending after World War II did not revert to its 1940 level. Finally, note the rise in spending beginning in 1947 and continuing upward in the following decades.

Even after World War II, wars contributed to the growth of government spending. During the time in question the United States was involved in the Korean War (1950–1953), the Vietnam War (1961–1975), and more recently the wars in Iraq and Afghanistan. But these were not the all-

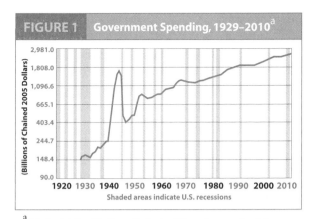

FIGURE 1   Government Spending, 1929–2010[a]

Shaded areas indicate U.S. recessions

[a]"Chained dollars" in the vertical axis of Figure 1 means the dollar amounts used in the graph have been adjusted for inflation to equal the value of the dollar in 2005. In other words, the amounts are "chained" to 2005 dollars.

Source: U.S. Department of Commerce: Bureau of Economic Analysis.

out struggles of World War I and World War II. Spending for the war in Iraq in 2007, for example, was less than 5 percent of GDP. At its height in 1944, spending to fight World War II was greater than 50 percent of GDP.

For a more complete explanation of the rise in spending, it is necessary to look beyond the costs of war. Table 1 provides a snapshot of changes in federal spending since 1960. Spending on transfer payments has increased as a percentage of federal spending. The largest change in transfer spending is accounted for by increases in spending on Social Security, health care, welfare, and payments to people with disabilities. There has been a decrease in the percentage of federal spending on the purchase of goods and services for general government

TABLE 1   Distribution of Federal Spending: 1960, 2000, 2010

	1960	2000	2010
	Percent of the federal budget	Percent of the federal budget	Percent of the federal budget
Transfer payments	14	55	58
Purchases of goods and Services	76	33	37
Interest on the national debt	10	12	5

Sources: http://www.usgovernmentspending.com

Is the Growth of the Federal Government Good for the Economy?

321

operations.

These changes in federal spending reflect a trend in legislators' choices, beginning in the 1930s. In 1935 Congress approved a major new entitlement program called Social Security. An **entitlement** results from a governmental promise that certain benefits will be provided to individuals who meet the entitlement program's criteria—a particular age or income level, for example. Another entitlement program—Medicare—was approved 30 years later. Here is some background on these events.

On June 8, 1934, a year after the worst days of the Great Depression, President Franklin D. Roosevelt announced his desire to have Congress approve the Social Security program. Congress passed the Social Security Act and President Roosevelt signed it into law on August 14, 1935. Unlike temporary welfare payments, Social Security created a permanent social insurance program. It was designed originally to pay retired workers aged 65 or older a continuing income.

President Harry S. Truman followed Roosevelt in office. Truman was an early supporter of government-provided health insurance for the elderly. He tried and failed to obtain Congressional support for a national health insurance program in 1945 and 1948. By 1964, things had changed. President Lyndon

B. Johnson won a landslide victory in the 1964 election. When he took office he launched a plan to create a "Great Society." The Great Society he envisioned would be one served by a wide range of federally sponsored social welfare programs. His political party held large majorities in both houses of Congress. On July 30, 1965, President Johnson signed a new program into law as an amendment to the original Social Security legislation. The new program was Medicare—a program to provide health care insurance for people aged 65 and over.

Like Social Security, the Medicare program expanded over time to provide additional benefits such as health insurance for the disabled and insurance coverage for prescription drugs. In 2008, nearly 60 million people received Social Security payments, totaling more than $615 billion, and more than 7 million people received Supplemental Security Income (SSI) payments, totaling more than $43 billion. More than 47 million Americans currently receive Medicare. Spending on Medicare in 2010 was $520.4 billion.

Expenditures Outpace Revenues

As the federal government has expanded its commitments, a problem has begun to emerge. Figure 2 shows that federal government

President Lyndon B. Johnson signs the Medicare Bill, seated next to former President Harry S. Truman, July 30th 1965.

expenditures, as of 2010, amount to about $3,400 billion. Figure 3 shows that federal receipts (tax revenue), as of 2010, amount to about $2,300 billion. Federal tax receipts are not keeping pace with federal spending.

Why Is Spending on Social Security and Medicare Increasing at a Fast Pace, and Why Might That Be a Problem?

Today nearly 60 million Americans depend on Social Security during their retirement years. Social Security also provides benefits to widows and people with disabilities. Until recently the system has functioned well, in part because the number of people in the workforce has been substantially larger than the number of people in retirement. This situation is changing.

The underlying change is demographic. America had relatively low birth rates in the years of the Great Depression and during World War II. As people from these generations retired, they put relatively little stress on the Social Security system.

After World War II, however, the birthrate skyrocketed, producing what is often called the Baby Boom generation. Now the Baby Boomers are at retirement age. They are beginning to receive Social Security payments and Medicare benefits. However, there are fewer workers in the work force to support this large number of retirees. The number of workers per retiree is currently 3.3; that number is projected to fall to 2.2 in 2041. In 1950, by contrast, there were 16 workers for every recipient of Social Security benefits.

Moreover, owing to improvements in health care, Baby Boomers today are likely to spend many more years in retirement than earlier retirees did. In 1935, when the retirement age was set at 65, the average life expectancy for an American was nearly 62 years. Today, the average life expectancy is more than 78 years.

Federal spending on entitlement programs is expected to increase dramatically in the coming decades, particularly for Social Security and Medicare. Taken together, these programs currently account for nearly half of all federal spending, not counting interest paid on the debt. The problem this situation raises is that, unless something changes, paying for Social Security and Medicare will require such a large portion of federal spending that the federal government will be able to do little except pay for those programs. Funding for national defense, education, transportation, environmental protection, and other matters of priority to many Americans may be crowded out by entitlement commitments.

Why Federal Spending Increases: The Role of Interest Groups, Legislators, and Incentives

Federal spending has also increased in areas other than the major entitlement programs. In part, the explanation for this steady increase in federal spending is straightforward. The United States has taken on costly international responsibilities since World War II, and at home it has increased federal spending on transportation, space exploration, education, environmental

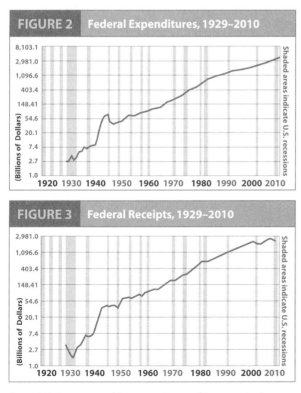

Source: U.S. Department of Commerce: Bureau of Economic Analysis.

Is the Growth of the Federal Government Good for the Economy?

323

protection, and other areas. But merely listing areas of expanded governmental activity does not explain how support for increased spending comes about. It does not always come about because the general public strongly favors the programs in question. Instead, support often arises from interest groups. **Interest groups** are voluntary organizations of like-minded citizens who advocate for legislation that specifically benefits the members of their groups. Their frequent success illustrates a key principle of the economic way of thinking: people respond predictably to incentives. **Incentives** are rewards that encourage people to take a certain action.

Interest groups seeking economic assistance from the federal government include business owners, farmers, consumers, the elderly, environmentalists, labor unions, teachers, and so on. The U.S. Chamber of Commerce and the AFL-CIO are specific examples. Interest groups often *lobby* legislators, in the state capitols and in Congress. *Lobbying* means meeting with legislators to urge the legislators to support policies that the interest group supports.

Many Americans have at least some interest in policy issues under consideration by legislators, of course, but interest groups are distinctive because they have *concentrated interests*. They focus their attention sharply on policy issues that will affect them specifically, and they spend time and money to influence political outcomes related to those issues. There is nothing illegal about that. But the outcomes interest groups seek may be economically inefficient. That is, they may produce benefits for the interest group at the expense of others. When government policies cause inefficiencies of this sort, they are said by economists to be examples of **government failure**. Government failure helps to explain recent increases in government spending.

Consider, for example, interest-group activity on behalf of dairy farmers. Many dairy farmers join interest groups that advocate for government price supports for milk. Price supports are established by laws and regulations that set the price of milk above the market price. Interest groups advocating for price supports may argue that they wish to protect family farms

Leading businessmen and industrialists gather at the United States Chamber of Congress annual meeting, 1937. The Chamber of Congress is an example of an interest group.

by using price supports to give farmers more income. Legislators have an incentive to respond favorably to such advocacy. Interest groups create incentives for legislators by their activities: educating voters through advertising, making campaign contributions, and turning out voters who will support helpful candidates on Election Day.

The incentives legislators face can make it difficult for them to resist the wishes of interest groups. In exchange for supporting policies favored by interest groups, legislators may obtain benefits—campaign contributions, volunteer workers, votes—which may help them to be reelected.

But, you might say, dairy-state legislators must understand that price supports will harm consumers by increasing the price they pay for milk. Why take the risk of angering voters who are not dairy farmers? The legislators, however, probably are willing to bet that that risk is not great. Few consumers will notice the increase in the price of milk they buy. The increase probably will be only a few pennies per purchase. That is because the total cost of the price- support program will be spread out, or *diffused*, over millions of consumers, and over time. The benefits of the program, on the other hand, will be concentrated in the present, for dairy farmers and for the legislators who enjoy their support. *Concentrated benefits* to interest groups paired with *diffused* costs spread out over millions of consumers can produce economically inefficient policies.

The example of price supports for dairy farmers is not unique. Interest groups and incentives also help to explain increases in entitlement spending. When the Social Security program was enacted in 1935, many legislators gained benefits in the form of support from voters who benefitted from the program. And the costs of the program were spread out—over millions of workers, in the form of a payroll tax, and over time. Since 1935, interest groups have pushed, with considerable success, for extending and increasing Social Security benefits. In 1957, Congress broadened the program to include

disability insurance benefits for severely disabled workers. In 1972, Congress approved automatic cost-of-living adjustments in benefit payments.[2]

Legislative action can cut both ways, of course. In response to the funding crisis that seems to be implied by changes in entitlement spending, Congress also has acted to raise the payroll tax that supports Social Security and to increase the retirement age. In spite of these changes, however, the future looks challenging. Social Security began as program from which few Americans received benefits, supported by tax revenue from many workers. It has now become a program from which many Americans receive benefits, supported by fewer workers.

HISTORICAL QUESTIONS & ECONOMIC ANSWERS

Who pays Social Security taxes?

Everybody who works. Social Security is financed through a payroll deduction (FICA) tax. The FICA notation is what Rachel saw on her first paycheck receipt. The section called "FICA" represented her payment into Social Security. If you receive a paycheck, you will find FICA on your pay stub.

How does Social Security differ from a private pension program?

From the days when Social Security was first proposed in 1934, it has been described as an old-age pension program. Many Americans imagine that they have an "account" into which they have made contributions during their working years and from which they will eventually be able to draw benefits. The Social Security Administration mails a statement to older Americans that tells them how much money they have contributed and provides an estimate of the amount of their future payments.

But Social Security operates differently from a private pension program. In a private pension program, individuals make regular payments into the program over several years. A pool of savings is built up. The idea is that not everyone will retire at the same time. The benefits will be paid out gradually. In the meanwhile, these savings accumulate and grow as they are invested in stocks and bonds. A well-managed pension plan takes in more in payments and in investment earnings than it pays out. The amount of money in the private pension program will have ups and downs with changes in the stock and bonds markets, but it should be sustainable.

So, how *does* Social Security work?

Social Security was designed from the beginning as a "pay as you go" system. It is funded by payroll taxes paid by current workers. These funds are used to pay for the benefits of current retirees. For several years, Social Security built up a trust fund—a surplus of income over expenditures—in anticipation of the forthcoming Baby Boom generation of retirees. This surplus is expected to begin declining in 2016. By 2037, unless something changes, the Social Security trust fund will be exhausted.[3] Tough decisions will need to be made regarding benefit levels and payroll taxes.

Increases in entitlement spending will add to the federal debt and the budget deficit. What is the difference between the two?

When the federal government's annual spending is greater than the revenue it collects, the outcome is called a **deficit**. This means the taxes

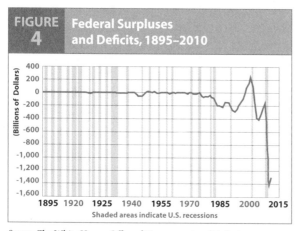

FIGURE 4 **Federal Surpluses and Deficits, 1895–2010**

Shaded areas indicate U.S. recessions

Source: The White House: Office of Management and Budget.

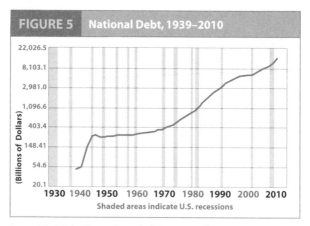

FIGURE 5 **National Debt, 1939–2010**

Shaded areas indicate U.S. recessions

Source: The White House: Council of Economic Advisors.

and fees collected by the government do not cover its expenditures. When the federal government's annual spending is less than the revenue it collects, the outcome is a **surplus**. Figure 4 shows federal deficits and surpluses since 1895. The federal government has had a balanced budget—no deficit or surplus—through much of its history. However, deficits began to increase dramatically in the 1970s. We returned to surpluses in the 1990s, but in 2009 the federal deficit nearly dropped off the chart, reaching $1.4 trillion. Much of this increase in the deficit came in response to the deep recession of 2007–2009. The deficit for 2010 declined to $1.3 trillion and is expected to increase to nearly $1.5 trillion in 2011.[4]

Some people confuse deficits with debt. "Deficit" refers to an annual shortfall. When government revenues fall short of expenditures in a given year, the U.S. Treasury does the same thing individuals do when they spend more money than they have—it borrows money. The amount of the annual shortfall is the deficit. As the government runs a deficit year after year, it accumulates debt. The **national debt** is the amount of money the federal government owes—the sum total of the deficits it has accumulated. Figure 5 shows the level of the national debt since 1939. It is the mirror image of the deficits shown in Figure 4. The national debt begins to accelerate in the 1970s. Growth slows in the 1990s; it takes off again in 2000, with a large jump between 2008 and 2010. The current level of the national debt is about $12 trillion.

How do deficits and debts affect the economy?

It depends. Small deficits may be unimportant, in relation to the overall size of the economy. When the economy falls into recession, deficit spending, even on a large scale, may help to stimulate economic activity and recovery. But large, sustained deficits are another matter. As they push the national debt upward, they may create the following problems:

- If the government raises taxes to pay for the rising costs of interest on the national debt, personal savings will be reduced. Some tax increases may discourage people from working.

- Rising costs of interest on the national debt could force reductions in spending on important government programs such as transportation, health care, environmental protection, and defense.

- Inflation rates may go up, as they did in the 1970s. Government-issued bonds are used to pay for the deficits. If deficits are increasing faster than the overall economy is growing, we wind up with too many dollars chasing too few goods and services. The result may be a surge in inflation.

- Individuals and financial institutions may decide to use a growing portion of their savings for purchases of government debt. That decision would be encouraged by the increased availability of government bonds, sold by the government to raise funds to pay for each deficit. More investment in government bonds—rather than investment in capital goods such as factories—may lead to fewer jobs and a general slowing of economic growth.

QUESTIONS for DISCUSSION

1. In your own words, explain what an entitlement program is.
2. Make up a new example of an entitlement program. Never mind if it is realistic or not. Let your imagination—or your interests—be your guide.
3. Since about 1920, how has government spending compared with government revenues?
4. Why does the future of the Social Security and Medicare programs appear to be uncertain? Explain your answer.
5. Why do legislators and other politicians choose to spend so much money?
6. What is the federal deficit? How is it different from the national debt?
7. What has happened recently to federal deficits and the national debt?
8. What are some risks associated with persistently high deficits and a large national debt?

Three Presidents Comment on the Economic Role of Government

T he following are statements from three U.S. presidents. Read the statements to learn what each president thinks the proper role of the government in the economy should be.

Thomas Jefferson's' First Inaugural Address, March 4, 1801

… Kindly separated by nature and a wide ocean from the exterminating havoc of one quarter of the globe, … possessing a chosen country, with room enough for our descendants to the thousandth and thousandth generation, … with all these blessings, what more is necessary to make us a happy and a prosperous people? Still one thing more, fellow citizens, a wise and frugal government, which shall restrain men from injuring one another, shall leave them otherwise free to regulate their own pursuits of industry and improvement, and shall not take from the mouth of labor the bread it has earned. This is the sum of good government; and this is necessary to close the circle of our felicities.

Franklin D. Roosevelt's Message to Congress, June 8, 1934

Security was attained in the earlier days through the interdependence of members of families upon each other and of the families within a small community upon each other. The complexities of great communities and of organized industry make less real these simple means of security. Therefore, we are compelled to employ the active interest of the Nation as a whole through government in order to encourage a greater security for each individual who composes it . . . . This seeking for a greater measure of welfare and happiness does not indicate a change in values. It is rather a return to values lost in the course of our economic development and expansion . . .

President Lyndon B. Johnson, Regarding Medicare, January 7, 1965

Thirty years ago, the American people made a basic decision that the later years of life should not be years of despondency and drift. … Since World War II, there has been increasing awareness of the fact that the full value of Social Security would not be realized unless provision were made to deal with the problem of costs of illnesses among our older citizens. . . . Compassion and reason dictate that this logical extension of our proven Social Security system will supply the prudent, feasible, and dignified way to free the aged from the fear of financial hardship in the event of illness.

PRIMARY SOURCE QUESTIONS for DISCUSSION

1. What should the role of government in the economy be, according to President Jefferson?
2. How did President Roosevelt's speech express his support for Social Security?
3. How did President Johnson express his support for Medicare?
4. Which president to you tend to agree with? Why?

What Should We Do Now?

Mr. Ben Bernanke, Chairman of the Federal Reserve Board, is well aware of the problems today's generation faces regarding increases in entitlement spending. Here is what he had to say about the future of Social Security and Medicare:

> The arithmetic is, unfortunately, quite clear. To avoid large and unsustainable budget deficits, the nation will ultimately have to choose among higher taxes, modifications to entitlement programs such as Social Security and Medicare, less spending on everything else from education to defense, or some combination of the above. These choices are difficult, and it always seems easier to put them off—until the day they cannot be put off any more.[5]

Here are some details related to Mr. Bernanke's point. Estimates of future growth in entitlement spending consistently predict sharply rising expenditures in coming decades. Figure 6 shows expected growth in Social Security spending over the next two decades. In 2008, Social Security spending was about 4.3 percent of Gross Domestic Product (GDP). (**GDP** is the value of all goods and services produced in the borders of the United States.) This figure is expected to increase to about 6 percent of GDP by 2030. Similarly, Medicare and Medicaid spending will increase over the long term. In 2008, spending on Medicare and Medicaid amounted to about 2.7 percent and 1.4 percent of GDP, respectively. The Office of Management and Budget estimates that in 2030 Medicare spending will be 5.0 percent of GDP and Medicaid spending will be 2.4 percent of GDP.

The chart shows that entitlement spending, if left unchanged, will take up a

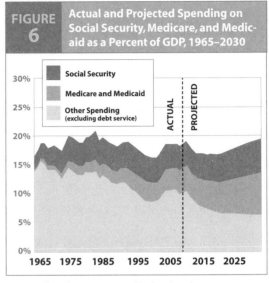

FIGURE 6 — Actual and Projected Spending on Social Security, Medicare, and Medicaid as a Percent of GDP, 1965–2030

Source: Office of Management and Budget (2008).

much larger portion of the economy in 2030 than it did in 2008. What might be some ways to "bend" the spending projections downward? Here are three proposals developed by hypothetical "think tanks" (policy-study organizations):

Think Tank A: The best way to reduce the increase in entitlement spending is to raise the retirement age. When Social Security was approved in 1935, the retirement age was set at 65, while life expectancy was 63. Today, the typical person claiming Social Security benefits at age 62 lives into his or her early or mid-80s. Our research suggests that raising the age of retirement—the time at which an individual becomes eligible for full Social Security benefits—from age 66 to age 69 will provide significant savings without reducing annual benefits.

Think Tank B: The best way to reduce the increase in entitlement spending is to reduce the annual benefits while keeping the same retirement age. Social Security was never intended to provide a primary source of income for people in retirement. It was designed on the assumption that people need to save money during their working years to provide for most of what they will need in retirement. We make two proposals. First, we recommend a gradual reduction in the annual increases in Social Security payments. For example, Social Security payments include Cost of Living Allowances (COLAs) to adjust payments for inflation. Reducing the amount of the COLAs will provide significant savings. Second, we recommend reducing annual benefits for individuals with high incomes. These folks should be able to save enough money to provide for their own retirement needs. They don't need to be supported by low-income taxpayers.

Think Tank C: The best way to reduce the increase in entitlement spending is to raise taxes. In 2010, individuals paid a 6.2 percent Social Security tax on earnings up to $106,800. We propose lifting this cap and gradually expanding the Social Security tax to apply to all earned income. After all, under the new health care reforms, Medicare taxes are already increasing for taxpayers earning over $200,000 and for couples earning over $250,000. Why not continue down that path? This change would allow us to keep the retirement age where it is and not reduce annual benefits to retirees.

THEN & NOW QUESTIONS for DISCUSSION

1. What is likely to happen if entitlement spending is not reduced?
2. Think Tanks A, B, and C proposed solutions to the problem if entitlement spending. Which of these solutions do you favor? Can you think of a different solution? Explain your answer.
3. Using the economic way of thinking, explain why politicians might want to drag their feet on fixing entitlement spending.

Web Resources

Statistics on government spending
http://www.usgovernmentspending.com

A rich source of charts and graphs on federal and state spending today and in the past.

Social Security
http://www.ssa.gov/history

Detailed information on the history of Social Security.

Federal Reserve Bank of St. Louis
http://research.stlouisfed.org/fred2

Allows downloading of economic data including data on government expenditures. Great source for graphs.

The Office of Management and Budget
http://www.whitehouse.gov/omb

The website allows you to keep up with the latest federal budget projections and much more.

CHAPTER 1

1. Esther. B. Fein, "Talking History with David McCullough: Immersed in Facts, the Better to Imagine Harry Truman's Life," *New York Times*, August 12, 1992. Emphasis added.

2. Paul Heyne, *The Economic Way of Thinking* (New York: Macmillan, 1994), p. 8.

3. Adam Smith [1776], *The Wealth of Nations* (Indianapolis: Liberty Fund, 1982), Book I, Ch. 2, pp. 26-27.

4. Ibid., Book IV, Ch. 2, pp. 456-457.

5. G. M. Trevelyan, *A Shortened History of England* (Baltimore: Penguin Books, 1960), pp. 478-481.

CHAPTER 2

1. Kieran Doherty, Sea Venture: *Shipwreck, Survival, and the Salvation of Jamestown* (New York: St. Martin Press, 2008).

2. Gary M. Walton and Hugh Rockoff, *History of the American Economy with Economic Applications*, 10th ed. (Mason, Ohio: Thomson South-Western, 2004), p. 102.

3. Adam Smith [1776], *The Wealth of Nations*, Edwin Cannan, ed. (London: Methuen, 1904), Book I, Ch. 8. Available at http://www.econlib.org/library/Smith/smWN.html

4. Ibid., Editor's Introduction, Book I, p. 56.

5. Ibid., Book IV, Ch. 2.

6. Gary M. Walton and Hugh Rockoff, *History of the American Economy with Economic Applications*, 10th ed. (Mason, Ohio: Thomson South-Western, 2004), p. 102.

7. John Smith, *The Generall Historie of Virginia, New-England, and the Summer Isles* (Chapel Hill, N.C.: University of North Carolina Press, 2006). Available at http://docsouth.unc.edu/southlit/smith/smith.html

8. John Pinkerton, *A General Collection of the Best and Most Interesting Voyages and Travels in All Parts of the World: Many of Which Are Now First Translated into English*; Digested on a New Plan (London: Longman, Hurts, Rees, and Orme, 1912), p. 91.

9. Philippe Legrain, *Aftershock: Reshaping the World Economy after the Crisis* (Boston: Little, Brown, 2010).

10. Sherry Lee, "China's Unequal Wealth-Distribution Map Causing Social Problems," *China Post*, June 28, 2010. Available at HTTP://www.chinapost.com.tw/commentary/the-china-post/special-to-the-china-post/2010/06/28/262505/p3/China%27s-unequal.htm

CHAPTER 3

1. John Harrower, *The Journal of John Harrower, An Indentured Servant in the Colony of Virginia*, 1773-1776 (New York: Holt, Rinehart, and Winston, 1963), pp. 14-19, 38-42.

2. Available at http://www.virtualjamestown.org/

3. David S. Landes, *The Wealth and Poverty of Nations* (New York: W.W. Norton & Co., 1999).

4. Samuel Eliot Morison, *The Oxford History of the American People* (New York: Oxford University Press, 1965), p. 82.

CHAPTER 4

1. See hhttp://www.history.org/almanac/people/bios/biogree.cfm

2. T.G. Burnard, "Prodigious Riches: The Wealth of Jamaica before the American Revolution," Economic History Review, 2nd series (August 2001), pp. 506-524).

3. Gary M. Walton and Hugh Rockoff, *History of the American Economy*, 9th ed. (Mason, Ohio: South-Western/ Thomson Learning, 2002), p. 112.

4. Samuel Eliot Morison, *The Oxford History of the American People* (New York: Oxford University Press, 1965), p. 12.

5. Gary M. Walton and Hugh Rockoff, *History of the American Economy*. 9th ed. (Mason, Ohio: South-Western/ Thomson Learning, 2002), p. 133.

6. Robert M. Calhoon, "Loyalty and Neutrality," in Jack P. Greene and J. R. Pole, eds., *A Companion to the American Revolution* (Malden, Massachusetts: Blackwell Publishing Ltd. 2000), p. 235.

CHAPTER 5

1. Washington Irving, *George Washington: A Biography*, Charles Neider, ed. (New York: Da Capo Press), p. 639.

2. *The Federalist No. 15*: "Insufficiency of the Present Confederation to Preserve the Union," *Independent Journal*, December 1, 1787.

CHAPTER 6

1. Michael Allen, "The Riverman as Jacksonian Man," *The Western Historical Quarterly* (August 1990), pp. 305-320, esp. 319-320. Available at http://www.jstor/stable/969705

2. Mark C. Schug, Jean Caldwell, and Tawni Hunt Farrarini, *Focus: Understanding Economics in U.S. History* (New York: National Council on Economic Education, 2006), p. 153.

3. Article I, Section 8.

4. John Luther Ringwalt, *Development of Transportation Systems in the United States* (Philadelphia: Railway World Office, 1888), p. 47.

5. James Mak and Gary M. Walton, "The Persistence of Old Technologies: The Case of Flatboats," *The Journal of Economic History* (June 1973), pp. 444-451.

6. Archiving Industry, "Power of Steam: Railways." Available at http://www.archiving industry,com/Industrydata/steam.htm

7. Nathaniel Hawthorne, "The Canal Boat," *New England Magazine* (December 1835), pp. 398-409. Available at http://www.history.rochester.edu/canal/bib/hawthorne/canalboat.htm

8. Adam Shell, "Buffett: Railroad Business Is 'In Tune with the Future,'" *USA Today*, November 4 2009. Available at http://www.usatoday.com/money/c ompanies/management/2009-11-04-buffett-interview_N.htm

9. CSX Railroad, "Clean Air." Available at http://www..csx.com/index.cfm/about-csx/projects-and-partnerships/clean-air/

CHAPTER 7

1. Louis Hughes, *Thirty Years a Slave: From Bondage to Freedom: The Institution of Slavery as Seen on the Plantation and in the Home of the Planter* (Milwaukee: South Side Printing Co., 1897), p. 209.

2. Debates in the Federal Convention of 1787, as reported by James Madison, *Documents Illustrative of the Formation of the Union of the American States* (Washington, D.C.: U.S.Government Printing Office, 1927), pp. 589-590.

3. James Gwartney, Robert Lawson, and Walter Block, *Economic Freedom of the World, 1975-1995* (Vancouver: Fraser Institute, 1996), p. 12.

4. Adam Smith [1776], *The Wealth of Nations* (Indianapolis: Liberty Fund, 1982), Book I, Ch. 8.

5. Robert Fogel and Stanley Engerman, Time on the Cross: *The Economics of American Negro Slavery* (Boston: Little, Brown and Co., 1974).

6. Ibid.

CHAPTER 8

1. Elizabeth Brown Pryor, "Robert E. Lee's 'Severest Struggle,'" *American Heritage* (Winter 2008), pp. 18-25. Available at http://www.americanheritage.com/articles/magazine/ah/2008/3/2008_3_18.shmtl

2. Dick Weeks, "The Price in Blood! Casualties in the Civil War." Available at http://www.civilwarhome.com/casualties.htm

3. Roger L. Ransom, *The Confederate States of America: What Might Have Been* (New York: W.W. Norton & Co., 2005), p. 27.

4. After resigning his U.S. Army commission, Lee was appointed General by the CSA.

5. Claudia D. Golding and Frank D. Lewis, "The Economic Cost of the Civil War: Estimates and Implications," *The Journal of Economic History* (June 1975), pp. 299-326).

6. Jeremy Atak and Peter Passell, *A New Economic View of American History*, 2d ed. (New York: W.W. Norton & Co., 1994), pp. 262-63.

7. Steven Davis, Kevin M. Murphy, and Robert H. Topel, *War in Iraq versus Containment: Weighing the Costs* (Chicago: University of Chicago Graduate School, March 20, 2003). Available at http://gsbwww.uchicago.edu/fac/steven.davis/research/

8. Peter Orszag, Estimated Costs of U.S. *Operations in Iraq and*

CHAPTERS 9–13

Afghanistan and of Other Activities Related to the War on Terrorism (Washington, D.C.: Congressional Budget Office, October 24, 2007), p. 4.

9. Linda J. Bilmes and Joseph E. Stigler, The *Three Trillion Dollar War: The True Cost of the Iraq Conflict* (New York: W.W. Norton & Co., 2008), pp. 10–16.

CHAPTER 9

1. Margaret Mitchell, *Gone with the Wind* (New York: Scribner's, 1936), p. 193. See also E. Lee Spence, "Discovery of the 'Real' Rhett Butler," available at http://knol.google.com/k/dr-e-lee-spence/discovery-of-the-real-rhett-butler-by/9a3pk7ykcgda/3#

2. Samuel Eliot Morison, *The Oxford History of the American People* (New York: Oxford University Press, 1965), p. 618.

3. Ibid., pp. 653-54.

4. Department of Veterans Affairs, Office of Public Affairs, Washington, D.C. Available at http://www.l.va.gov/opa/publications/factsheets/fs_americas_wars.pdf

5. Claudia D. Goldin and Frank D. Lewis, "The Economic Cost of the Civil War: Estimates and Implications," *Journal of Economic History* (June 1975), pp. 299-326.

6. Stanley Lebergott, *The Americans: An Economic Record* (New York: W.W. Norton & Co., 1984), esp. pp. 246-248.

7. Roger Ransom, "Economics of the Civil War," in Robert Whaples, ed., *EH.Net Encyclopedia* (August 24, 2001). Available at http://eh.net/encyclopedia/article/ransom.civil.war.us

8. Denise L. Amos, "Minorities Finding Opportunities in the South," *St. Petersburg Times*, September 26, 1992.

9. William Frey, *The New Great Migration: Black Americans Return to the South, 1965-2000* (Washington, D.C.: Brookings Institution, 2004).

10. U.S. Department of Commerce, Bureau of Economic Analysis. Released September 2010. Available at http://bber.unm.edu/econ/us-pci.htm

CHAPTER 10

1. National Archives, Teaching with Documents: The Homestead Act of 1862. Available at http://www.Archives.gov/education/lessons/homestead-act/

2. Library of Congress: American Memory WPA Life History. Available at http://memory.loc.gov/cgi-bin/query

3. Stanley Lebergott, *The Americans: An Economic Record* (New York: W.W. Norton & Co., 1984), p. 270.

4. Gary M. Anderson and Deloris T. Martin, "The Public Domain and Nineteenth-Century Transfer Policy," *Cato Journal* (Winter 1987), pp. 905-923.

5. Atif Lian and Amir Sufi, "The Effects of Fiscal Stimulus: Evidence from the 2009 'Cash for Clunkers' Program," Social Science Research Network File: SSRN-id1670759 (September 2010). Available at http://papers.ssrn.com/sol3/papers.cfm?abstract_id=1670759

CHAPTER 11

1. Source: http://www.greatdreams.com/lakota/sitting-bull.htm

2. Samuel Eliot Morison, *The Oxford History of the American People* (New York: Oxford University Press, 1965), p. 446.

3. Ibid., pp. 446–447.

4. Terry L. Anderson, *Sovereign Nations or Reservations: An Economic History of American Indians* (San Francisco: Pacific Institute for Public Policy, 1995), p. 70.

5. Bruce L. Benson, "Customary Indian Law: Two Case Studies," in *Property Rights and Indian Economics*, Terry L. Anderson, ed. (Boston Way, Lanham, Maryland: Rowman & Littlefield, 1992), p. 34.

6. Source: National Achieves, Washington D.C.: http://www.ourdocuments.gov/

7. Christine Negroni, "In Missouri, Investors Seek a Profit in Branson Airport," *New York Times*, April 21, 2009. http://www.nytimes.com/2009/04/21/business/21branson.html

CHAPTER 12

1. Julie Fanselow, *Traveling the Lewis and Clark Trail*, 4th ed. (Guilford, Connecticut: Falcon Press, 2007), p. 112.

2. John Fire Lame Deer and Richard Erdoes, *Lame Deer, Seeker of Visions: The Life of a Sioux Medicine Man* (New York: Simon & Schuster, 1972), p. 130.

3. Edward L. Ayers et al., *American Anthem* (Orlando, Florida: Holt, Rinehart, and Winston, 2009), p. 439.

4. Frank H. Mayer and Charles B. Roth, "The Buffalo Harvest." Available at http://www.pbs.org/weta/thewest/resources/archives/five/buffalo.htm

5. Ibid.

6. Armen A. Alchian, "Property Rights," in David R. Henderson, ed., *The Concise Encyclopedia of Economics* (Indianapolis: Liberty Fund), pp. 422-425. Available at http://www.econlib.org/library/Enc/PropertyRights.html

7. John Fire *Lame Deer* and Richard Erdoes, *Lame Deer, Seeker of Visions: The Life of a Sioux Medicine Man* (New York: Simon & Schuster, 1972), p. 130.

8. Frank H. Mayer and Charles B. Roth, "The Buffalo Harvest." Available at http://www.pbs.org/weta/the west/resources/archives/five/buffalo.htm

9. Ibid.

10. Ibid.

11. Quoted in "Bison Back from the Brink of Extinction," The Canadian Encyclopedia. Available at http://www.canadianencyclopedia.ca/index.cfm?PgNm=TCE&Params-MlARTM00l2570

12. Robert Miller, "Indian Treaties as Sovereign Contracts." Available at http://lawlib.lclark.edu/blog/native_america/?page_id=8

13. Bison Central, "Industry Data & Statistics." Available at http://www.bisoncentral.com/indexphp?s=&c=14d=105&a=1064&w=2&r=Y

14. W.B. Hazen, "Wanton Butchery: The Evils of Buffalo Hunting," letter to the *New York Times*, January 26, 1872, reprinted in the Congressional Globe, April 6, 1872, p. 179. Available at http://books.google.com/books?id=qkMFAAAAYAAJ&printsec=frontcover&source=gbs_ge_summary_r&cad=0#v=onepage&q&f=false

15. Discovery News, "Oceans' Fish Could Disappear by 2050," May 17, 2010. Available at http://news.discovery.com/earth/oceans-fish-fishing-industry.html

16. State of Maine Department of Marine Resources, "Historical Maine Yellowtail Flounder Landings," June 30, 2010. Available at http://www.maine.gov/dmr/commercialfishing/documents/yellowtail.table.pdf

CHAPTER 13

1. Public Broadcasting System, "People and Events: Theodore Judah (1826-1863)." Available at http://www.pbs.org/wgbh/amex/tcrr/peopleevents/p_judah.html

2. Gary M. Walton and Hugh Rockoff, *History of the American Economy*, 10th ed. (Mason, Ohio: Thomson South-Western, 2005), ch. 16.

3. Robert Higgs, "To Get More of Something (e.g., Unemployment), Subsidize It," Novemner 21, 2008. Available at http://www.independent.org/blog/?p=551

4. William C. Wood, "Primary Benefits, Secondary Benefits, and the Evaluation of Small Business Assistance programs," *Journal of Small Business Management* (July 1994), pp. 65-75.

5. Albert Fishlow, *American Railroads and the Transformation of the Ante-bellum Economy* (Cambridge, Massachusetts: Harvard University Press, 1965), p. 204.

6. Stanley Lebergott, *The Americans: An Economic Record* (New York: W.W. Norton & Co., 1984), p. 277.

7. Kenneth D. Frederick, "Water Resources: Increasing Demand and Scarce Supplies," in Kenneth D. Frederick and Roger A. Sedjo, eds., *America's Renewable Resources: Historical Trends and Current Challenges* (Washington, D.C.: Resources for the Future, 1991), p. 40.

8. Gary M. Walton and Hugh Rockoff, History of the American Economy, 10th ed. (Mason, Ohio: Thomson South-Western, 2005), ch. 16.

9. Richard Florida, "The Rise of the Creative Class," *Washington Monthly* (May 2002). Available at http://www.washingtonmonthly.com/features/2001/0205.florida.html

10. Michele Hoyman and Christopher Faricy, "It Takes a

Village: A Test of the Creative Class, Social Capital, and Human Capital Theories," *Urban Affairs Review* (January 2009). Available at http://ssrn.com/abstract=1313563

CHAPTER 14

1. *New York Times*, "Repudiation Has Won," July 10, 1896. Available at http://www.nytimes.com/learning/general/onthisday/big/0709.html#article

2. William Jennings Bryan, "Cross of Gold," speech delivered at the Democratic National Convention, July 8, 1896. Available at http://historymatters.gmu.edu/d/5354/

3. Price Deflator, Series ca13, Historical Statistics of the United States. Available at http://hsus.cambridge.org/HSUSWeb/HSUSEntryServlet

4. William C. Wood, "The Gold at Fort Knox," *Journal of Economic Education* (Autumn 1994), pp. 343-348.

5. Hugh Rockoff, "The 'Wizard of Oz' as a Monetary Allegory," *Journal of Political Economy* (August 1990), pp. 739-760.

6. William Jennings Bryan, "Cross of Gold," speech delivered at the Democratic National Convention, July 8, 1896. Available at http://historymatters.gmu.edu/d/5354/

7. Scott Lanman and Craig Craig, "Fed Mulls Raising Inflation Expectations to Boost Economy," Bloomberg News Service, October 13, 2010. Available at http://www.bloomberg.com/news/2010-10-13/fed-considers-raising-inflation-expectations-to-boost-economy.html

CHAPTER 15

1. Daniel M. G. Raff and Lawrence H. Summers, "Did Henry Ford Pay Efficiency Wages?" Working Paper No. 2101 (Cambridge, Massachusetts: National Bureau of Economic Research, December 1986).

2. Ida Tarbell, "The Rise of Standard Oil," *McClure's Magazine*, vol. 20, no. 2 (1902), p. 121.

3. John D. Rockefeller, *Random Reminiscenses of Man and Events* (New York: Doubleday & Co., 1909).

4. Robert B. Reich, "Don't Blame Wal-Mart," *New York Times*, February 28, 2005. Available at http://www.nytimes.com/2005/02/28/opinion/28reich.html

5. Emek Basker, "Selling a Cheaper Mousetrap," *Journal of Urban Economics* (September 2005), pp. 203-229.

6. Richard Vedder and Wendell Cox, *The Wal-Mart Revolution* (Washington, D.C.: AEI Press, 2006), pp. 118-119.

CHAPTER 16

1. Gary M. Walton and Hugh Rockoff, *History of the American Economy*, 9th ed. (Mason, Ohio: South-Western Thomson Learning, 2002), pp. 370-71.

2. Naomi R. Lamoreaux, *The Great Merger Movement in American Business*, 1895-1904 (Cambridge: Cambridge University Press, 1985), p. 2.

3. Stanley Lebergott, *The Americans: An Economic Record* (New York: W. W. Norton & Co., 1984), p.329.

4. Werner Troeskenn and Karen Clay, "Did the Trusts Have Market Power? Evidence from Distilling, 1881-1898." Available at http://eh.net/Clio/Conferences/ASSA/Jan_00/Troesken.html

5. Gerald Gunderson, *An Entrepreneurial History of the United States* (Washington, D.C.: Beard Books, 2005), p. 132.

6. Ibid.

7. Ellen Torelle, *The Political Philosophy of Robert M. La Follette* (Madison, Wisconsin: The Robert M. La Follette Co., 1920), p. 93.

CHAPTER 17

1. William Sprague papers, Rhode Island Historical Society. Available at http://www.rihs.org/mssinv/Mss733.htm

2. Robert Allen Palmatier, Speaking of Animals: A Dictionary of Animal Metaphors (Westport, Connecticut: Greenwood Press, 1995), p. 414.

3. William McChesney Martin, quoted in Gregory N. Mankiw, "How to Avoid Recession? Let the Fed Work," *New York Times*, December 23, 2007. Available at http://www.nytimes.com/2007/12/23/business/23view.html?ex=1356066000&en=3337604c8708710a&ei=5090&partner=rssuserland&emc=rss

4. Federal Reserve Bank of New York City, "Founding of the Federal Reserve Bank." Available at

http://www.ny.frb.org/aboutthefed/history_article.html

CHAPTER 18

1. "Jewish Massacre Denounced," *New York Times*, April 28, 1903, p.6.

2. "Sinking the Unsinkable," December 18, 2005. Available at http:www.snopes.com/history/titanic/unsinkable.asp

3. Raymond L. Cohn, "Immigration to the United States," *EH.Net Encyclopedia of Economic and Business History*. Available at http://eh.net/encyclopia/article/cohn.immigration.us

4. Barry Chiswick, "The Effect of Americanization on the Earnings of Foreign-Born Men," *Journal of Political Economy* (October 1978), pp. 897-921.

5. Sindya Bahnoo, "How the Men Reacted as the *Titanic* and the *Lusitania* Went Under," *New York Times*, March 1, 2010. Available at http://www.nytimes.com/2010/03/02/science/02ships.html

6. Matt Richtel, "Google's 'Immigration Fixer,'" *New York Times*, April 13, 2009. Available at http://bits.blogs.nytimes.com/2009/04/13googles-immigration-fixer/?scp=1&sq=richtel%20immigration&st=cse

7. James P. Smith, "Immigrants and the Labor Market," *Journal of Labor Economics* (April 2006), pp. 203-233.

CHAPTER 19

1. Joshua Zeitz, Flapper: *A Madcap Story of Sex, Style, Celebrity, and the Women Who Made America Modern* (New York: Three Rivers press, 2007), p-p. 1-4.

2. Milton Friedman and Anna J. Schwartz, *Monetary Trends in the United States and the United kingdom* (Chicago: University of Chacago Press, 1982), p. 125.

3. Robert W. Dimand and John Geanakopolos, *Celebrating Irving Fisher: The Legacy of a Great Economist* (Oxford: Blackwell, 2005).

4. J. Bradford DeLong and Andrei Shleifer, "The Stock Market Bubble of 1929: Evidence from Closed-End Funds," *Journal of Economic History* (September 1991), pp. 675-700.

5. Gary M. Walton and Hugh Rockoff, History of the American Economy with Economic Applications, 11th ed. (Mason, Ohio: Cengage, 2010), p. 436.

6. Bernard M. Baruch, The Public Years (Canada: Holt, Rinehart, and Winston, 1960), quoted in David M. Frankel, "Adaptive Expectations and Stock Market Crashes," *International Economic Review* (May 2008), pp. 595-619).

7. Jon Hilsenrath, "Fed Debates New Role: Bubble Fighter," *Wall Street Journal*, December 2, 2009. Available at http://online.wsj.com/articleSB125970281466871707.html

CHAPTER 20

1. Ohio Department of Aging, "Great Depression Story Project," vol. 1. Available at http://aging.ohio.gov/nes/greatdepressionstoryproject/volume1.aspx

2. Robert Barro, "What Are the Odds of a Depression?" *Wall Street Journal*, March 4, 2009, p. A-15.

3. Ibid.

4. Milton Friedman and Anna J. Schwartz, *A Monetary History of the United States*, 1867-1960 (Princeton: Princeton University Press, 1971).

CHAPTER 21

1. Leon Alligood, "Civilian Conservation Corp Honored," USA Today, March 18, 2008. Available at http://www.usatoday.com/news/nation/2008-03-18-ccc75th_N.htm

2. Stanley Lebergott, *The Americans: An Economic Record* (New York: W.W. Norton & Co., 1984), p. 461.

3. Frederic Bastiat [1848], "What Is Seen and What Is Not Seen," in Seymour Cain, trans., and George B. de Huszar, ed., *Selected Essays on Political Economy* (New York: The Foundation for Economic Education, 1995). Available at http://www.econlib.org/library/Bastiat/basEss.html

CHAPTER 22

1. Stanley Lebergott, *The Americans: An Economic Record* (New York: W. W. Norton & Co., 1984), p. 370.

2. Jonathan Hughes and Louis P. Cain, *American Economic History*,

NOTES

CHAPTERS 23–27

6th ed. (Boston: Addison Wesley/ Pearson Education, Inc., 2003), pp. 420-21.

3. Samuel Eliot Morison, *The Oxford History of the American People* (New York: Oxford University Press, 1965), p. 843.

CHAPTER 23

1. Tony Marcano, "Famed Riveter in War Effort, Rose Monroe Dies at 77," *New York Times*, June 2, 1997. Available at http://www. nytimes.com/1997/06/02/us/famed-riveter-in-war-effort-rose-monroe-dies-at-77.html

2. Robert Whaples, "Hours of Work in U.S. History," *EH.Net Encyclopedia.* Available at http:// eh.net/encyclopedia/article/whaples. work.hours.us

3. Claudia Goldin, The Role of World War II in the Rise of Women's Employment," *American Economic Review* (September 1991), p. 743.

4. *Statistical Abstract of the United States, 1950* (Washington, D.C.: U.S. Government Printing Office), Table 209, p. 175.

5. Claudia Goldin, "The Role of World War II in the Rise of Women's Employment," *American Economic Review* (September 1991), p. 750.

6. Ibid., p. 755.

7. William Breit and Kenneth G. Elzinga, "Ezra Pound and the GNP," *Southern Economic Journal* (January 1980), pp. 904-912.

8. "Oprah Winfrey." Available at http://www.biography.com/articles/ Oprah-Winfrey-9534419

9. Robert H. Frank and Philip J. Cook, *The Winner-Take-All Society: Why the Few at the Top Get So Much More Than the Rest of Us* (New York: Penguin Books, 1996).

CHAPTER 24

1. Mark C. Schug, Jean Caldwell, and Tawni Hunt Ferrarini, Focus: *Understanding Economics in the U.S. Economy* (New york: National Council on Economic Education, 2006), p. 388.

2. Employment Act of 1946, ch. 33, section 2, 60 Stat. 23, 15 U.S.C. 1021.

3. *Economic Report of the President, 1946* (Washington, D.C.: U.S. Government Printing Office).

4. Real per capita disposable income, from the Bureau of Economic Analysis, U.S. Commerce Department.

5. boomerslife.org, "Baby Boom Population." Available at http:// www.boomerslife.org/baby_boom_ population_us_census-bureau_by_ state.htm

6. Quoted in Richard Goldstein, "Edith Shain, Who Said Famous Kiss Came Her Way, Dies at 91," *New York Times*, June 24, 2010. Available at http://www.nytimes. com/2010/06/24/nyregion/24shain. html

7. Florie Meeks, "Spring Resident Recounts 'The Kiss' That Signified the End of World War II," *Houston Chronicle*, September 12, 2007. Available at http://www.chron. com/disp/story.mpl/nb/spring/ news/5130483.html

8. Richard Goldstein, "Edith Shain, Who Said Famous Kiss Came Her Way, Dies at 91," *New York Times*, June 24, 2010. Available at http:// www.nytimes.com/2010/06/24/ nyregion/24shain.html

9. Florie Meeks, "Spring Resident Recounts 'The Kiss' That Signified the End of World War II," *Houston Chronicle*, September 12, 2007. Available at http://www.chron. com/disp/story.mpl/nb/spring/ news/5130483.html

10. Steve Gillon and Nancy Singer Olaguera, Boomer Nation: *The Largest and Richest Generation Ever, and How It Changed America* (New York: Free Press, 2004), p. 318.

11. Ben Stein, "Living Hand to Mouth—and Barely Getting By," February 3, 2006. Available at http:// finance.yahoo.com/expert/article/ yourlife/2449

CHAPTER 25

1. Linda Gorman, "Discrimination," in David R. Henderson, ed., *The Concise Encyclopedia of Economics* (Indianapolis: Liberty Fund, 2008), p. 118.

CHAPTER 26

1. Information Control Division, Office of Military Government for Germany (U.S.), *Me and Mr. Marshall* (1949). Available at http://www.marshallpalnimages.com/ me-and-marshall

2. Barry Eichengreen, *The European Economy Since 1945: Coordinated Capitalism and Beyond* (Princeton: Princeton University Press, 2006), p. 3.

3. David Luhnow, "Global Aid Is No Relief for Small Haitian Businesses," *Wall Street Journal*, March 3, 2010. Available at http:// online.wsj.com/article/SB100014 24052748704486504575097783 3544905868.html?mod=WSJ_hps_ MIDDLESecondNews

4. Piers Vitebsky, *The Reindeer People: Living with Animals and Spirits in Siberia* (Boston: Houghton Mifflin Harcourt, 2005), p. 382.

5. R. Glenn Hubbard and William Duggan, *The Aid Trap: Hard Truths About Ending Poverty* (New York: Columbia University Press, 2009), pp. 90-91.

6. Curt Tarnoff and Larry Nowels, "Foreign Aid: An Introductory Overview of U.S. Programs and Policy" (Washington, D.C.: U.S. Department of State, April 15, 2004). Available at http://fpc.state. gov/documents/organization/31987. pdf

7. Barry Eichengreen, *The European Economy Since 1945: Coordinated Capitalism and Beyond* (Princeton: Princeton University Press, 2006).

8. J. Bradford DeLong and Barry Eichengreen, "The Marshall Plan: History's Most Successful Structural Adjustment Program," in Rudiger Dornbusch et al., eds., *Postwar Economic Reconstruction and Lessons for the East Today* (Cambridge, Massachusetts: MIT Press, 1993), p. 189.

9. Tyler Cowan, "The Marshall Plan: Myths and Realities," in Doug Bandow, ed., *U.S. Aid to the Developing World* (Washington, D.C.: Heritage Foundation, 1985), pp. 61-74.

10. J. Bradford DeLong and Barry Eichengreen, "The Marshall Plan: History's Most Successful Structural Adjustment Program," in Rudiger Dornbusch, et al., eds., *Postwar Economic Reconstruction and Lessons for the East Today* (Cambridge, Massachusetts: MIT Press, 1993), pp. 210-221.

11. Glenn Hubbard, "Think Again: A Marshall Plan for Africa," *Foreign Policy* (August 13, 2009). Available at http://www.foreignpolicy. com/articles/2009/08/13/think_ again_aid_to_africa

12. Blaine Harden, *Africa: Dispatches from a Fragile Continent* (London: Flamingo, 1992), pp. 178-180. Cited in Christopher Coyne, "The Economic Problem of Humanitarian Action," available at http://econ.as.nyu.edu/docs/ IO/16666/Coyne_20101108.pdf

13. Glenn Hubbard, "Think Again: A Marshall Plan for Africa," *Foreign Policy* (August 13, 2009). Available at http://www.foreignpolicy. com/articles/2009/08/13/think_ again_aid_to_africa

CHAPTER 27

1. Johnson Products, "Passing the Baton: George E. Johnson, Sr., to Be Honored June 12 by New Owners of Johnson Products," news release, May 31, 2010. Available at http:// johnsonproductsmedia.wordpress. com/2010/05/31/passing-the-baton-george-e-johnson-sr-to-be-honored-june-12--by-new-owners-of-johnsn-products/

2. Stephen Hahn, *A Nation Under Our Feet: Black Political Struggles in the Rural South from Slavery to the Great Migration* (Cambridge, Massachusetts: Belknap Press, 2003).

3. Robert A. Margo, "Historical Perspectives on Racial Economic Differences: A Summary of Recent Research," *National Bureau of Economic Research Reporter* (Winter 2005). Available at http://www.. ber.org/reporter/winter05/margo. html#N_3_

4. Mary Patillo-McCoy, *Black Picket Fences: Privileges and Peril among the Black Middle Class* (Chicago: University of Chicago Press, 2000), pp. 14-15.

5. Pew Research Center, "Inside the Middle Class: Bad Times Hit the Good Life," April 9, 2008. Available at http://pewsocialtrends. org/pubs/706/middle-class-poll

6. Julia B. Isaacs, "Economic Mobility of Black and White Families," in Julia B. Isaacs, ed., *Getting Ahead or Losing Ground: Economic Mobility in America* (Washington, D.C.: Brookings Institution and Pew Charitable Trusts, February 2008), p. 76.

334   Notes

7. Ewing Marion Kauffman Foundation, "The Entrepreneur Next Door: Characteristics of Individuals Starting Companies in America," September 2002. Available at http://www.kauffman.org/uploadedFiles/psed_brochure.pdf

8. Booker T. Washington, "Atlanta Compromise Speech," September 18, 1895. Available at http://historymatters.gmu.edu/d/39/

9. W.E.B. Du Bois, quoted in "American Thinkers on Values." Available at http://www.america.gov/st/peopleplace-english/2006/june/2008081313605SrenoD0.3074304.html

10. W.E.B. Du Bois, *John Brown* (Philadelphia: George W. Jacobs & Co., 1909), p. 383.

11. Janes P, Smith and Finis R. Welch, "Black Economic Progress after Myrdal," *Journal of Economic Literature* (June 1989), p. 521.

12. William H. frey, "The New Great Migration: Black Americans' Return to the South, 1965-2000" (Washington, D.C.: The Brookings Institution, 2004). Available at htpp://www.brookings.edu/urban/pubs/20040524_Frey.pdf

13. Mike Householder and Jeff Karoub, "Motown Sounds Strong at 50," *Seattle Times*, September 13, 2009. Available at http://seattletimes.nwsource.com/html/musicnightlife/2009834281_motown13html?syndication=rss

14. Isabel Wilkerson, *The Warmth of Other Suns: The Epic Story of America's Great Migration* (New York: Random House, 2010).

15. Tavis Smiley, interview with Isabel Wilkerson, October 6, 2010. Available at http://www.pbs.org/kcet/tavissmiley/archive/201010/20101006_wilkerson.html

16. Ibid.

CHAPTER 28

1. Becky Sheaves, "The Twins Brought Up on Either Side of the Iron Curtain . . . But Who Lived Identical Lives," The Daily Mail, December 20, 2007. Available at http://www.dailymail.co.uk/femail/article-503775/The-twins-brought-Iron-Curtain-lived-identical-lives.html

2. Ibid.

3. John Rodden, "Going Bananas," *Commonweal*, March 24, 1995. Available at http://www.thefreelibrary.com/Going+bananas.-a016723808

4. Gareth Dale, *Between State Capitalism and Globalization: The Collapse of the East German Economy* (Bern: Peter Lange Publishing, 2004), p. 213.

5. Mary Elise Sarotte, "How It Went Down: The Little Accident That Toppled History," *Washington Post*, November 1, 2009. Available at http://www.washingtonpost.com/wp-dyn/content/article/2009/10/30/AR2009103001846.html?sid=ST2009103101419

6. Bryan Caplan, "Communism," in David R. Henderson, ed., *The Concise Encyclopedia of Economics* (Indianapolis: Liberty Fund, 2008), pp. 66-69. Available at http://www.econlib.org/library/Enc/Communism.html

7. Andreas Ramos, "The Fall of the Berlin Wall: A Personal Account." Available at http://andreas.com/berlin.html

8. U.S. Department of Commerce, Bureau of Economic Analysis, "Disposable Personal Income Per Capita." Available at http://www.bea.gov/regional/remdmap/REMDMap.aspx

9. Michael Burda, "Half Empty or Half Full? East Germany Two Decades Later," *Centre for Economic Policy Research*, November 9, 2009. Available at http://www.voxeu.org/index.php?q=node/4180

10. Becky Sheaves, "The Twins Brought Up on Either Side of the iron Curtain . . . But Who Lived Identical Lives," *The Daily Mail*, December 20, 2007. Available at http://www.dailymail.co.uk/femail/article-503775/The-twins-brought-Iron-Curtain-lived-identical-lives.html

CHAPTER 29

1. Jonathan Hughes and Louis P. Cain, *American Economic History*, 6th ed. (Boston: Addison Wesley/Pearson Education Inc., 2003), p. 612.

2. Ibid., pp. 614-616.

CHAPTER 30

1. Biography.com, "Bill Gates Biography." Available at http://www.biography.com/articles/Bill-Gates-9307520

2. Robert M. Solow, "We'd Better Watch Out," *New York Times Book Review*, July 12, 1987, p. 36.

3. Daniel Cohen, Pietro Garibaldi, and Stefano Scarpetta, eds, *The ICT Revolution: Productivity Differences and the Digital Divide* (New York: Oxford University Press, 2004).

4. Institute of Physics, "Your Car Has More Computing Power Than the System That Guided Apollo Astronauts to the Moon." Available at http://www.physics.org/facts/apollo-really.asp

5. Carl Shapiro and Hal R. Varian, *Information Rules* (Cambridge, Massachusetts: Harvard Business Press, 1999), p. 184.

6. Ian Peter, "History of the World Wide Web," 2003. Available at http://www.nethistory.info/History%20of%20the%20Internet/web.html

7. Stephen D. Oliner and Daniel E. Sichel, "The Resurgence of Growth in the Late 1990s: Is Information Technology the Story?" *The Journal of Economic Perspectives* (Autumn 2000), pp. 3-22.

8. Robert J. Gordon, Does the 'New Economy' Measure Up to the Great Inventions of the Past?" *The Journal of Economic Perspectives* (Autumn 2000), pp. 49-74.

9. Internet Society, "A Brief History of the Internet." Available at http://www.isoc.org/internet/history/brief.shtml

10. Joseph Schumpeter [1942], *Capitalism, Socialism, and Democracy* (New York: Harper, 1975), p. 84.

11. Rebecca Sato, "Will a Computer 'Symbiote' Be Implanted in Future Human Brains?" *The Daily Galaxy*, June 25, 2008. Available at http://www.dailygalaxy.com/my_weblog/2008/06/researchers-dev.html

12. "Ken Olsen," available online: http://www.snopes.com/quotes/kenolsen.asp

13. Edgar H. Schein, *DEC Is Dead, Long Live DEC: The Lasting Legacy of Digital Equipment Corporation* (San Francisco: Berrett-Koehler Publishers, 2003), p. 39.

14. Carmen M. Reinhart and Kenneth Rogoff, *This Time Is Different: Eight Centuries of Financial Folly* (Princeton: Princeton University Press, 2009).

CHAPTERS 28–32

15. Richard Wray, "Time Warner and AOL to Demerge at End of Year," *The Guardian*, May 28, 2009. Available at http://www.guardian.co.uk/technology/2009/may/28/time-warner-aol-separate

16. Chet Dembeck, "AOL and Time Warner to Merge in Blockbuster Deal," *E-Commerce Times*, January 10, 2000. Available at http://www.ecommercetimes.com/story/2168.html?wlc=1284562862

CHAPTER 31

1. Alan S. Blinder, "Free Trade," in David R. Henderson, ed., *The Concise Encyclopedia of Economics* (Indianapolis: Liberty Fund, 2008), pp. 205-207.

2. Adam Smith [1776], *The Wealth of Nations* (Indianapolis: Liberty Fund, 1992), Book IV, Ch. 2, p. 458.

3. *Wall Street Journal*, "The Teamster Tariffs," August 21, 2010.

CHAPTER 32

1. Source: http://www.friendscafe.org/scripts/sl/104.php

2. Thomas R. Saving, "Social Security," in David R. Henderson, ed., *The Concise Encyclopedia of Economics* (Indianapolis: Liberty Fund, 2008), p. 463.

3. Social Security and Medical Board of Trustees, "Status of the Social Security and Medicare Administration, 2010." Available at http://www.ssa.gov/oact/trsum/index.html

4. Congressional Budget Office, *The Budget and Economic Outlook: Fiscal Years 2011 to 2021* (Washington, D.C.: Congress of the United States, 2011). Available at http://www.cbo.gov

A

absolute advantage: The ability of a business or an individual to produce more units of a good or service than some other producer, using the same quantity of resources. See also **comparative advantage.**

aggregate demand: The sum or total amount of production desired by all sectors of the economy.

aggregate supply: The sum or total of all the goods and services that producers want to provide.

Agricultural Adjustment Administration (AAA): An agency established in 1933 as part of the New Deal. Its purpose was to reduce production of livestock and crops order to raise prices and thus benefit farmers. In 1937, the U.S. Supreme Court ruled that the AAA was unconstitutional; Congress revised and re-enacted portions of the AAA legislation in 1938.

American Federation of Labor (AFL): A national labor union founded in 1886. The AFL stressed workplace issues: better wages, shorter work days and weeks, and worker safety. The AFL merged with the Congress of Industrial Organizations in 1955.

American Stock Exchange: A market for buying and selling ownership shares in corporations, operated in New York City, beginning in 1908; it is currently known as NYSE Amex Equities.

anti-piracy measures: Laws and enforcement actions designed to prevent robbery and violence at sea. This term also refers to laws and enforcement actions intended to prevent unauthorized reproduction or distribution of intellectual property such as movies, books, and other copyrighted material.

arbitration: A way of settling disputes by mutual agreement, outside the courts.

Articles of Confederation: The first constitution of the United States, adopted in 1789; supplanted in 1789 by the U. S. Constitution. The Articles established a weak role for the federal government and a strong role for state governments.

artisan: A skilled worker who makes things by hand—for example, a seamstress, blacksmith, glassblower, baker, jeweler, cobbler.

B

Baby Boom: A large increase in the number of births in the United States from 1946 to 1964.

Bank Holiday: On March 6, 1933, in response to a wave of bank failures, President Franklin Delano Roosevelt issued a proclamation ordering the immediate closing of all American banks. During this time of closure, known as a Bank Holiday, banks were not permitted to conduct any transactions. Banks subsequently reopened according to new rules established by the Emergency Banking Act.

bank run: A situation in which a bank's customers seek to withdraw all their deposits at once.

Beard-Hacker Thesis: The contention (developed by Charles Beard and Louis M. Hacker) that the American Civil War shifted the U.S. economy toward rapid industrialization.

benefits: Positive consequences resulting from a choice. Benefits may be monetary or non-monetary.

Berlin Wall: A concrete barrier separating East Berlin from West Berlin in Germany from 1961 to 1989.

blacklist: A list of names of individuals, intended to identify them as undesirable; workers who supported labor unions were sometimes "blacklisted" by employers before such practices were outlawed.

bond: a certificate issued by a government or a corporation promising to repay borrowed money, plus interest, to the owner of the bond. Bonds acknowledge loans made by investors (individuals or institutions).

Boston Tea Party of 1773: An act of rebellion carried out on December 16, 1773, in which a group of colonists boarded British ships docked at Boston Harbor and destroyed the ships' cargoes of tea by throwing the tea into the water. The Tea Party was the culmination of a resistance movement by the colonists against the Tea Act of 1773.

business cycle: The pattern of up-and-down movements that occur in economic activity over time. The business cycle is measured in part by increases or decreases in Gross Domestic Product (GDP).

C

canal: An artificial waterway constructed to allow for inland passage of boats or ships.

cartel: A group of producers acting together in an effort to restrict production and control the prices of their products.

Cash for Clunkers: The popular term for a U.S. government program officially called the Car Allowance Rebate System (CARS). Created by Congress in 2009, Cash for Clunkers offered financial incentives for Americans to purchase new, more fuel-efficient cars when trading in older cars that were less fuel-efficient.

central authority: A high-level concentration of government power, as contrasted with power dispersed among different government branches and localities.

central planning: A form of economic control under which a government decides in advance what goods should be produced, how they should be produced, and how they should be allocated among people.

Charleston: A popular dance of the 1920s, considered uninhibited and provocative at the time.

checks and balances: A structure built into the U.S. Constitution intended to limit the central government's power by distributing decision-making authority across different branches of government.

Choctaw: American Indian people who lived in what is today Mississippi, western Alabama, and eastern Louisiana.

civil society: An arena in which people interact with one another voluntarily on the basis of shared interests and purposes. Churches, labor unions, business associations, charitable organizations, book clubs, garden clubs, and bowling leagues are among the many organizations that make up civil society.

Civilian Conservation Corps (CCC): An agency established in 1933 as part of the New Deal, designed to help unemployed, unmarried men, aged 18–25, by employing them in conservation-related projects on public land throughout the United States.

Clayton Antitrust Act: This federal law passed in 1914 included a section declaring that unions could not be considered as unlawful "combinations," except upon proof of certain prohibited conduct. It also stated that strikes, boycotts, and labor-union picketing were not violations of federal law.

collective bargaining: A process of negotiation between representatives of a union and representatives of management, aimed at reaching an agreement on wages, working conditions, and related matters.

Comanche: American Indian people who lived across parts of what is today Arizona, Colorado, Kansas, Texas, and Oklahoma.

command economy: An economy in which the government or some other central authority makes the decisions about what goods and services will be produced, how they will be produced, and how they will be distributed. Contemporary examples of command systems are Cuba and North Korea.

Commerce Clause: Article I, Section 8, Clause 3 of the U.S. Constitution, which states that Congress shall have power "To regulate Commerce with foreign Nations, and among the several States, and with the Indian Tribes." The Commerce Clause took the power to impose tariffs away from the states and created a "free trade zone" within the United States.

communism: An economic and political theory that calls for a society in which property is publicly owned and government power is concentrated in a single political party whose leaders control the economy and society generally. In the 20th century, the Soviet Union controlled a powerful communist empire until its collapse in 1991. Today, North Korea and Cuba

are communist nations, and there are communist political parties in various parts of the world.

comparative advantage: The ability of a business in one nation to produce a good or service at a lower opportunity cost than a business in another nation.

competition: In business, rivalry among producers and suppliers, acting independently, in their efforts to win customers by offering the best deal. In a market economy, competition acts as a control on self-interested behavior by guiding the market toward high-quality products and services offered at low (that is, competitive) prices.

concentrated interests: The focus of interest groups on policy issues that directly affect them. Interest groups spend time and money to influence political outcomes related to such issues.

Congress of Industrial Organizations (CIO): A federation of labor unions led by John L. Lewis, president of the United Mine Workers of America. The CIO held its first convention in 1938; it merged with the American Federal of Labor (AFL) in 1955.

conquistadores: Spanish soldiers who conquered native people and brought much of the Americas under the control of Spain following Europe's discovery of the Americas.

Consumer Price Index (CPI): A statistic calculated by the Bureau of Labor Statistics (BLS), the CPI represents changes in the prices of goods and services commonly bought by consumers. It is widely used as a measure of inflation.

contract: A legally binding agreement between consenting people; contracts can be enforced by the courts.

Contract Clause: Article I, section10, clause 1 of the U.S. Constitution, which states that "No state shall…pass any…law impairing the Obligation of Contracts," thus ensuring that contracts, including those dealing with debts, can be enforced.

corporation: A business owned by shareholders who possess ownership rights to the firm's profits.

cost: What people pay to buy something—

as in *That skateboard will cost you $78.* Also, a consequence resulting from a choice or an act—as in *That speeding ticket is going to cost you $160.* Costs may be non-monetary—as in Learning Spanish cost me a lot of effort. See also **opportunity cost**.

cotton gin: A machine invented by Eli Whitney; used to quickly separate cotton fibers from cotton seeds, a job previously done, less efficiently, by hand.

creative class: People whose work involves creating new goods and services. Members of the creative class include engineers, designers, film makers, writers, and entrepreneurs. They differ from other workers who are paid primarily to do their jobs according to plans others have designed.

creative destruction: A concept developed by Joseph Schumpeter to describe innovation that spurs economic growth while sharply reducing or destroying the value of companies using older technology. The development of word processing, for example, has improved productivity while largely doing away with electric typewriters

D

deficit: In governments or private-sector firms, an excess of spending over income in a given time period. See also national debt.

deflation: A sustained decrease in the average price level of all goods and services produced in an economy.

demand: The amount of a good or service that consumers are willing and able to purchase at specific prices.

depression: A period of prolonged economic contraction. Informally, a long, deep economic slump. A depression is measured in part by decreases in Gross Domestic Product (GDP) and high levels of unemployment. See also **Great Depression**.

diffused costs: Costs spread out over many consumers or taxpayers, and over time. Costs of government programs, for example, are diffused.

direct benefit: A positive result that goes entirely to the individuals involved in a transaction.

dot-com bubble: The rapid and unsustainable increase in technology stock prices from 1995 to 2000.

Dred Scott v. Sanford: An 1857 decision of the U.S. Supreme Court which declared that enslaved African Americans were not protected under the U.S. Constitution and were not citizens. The decision held that Congress had no authority to prohibit slavery in U.S. territories that had not yet become states.

dumping: The sale of a product in another nation at a price lower than the price charged in the producer's home markets.

E

earnings crossover: A point at which an immigrant group's average earnings equal, and then begin to exceed, average earnings of the native born.

economic expansion: A period of economic growth; a time when people spend and receive more and more money. Economic expansion is measured in part by increases in Gross Domestic Product (GDP).

economic freedom: An environment in which individuals make choices, engage voluntarily in exchanges with others, enter and compete in markets, and possess and use private property, as long as their actions do not harm others.

economic growth: An increase in the production of goods and services over time. Economic growth is often measured by changes in Gross Domestic Product (GDP).

economic recovery: A period of economic expansion following an economic downturn. Economic recovery is measured in part by increases in Gross Domestic Product (GDP). [

economic way of thinking: An approach to analyzing human behavior by reference to individual choices, costs, incentives, rules of the game, gains from trade, and unintended consequences.

economics: The study of human behavior that emphasizes choices people make about how to use scarce resources.

economies of scale: In manufacturing, the ability to reduce the average cost for each unit of production by spreading costs out over many units and over a long period of time.

emancipation: Obtaining political rights and freedom. The term is often associated with granting freedom to enslaved African Americans.

employed: Adults who are working in either full-time or part-time jobs.

Employment Act of 1946: Legislation giving the federal government responsibility for maintaining economic growth and job opportunity.

entitlements: Payments of income to recipients who do not provide any goods or services in return for the payments. Social Security payments are an example.

equity: In real estate, the value of a home minus the debt owed.

external benefit: An advantage or positive result that goes to people other than those who benefit directly from an action. For example, homeowners who paint their homes or make other outside improvements provide an external benefit to neighbors. See also externality.

externality: A positive or negative effect of a transaction on somebody who is not directly involved in the transaction. Informally: a spillover effect.

entrepreneur: An individual who starts up a new enterprise, assuming the risks involved.

exports: Goods and services produced by people in one country and sold to people in another country.

F

Federal Baseball Club of Baltimore, Inc. v. National League of Professional Baseball Clubs: A 1922 U.S. Supreme Court case in which the Court ruled that major league baseball was not engaged in interstate commerce and was not a monopoly as defined by the Sherman Antitrust Act.

Federal Deposit Insurance Corporation (FDIC): A corporation sponsored by the U.S. government that insures bank deposits in order to maintain public confidence in the banking system.

federal funds rate: The interest rate banks charge one another for loans. This is a key interest rate controlled by the Federal Reserve.

Federal Insurance Contributions Act (FICA): A federal law establishing a tax to be withheld from paychecks, to finance the Social Security and Medicare programs.

Federal Reserve Act of 1913: A federal law that set up a central bank, the Federal Reserve System, to regulate banking and the supply of money.

Federal Reserve System: The U.S. central bank, designed as an independent agency to coordinate the activities of all financial institutions in the country. It is commonly called the Fed.

Federalist Papers: A series essays written by Alexander Hamilton, James Madison, and John Jay, between 1787 and1788. These essays advocated for ratification of the U.S. Constitution.

financial economy: The banks and other money-handling institutions of a society, together with the money and financial assets they hold and manage. See also the **real economy**.

financial institution: An organization, such as a bank or a brokerage firm, that collects funds and provides services for the management, investment, and safekeeping of funds.

financial panic: A response that occurs when banks or other financial institutions suddenly lose a large amount of their value, causing fear and widespread losses among their customers. In the case of a bank panic, depositors rush to withdraw money from their accounts, fearing that their bank is about to fail. In the case of a stock market panic, share holders rush to sell their stocks, fearing that the market is about to collapse, thus pushing share prices down even faster.

fiscal policy: The use of taxation and government spending to increase or decrease total demand in an economy for goods and services.

fixed cost: In business, the cost that business owners incur whether they produce nothing, a little, or a lot. Some examples are the cost of rent, insurance, and salaries. In personal finance, costs that must be paid at regular intervals. Rent or mortgage payments are examples of fixed costs in this sense. See also **variable cost**.

flapper: A rebellious and independent young woman, particularly in the 1920s in the United States.

forced saving: An involuntary reduction in people's spending.

foreign aid: A granting of money or resources from a donor nation to a recipient nation.

free trade zone: An area within which trade barriers such as tariffs and quotas are reduced or eliminated in order to foster specialization and trade.

French and Indian War: A war between Britain and France in North America, lasting from 1755–1763.

G

gender gap: A difference in earnings or participation rates between men and women in labor markets.

General Agreement on Tariffs and Trade (GATT): An international agreement which substantially reduced tariff barriers on manufactured goods in major industrial countries following World War II.

gentlemen's agreement: In business usage, a form of collusion in which business owners coordinate their business practices to protect each other from competition. For example, they might agree to set prices at a certain level and not engage in underselling each other.

Gibbons v. Ogden: An 1824 decision by the U.S. Supreme Court which confirmed the power of the federal government to regulate interstate commerce.

G.I. Bill: Legislation passed in 1944 that provided financial support for college or vocational education for returning World War II veterans, as well as one year of unemployment compensation. It also provided loans to enable veterans to buy homes and start businesses.

globalization: The expansion of international trade, communications, and transportation across regions, nations, and cultures.

gold standard: A system (now abandoned) under which the U.S. government once maintained the value of the dollar constant, relative to the price of gold.

government failure: Policy choices made by government that result in inefficiency.

Great Contraction: The sharp reduction in the money supply from 1929 to 1933, thought to have dramatically worsened the economic downturn that became the Great Depression.

Great Depression: A financial and industrial slump marked by declining Gross Domestic Product and high rates of unemployment that brought great hardship to the United States from 1929 to about 1939.

Great Society: An American society envisioned by President Lyndon B. Johnson, in which poverty would be reduced by a wide range of federally sponsored social welfare programs.

Greater Fool Theory: The idea that buying stocks at unreasonably high prices can still be a winning strategy if those stocks can be sold later at an even higher price (to a "greater fool" than the original buyer).

Gross Domestic Product (GDP): The market value of all final goods and services produced within the borders of a nation during a specific period of time, such as a quarter or a year. GDP is often used to measure economic growth and to mark periods of economic expansion and contraction.

H

Homestead Act of 1862: Legislation passed by Congress, typically offering qualified homesteaders ownership of 160 acres land. The law required the potential owner to submit an application, to file for deed of title (proving ownership), and then to improve the land and live on it for five years.

horizontal integration: A form of business expansion which occurs when a firm increases its operations at a given point in the supply chain. For example, an owner of line of discount retail stores might wish to expand his or her business by acquiring other retail operations. See also **vertical integration**.

human capital: The knowledge, skills, and work habits that enable workers to be productive.

hunter-gatherers: People who obtain their food by hunting game and finding edible plants.

I

immigration: Leaving one's country to settle in a different country.

imports: Goods and services bought from people in another country.

incentive: A benefit offered to encourage people to act in certain ways. Incentives can be monetary, such as a paycheck, or non-monetary, such as praise.

income inequality: A measure of unequal earnings among residents of a society. Income inequality is always present, but it may increase or decrease over time and may vary sharply across societies.

indenture: Historically, a legal contract in which an individual agreed to provide labor for a period of years in return for passage across the Atlantic, plus room, board and other considerations. Today, an indenture is a legal document issued to lenders.

indentured servitude: Work performed according to the terms of an indenture—for example, farm labor for a period of five years.

Industrial Revolution: The transition of a society from agriculture to manufacturing as its major source of economic activity. In the United States, the Industrial Revolution occurred (approximately) between 1820 and 1870.

inflation: A sustained increase in the average price level of all the goods and services produced in an economy.

Information Revolution (or Information and Communications Technology Revolution): the transformation of a society resulting from widespread use of low-cost information and communication technology; dated as approximately 1955 to the present in the United States.

infrastructure: Basic facilities such as roads, ports, bridges, airports, and railways that support economic activity.

interest group: A voluntary organization of like-minded citizens who advocate for the members of their group. Interest groups include business owners, farmers, consumers, the elderly, environmentalists, and so forth.

International Workers of the World (IWW): A militant labor union of socialists, anarchists, and trade unionists, formed in 1905; widely known as the Wobblies.

investment: The use of income today in a way that may yield gains in the future. For example: a business invests when it spends some of its income to build a factory or buy new equipment. An individual invests when she deposits some of her income in a retirement account, or improves her knowledge and skills through continuing education or training.

investors: Individuals and firms who use income in a way that may yield gains in the future—for example, by purchasing stocks and bonds or by spending money to improve productivity.

invisible hand: A metaphor created by Adam Smith in *The Wealth of Nations*. As used by Smith and subsequently by other economists, the term suggests that the operation of free markets promotes positive social outcomes even when those outcomes are not intended by individuals involved. The positive outcomes occur, Smith claimed, as if the market transactions had been guided toward those ends by an invisible hand.

Iroquois: American Indian people who lived in what is today the northeastern United States and southeastern Canada.

J–K-L

Jim Crow laws: Local and state laws in force in the South from about 1876 to 1965, requiring that African Americans be segregated from white Americans in most public settings.

Kansas-Nebraska Act of 1854: This legislation created the territories of Kansas and Nebraska. It repealed the Missouri Compromise of 1820 and allowed settlers in Kansas and Nebraska to decide whether they would or would not allow slavery within their territorial borders.

Knights of Labor: A national labor union established in 1869, reaching its membership peak in 1886 with 700,000 members. The organization accepted workers from all workplace backgrounds and had a large social agenda.

labor force: The category of all adults who are working (the employed) plus those who are seeking work but unable to find it (the unemployed). The size of the labor force can change over time as the economy expands and contracts and as people make choices about work and other priorities.

labor force participation: The percentage of adults employed or seeking employment.

labor market: Any place or situation in which employers are trying to hire workers at various wages and workers are trying to find jobs at various wages. See also market.

labor union: An organization of employees, established for the purpose of improving wages, fringe benefits, and working conditions. Unions negotiate with employers on behalf of all unionized employees in a given company rather than having each employee negotiate an employment contract on his or her own behalf.

land grants: Land provided by government to an individual, a company, or another government. The U.S. government, for example, gave land grants to railroad companies beginning in the 1860s.

Law of One Price: An economic principle which states that identical goods should sell everywhere for the same price.

life expectancy: The average number of years that a member of a group is expected to live.

lobbying: The effort by members of interest groups to inform legislators about how policies may affect their group. Lobbying also includes efforts to persuade legislators to support or oppose various government policies.

Loewe v. Lawler: Also referred to as the Danbury Hatters' Case, this 1908 Supreme Court case addressed the application of antitrust laws to labor unions. The Court's decision held that boycotts led by labor unions were a violation of the Sherman Antitrust Act because such actions restrained interstate commerce.

loose money: A policy of increasing the supply of money in order to create inflation.

M

market: Any place or situation in which people buy and sell goods and services. Markets can arise when people meet face-to-face or through technological arrangements such as telephone conversations.

market economy: An economy based on individuals' choices and voluntary exchange; consumers are free to spend their money as they wish, to enter into businesses or to sell their labor as they think best. In market economies, prices are determined by supply and demand; information suggested by rising or falling prices guides decisions about how to allocate goods, services, and productive resources.

market price: The price at which the quantity demanded by buyers equals the quantity supplied by sellers.

marriage bars: Formal or informal policies against employing married women, sometimes extending to the firing of single women who became married while on the payroll. Marriage bars began to disappear in the United States during World War II.

Marx, Karl: A German political philosopher and economist (1818-1883); the founder of modern communism.

Medicare: An entitlement program which provides health care insurance for people aged 65 and over.

***Mein Kampf (My Struggle,* in English):** A book by Adolf Hitler (1889-1945), the chancellor of Nazi Germany from 1933-1945. *Mein Kampf* outlines Hitler's life story and his political philosophy.

mercantilism: A loosely defined set of ideas that identified the wealth of a nation with its possession of gold and silver. Mercantilism suggested that colonies have an obligation to assist the mother country in gaining wealth and that the government of the mother country should managing the overall economy by offering monopolies and subsidies and by intervening in trade.

Metcalfe's Law: A law attributed to Robert Metcalfe which states that when the number of users of a network doubles, the value of the network quadruples.

middle class: A vaguely defined category of people who have higher than poverty-level incomes but are not considered wealthy.

Misery Index: A measure of economic pain, calculated by adding the unemployment rate to the rate of inflation. Higher sums mean more economic pain.

Missouri Compromise of 1820: This legislation preserved a balance of power between slave states and free states. It did so by admitting Maine as a free state and Missouri as a slave state to the Union. The result at the time was an even balance between 12 free and 12 slave states. This legislation also prohibited slavery in the former Louisiana Territory north of the 36° 30′ latitude line except within the boundaries of the proposed state of Missouri. In 1854, the Missouri Compromise was repealed by the Kansas-Nebraska Act.

mixed economy: An economy that has some characteristics of a command economy and some characteristics of a market system. Many modern economies are mixed economies.

money: Anything commonly accepted as payment for goods and services.

money supply: The total quantity of money in the economy. Money resulting from loans is part of the money supply, along with coins, currency, and deposits in savings accounts and checking accounts. Bank lending affects how much money there is in the economy overall.

monetary policy: Government actions that influence the money supply and the banking system, exercised to influence the economy. In the United States, monetary policy is conducted by the Federal Reserve System.

monopoly: An market that is difficult to enter, typically with only one supplier producing a unique product.

monopsony: An industry in which there is only one buyer but many sellers. Monopsony is a form of monopoly power. In the United States, major league baseball is a monopsony.

mortgage: A long-term loan used to buy a house, allowing the borrower to live in the house as long as payments are made on the loan.

muckrakers: Journalists or other writers who investigate and publish reports alleging criminal behavior and corruption among elected officials, political leaders, and business leaders.

multiplier effect: The effect that occurs when one person's spending is received as income by another person, who in turn uses some of that income in new spending. If this process goes through repeated rounds, total income will increase. The multiplier effect also can work in reverse, when reductions in spending cause a reduction in income for others.

N

national debt: The amount of money the U.S. government owes—the sum total of the deficits it has accumulated.

National Labor Relations Act of 1935: Also known as the Wagner Act, this legislation gave workers new legal protections to organize unions for the purpose of collective bargaining. It also established the National Labor Relations Board (NRLB), which enforces the rights of employees to organize and bargain.

National Monetary Commission: A panel created in 1908 to recommend ways to prevent future bank panics; the panel's recommendations resulted in the creation of the Federal Reserve System.

National Recovery Administration (NRA): An agency established as part of the New Deal in 1933. Its goal was to reduce competition by bringing industry, labor, and government together to set prices and to create and implement codes of business practices. In 1935, the U.S. Supreme Court held that the NRA was unconstitutional.

National Youth Administration: This was a New Deal program established in 1935 to provide jobs, study programs, and job training programs for young men and women of high school and college ages.

natural experiment: An opportunity to observe how a social system reacts to an externally imposed change.

natural resources: Natural resources are the productive elements available from the environment; they include land, water, wildlife, timber, and climate. As an economy's access to natural resources improves, it becomes capable of producing more output.

Navigation Acts: A series of laws regulating trade between Britain and the colonies, beginning in 1651.

network: Interconnected systems of devices or people.

New Deal: A term used to describe programs introduced by the President Franklin Delano Roosevelt in his efforts to reduce the economic impact of the Great Depression. New Deal programs included new regulations in agriculture, banking, labor, and welfare.

New Economic Policy: A 1971 program of wage and price controls approved by President Richard M. Nixon, intended to reduce inflation.

New South: A term used to describe economic changes in the South in the decades following the Civil War. Today the economy of the South includes agriculture and manufacturing as well as a large service sector.

Norris-La Guardia Act of 1932: Federal legislation outlawing "yellow dog contracts" illegal. A yellow dog contract is one in which an employee promises not to become a member of any labor organization. The Norris-La Guardia Act also limited the ability of federal courts to issue injunctions in labor disputes.

North American Free Trade Agreement (NAFTA): A regional trade agreement (RTA) established in 1994 under President William Clinton. Under the terms of NAFTA, the United States, Canada, and Mexico agreed to reduce trade barriers.

O–P–Q

ocean resources: Anything valuable from the seas, such as fish, petroleum, plant food, and salt.

opportunity cost: The value of the next-best alternative, or what someone gives up by choosing one alternative over another.

Organization of Oil and Petroleum Exporting Countries (OPEC): A cartel of oil-exporting nations founded in 1960 to manage the supply of oil in an attempt to set the price of oil on world markets.

ostracism: A punishment that involves banishing an individual from the group; used by some American Indian people to enforce traditional rules.

outsourcing: A form of trade in which one firm enters into an agreement with another firm (frequently in another country) to provide services (usually at a lower rate of pay) that might otherwise be performed by in-house workers.

paper profits: Gains that occur when a stock has gone up in value but has not yet been sold at a profit; until the stock is actually sold, the stock may drop in value, eliminating the gain.

per capita income: A calculation which divides the total income of a nation by population, yielding a per-person figure. It is often associated with per capita Gross Domestic Product (GDP), which is a calculation of total GDP divided by the number of people in the nation.

physical capital: Tools made by individuals—such as machines, construction equipment, factories, delivery trucks, roads and so forth—used to produce goods and services.

pogrom: A violent riot directed against an identified ethnic group, particularly Jews in Central or Eastern Europe during the early part of the 20th century.

popping a bubble: Government action to reduce the price of an investment thought to be unsustainably high.

post road: A highway designated for the transport of mail. The U.S. Constitution gave Congress the authority to establish post roads.

primary effects: The immediate and visible effects of an action. See also **secondary effects**.

private property: Things owned by individuals and businesses; in the United States and other countries that protect property rights, owners of property can control, use, and transfer their possessions, subject to rules intended to prevent harm to others.

privatization: Transferring ownership of property from government to individual or private-sector owners.

property rights: The exclusive authority of a property owner to determine how his or her property will be used. Property rights may be held by individuals, groups, or governments.

productivity: A measure of efficiency, based on the amount of goods or services that a person can produce with a given quantity of resources in a given period of time.

profit: The money left over after costs have been subtracted from revenues. Profits serve as an important incentive in a market economy.

profit motive: The desire to earn profits—often prompting businesses to produce or supply the goods and services consumers want. Businesses that satisfy consumers and produce efficiently are rewarded with profits.

public sector unions: Labor unions whose members are local, state, and federal government employees.

Pueblo: American Indian people who had settled in what is today an area including parts of New Mexico, Utah, Colorado, Arizona, and Nevada.

Quebec Act of 1774: This act of Parliament enlarged the size of Quebec, thus reducing western land areas available for settlement by colonial Americans.

quota: A restriction on the amount of a product that may be imported during a period of time.

R

real economy: The real economy is that part of the economy concerned with actually producing goods and services, as opposed to the part of the economy that is concerned with buying and selling on the financial markets (see **financial economy**). For example, the real economy produces houses, while the financial economy provides loans that enable people to buy houses. The real economy includes all of a society's human capital, physical capital, natural resources, and technological knowledge.

recession: A period of economic contraction; a time when people spend and receive less money. A recession is measured in part by decreases in Gross Domestic Product (GDP).

Regional Trade Agreements (RTAs): Trade agreements among a limited number of nations, designed to reduce trade barriers. The North American Free Trade Agreement (NAFTA) is an example.

reserves: Funds that banks set aside for use in managing the day-to-day operations of the bank or for an emergency. These funds are not lent to customers. Today, banks keep some of their reserves in their own bank vaults, but they keep most reserves in the form of deposits with the Federal Reserve.

Roaring Twenties: The decade of 1920-1929, marked in the United States by rapid social change and economic growth.

robber baron: A derogatory term used by journalists and politicians to describe 19th-century industrialists such as Andrew Carnegie and John D. Rockefeller.

Roosevelt, Franklin Delano: The 32nd president of the United States, serving from 1933-1945. Known for his New Deal programs, intended to help lift the United States out of the Great Depression, and for his leadership in the time of World War II.

Roosevelt, Theodore: The 26th president of the United States, serving from 1901-1909. Known for initiating antitrust legislation.

rules of the game: The formal and informal regulations that govern the economic system. These rules are often set by government; they often act as incentives, influencing people's behavior. Tax laws and other regulations are examples.

S

scalable output: A type of production that can be increased in size at little or no additional cost.

scarcity: The lack of enough resources

to satisfy economic wants. Scarcity exists because human wants are always greater than the resources available to satisfy them.

secondary effects: The unexpected or indirect effects of an action that become known with the passage of time. See also **unintended consequences**.

self-interested behavior: Purposeful action people engage in to make themselves better off, in material or non-material ways. Self-interested behavior might include working overtime, to earn more money; it might include volunteer work at a community hospital. The key is whether the acts in question do serve the interests of the person performing them. The notion of self-interested behavior is tied closely to the thinking of Adman Smith, who drew a distinction between self-interested behavior and selfish (or greedy) behavior.

sharecropping: A system of agricultural land use in which a landowner allows a tenant to farm land in return for a share of the crop produced on the land.

Sherman Antitrust Act of 1890: A federal law designed to break up monopolies or companies attempting to form monopolies. The Sherman Act authorized the U.S. attorney general to initiate lawsuits against firms regarded as trying to restrain trade by reducing competition.

shoestring or "on a shoestring" financing: Financing (for the purchase of a car or a home, for example) that amounts to little and is casually provided. Financing the purchase of a used car by borrowing $200 from a friend and assuming you'll figure out later how to come up with the rest of the money would be an example of buying "on a shoestring."

smokestack chasing: An economic development strategy that involves attracting heavy industries through the use incentives paid for by tax revenue.

Smoot-Hawley Tariff: Federal legislation passed in 1930, increasing tariffs on many goods imported into the United States.

social contract: An unwritten agreement or consensus among people in a given society, indicating basic values and mutual obligations. Because there is no written form of the social contract, references to its contents are often subject to dispute.

Social Security: An entitlement program to pay retired workers aged 65 or older a continuing income. The Social Security program also provides other benefits including payments to people who are disabled and to spouses or children of a worker who has died.

socialism: A political and economic theory that calls for government ownership of industry, and for social policies aimed at promoting equality. Socialist political parties have been influential in Europe and other parts of the world throughout much of the 20th century.

specialization: Confining oneself (or one's business) to providing a narrower range of goods and services than one consumes, and then trading for (purchasing) other goods and services. People who specialize do not try to be self-sufficient. A lawyer provides legal services, for example, and she needs medical services from time to time; but she does not try to act as her own doctor. Farmers in Iowa specialize in growing corn; if they want to consume oranges, they buy oranges grown by farmers in Florida. Specialization increases productivity; it also increases interdependence.

speculative bubble: An unsustainable increase in prices, as when prices in a market increase in the absence of fundamental reasons suggested by the real economy. "Stock price bubbles" or "housing price bubbles" are examples.

speculator: A high-risk investor; someone who tries to earn income by buying financial products like stocks and betting on the movements of prices.

stagflation: Stagnant economic growth (including high unemployment rates) combined with high levels of inflation. The term was first used to describe the U.S. economy of the 1970s.

starving time: The time during the winter of 1609-1610 in which the Jamestown Colony in Virginia lost more than half its settlers because of lack of food.

strike: An effort by a union to withhold its labor from an employer, typically in an attempt to obtain concessions in contract negotiations.

stock: Shares of ownership in a corporation. A corporation sells stock in order to obtain money to run or expand the business. Stock buyers purchase stocks in hopes of earning a financial gain.

subsidy: A form of financial assistance—a special economic favor—provided by government to a business, to individuals, or to some group. Subsidies are often used by government to encourage the production of a good or a service.

subsidy wars: Competition between states and localities to attract new business by offering or subsidies to companies that are relocating or building new facilities.

supply: The amount of a good or service that producers are willing and able to sell at specific prices.

surplus: An excess of production or supply over demand; also, an excess of income or assets over spending.

T

Takings Clause of the Fifth Amendment: The last clause of the Fifth Amendment to the U.S. Constitution, which concludes with the statement: "nor shall private property be taken for public use, without just compensation." This clause provides protection for private property owners against arbitrary government seizure.

tariff: A tax charged on imports.

Taxation Clause: Article I, Section 8, of the U.S. Constitution, which gives Congress the power "to lay and collect taxes."

Tea Party of 2010: An organization of political activists who favor balancing the federal budget, reducing taxes, and reducing the size of the federal government. See also the **Boston Tea Party of 1773**.

The Great Migration: A large-scale movement of African Americans out of the South between 1910 and 1930.

tight money: A policy of keeping the supply of money steady in order to avoid inflation.

ton-mile: A transportation measure equal to one ton of cargo (2,000 pounds) transported one mile. To get the total ton-miles involved in a trip, the weight of the cargo in tons is multiplied by the length of the trip in miles.

too big to fail: A phrase sometimes used to describe a company so large that its bankruptcy would be politically unacceptable.

Townshend Acts: A series of laws passed by the British Parliament, beginning in 1767, intended to raise revenue and to enforce trade restrictions on Britain's American colonies. The Acts placed new taxes on English manufactured goods entering America, including tea, glass, paper, and pigments for paint. The Townshend Acts were met with resistance, which culminated in the Boston Massacre of 1770.

trade: The action of buying and selling goods and services, within a nation or internationally.

transcontinental railroad: A railroad across America, connecting the Atlantic Coast and the Pacific Coast; completed in 1869.

transfer payments: Payments by government to recipients who do not provide any goods or services in return. Examples include Social Security payments, unemployment compensation, and payments to people with disabilities.

transportation: The movement of people, goods, and services from one location to another.

Transportation Act: A law passed by the British Parliament in 1718, under which Britain began sending imprisoned convicts to be sold as indentured servants in the American colonies.

treaties: Formal agreements negotiated between sovereign nations.

trust: A form of business organization in which individuals (trustees) are given legal authority to administer the organization for the advantage of its shareholders.

trust busting: An informal term for legal actions taken by government to break up large corporations or trusts by enforcing anti-trust laws; trust buster:

a political figure who engages in trust busting.

turnpike: Originally, a road that required payment of a toll for passage; today the term may also apply to toll-free roads.

unalienable rights: Rights that cannot be taken away, surrendered, or sold to others. The term "unalienable rights" is used in the Declaration of Independence, which states that unalienable rights to life, liberty, and the pursuit of happiness are given to "all men" by their creator—that is, they are not a gift from government.

U–V

unemployed: Adults who are seeking work but unable to find it.

unemployment rate: The percentage of the labor force that is unemployed.

unintended consequences: Results that are not expected or predicted. The term is often used in reference to government policies that produce unwelcome results.

variable cost: In business, a cost that varies as the level of output changes. Examples include the cost of raw materials used in production or the wages paid for additional hourly workers. In personal finance, a cost that varies depending on choices people make about spending for non-essentials—entertainment and recreational travel, for example. See also **fixed cost**.

vertical integration: A form of business expansion which occurs when a firm acquires resources all along the chain of production. An auto manufacturer engaged in vertical integration would acquire iron ore mines, railroads, battery factories and so forth, for use in automobile production. See also **horizontal integration**.

visa: A document issued by a nation that grants a foreign traveler the right to enter and remain for an indicated time.

voluntary exchange (or voluntary trade): Transactions entered into freely, in which both sides anticipate that the benefits of the exchange will outweigh the costs. Buying a cup of coffee is an example of a voluntary exchange.

voluntary export restraints: Restrictions

imposed on cars imported from Japan in 1981.

W–Y

wage rate: The rate of pay a worker earns—often stated per hour, month, or year. In market economies, wage rates are determined in large part by the interaction of supply and demand.

Wealth of Nations: Adam Smith's famous book, published in Scotland in 1776; widely regarded as the foundation of modern economic theory. The complete title of the book is *An Inquiry into the Nature and Causes of the Wealth of Nations*.

weapons of mass destruction: weapons capable of killing people in huge numbers—for example, nuclear, chemical, and biological weapons.

Whip Inflation Now (WIN): A program approved by President Gerald Ford in 1974 that encouraged people to reduce spending and save money in order to fight inflation.

wildcat money: Currency issued by private banks, subject to complete loss of value if the issuing bank failed.

winner-take-all society: A society characterized by a high level of inequality in income and wealth, in which relatively few high earners receive unusually large gains.

Works Progress Administration (WPA): Established in 1935, this was the largest of the New Deal programs. It employed millions of people in building public buildings and roads. It also operated arts, drama, media, and literacy programs.

World Trade Organization (WTO): An international organization which succeeded the **General Agreement on Tariffs and Trade** in 1995. With 153 members, the WTO is now a forum in which member countries negotiate reductions in trade barriers.

Yalta Conference: A meeting between the Allied leaders Churchill, Roosevelt, and Stalin in 1945 at Yalta, a port on the Black Sea. At the conference the leaders planned the final stages of World War II and agreed to territorial divisions of Europe for the post-war era.

Image

> The following abbreviations are used for sources from which several images were obtained:
>
> CORBIS . . . . Corbis Corporation
> LOC . . . . Library of Congress Prints and Photographs Division
> NPS . . . . National Park Service, Colonial National Historic Park
> NWPA . . . . North Wind Picture Archives

Chapter 1: 1 LOC; 4 Oksana Struk/iStockphoto; 6 Oscar Williams/Dreamstime. **Chapter 2**: 11 LOC; 13 B.F. Gribble; 14 Sidney King/NPS; 17 Sidney King/NPS. **Chapter 3**: 21 NPS; 26 Sidney King/NPS. **Chapter 4**: 31 NPS; 32 NPS; 35 LOC. **Chapter 5**: 41 Timothy Nichols/Dreamstime; 42 U.S. Capitol Historical Society; 45 NWPA. **Chapter 6**: 53 NWPA. **Chapter 7**: 61 NWPA. **Chapter 8**: 71 LOC; 74 LOC. **Chapter 9**: 79 LOC; 82 LOC; 83 NWPA; 86 LOC. **Chapter 10**: 91 LOC; 93 NWPA; 95 NWPA; 99 LOC. **Chapter 11**: 103 NWPA; 107 John Mix Stanley, photograph Ad Meskens. **Chapter 12**: 113 LOC; 115 Dreamstime. **Chapter 13**: 121 H. Charles McBarron/American Oil Company; 125 LOC. **Chapter 14**: 131 LOC; 132 LOC; 137 LOC; 138 LOC. **Chapter 15**: 141 Ken Cole/Dreamstime; 142 LOC; 143 LOC; 147 LOC; 149 (both) LOC. **Chapter 16**: 153 LOC; 154 LOC; 155 LOC; 159 LOC; 160 Wisconsin Historical Society—Image ID 5587. **Chapter 17**: 163 LOC; 164 LOC. **Chapter 18**: 171 LOC; 177 LOC. **Chapter 19**: 181 LOC; 182 LOC; 183 Bettmann/CORBIS; 185 LOC; 188 LOC. **Chapter 20**: 191 LOC; 192 The Bancroft Library/USC, Berkeley; 194 LOC; 198 (left) LOC; 198 (right) AP Photo/Nick Ut. **Chapter 21**: 201 Paul Bieler/USDA Forest Service/Oregon State University Archives; 202 USDA NRCS; 205 Bettmann/CORBIS; 206 Bettmann/CORBIS; 208 Milton R. Halladay.

Chapter 22: 212 LOC; 213 LOC. **Chapter 23**: 223 LOC; 226 LOC; 229 (left) © 1943 Saturday Evening Post and Curtis Publishing Company; 229 (right) LOC. **Chapter 24**: 235 FDR Library Photo Collection; 237 Bettmann/CORBIS; 239 Orlin C. Munns; 240 Bill Rich; 241 State Museum of Pennslyvania. **Chapter 25**: 250 Bettmann/CORBIS. **Chapter 26**: 255 Bettmann/CORBIS; 256 George C. Marshall Foundation; 257 (top) George C. Marshall Foundation; 257 (bottom) Hulton-Deutsch Collection/CORBIS; 258 Bettmann/CORBIS; 260 George C. Marshall Foundation; 262 The Phoenix Gazette. **Chapter 27**: 265 LOC; 266 Johnson Products Company; 267 LOC; 272 Birmingham, Ala. Public Library Archives, Cat. # OVH 118. **Chapter 28**: 275 Sue Ream; 278 Jurgen Ludwig; 282 Birgit Kinder. **Chapter 29**: 285 LOC; 286 Bettmann/CORBIS. **Chapter 30**: 297 Benis Arapovi/Dreamstime; 299 (left) IBM; 299 (right) Nokia Corporation; 300 Tim Patterson; 302 Amazon.com. **Chapter 31**: 307 World Trade Organization; 309 Jeffrey Markowitz/Sygma/CORBIS; 312 Steve Jurvetson; 316 LOC. **Chapter 32**: 319 LOC; 322 National Archives and Records Administration; 324 LOC.

Maps, tables, and figures by Jeremy C. Munns

All other images are in the public domain or not under copyright.

Text

Chapter 3: P. 28 Primary Source, Indenture Signed by Richard Lowther. © Copyright 2011 by Crandall Shifflett. All rights reserved. A part of Virtual Jamestown. XML searching and web delivery provided by the University of Virginia Library's Electronic Text Center. **Chapter 5**: P. 47 Figure 1, Real GDP, 1790–1850. Reprinted with the permission of MeasuringWorth. **Chapter 7**: P. 67 Primary source, letter written by Eli Whitney to his family. Courtesy of Eli Whitney Papers, Manuscripts and Archives, Yale University Library. **Chapter 8**: P. 75 Table 2, Direct Costs of the Civil War, in 1860 Dollars. Reprinted with the permission of Cambridge University Press. **Chapter 9**: P. 84 Table 1, Real Growth in Gross Domestic Product Before and After the Civil War. Reprinted with the permission of MeasuringWorth. **Chapter 11**: P. 105 Map 1, Historic Locations of American Indian Tribes. Courtesy of the University of Texas Libraries, The University of Texas at Austin. P. 111 Table 1, Major Private or Partially Private Airports. Reprinted with the permission of Elsevier B.V. **Chapter 12**: P. 115 Table 1, Buffalo Population, Selected Years, 1800–2010. Courtesy of the University of Oklahoma. P. 116 Table 2, Plains Indian Tribes: Selected Population Statistics from First Contact with

White Americans to 1990. Reprinted with the permission of Cambridge University Press. **Chapter 13**: P. 123 Table 1, Production per Person and Railroad Mileage, 1870–1900. From *Historical Statistics of the United States, Millennial Edition Online*. Reprinted with the permission of Cambridge University Press. P. 128 Primary source, "Crazy Judah's" Railroad Plan. Reprinted with the permission of the Museum of the City of San Francisco. P. 129 Table 2, Top Five and Bottom Five Creative Cities (Among 49 Cities Over 1 Million Population). Reprinted by permission of Basic Books, a member of the Perseus Book Group. **Chapter 14**: P. 134 Table 1, Inflation in the United States, Five-Year Averages, 1860–1910. From *Historical Statistics of the United States, Millennial Edition Online*. Reprinted with the permission of Cambridge University Press. **Chapter 15**: P. 144 Table 1, Production of Ford's Model T. Reprinted with the permission of Wayne State University Press. P. 146 Table 2: Estimated Average Weekly Hours Worked in Manufacturing. Reprinted with the permission of EH.Net Encyclopedia. P. 146 Figure 2, Nonfarm Employees Real Annual Earnings in 1914 Dollars. Reprinted with the permission of David R. Henderson. P. 151 Figure 3, Wal-Mart Shoppers by Income Levels. Reprinted with permission of the American Enterprise Institute for Public Policy Research, Washington, D.C. **Chapter 18**: P. 175 Table 1, Labor Force and Wage Statistics, 1880–1920. From *Historical Statistics of the United States, Millennial Edition Online*. Reprinted with the permission of Cambridge University Press. P. 176 Table 2, Survival Rates on the *Titanic*. Reprinted with the permission of Chuck Anesi. P. 178 Table 3: Major U.S. Firms Founded by Immigrants: Published by the Associated Press. Reprinted with the permission of ZDNet Research. P. 179 Table 5, Education Levels of Recent Male Immigrants, by Category. Reprinted with the permission of the University of Chicago Press. **Chapter 19**: P. 184 Figure 1, Stock Prices and the Value of Production, 1920–1940. From *Historical Statistics of the United States, Millennial Edition Online*. Published with the permission of Cambridge University Press. **Chapter 20**: P. 193 Figure 1, Selected Panics and the Great Depression. From *Historical Statistics of the United States, Millennial Edition Online*. Reprinted with the permission of Cambridge University Press. **Chapter 21**: P. 204 Table 1, Bank Failures by Year, 1921–1936. From *Historical Statistics of the United States, Millennial Edition Online*. Reprinted with the permission of Cambridge University Press. **Chapter 22**: P. 212 Figure 1, Percent of Union Membership in the U.S. Workforce. Reprinted with the permission of the *Industrial and Labor Relations Review*. P. 215 Table 1, Annual Average Earnings of Nonfarm Workers (in 1914 Dollars). Reprinted with the permission of W. W. Norton & Company, Inc. P. 215 Table 2,

Estimated Hours Worked per Week in Manufacturing, 1900–1929. Reprinted with the permission of EH.Net. **Chapter 23**: P. 227 Table 1, Labor Force Participation by Men and Women, 1900–2000. From *Historical Statistics of the United States, Millennial Edition Online*. Reprinted with the permission of Cambridge University Press. **Chapter 24**: P. 238 Figure 3, The Baby Boom and Surrounding Years. From *Historical Statistics of the United States, Millennial Edition Online*. Reprinted with the permission of Cambridge University Press. P. 242 Table 1, Top Ten Best Movies of the Baby Boomer Generation reprinted with the permission of Examiner.com, Paul Brand, author. Top Ten Films of 2000–2010. Reprinted with the permission of Box Office Mojo. P. 243 Figure 4, First Grade Enrollment, 1940–1995. From *Historical Statistics of the United States, Millennial Edition Online*. Reprinted with the permission of Cambridge University Press. **Chapter 26**: P. 259 Table 1, Marshall Plan Expenditures by Nation, in Millions of Dollars. Reprinted with the permission of Palgrave Macmillan. P. 263 Figure 1, Per Capita GDP, 1870–2003. Reprinted with the permission of Oxford University Press. **Chapter 27**: P. 268 Figure 1, School Enrollments by Race, 1850–1950. From *Historical Statistics of the United States, Millennial Edition Online*. Reprinted with the permission of Cambridge University Press. P. 269 Table 1, Occupational Distribution of African Americans, 1880–1970. Reprinted by permission of the publisher from *Harvard Encyclopedia of American Ethnic Groups* edited by Stephan Thernstrom, Ann Orlov and Oscar Handlin, p. 21, Cambridge, Mass.: The Belknap Press of Harvard University Press, Copyright © 1980 by the President and Fellows of Harvard College. P. 270 Table 2, African American College Participation. From *Historical Statistics of the United States, Millennial Edition Online*. Reprinted with the permission of Cambridge University Press. P. 273 Household/Karoub quotes in Householder/Karoub, "Motown Sounds Strong at 50," *Seattle Times*, September 13, 2009. Reprinted with the permission of The Associated Press. **Chapter 28**: P. 280 Figure 2, Comparative GDP Growth Rates for the East and West Germany, 1950–1989. Reprinted with the permission of Akademie Verlag GmBH. P. 282 Primary source, Andreas Ramos quotation. Reprinted with the permission of the author, Andreas Ramos. P. 283 Table 1, Durable Goods Ownership in East and West Germany, 1993–2007. Reprinted with the permission of the author, Michael Burda. **Chapter 30**: P. 304 Primary Source, Schein and Olsen quotations in Edgar H. Schein's interview with Ken Olsen. Reprinted with the permission of Berrett-Koehler Publishing. **Chapter 31**: P. 313 Table 1, Top U.S. Exports and Imports for 2008. Reprinted with the permission of the International Monetary Fund.